Fodor's 2nd Edition

Cuba

The Guide for All Budgets, Completely Updated, with Many Maps and Travel Tips

D0971479

Where to Stay, Eat,
and Explore

On and Off
the Beaten Path

When to Go,
What to Pack

Post-it® Flags,
Web Sites, and More

Fodor's Travel Publications • New York, Toronto, London, Sydney, Auckland
www.fodors.com

Fodor's Cuba

EDITOR: Laura M. Kidder

Editorial Contributors: David Dudenhoefer, George Semler, Michael B. DeZayas

Editorial Production: Tom Holton

Maps: David Lindroth, Mapping Specialists Ltd., *cartographers;* Rebecca Baer and Bob Blake, *map editors*

Design: Fabrizio La Rocca, *creative director;* Guido Caroti, *art director;* Jolie Novak, *senior picture editor;* Melanie Marin, *photo editor*

Cover Design: Pentagram

Production/Manufacturing: Angela L. McLean

Cover Photo: Jan Butchofsky-Houser

Copyright

Second Edition

ISBN 0–676–90189–1

ISSN 1091–4749

Important Tip

Although all prices, opening times, and other details in this book are based on information supplied to us at press time, changes occur all the time in the travel world, and Fodor's cannot accept responsibility for facts that become outdated or for inadvertent errors or omissions. So **always confirm information when it matters,** especially if you're making a detour to visit a specific place.

Special Sales

Fodor's Travel Publications are available at special discounts for bulk purchases for sales promotions or premiums. Special editions, including personalized covers, excerpts of existing guides, and corporate imprints, can be created in large quantities for special needs. For more information, contact your local bookseller or write to Special Markets, Fodor's Travel Publications, 280 Park Avenue, New York, NY 10017. Inquiries from Canada should be directed to your local Canadian bookseller or sent to Random House of Canada, Ltd., Marketing Department, 2775 Matheson Boulevard East, Mississauga, Ontario L4W 4P7. Inquiries from the United Kingdom should be sent to Fodor's Travel Publications, 20 Vauxhall Bridge Road, London SW1V 2SA, England.

PRINTED IN THE UNITED STATES OF AMERICA

10 9 8 7 6 5 4 3 2 1

CONTENTS

Maps

ON THE ROAD WITH FODOR'S

The more you know before you go, the better your trip will be. Cuba's most fascinating small museum (or its most entrancing salsa club or enticing *criollo* restaurant) could be just around the corner from your hotel, but if you don't know it's there, it might as well be on the other side of the globe. That's where this book comes in. It's a great step toward making sure your next trip lives up to your expectations. As you plan, check out the Web as well. Guidebooks have been helping smart travelers find the special places for years; the Web is one more tool. Whatever reference you consult, be savvy about what you read, and always consider the source. Images and language can be massaged to make places appear better than they are. And one traveler's quaint is another's grimy. Here at Fodor's, and at our on-line arm, Fodors.com, our focus is on providing you with information that's not only useful but accurate and on target. Every day Fodor's editors put enormous effort into getting things right, beginning with the search for the right contributors—people who have objective judgment, broad travel experience, and the writing ability to put their insights into words. There's no substitute for advice from a like-minded friend who has just come back from where you're going, but our writers, having seen all corners of Cuba, are the next best thing. They're the kind of people you'd poll for tips yourself if you knew them.

Freelance journalist and travel hack **David Dudenhoefer** spent most of the 1990s writing about things Latin American from his base in San José, Costa Rica. In addition to writing the central Cuba chapter and updating the Cuba Smart Travel Tips section, he has worked on five Fodor's guides and contributed articles and photos to dozens of newspapers and magazines published on both sides of the Rio Grande.

Barcelona-based journalist **George Semler,** who covered Havana and western Cuba, has been writing about Spain, France, and North Africa since the early '70s. Author of books on Madrid and Barcelona, George has reported on gastronomy, music, theater, poetry, fly-fishing, and baseball in both English and Spanish for the *Los Angeles Times, Saveur, Sky, Forbes FYI, The International Herald Tribune,* and *El Pais.* He's presently writing a book on the Pyrénées.

Michael de Zayas, a twentysomething Cuban-American writer, had the trip of his life covering eastern Cuba: along the way he met some members of his family for the first time. He's also written for Fodor's guides on Spain, Chile, Argentina, Mexico, Central America, the Caribbean, the Bahamas, and New York City—which is where he lives between travels. Michael spent five years with the *Miami Herald* and often writes about travel for the *New York Post.*

Don't Forget to Write

Your experiences—positive and negative—matter to us. If we have missed or misstated something, we want to hear about it. We follow up on all suggestions. Contact the Cuba editor at editors@fodors.com or c/o Fodor's, 280 Park Avenue, New York, NY 10017. And have a fabulous trip!

Karen Cure
Editorial Director

World Time Zones

Numbers below vertical bands relate each zone to Greenwich Mean Time (0 hrs.).
Local times frequently differ from these general indications,
as indicated by light-face numbers on map.

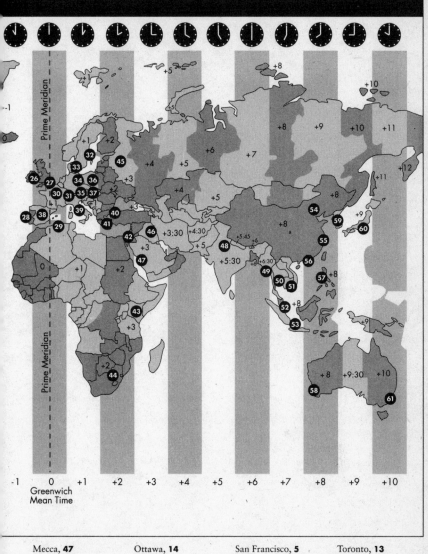

Mecca, **47**
Mexico City, **12**
Miami, **18**
Montréal, **15**
Moscow, **45**
Nairobi, **43**
New Orleans, **11**
New York City, **16**

Ottawa, **14**
Paris, **30**
Perth, **58**
Reykjavík, **25**
Rio de Janeiro, **23**
Rome, **39**
Saigon (Ho Chi Minh City), **51**

San Francisco, **5**
Santiago, **21**
Seoul, **59**
Shanghai, **55**
Singapore, **52**
Stockholm, **32**
Sydney, **61**
Tokyo, **60**

Toronto, **13**
Vancouver, **4**
Vienna, **35**
Warsaw, **36**
Washington, D.C., **17**
Yangon, **49**
Zürich, **31**

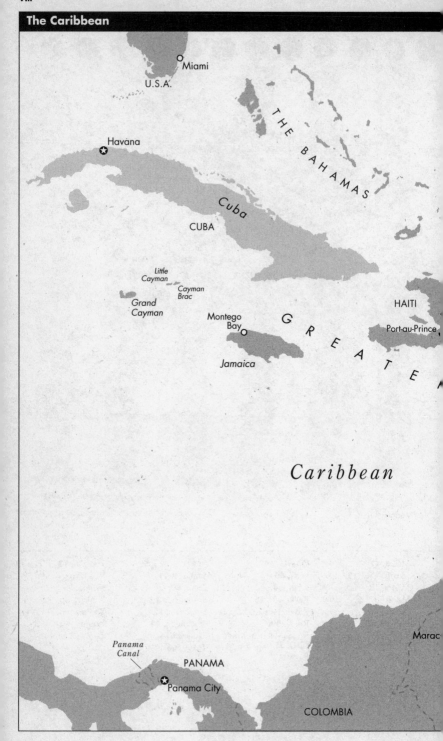

Miami

U.S.A.

THE BAHAMAS

Havana

Cuba

CUBA

Little
Cayman

Cayman
Brac

Grand
Cayman

Montego
Bay

G R E A T E

HAITI

Port-au-Prince

Jamaica

Caribbean

Panama
Canal

PANAMA

Panama City

Marac

COLOMBIA

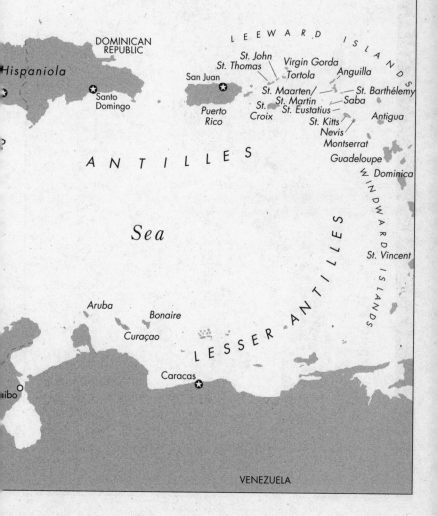

0   200 miles

0   300 km

N

ATLANTIC OCEAN

Turks and Caicos Islands

L E E W A R D   I S L A N D S

DOMINICAN REPUBLIC

Hispaniola

St. John

St. Thomas

Virgin Gorda

Tortola

Anguilla

San Juan

Santo Domingo

St. Maarten/   *St. Barthélemy*

St. Martin   *Saba*

St. Croix

St. Eustatius

Puerto Rico

St. Kitts

Antigua

Nevis

Montserrat

A N T I L L E S

Guadeloupe

Dominica

W I N D W A R D   I S L A N D S

Sea

St. Vincent

Aruba

Bonaire

Curaçao

L E S S E R   A N T I L L E S

Caracas

ibo

VENEZUELA

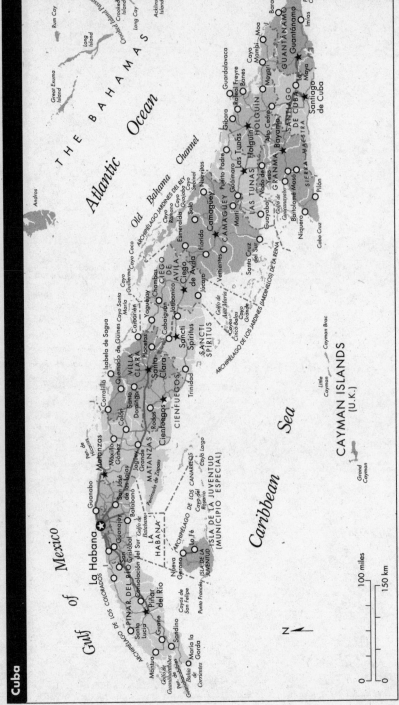

Cuba

ESSENTIAL INFORMATION

ADDRESSES

Addresses are frequently cited as street names with numbers and/or locations, as in: "Calle Concordia, e/Calle Gervasio y Calle Escobar" or "Calle de los Oficios 53, esquina de Obrapía." It's helpful to know the following terms and abbreviations: "e/" is *entre* (between); *esquina de* (sometimes seen as "esq. de") is "corner of"; and *y* is "and." Some streets have pre- and post-revolutionary names; both are often cited on local maps and on maps and in text throughout this guide.

AIR TRAVEL

Dozens of international airlines now serve Cuba, although air travel to the island is still dominated by charter flights. Many of these originate in Canada, Mexico, and Europe and are part of package deals that include stays in one of Cuba's burgeoning number of all-inclusive resorts. Flying within Cuba is extremely affordable by North American and European standards, and routes connect most major cities in the country.

Although there's still no regular commercial service from the United States to Cuba (Americans flouting the embargo often fly to the island from elsewhere in the Caribbean or from Canada, Mexico, or Central America), new rules have cleared the way for more direct charter flights between the two nations. Note that U.S. citizens still require special permission from the Treasury Department to travel to the island (☞ Americans and Cuba, *below*).

AIRPORTS

In addition to its main hub, Aeropuerto Internacional José Martí in Havana, Cuba has seven international airports—in Varadero, Cayo Largo, Cienfuegos, Ciego de Ávila, Camagüey, Holguín, and Santiago de Cuba—and several smaller, regional hubs.

BOOKING

When you book, **look for nonstop flights** and **remember that "direct" flights stop at least once.** Try to avoid connecting flights, which require a change of plane. For more booking tips and to check prices and make on-line flight reservations, log on to www.fodors.com.

CARRIERS

Cubana, the national carrier, has both domestic and international flights on mostly Russian-built aircraft. Service is adequate but somewhat below North American and European standards. The airline offers direct service between Havana and Toronto and Montréal, Canada; Cancún and Mexico City, Mexico; most Central and South American capitals; several Caribbean islands; and half a dozen European cities. Domestic service includes daily flights between Havana and Santiago de Cuba, Camagüey, and Holguín as well as less frequent flights to a dozen more destinations, among them Cayo Largo, Cienfuegos, and Baracoa. (Note that it's illegal for U.S. citizens to fly on Cubana, as it constitutes a cash payment to the Cuban government—a trade-embargo no-no.)

Several major foreign carriers, which are undoubtedly more comfortable than Cubana, also serve the island. These include British Airways, which has weekly flights (on Saturday) from Gatwick to Nassau, Bahamas, and on to Havana, and Iberia, which flies nonstop from Madrid to Havana daily. LTU and Condor offer weekly flights to Havana and Varadero from several German cities. Martinair has weekly flights to Havana and Varadero from Amsterdam. The Panamanian carrier Copa has daily flights from Panama City to Havana. Grupo Taca flies to Havana several times a week from San José, Costa Rica, with connections from the rest of Central America. Aeropostal offers weekly flights from Caracas, Venezuela; Air Jamaica flies from Kingston; Mexicana flies from Mexico City, and Air France, from Paris.

Air Transat offers flights and packages from Montréal and Toronto to Varadero, Cayo Largo, Cienfuegos, Ciego de Ávila, Camagüey, Holguín, and Santiago de Cuba. It also flies from Vancouver, Edmonton, and Calgary to Varadero and Ciego de Ávila. Skyservice Airlines (whose flights are booked through Sunquest/Alba Tours) flies from Toronto—with connections from several nearby cities—to Varadero, Cayo Largo, Cienfuegos, Ciego de Ávila, Camagüey, Holguín, and Santiago. Numerous Canadian tour companies sell packages that include flights with these airlines, among them Carlson Wagonlit, Regent Holidays, and Sell Off Vacations. The Costa Rican airline Lacsa also offers direct flights between Toronto and Havana.

Marazul Tours—which has been running charters between the United States and Cuba since 1979—offers weekly flights to Havana from Miami, New York, and Los Angeles. The Coral Gables–based tour operator Caribbean Family & Travel Services arranges flights through its charter company, Tico Travel in Fort Lauderdale. There are daily flights from Miami to Havana and weekly flights from Los Angeles and New York. Note that only certain Americans qualify for licensed travel to Cuba (☞ Americans and Cuba, *below*).

▶ AIRLINES/CHARTERS FROM CANADA: **Air Transat** (☎ 33/30–1326 in Cayo Coco, WEB www.airtransat.com). **Carlson Wagonlit** (☎ 416/929–1980 in Toronto or 514/871–8330 in Montréal, WEB www.carlsonwagonlit. ca). **Cubana** (☎ 416/967–2822 in Toronto or 514/871–1222 in Montréal). **Cubanacán** (☎ 416/601–0343 in Toronto). **Lacsa** (☎ 416/968–2222 in Toronto or 800/225–2272 in North America, WEB www. grupotaca.com). **Regent Holidays** (☎ 416/673–3343 in Toronto, WEB www.regentholidays.com). **Sell Off Vacations** (WEB www.selloffvacations. com). **Skyservice Airlines** (☎ 877/ 485–6060 in the U.S. and Canada).

Sunquest/Alba Tours (☎ 877/485–6060, WEB www.sunquest.ca).

▶ AIRLINES/CHARTERS FROM THE CARIBBEAN AND LATIN AMERICA: **Aerocaribe** (☎ 98/84–2000 in Cancún, WEB www.aerocaribe.com). **Aeropostal** (☎ 509–3666 in Caracas). **Air Jamaica** (☎ 888/359–2475 in Jamaica or 800/523–558 in the U.S.). **Copa** (☎ 507/227–5000 in Panama City, WEB www.copaair.com). **Cubana** (☎ 5/250–6355 in Mexico City; 9/887–7210 in Cancún; 809/549–0345 or 809/227–2040 in Santo Domingo; 876/978–3110 in Kingston; 242/377–8752 in Nassau; 507/227–2291 in Panama City; 506/290–5095 in San José). **GrupoTaca** (☎ 800/225–2272 in North America or 506/296–0909 in Costa Rica, WEB www.grupotaca.com). **Mexicana** (☎ 800/531–7921 in North America or 5/428–0990 in Mexico City, WEB www.mexicana.com).

▶ AIRLINES FROM EUROPE: **Air France** (☎ 33/082–082–0820 in Paris, WEB www.airfrance.com). **British Airways** (☎ 0345/222111 in London, WEB www.britishair.com/uk). **Condor** (WEB www.condor.de). **Cubana** (☎ 020/7734–1165 in London, WEB www.cubana.cu). **Iberia** (☎ 904/400500 in Madrid, WEB www. iberia.es). **LTU** (☎ 94/18–888 in Düsseldorf, WEB www.ltu.de). **Martinair** (☎ 31/0/2060–11222 in Amsterdam, WEB www.martinair.com).

▶ CHARTERS FROM THE U.S: **Marazul Tours** (✉ 8324 S.W. 40 St., Miami, FL 33155, ☎ 305/559–3616 or 800/223–5334, WEB www.marazultours. com; ✉ Tower Plaza Mall, 4100 Park Ave., Weehawken, NJ 07087, ☎ 201/319–3900). **Tico Travel** (✉ 161 E. Commercial Blvd., Fort Lauderdale, FL 33334, ☎ 800/493–8426, WEB www.destinationcuba.com).

CHECK-IN & BOARDING

Most carriers require you to check in two hours before your scheduled departure time for domestic flights and 2½ to 3 hours before international flights. Always ask your carrier about its check-in policy.

Assuming that not everyone with a ticket will show up, airlines routinely overbook planes. When everyone does, airlines ask for volunteers to give up their seats. In return, these volunteers usually get a certificate for a free flight and are rebooked on the next flight out. If there are not enough volunteers, the airline must choose who will be denied boarding. The first to get bumped are passengers who checked in late and those flying on discounted tickets, so **get to the gate and check in as early as possible,** especially during peak periods.

Always **bring a government-issued photo I.D. to the airport;** even when it's not required, a passport is best.

CUTTING COSTS

You'll often get the best rates on flights to Cuba, particularly from Canada (Toronto handles most of the traffic), if you **book a charter flight—** whether you opt only to purchase seats on a plane or to buy a complete package that includes airfare, hotel, and transfers to and from the airport. If charter-flight scenarios don't appeal to you—and you aren't the type who likes to wait for last-minute deals—know that the least expensive airfares to Cuba must usually be purchased in advance and are nonrefundable.

It's smart to **call a number of airlines,** and when you're quoted a good price, **book it on the spot**—the same fare may not be available the next day. Always **check different routings** and look into using different airports. Travel agents, especially low-fare specialists (☞ Discounts & Deals, *below*), are helpful.

ENJOYING THE FLIGHT

For more legroom, **request an emergency-aisle seat.** Don't sit in the row in front of the emergency exit or in front of a bulkhead, where seats may not recline. If you have dietary concerns, **ask for special meals when booking.** These can be vegetarian, low-cholesterol, or kosher, for example. On long flights, try to maintain a normal routine, to help fight jet lag. At night, **get some sleep.** By day, **eat light meals, drink water** (not alcohol), and **move around the cabin** to stretch your legs. For additional jet-lag tips consult *Fodor's FYI: Travel Fit & Healthy* (available at bookstores everywhere).

HOW TO COMPLAIN

If your baggage goes astray or your flight goes awry, complain right away. Most carriers require that you **file a claim immediately.**

AMERICANS AND CUBA

Although there are restrictions in place owing to the U.S. trade embargo, technically, it's not illegal for Americans to travel to Cuba; what *is* illegal is spending money in the country. American companies cannot conduct business with companies in Cuba, and neither can individual Americans. Hence, credit cards issued by U.S. companies and insurance policies provided by U.S. insurers are not valid here; American airlines do not offer commercial service to Cuba (though there is charter-flight service from New York, Miami, and Los Angeles); and the only American tour operators and travel agents offering packages directly to the island are those working with groups licensed by the U.S. Department of the Treasury's Office of Foreign Assets Control (OFAC).

Restrictions on individuals and businesses are contained within the Cuban Assets Control Regulations, first enacted in 1963 under the Trading with the Enemy Act, but revised through the years. For complete details on the latest regulations and on licenses for travel to Cuba contact the OFAC. The Treasury Department has a helpful Web site, and, in an effort to help explain the restrictions further, the U.S. State Department has also developed a useful Web site.

LICENSED TRAVEL TO CUBA

For official travel to Cuba, **look into OFAC general and specific licenses.** Those who qualify for a general license need not inform the OFAC in advance of their visit or obtain a written OFAC license. Specific licenses are more complicated: if you qualify, you must obtain a written license by writing to the OFAC stating your name and title, when you plan to travel, and the length and purpose of your visit; you must also provide details on your background.

If you have either type of license, the maximum that you can spend each day on transportation, food, lodging, and other basics is $158. Note that this sum is for Havana only; elsewhere the per diem total is $125, except for Guantánamo Bay, where it's $58. Also, there are precise guidelines on how much of each per diem total should be spent on hotel and other expenses. You can also return to the United States with Cuban products whose value totals no more than $100 (educational and informational material, film, CDs, and books are exempt). **Save your receipts,** as a Cuban stamp in your passport will no doubt raise red flags with U.S. Customs officials. Always **check on rules on travel to Cuba right before your trip;** these rules are subject to sudden changes.

The following U.S. travelers qualify for an OFAC general license: government personnel on official business; journalists and their support staff who are employed full time by a publication or broadcast company (such travelers should have a company ID with a photograph, business cards, and a letter—on company letterhead—verifying full-time employment); fully hosted travelers; and individuals visiting close relatives (such trips are limited to once a year, though exceptions are made—via a specific license—for humanitarian reasons).

The following Americans can apply for a specific license: those involved in business, academic, international-relations, and human-rights research; people visiting close relatives more than once in a 12-month period for extreme humanitarian reasons; freelance journalists; graduate students; professors who will be lecturing at educational institutions; athletes who will be competing in events; and artists and performers who will be participating in exhibitions or concerts. Those accompanying licensed humanitarian donations (as specified by the U.S. Department of Commerce's Office of Export Administrations) also qualify for a specific license.

Licenses are also available for individuals or establishments affiliated with a U.S.-based religious organization. Such licenses must be renewed every two years. Travelers associated with a licensed organization are free to travel to Cuba as long as they carry a letter from the organization stating its license number and that the individual is affiliated with the organization and is traveling for the purpose of religious activity in Cuba under the organization's auspices.

FULLY HOSTED TRAVELERS

Fully hosted travelers are defined as those who spend no money on their Cuba trip, as they're guests of a non-U.S. entity. Although such people qualify for travel under a general license, the guidelines and restrictions for such trips are more complex. Further, the $100 Cuban-goods import allowance does not apply, and you may be required to provide proof supporting your claim to being fully hosted. The OFAC warns that fully hosted travelers will be under intense scrutiny by State Department, Treasury Department, customs, and immigration officials. If you're planning a fully hosted trip to Cuba, **be sure that you meet all the requirements and have all the necessary documentation.**

UNLICENSED TRAVEL TO CUBA

Cuba's romantic history, culture, and people have left an indelible imprint on the American psyche, making the idea of a leisure junket to the island very tempting. Many U.S. citizens visit Cuba by going through third countries such as Canada, Mexico, the Bahamas, or Costa Rica (usually by using third-country tour operators and travel agents to arrange their trips). Such travelers enter Cuba on $20 tourist cards, which they purchase from their airline or travel agent; Cuban officials stamp these cards rather than passports. Although few people have been prosecuted for violating the restrictions, **be aware that there are stiff penalties on the books for unlicensed travel to Cuba.** The fines can be severe: for businesses, they're as much as $1 million, for individuals, up to $250,000. In certain circumstances, penalties include up to 10 years in jail. The Bush administration has made moves to curb illegal travel to Cuba by imposing fines of several thousand dollars on Americans caught arriving from Cuba in Canadian airports.

➤ INFORMATION: **U.S. Department of the Treasury, Office of Foreign Assets Control** (☎ 202/622–2520 in Washington D.C. or 305/810–5140 in

Miami, WEB www.treas.gov/ofac). **U.S. State Department** (WEB www.state. gov/www/regions/wha/cuba/travel/ index.html).

BIKE TRAVEL

Since the collapse of the Soviet Union, cycling has become a main means of transport in Cuba, and you'll see lovers out on a date, grandmothers with groceries, and farmers hauling crops from the fields on bicycles. Cuban tour operators offer everything from short trips to island-wide treks. You'll find bicycle-rental shops—well-stocked with spare parts and supplies—in all major cities and tourist centers. Still, as country roads are rough (and can take you miles from the nearest shop), it's wise to bring your own emergency repair supplies.

BIKES IN FLIGHT

Most airlines accommodate bikes as luggage, provided they're dismantled and boxed. Airlines sell bike boxes, which are often free at bike shops, for about $5 (it's at least $100 for bike bags). International travelers can sometimes substitute a bike for a piece of checked luggage at no charge; otherwise, the cost is about $100. Canadian airlines charge $25–$50.

BOAT & FERRY TRAVEL

There's boat and ferry service from the Cuban mainland to several off-shore keys. For details on such service, *see* the A to Z section at the end of each chapter.

BUS TRAVEL

Cubans rely a great deal on an unreliable bus system—one with crowded, badly maintained vehicles and slow service. Even long-distance buses, called *especiales,* are well below North American and European standards. Demand for service is so great and seats (and fuel) so scarce that not only are old farm trucks pressed into public-transport service but also state-owned trucks, by law, must pick up Cuban citizens hitching rides. For these reasons, public buses aren't the best option for most visitors. Nevertheless, the bus company Astro reserves a few seats on its especiales for non-Cubans.

Your best option, however, is the tourist bus company Víazul, which

has comfortable, air-conditioned vehicles that depart fairly punctually. It offers daily service between Havana and Varadero (three per day), Viñales (one per day), Trinidad (two per day), and Santiago de Cuba (two per day). There's also daily service between Varadero and Trinidad and between Trinidad and Santiago de Cuba. Fares range from $10 (Havana–Varadero) to $51 (Havana–Santiago). Note that most cities have two types of terminal: the *terminal de omnibus interprovincial* serves especiales, including those run by Astro and Víazul (which also sometimes has its own terminals); the *terminal de omnibus intermunicipal* serves buses to nearby towns and beaches.

➤ BUS INFORMATION: **Astro** (☎ 7/ 870–9401). **Víazul** ☎ 7/881–1413 in Havana, 5/61–4886 in Varadero, 419/2404 in Trinidad, 226/62–8484 in Santiago de Cuba, WEB www. viazul.cu).

PAYING

Though public buses charge Cubans in pesos, tourists must pay much inflated prices in U.S. dollars. You'll need cash for Astro buses; Víazul accepts non-U.S. credit cards.

RESERVATIONS

The only way to reserve seats is to purchase tickets at bus stations; this should be done several days ahead of time in high season. For much of the year, however, tickets are available only on the day you plan to depart or the day before. In Havana, you can buy Víazul tickets at Infotur offices as well as at bus stations.

BUSINESS HOURS

Banks are open weekdays 9–3, and offices are usually open weekdays 8–noon and 1–5. Museums are generally open weekdays 9–5, with slightly shorter hours on weekends (e.g., 10–4 or simply an afternoon or morning off); some close on Monday. Most shops conduct business Monday–Saturday 9–6, though some may close for an hour at lunchtime. Many gas stations are open 24 hours.

CAMERAS & PHOTOGRAPHY

Cuba, with its unusual cityscapes and its majestic landscapes, is a photographer's dream. Cubans seem amenable to having picture-taking tourists in their midst, but you should always **ask permission before photographing individuals.** If you're bashful about approaching strangers, **photograph people with whom you interact**: your waiter, your desk clerk, the vendor selling you crafts. Even better, have a traveling companion or a passerby photograph you *with* them. Many Cubans will ask you to mail copies of the photos back to them, and, out of courtesy, you should do your absolute best to comply. You should also comply with the government's ban on photographing military or police installations or personnel and harbor, rail, or airport facilities. Note that there's often a charge for taking pictures and shooting video at museums and other sights.

Frothy waves in a turquoise sea and palm-lined crescents of beach are relatively easy to capture on film if you **don't let the brightness of the sun on sand and water fool your light meter.** You'll need to compensate or else work early or late in the day when the light isn't as brilliant and contrast isn't such a problem. Try to **capture expansive views** of waterfront, beach, or village scenes; consider shooting down onto the shore from a clearing on a hillside or from a rock on the beach. Or **zoom in on something colorful,** such as a delicate tropical flower or a craftsman at work.

Bring high-speed film to compensate for low light under the tree canopy on jungle or forest trips. **Invest in a telephoto lens to photograph wildlife:** even standard zoom lenses of the 35–88 range won't capture a satisfying amount of detail. Casual photographers should **consider using inexpensive disposable cameras** to reduce the risks inherent in traveling with sophisticated equipment. One-use cameras with panoramic or underwater functions can also be nice supplements to a standard camera and its gear.

The *Kodak Guide to Shooting Great Travel Pictures* (available at bookstores everywhere) is loaded with tips.

➤ Photo Help: **Kodak Information Center** (☎ 800/242–2424).

EQUIPMENT PRECAUTIONS

Don't pack film and equipment in checked luggage, where it is much more susceptible to damage. X-ray machines used to view checked luggage are becoming much more powerful and therefore are much more likely to ruin your film. Always **keep film and tape out of the sun.** Carry an extra supply of batteries, and **be prepared to turn on your camera or camcorder** to prove to security personnel that the device is real. Always **ask for hand inspection of film,** which becomes clouded after repeated exposure to airport X-ray machines, and **keep videotapes away from metal detectors.**

FILM & DEVELOPING

There are film labs in every city, but it's best to **process film back home.** Developing it in Cuba is expensive and time-consuming, and you may not want to trust your prize photos to the island's poorly equipped labs. Although the government-owned Photo Service chain sells film and basic camera gear, supplies of everything are limited. **Bring more film and videotapes than you expect to use,** as well as extra batteries and other equipment.

CAR RENTAL

Renting a car is an expensive proposition: gas prices are high, and rental rates are $60–$90 a day including insurance. Further, if all your credit cards are issued by U.S. banks, you'll also have to make a security deposit of $200–$300. If you're on a tight budget, consider traveling longer distances by bus or plane and/or picking one city as a base from which to make short side trips by cab.

If you're traveling during a holiday period, **make sure that a confirmed reservation guarantees you a car.** Before setting out, **check the car carefully for defects,** and **make sure your car has a jack and spare tire.** The two biggest agencies are Havanautos and Transautos, and because they have the most branches, they can get another vehicle to you fairly quickly if you have problems. Smaller agencies such as Micar and Vía may offer lower rates, whereas Rex specialized in luxury vehicles. Cubacar and Veracuba offer moderate rates.

➤ LOCAL AGENCIES: **Cubacar** (☎ 7/ 33–2277 in Havana, WEB www. cubacar.cubanacan.cu). **Havanautos** (☎ 7/203–9318 in Havana, WEB www. havanautos.cubaweb.cu). **Micar** (☎ 7/204–2444 in Havana). **Rex** (☎ 7/33–9160 in Havana). **Trans-autos** (☎ 7/204–5532 in Havana. **Transtur** (☎ 7/861–6788 in Havana, WEB www.transtur.cubaweb.cu). **Veracuba** (☎ 7/33–0600 in Havana, WEB www.cubanacan.cu). **Vía Rent a Car** (☎ 7/33–9781 in Havana).

CUTTING COSTS

Because all agencies are state owned, prices are basically set. Still some of the smaller agencies may offer slightly better rates.

INSURANCE

When driving a rented car you are generally responsible for any damage to or loss of the vehicle as well as for any property damage or personal injury that you may cause. If you're a visitor from anywhere but the United States, see what coverage your personal auto-insurance policy and credit cards already provide before you rent. U.S. visitors should definitely purchase auto insurance locally.

REQUIREMENTS & RESTRICTIONS

You must be 21 years old and have a valid national driver's license or an international driver's license to rent an automobile.

SURCHARGES

Before you pick up a car in one city and leave it in another, **ask about drop-off charges or one-way service fees,** which can be substantial. Note, too, that some rental agencies charge extra if you return the car before the time specified in your contract. In Cuba you often pay for whatever gas is in the tank upon renting the car, and you're not necessarily expected to bring the tank back full or pay a hefty refueling fee if you fail to do so.

CAR TRAVEL

The good news is that most main roads are well maintained, and once you're out of the cities traffic is light.

The bad news is that signage is very poor; it's easy to get lost, so **get good road maps.** If your arsenal of maps and the directions in this guide aren't enough to get you where you're going, **be a bold and artful traveler: use the time-honored method of asking a local for directions** (pointing to maps and gesturing if need be).

EMERGENCY SERVICES

Roadside assistance is handled primarily through car rental companies, so be sure to **ask your rental agent for the most up-to-date emergency number.**

GASOLINE

Gas costs about $1 a liter (roughly $4 a gallon). There are state-run Servi-Cupet, Cupet-Cimex, and Oro Negro stations spread out along major routes; many are open 24 hours a day. Nonetheless, it's best to start a long journey with a full tank. These stations, which only accept payment in dollars, also sell snacks and beverages.

PARKING

Parking is easy in most Cuban cities. On-street spaces are plentiful, and many hotels have large lots. Never leave valuables unattended in your car, and don't leave a car on an unguarded street overnight.

ROAD CONDITIONS

Most roads are well maintained. The country's main artery, the six-lane Autopista Nacional, runs from Havana to Ciego de Ávila before hitting the two-lane Carretera Central, which runs to El Oriente, the island's eastern portion. The Autopista Nacional also runs westward from Havana into Pinar del Río. Cuba has tolls on some routes; a trip on the Matanzas–Varadero Expressway, for example, costs $2.

RULES OF THE ROAD

Driving is on the right side of the road. Speed limits range from 40 kph (25 mph) around schools to 100 kph (60 mph) on main highways. As anywhere, **avoid drinking and driving.** Cuba's police force is efficient by Caribbean and Latin American standards; you're likely to get caught if you break any laws. Note that any fines you incur for traffic violations will be deducted from your rental car deposit.

It may be illegal in some parts of the world, but hitchhiking is a common mode of transportation in Cuba. Although you should exercise caution about picking people up, note that most hitchhikers are ordinary folk simply trying to get to work or pay a visit to relatives. Sharing the ride with them can put you in greater touch with the country and get you some much-needed navigational assistance.

CHILDREN IN CUBA

It's quite safe to travel the island with your kids. What's more, Cubans love children and will shower attention on them, so you may find yourselves interacting with locals a great deal. Many beach resorts have children's programs that can keep the little ones busy most of the day and part of the evening. If you're renting a car, don't forget to **arrange for a car seat** when you reserve. For general advice about traveling with children, consult *Fodor's FYI: Travel with Your Baby* (available in bookstores everywhere).

Let older children join in on planning as you outline your trip. **Scout your library for picture books, storybooks, and maps about places you'll be going.** Try to **explain the concept of foreign language**; some kids, who may have just learned to talk, are thrown when they can't understand strangers and strangers can't understand them. On sightseeing days try to **schedule activities of special interest to your children.** If you're renting a car, don't forget to **arrange for a car seat** when you reserve.

FLYING

If your children are two or older, **ask about children's airfares.** As a rule, infants under two not occupying a seat fly at greatly reduced fares or even for free. When booking, **confirm carry-on allowances** if you're traveling with infants. In general, for babies charged 10% of the adult fare you're allowed one carry-on bag and a collapsible stroller; if the flight is full, the stroller may have to be checked or you may be limited to less.

Experts agree that it's a good idea to use safety seats aloft for children weighing less than 40 pounds. Airlines set their own policies: some carriers require that the child be ticketed, even if he or she is young enough to ride free, since the seats must be strapped into regular seats. Do **check your airline's policy about using safety seats during takeoff and landing.** And since safety seats aren't allowed everywhere in the plane, get your seat assignments early.

When reserving, **request children's meals or a freestanding bassinet** if you need them. But note that bulkhead seats, where you must sit to use the bassinet, may lack an overhead bin or storage space on the floor.

LODGING

Most hotels in Cuba allow children under a certain age to stay in their parents' room at no extra charge, but others charge for them as extra adults; be sure to **find out the cutoff age for children's discounts.**

PRECAUTIONS

Children should have all their inoculations up to date before leaving home. Make sure that health precautions, such as what to drink and eat, are applied to the whole family. Not cramming too much into each day will keep the whole family healthier while on the road.

SIGHTS & ATTRACTIONS

Places that are especially appealing to children are indicated by a rubber-duckie icon (☺) in the margin.

SUPPLIES & EQUIPMENT

Pack things to keep your children busy while traveling. For children of reading age, **bring books from home;** locally, literature for kids in English is hard to find.

It's a good idea to **pack first-aid supplies and a few basic over-the-counter children's medicines.** Obviously, you should also bring an ample supply of any prescription medicines your child may be taking. Although Cuban diapers are available at reasonable prices (less than 50¢ each), they're shabbily made and may not offer the absorbancy you are used to;

you may find other supplies lacking—in both quantity and quality. If you're traveling with an infant, **bring diapers, formula, and all other essential gear.**

COMPUTERS ON THE ROAD

If you're traveling with a laptop, you're supposed to fill out a declaration form for it upon entering Cuba, though it's unlikely anyone will ask you to do so. Carry a spare battery, extra disks, a universal adapter plug, and a converter if your computer isn't dual-voltage. Note that blackouts and electrical surges are sometimes a problem, so saving your work more frequently is a good idea. **Keep your disks out of the sun** and **avoid excessive heat for both your computer and disks.**

Because the telecommunications system isn't as advanced as those in Europe and North America, Internet access isn't widely available. If you do tap into the Web, be prepared for your surfing expedition to be expensive and slow. Cybercafés have begun to appear in Cuba's more visited areas. Havana's famous Capitolio has a small Internet café off its foyer. In addition, nonguests can use the business centers in Havana's Hotel Nacional and Hotel Habana Libre for a hefty fee. In Trinidad, the restaurant Las Begonias has a few computers hooked up to the Internet. *Correos* (post offices) in some large towns also offer e-mail service.

➤ BUSINESS CENTERS AND CYBERCAFÉS: **Las Begonias** (⊠ Antonio Maceo y Simón Bolívar, Trinidad, ☎ no phone). **Capitolio** (⊠ Paseo de Martí/Prado, Havana, ☎ 7/862–8504 or 7/862–6536). **Hotel Habana Libre** (Calle 23/La Rampa y Calle L, Vedado, Havana, ☎ 7/33–4011). **Hotel Nacional** (Calle O y Calle 21, Vedado, Havana, ☎ 7/33–3564 through 7/33–3567).

CRUISE TRAVEL

The trade embargo bars U.S. lines from offering cruises to Cuba. Since the mid-1990s, however, some European lines have been stopping in Havana and/or Santiago de Cuba as part of itineraries that also include stops in Jamaica, Grand Cayman, and the Dominican Republic. West Indies Cruising Ltd. offers trips on the *Valtur Prima*; these depart from Montego Bay, Jamaica, and stop in Havana, and you can book them though itravel2000. The Mexican line Riviera Holiday Cruises runs two inexpensive cruises per week from Cancún to Havana, one from Friday to Sunday, one from Monday to Thursday, with an option to stay in Cuba and return on another cruise. The Toronto-based Cuba Cruise Corp. offers cruises year-round to Havana on MV *La Habana*, which departs from Nassau, Bahamas. To learn how to plan, choose, and book a cruise-ship voyage, consult *Fodor's FYI: Plan & Enjoy Your Cruise* (available in bookstores everywhere).

➤ CRUISE LINES: **Cuba Cruise Corp.** (☎ 800/387–1387 in the U.S. and Canada or 416/964–2569, WEB www.cubacruising.com). **itravel2000** (☎ 800/859–2920, WEB www.itravel200.com). **Riviera Holiday Cruises** (☎ 529/887–3414, WEB www.rivieraholidaycruises.com).

CUSTOMS & DUTIES

When shopping, **keep receipts** for all purchases. Upon reentering the country, **be ready to show customs officials what you've bought.** If you feel a duty is incorrect or object to the way your clearance was handled, note the inspector's badge number and ask to see a supervisor. If the problem isn't resolved, write to the appropriate authorities, beginning with the port director at your point of entry.

IN CUBA

Expect X-ray machines and a thorough search by officials in military fatigues or blue uniforms upon your arrival. You many enter Cuba with three bottles of liquor, a carton of cigarettes, 50 cigars, gifts totaling no more than $100 in value, and prescription medicines (for personal consumption) either in their original bottles or in other bottles accompanied by a doctor's prescription. Be sure to register valuable items (such as a laptop) in your home country and declare them and large amounts of foreign currency upon entering Cuba.

Firearms aren't allowed, and Cuban authorities may confiscate written or visual material viewed either as "pornographic" or "counterrevolutionary." Don't even think of bringing illegal drugs into Cuba, which is remarkably drug-free and has among the region's stiffest penalties for offenders.

IN AUSTRALIA

Australian residents who are 18 or older may bring home $A400 worth of souvenirs and gifts (including jewelry), 250 cigarettes or 250 grams of tobacco, and 1,125 ml of alcohol (including wine, beer, and spirits). Residents under 18 may bring back $A200 worth of goods. Prohibited items include meat products. Seeds, plants, and fruits need to be declared upon arrival.

➤ INFORMATION: **Australian Customs Service** (Regional Director, ✉ Box 8, Sydney, NSW 2001, Australia, ☎ 02/9213–2000, FAX 02/9213–4000, WEB www.customs.gov.au).

IN CANADA

Canadian residents who have been out of Canada for at least seven days may bring home C$750 worth of goods duty-free. If you've been away fewer than seven days but more than 48 hours, the duty-free allowance drops to C$200; if your trip lasts 24–48 hours, the allowance is C$50. You may not pool allowances with family members. Goods claimed under the C$750 exemption may follow you by mail; those claimed under the lesser exemptions must accompany you. Alcohol and tobacco products may be included in the seven-day and 48-hour exemptions but not in the 24-hour exemption. If you meet the age requirements of the province or territory through which you reenter Canada, you may bring in, duty-free, 1.14 liters (40 imperial ounces) of wine or liquor *or* 24 12-ounce cans or bottles of beer or ale. If you are 19 or older you may bring in, duty-free, 200 cigarettes and 50 cigars. Check ahead of time with the Canada Customs Revenue Agency or the Department of Agriculture for policies regarding meat products, seeds, plants, and fruits.

You may send an unlimited number of gifts worth up to C$60 each duty-free to Canada. Label the package UNSOLICITED GIFT—VALUE UNDER $60. Alcohol and tobacco are excluded.

➤ INFORMATION: **Canada Customs Revenue Agency** (✉ 2265 St. Laurent Blvd. S, Ottawa, Ontario K1G 4K3, Canada, ☎ 204/983–3500 or 506/636–5064; 800/461–9999 in Canada, WEB www.ccra-adrc.gc.ca).

IN NEW ZEALAND

Homeward-bound residents 17 or older may bring back $700 worth of souvenirs and gifts. Your duty-free allowance also includes 4.5 liters of wine or beer; one 1,125-ml bottle of spirits; and either 200 cigarettes, 250 grams of tobacco, 50 cigars, or a combination of the three up to 250 grams. Prohibited items include meat products, seeds, plants, and fruits.

➤ INFORMATION: **New Zealand Customs** (Custom House, ✉ 50 Anzac Ave., Box 29, Auckland, New Zealand, ☎ 09/300–5399, FAX 09/359–6730), WEB www.customs.govt.nz.

IN THE U.K.

From countries outside the European Union, including Cuba, you may bring home, duty-free, 200 cigarettes or 50 cigars; 1 liter of spirits or 2 liters of fortified or sparkling wine or liqueurs; 2 liters of still table wine; 60 ml of perfume; 250 ml of toilet water; plus £145 worth of other goods, including gifts and souvenirs. If returning from outside the EU, prohibited items include meat products, seeds, plants, and fruits.

➤ INFORMATION: **HM Customs and Excise** (✉ St. Christopher House, Southwark, London, SE1 OTE, U.K., ☎ 020/7928–3344, WEB www.hmce.gov.uk).

IN THE UNITED STATES

Normally U.S. residents who have been out of the country for at least 48 hours (and who have not used the $400 allowance or any part of it in the past 30 days) may bring home $400 worth of foreign goods duty-free. With Cuba, however, all these bets are off. Licensed travelers (☞ Americans and Cuba, *above*) are limited to a total of $100 worth of

Cuban products. Unlicensed travelers caught bringing Cuban items into the country should be prepared to have the goods confiscated and to face possible fines and/or other penalties.

➤ INFORMATION: **U.S. Customs Service** (✉ 1300 Pennsylvania Ave. NW, Room 6.3D, Washington, DC 20229, WEB www.customs.gov; inquiries ☎ 202/354–1000; complaints c/o ✉ 1300 Pennsylvania Ave. NW, Room 5.4D, Washington, DC 20229; registration of equipment c/o Office of Passenger Programs, ☎ 202/927–0530).

DINING

Forty years of socialism, isolation, and hard economic times have taken their toll, often leaving Cuban food (and service in restaurants) uninspired and uninspiring. (Even Castro has remarked about the bad service given by Cuban waiters and waitresses.) Many of the country's best chefs and restaurateurs followed their upper- and middle-class clients into exile after the Revolution, and even local *comida criolla* (creole cuisine) isn't as good as the Cuban food served in the exile communities of Miami, New York, or Puerto Rico.

As the economy has become increasingly reliant on tourism, the government has made efforts to improve the quality of both the service and the food in state-run restaurants. Foreign management of hotels and their restaurants, through joint ventures with the Cuban government, is also helping matters.

Unless otherwise noted, the restaurants listed in this guide are open daily for lunch and dinner. Most hotel restaurants serve buffet-style breakfasts from 7 AM to 10 AM and dinners from 7 PM to 10 PM. Better meals— sometimes only dinner—are served in *paladares,* tiny eateries in private homes that are allowed a maximum of only 12 seats and must be staffed by family members. Although there are restrictions on what can be served (seafood, for example, is officially forbidden at paladares), the food is usually fresh and relatively inexpensive (you can get a full meal for as little as $8), and the portions are often generous. Unfortunately, the government has closed many paladares in recent years, so most towns have only two or three; some have none at all. There are also a number of illegal paladares, toward which *jineteros* (street hustlers) will likely try to steer you. Although the food in these establishments can be good, in general you're better off avoiding all recommendations from the jineteros.

The restaurants we list (all of which are indicated with ✗) are the cream of the crop in each price category. Properties indicated by an ✗▥ are lodging establishments whose restaurant warrants a special trip.

CATEGORY	COST*
$$$$	over $20
$$$	$15–$20
$$	$10–$15
$	$5–$10
¢	under $5

*per person for a dinner entrée

PAYING

Dollars are almost always required in places frequented by tourists. In local establishments, which generally take only pesos (but will often accept your dollars and give you change in pesos), have small denominations on hand. Credit cards not issued by U.S. companies are accepted at government establishments but not in paladares.

RESERVATIONS & DRESS

Cuban meals are relaxed, and reservations are rarely required; we mention them only when they're essential or aren't accepted. Book as far ahead as you can, and reconfirm as soon as you arrive. Note that some restaurants frown on shorts for men and women both; beach attire is usually acceptable only on the beach. We mention dress requirements only when men are required to wear a jacket or a jacket and tie.

DISABILITIES & ACCESSIBILITY

Cuba has only recently—since the tourist boom of the 1990s—begun taking the needs of travelers with disabilities into account. Hence its infrastructure is dismal, with few ramps, curb dips, or wide doorways capable of accommodating wheelchairs; few realistic transportation options; and many cobblestone streets that can make getting around difficult. Your best bet for arranging a trip to Cuba is to work closely with a tour operator or travel agent who specializes in trips for people with disabilities.

RESERVATIONS

When discussing accessibility with an operator or reservations agent, **ask hard questions.** Are there any stairs, inside *or* out? Are there grab bars next to the toilet *and* in the shower/ tub? How wide is the doorway to the room? To the bathroom? For the most extensive facilities meeting the latest legal specifications, **opt for newer accommodations.**

TRAVEL AGENCIES

In the United States, the Americans with Disabilities Act requires that travel firms serve the needs of all travelers. Some agencies specialize in working with people with disabilities.

➤ TRAVELERS WITH MOBILITY PROBLEMS: **Access Adventures** (✉ 206 Chestnut Ridge Rd., Scottsville, NY 14624, ☎ 716/889–9096, dltravel@ prodigy.net), run by a former physical-rehabilitation counselor. **Accessible Vans of America** (✉ 9 Spielman Rd., Fairfield, NJ 07004, ☎ 877/ 282–8267, FAX 973/808–9713, WEB www.accessiblevans.com). **CareVacations** (✉ No. 5, 5110–50 Ave., Leduc, Alberta T9E 6V4, Canada, ☎ 780/ 986–6404 or 877/478–7827, FAX 780/ 986–8332, WEB www.carevacations. com), for group tours and cruise vacations. **Flying Wheels Travel** (✉ 143 W. Bridge St., Box 382, Owatonna, MN 55060, ☎ 507/451– 5005 or 800/535–6790, FAX 507/451– 1685, WEB www.flyingwheelstravel. com).

DISCOUNTS & DEALS

The most inexpensive way to visit Cuba is with a package that puts you in an all-inclusive beach hotel. (Don't confuse packages with guided tours: when you buy a package, you travel on your own, just as though you had planned the trip yourself.) Such establishments, however, may make you feel as if you were anywhere in the Caribbean rather than truly in Cuba. Further, you don't have much

flexibility to get out and really explore the country. **Ask your travel agent about split stays** between two or more hotels in different areas. You may be able to get bottom-line package rates, yet still experience the island and its people. Fly/drive packages, which combine airfare and car rental, are also often a good deal.

Be a smart shopper and **compare all your options** before making decisions. A plane ticket bought with a promotional coupon from travel clubs, coupon books, and direct-mail offers or on the Internet may not be cheaper than the least expensive fare from a discount ticket agency. And always keep in mind that what you get is just as important as what you save.

DISCOUNT RESERVATIONS

To save money, **look into discount reservations services** with toll-free numbers, which use their buying power to get a better price on hotels, airline tickets, even car rentals. When booking a room, always **call the hotel's local number** rather than the central reservations number—you'll often get a better price. Always ask about special packages or corporate rates.

➤ AIRLINE TICKETS: ☎ 800/AIR–4LESS.

➤ HOTEL ROOMS: **Turbotrip.com** (☎ 800/473–7829, WEB www. turbotrip.com).

ECOTOURISM

Centuries of agricultural exploitation have claimed much of Cuba's wilderness, but in recent decades the government has taken steps to protect what remains. The lowlands were deforested long ago, but patches of tropical forest still cling to hills and the upper slopes of mountain ranges such as Pinar del Río's Guaniguanico, the central Escambray range, and eastern Cuba's various *sierras*. Such highlands forests are home to parakeets, trogons, and other endemic species. The other surviving ecosystems are coastal, from the freshwater swamps—with their crocodiles and varied waterfowl—in the Península de Zapata to the keys in the Jardines del Rey, where flamingos, herons, and other rare birds abound. Though relatively new to the business, the

Cuban tour companies Horizontes, Gaviota, and Rumbos offer a variety of natural-history tours; Horizontes has the widest selection. There are also a number of wilderness-area lodges that have in-house nature guides.

➤ CONTACTS: **Gaviota** (☎ 7/66–6777 in Havana, WEB www.gaviota.cubaweb.cu). **Horizontes** (☎ 7/66–2161 in Havana, WEB www.horizontes.cu). **Rumbos** (☎ 7/66–2113 in Havana).

ELECTRICITY

Cuba uses both the North American system of 110 volts, 60 cycles, and the 220-volt European system. North American–style plugs are the norm here. If your appliances are dual-voltage (as many laptop computers are), you'll need only an adapter. However, if they're strictly 110 volts, as most appliances sold in in North America are, plugging them into a 220-volt outlet will destroy them. Outlets are often marked either 110 or 220, but if they aren't, **be sure to ask what the voltage is before plugging in appliance.** Consider buying a universal adapter; the Swiss Army knife of adapters, it has several types of plugs in one handy unit.

Although things have improved since the early 1990s, blackouts are still an occasional reality. Most hotels have a backup power system, but these are designed to keep electricity flowing only to lights in lounges and hallways and to emergency lamps in guest rooms.

EMBASSIES

➤ IN AUSTRALIA: **Cuban Embassy** (✉ Box 1412, Maroubra, NSW 2035, ☎ 61/2–9311–4611).

➤ IN CANADA: **Cuban Embassy** (✉ 388 Main St., Ottawa, ON, K1S 1E3, ☎ 613/563–0141).

➤ IN CUBA: **British Embassy** (✉ Calle 34, No. 704, Miramar, Havana, ☎ 7/204–1771). **Canadian Embassy** (✉ Calle 30, No. 518, Miramar, Havana, ☎ 7/204–2044). **U.S. Special Interests Section** (✉ c/o Swiss Embassy; Calle Calzada, e/Calle L y Calle M, Vedado, Havana, ☎ 7/33–3551 or 7/33–3026).

➤ IN THE UNITED KINGDOM: **Cuban Embassy** (✉ 167 High Holburn, London, WC1V6PA, ☎ 44/207–240–b2488).

➤ UNITED STATES: **Cuban Interests Section** (✉ 2630 16th St. NW, Washington, DC 20009, ☎ 202/797–8518 or 202/797–8522).

EMERGENCIES

All but the smallest hotels have their own nurses and doctors, who have access to medicines you won't find in most pharmacies or hospitals. Travelers who stay in *casas particulares* (private houses with rooms to rent) can head for 24-hour *clinicas internacionales* (international clinics), which have well-stocked pharmacies, or contact Asistur. A visit with a doctor at a clinic costs about $25; house calls can sometimes be made for an extra $25. Cuban nurses and doctors earn about $20 and $30 a month, and consequently appreciate tips. Traveler's insurance is available through Asistur, which can also help you with sorting out various medical, financial, legal, and other problems.

➤ CONTACTS: **Asistur** (✉ Paseo Martí/Prado 212, Havana, ☎ 7/33–8920, FAX 7/33–8087, WEB www.asistur.cubaweb.cu; Calle 31, No. 101, Varadero, ☎ 5/66–7277; ✉ Hotel Jagua, Calle 37, No. 1, Cienfuegos, ☎ 432/6402; ✉ Cayo Coco, ☎ 33/30–8150; ✉ Guardalavaca, ☎ 24/30148; ✉ Below Hotel Casa Grande, Parque Céspedes, Santiago de Cuba, ☎ 226/68–6128).

ENGLISH-LANGUAGE MEDIA

Outside of a few Havana bookshops and some hotel stores, it can be nearly impossible to find English-language books and international publications. (Note that markup on international newspapers and periodicals can be as much as four times the cover price.) Hotels and tourist offices throughout the country have bimonthly, monthly, and weekly publications with current information in English on arts events, movies, television, and other entertainment. *Business Tips on Cuba*, available at airports and hotels, is filled with useful information. *Prisma* is a bimonthly magazine that covers general subjects on Cuba, the

Caribbean, and Latin America. It also has a travel section. *Granma,* the official Communist Party newspaper, is the nation's most important daily. Although laced with socialist propaganda, it also offers an interesting Cuban perspective on international news and issues. A weekly edition, *Granma Internacional,* is published in English, French, German, Portuguese, and Spanish.

Guest rooms in most hotels have cable TV, which usually includes CNN (in Spanish and English) or similar European-based news programs. If your Spanish is good you might want to check out one of Cuba's two national TV stations; in some areas you can tune into programming from Florida and Jamaica. International radio programs—from the BBC to the U.S.-based, anti-Castro broadcasts (started under President Reagan) of Radio Martí—can also be heard. Radio Taíno is geared to tourists.

ETIQUETTE & BEHAVIOR

Cubans are an open, gregarious people. Despite the United States government restrictions on its citizens traveling to the island, Cubans receive Americans just like all other foreigners: with open arms. Although Cubans will talk about the current political and economic situations, they generally do so only in vague terms. It's probably best to avoid talking politics with locals unless they bring up the subject.

GAY & LESBIAN TRAVEL

Although reports of police harassment persist, Cuba's tolerance of gays and lesbians has improved tremendously since the 1960s, when gays were rounded up and jailed. Most gays and lesbians remain in the closet, but informal meeting places for them have begun popping up in Havana and other cities (Santa Clara has a very visible gay population, for example). Nevertheless, gay and lesbian travelers should be discreet about public displays of affection.

➤ GAY- & LESBIAN-FRIENDLY TRAVEL AGENCIES: **Different Roads Travel** (⊠ 8383 Wilshire Blvd., Suite 902, Beverly Hills, CA 90211, ☎ 323/

651–5557 or 800/429–8747, FAX 323/651–3678, lgernert@tzell.com). **Kennedy Travel** (⊠ 314 Jericho Turnpike, Floral Park, NY 11001, ☎ 516/352–4888 or 800/237–7433, FAX 516/354–8849, WEB www.kennedytravel.com). **Now Voyager** (⊠ 4406 18th St., San Francisco, CA 94114, ☎ 415/626–1169 or 800/255–6951, FAX 415/626–8626, WEB www.nowvoyager.com). **Skylink Travel and Tour** (⊠ 1006 Mendocino Ave., Santa Rosa, CA 95401, ☎ 707/546–9888 or 800/225–5759, FAX 707/546–9891, WEB www.skylinktravel.com), serving lesbian travelers.

GUIDEBOOKS

Plan well and you won't be sorry. Guidebooks are excellent tools—and you can take them with you. You may want to check out color-photo-illustrated *Fodor's Exploring Cuba,* thorough on culture and history.

HEALTH

DIVERS' ALERT

Divers take note: **don't fly within 24 hours of scuba diving.** Neophyte divers should have a complete physical exam before undertaking a dive. If you have travel insurance, **make sure your policy applies to scuba-related injuries,** as not all companies provide this coverage. Cuba has six decompression chambers scattered around the country, in case of a diving accident.

FOOD & DRINK

In Cuba the major health risk is traveler's diarrhea, caused by eating contaminated fruit or vegetables, or drinking contaminated water. So **watch what you eat.** Stay away from ice, uncooked food, and unpasteurized milk and milk products, and **drink only bottled water,** or water that has been boiled for at least 20 minutes, even when you're brushing your teeth. Make sure that fruit is thoroughly washed and/or peeled before eating it. Although Cuban lobsters are beyond reproach, avoid eating clams and mussels.

If you get diarrhea, drink plenty of purified water or tea—chamomile (*camomile*) is a good folk remedy. The doctors at the hotels and clinicas internacionales are experts at treating intestinal disorders. In severe cases, you can rehydrate yourself with a salt-sugar solution: ½ teaspoon salt (*sal*) and 4 tablespoons sugar (*azúcar*) per quart of water (*agua*).

MEDICAL PLANS

No one plans to get sick while traveling, but it happens, so **consider signing up with a medical-assistance company.** Members get doctor referrals, emergency evacuation or repatriation, hot lines for medical consultation, cash for emergencies, and other assistance.

➤ MEDICAL-ASSISTANCE COMPANIES: **International SOS Assistance** (WEB www.internationalsos.com; ✉ 8 Neshaminy Interplex, Suite 207, Trevose, PA 19053, ☎ 215/245–4707 or 800/523–6586, FAX 215/244–9617; ✉ 12 Chemin Riantbosson, 1217 Meyrin 1, Geneva, Switzerland, ☎ 4122/785–6464, FAX 4122/785–6424; ✉ 331 N. Bridge Rd., 17-00, Odeon Towers, Singapore 188720, ☎ 65/ 338–7800, FAX 65/338–7611).

OVER-THE-COUNTER & PRESCRIPTION REMEDIES

Since medical supplies in Cuba are short, **pack a small first-aid kit/medicine bag** with basic bandages and topical ointments as well as sunscreen; insect repellent; and your favorite brands of over-the-counter allergy, cold, headache, and stomach/diarrhea medicine. **Bring enough prescription medications to last the entire trip.** You may want to pick up some cheap vitamins, aspirin, and other common remedies at the discount drug store to give away, since most Cubans have a hard time getting even the most basic medicines.

PESTS & OTHER HAZARDS

Locals call the *almacigo* tree the "tourist tree" owing to its red, peeling bark (and its bulging trunk), a nod to Cuba's greatest health risk: the Caribbean sun. Use plenty of sunscreen.

There's some risk of contracting Hepatitis A, Hepatitis B, or the mosquito-carried dengue fever, though incidents of all three diseases are rare, and practically nonexistent in tourist zones. Visitors with allergies take note: the air quality in cities can be horrible, particularly in summer, when the thick, smoky exhaust from aging Eastern European trucks and buses mixes with choking dust and lingers in the humid air.

Most reports claim that—as a result of the Castro regime's authoritarian stance on health, drug addiction, and sexual mores—the risk of contracting AIDS in Cuba is minor. Other reports state that the disease is on the rise thanks to tourism-related prostitution. Other sexually transmitted diseases are fairly common. Extreme caution is advised in this area. Local condoms are of poor quality, so bring your own supply from home.

➤ HEALTH WARNINGS: **National Centers for Disease Control and Prevention** (CDC; National Center for Infectious Diseases, Division of Quarantine, Traveler's Health Section, ✉ 1600 Clifton Rd. NE, M/S E-03, Atlanta, GA 30333, ☎ 888/ 232–3228 or 877/394–8747, FAX 888/ 232–3299, WEB www.cdc.gov).

HOLIDAYS

There are 15 national holidays, all celebrating revolutionary events or heroes. The two largest are May Day (International Workers Day on May 1, which is celebrated throughout Cuba with parades and other activities) and National Revolution Day (on July 26, honoring the attack on Moncada Barracks in Santiago, which proved the spark for the Revolution). In addition, since Pope John Paul's visit to Cuba in 1998, Castro has allowed Cubans to openly celebrate Christmas.

Other national holidays are: January 1–2 (Liberation and Victory days), January 28 (José Martí), February 24 (Second War of Independence), March 8 (Women's/Mother's Day), March 13 (Students Attack), April 19 (Bay of Pigs Victory), July 30 (Martyrs of the Revolution), October 8 (Che Guevara), October 10 (First War of Independence), October 28 (Camilo Cienfuegos), December 2 (*Granma* landing), and December 7 (Antonio Maceo).

INSURANCE

Although it's impossible for Americans to get travel-insurance coverage for trips to Cuba, travelers from other countries should look into it. The most useful travel-insurance plan is a comprehensive policy that includes coverage for trip cancellation and interruption, default, trip delay, and medical expenses (with a waiver for pre-existing conditions).

Without insurance you will lose all or most of your money if you cancel your trip, regardless of the reason. Default insurance covers you if your tour operator, airline, or cruise line goes out of business. Trip-delay covers expenses that arise because of bad weather or mechanical delays. Study the fine print when comparing policies.

If you're traveling internationally, a key component of travel insurance is coverage for medical bills incurred if you get sick on the road. Such expenses are not generally covered by Medicare or private policies. U.K. residents can buy a travel-insurance policy valid for most vacations taken during the year in which it's purchased (but check pre-existing-condition coverage). British and Australian citizens need extra medical coverage when traveling overseas.

Always **buy travel policies directly from the insurance company**; if you buy them from a cruise line, airline, or tour operator that goes out of business you probably will not be covered for the agency or operator's default, a major risk. Before making any purchase, **review your existing health and home-owner's policies** to find what they cover away from home.

➤ TRAVEL INSURERS: In the U.S.: **Access America** (⊠ 6600 W. Broad St., Richmond, VA 23230, ☏ 800/284–8300, FAX 804/673–1491, WEB www.etravelprotection.com). **Travel Guard International** (⊠ 1145 Clark St., Stevens Point, WI 54481, ☏ 715/345–0505 or 800/826–1300, FAX 800/955–8785, WEB www.travelguard.com).

➤ INSURANCE INFORMATION: In the U.K.: **Association of British Insurers** (⊠ 51–55 Gresham St., London EC2V 7HQ, U.K., ☏ 020/7600–3333, FAX 020/7696–8999, WEB www.abi.org.uk). In Canada: **RBC Travel Insurance** (⊠ 6880 Financial Dr., Mississauga, Ontario L5N 7Y5, Canada, ☏ 905/791–8700, 800/668–4342 in Canada, FAX 905/816–2498, WEB www.royalbank.com). In Australia: **Insurance Council of Australia** (⊠ Level 3, 56 Pitt St., Sydney NSW 2000, ☏ 02/9253–5100, FAX 02/9253–5111, WEB www.ica.com.au). In New Zealand: **Insurance Council of New Zealand** (⊠ Level 7, 111–115 Customhouse Quay, Box 474, Wellington, New Zealand, ☏ 04/472–5230, FAX 04/473–3011, WEB www.icnz.org.nz).

LANGUAGE

Spanish is the official, and by far the most widely spoken, language. Many hotel personnel speak some English; German, Portuguese, Italian, and French are also often spoken at resorts. Outside of hotels and beyond cities, having a few rudimentary Spanish phrases in your repertoire will be very helpful.

LANGUAGES FOR TRAVELERS

A phrase book and language-tape set can help get you started. *Fodor's Spanish for Travelers* (available at bookstores everywhere) is excellent. If languages are your thing, you could take a Spanish course during your stay. In Havana, the José Martí School for Foreigners and the Mercadu SA offer courses that vary in length from one week to four months. Package trips can be arranged in the United States through Global Exchange.

➤ LANGUAGE COURSES: **Global Exchange** (⊠ 2017 Mission St., No. 303, San Francisco, CA, 94110, ☏ 800/497–1994, WEB www.globalexchange.org). **José Martí School for Foreigners** (⊠ Calle 16, No. 109, Miramar, Havana, ☏ 7/204–1697). **Mercadu SA** (Calle 13 951, esquina de Av. 8, Vedado, Havana, ☏ 7/33–3087 or 7/55–3784).

LODGING

Accommodations include large, modern hotels; smaller, restored colonial classics; and rooms in *casas particulares* (private homes). To improve its tourist infrastructure, the island has been entering into joint ventures with such foreign hoteliers as Spain's Sol Meliá. Local hotel chains includ Cubanacán and Gran Caribe, which have many traditional tourist properties; Horizontes and Gaviota, which offer more specialized or out-of-the way accommodations; Habaguanex, which has several boutique hotels in Old Havana; and Islazul, whose properties cater mostly to Cuban tourists. To get the best deal, **book your room in advance.**

Assume that hotels operate on the European Plan (**EP,** with no meals) unless we specify that they're **all-inclusive** (including all meals and most activities) or use the Continental Plan (**CP,** with a Continental breakfast daily), Breakfast Plan (**BP,** with a full breakfast daily), or Modified American Plan (**MAP,** with breakfast and dinner daily).

The lodgings we list (all of which are indicated by ⊡) are the cream of the crop in each price category. We always list the facilities that are available—but we don't specify whether they cost extra: when pricing accommodations, always ask what's included and what costs extra. Properties indicated by an ✕⊡ are lodging establishments whose restaurant warrants a special trip.

CATEGORY	COST*
$$$$	over $150
$$$	$125–$150
$$	$100–$125
$	$75–$100
¢	under $75

*for a double room in high season

CASAS PARTICULARES

Since 1996, Cubans have been allowed to rent out rooms to visitors. Homes with a license to rent will have a blue triangle on their front door or window. Havana now has hundreds of these casas particulares, and other towns frequented by foreigners have at least a few. The rates are excellent ($15–$35 daily, payable in cash, dollars only), and the accommodations are often charming. Some casas particulares are mansions that may have passed their heyday but still

have the power to impress; most offer such amenities as private baths and air-conditioning. A number of them are also licensed to serve meals to guests, and Cuban home cooking often puts the institutional buffets at the big hotels to shame.

Quality varies widely from one casa to the next, and you can't make reservations for them through a tour operator. A good strategy is to **book your first two nights at a tourist hotel, and then investigate nearby casas particulares.** Most of the buildings around Havana's Capri and Habana Libre hotels have rooms for rent in them—look for the blue triangles, and other signs. Shop around, and don't be shy, **ask to see the rooms before booking.** Just beware of recommendations from street hustlers; their desire to take you to a casa particular is based only on the commission they get, which will invariably affect the rate you pay.

HOSTELS

Although Cuba doesn't have a hostel network per se, international hostel organizations should be able to refer members to similar lodging options—in university dormitories—on the island. One-year membership in Hostelling International (HI) costs about $25 for adults (C$26.75 in Canada, £9.30 in the U.K., $30 in Australia, and $30 in New Zealand).

➤ ORGANIZATIONS: **Hostelling International—American Youth Hostels** (⊠ 733 15th St. NW, Suite 840, Washington, DC 20005, ☎ 202/783–6161, FAX 202/783–6171, WEB www.hiayh.org). **Hostelling International—Canada** (⊠ 400–205 Catherine St., Ottawa, Ontario K2P 1C3, Canada, ☎ 613/237–7884; 800/663–5777 in Canada, FAX 613/237–7868, WEB www.hostellingintl.ca). **Youth Hostel Association of England and Wales** (⊠ Trevelyan House, 8 St. Stephen's Hill, St. Albans, Hertfordshire AL1 2DY, U.K., ☎ 0870/8708808, FAX 01727/844126, WEB www.yha.org.uk). **Youth Hostel Association Australia** (⊠ 10 Mallett St., Camperdown, NSW 2050, Australia, ☎ 02/9565–1699, FAX 02/9565–1325, WEB www.yha.com.au). **Youth Hostels Association of New Zealand** (⊠ Level 3, 193

Cashel St., Box 436, Christchurch, New Zealand, ☎ 03/379–9970, FAX 03/365–4476, WEB www.yha.org.nz).

HOTELS

The construction of new hotels that gained momentum in the 1990s is continuing well into the new millennium (the island has almost 50,000 rooms and counting). All new hotels and resorts are up to North American and European standards, and many of the older ones have undergone renovations. Most new rooms are in massive beach resorts, which offer an array of services—from day tours to nightly entertainment and children's programs—and where all or most food and drink are included in the room rates. Rooms in all hotels invariably have air-conditioning and cable TV, and many have refrigerators and other modern conveniences. All hotels listed have private baths unless otherwise noted.

MAIL & SHIPPING

Although Cubans deeply distrust their postal system—and entrust letters to anyone they meet who may be leaving the country—mail service is fairly reliable, especially if you post letters from hotels. Stamps, however, are much less expensive in state post offices than in hotels. A postcard sent to anywhere in the Americas or Europe will cost no more than 50¢, a letter 75¢. It takes three or four weeks for mail to reach North America or Europe. There have been reports of mail censorship; if you want your card to eventually reach its destination, consider choosing your words carefully.

DHL Express is the international air courier service with the biggest presence in Cuba. It has desks at some major hotels and offices in Havana, Camagüey, Cienfuegos, Holguín, Pinar del Río, Santiago de Cuba, and Varadero. The company offers package and letter delivery to international points within 24 hours, but it will cost you dearly. Another option is Cubanacán Express.

➤ COURIER SERVICE: **Cubanacán Express** (Av. 31 y Calle 41, Playa, ☎ 7/204–7848). **DHL** (✉ Main office, Av. 1 y Calle 26, Miramar, Havana, ☎ 7/204–1578 for customer service).

MONEY MATTERS

Although the official *moneda nacional* (national currency) is the peso, the state has authorized the use of the U.S. dollar as legal tender. The government also issues a so-called *peso convertible,* which is on par with the U.S. dollar and which you can freely exchange back into dollars before leaving. Note that the letter "S" with one line through it is the symbol for pesos, while two lines signify dollars; (hence, that trinket that may appear to cost a shocking $100 may actually cost 100 pesos, or $5).

Fees throughout this guide are given for adults. Substantially reduced fees are almost always available for children, students, and senior citizens. For information on taxes, *see* Taxes, *below.*

BANKS & ATMS

The bank most travelers use is the Banco Financiero Internacional, which changes hard currencies into U.S. dollars and gives cash advances from credit cards not issued by U.S. banks. Other banks that serve foreigners are the Banco Nacional de Cuba and Banco Internacional de Comercio. There are some automatic teller machines in urban areas that accept international bank cards not issued through U.S. banks.

CREDIT CARDS

Credit cards—such as Visa and MasterCard—not affiliated with U.S. bank or companies are honored at government hotels, restaurants, and stores. Several other European and Latin American credit cards are also accepted.

Throughout this guide, the following abbreviations are used: **MC,** MasterCard and **V,** Visa.

CURRENCY EXCHANGE

U.S. dollars can be converted to pesos, but there are few opportunities for travelers to spend Cuban pesos. Most shops, restaurants, hotels, taxis, paladares, and casas particulares accept only dollars. City buses, street vendors, and restaurants that cater to Cubans charge pesos, but those packed buses are a pickpocket's paradise, and the meat served at the peso restaurants was probably turned down by the establishments that conduct business using dollars.

For the most favorable rates, **change money through banks.** Although ATM transaction fees may be higher abroad than at home, ATM rates are excellent because they are based on wholesale rates offered only by major banks. You won't do as well at exchange booths in airports or rail and bus stations, in hotels, in restaurants, or in stores. To avoid lines at airport exchange booths, **get a bit of local currency before you leave home.**

➤ EXCHANGE SERVICES: **International Currency Express** (☎ 888/278–6628 for orders, WEB www.foreignmoney. com). **Thomas Cook Currency Services** (☎ 800/287–7362 for telephone orders and retail locations, WEB www. us.thomascook.com).

TRAVELER'S CHECKS

Do you need traveler's checks? It depends on where you're headed. If you're going to rural areas and small towns, go with cash; traveler's checks are best used in cities. Lost or stolen checks can usually be replaced within 24 hours. To ensure a speedy refund, buy your own traveler's checks— don't let someone else pay for them: irregularities like this can cause delays. The person who bought the checks should make the call to request a refund.

Checks issued by U.S. banks can't be cashed in Cuba. Although it's nerve-wracking to travel with cash, it's the most convenient option (invest in a good money belt). Note, however, that some tour operators suggest that Americans traveling to Cuba unofficially through another country—say, Canada or Mexico—buy traveler's checks issued by a foreign company before leaving there for Cuba. Despite the fact that you're abroad, you should be able to get these checks in U.S. dollars, Cuba's de facto currency.

PACKING

For sightseeing, casual lightweight clothing and good walking shoes are appropriate; most restaurants don't require very formal attire. For beach vacations, you'll need lightweight sportswear, a bathing suit, a sun hat,

and lots of really good sunscreen. A sarong or a light cotton blanket makes a handy beach towel, picnic blanket, and cushion for hard seats, among other things.

Travel in forest areas will require long-sleeve shirts, long pants, socks, sneakers and/or hiking boots, a hat, a light waterproof jacket, a bathing suit, and plenty of insect repellent. Other useful items include a screw-top water container that you can fill with bottled water, a money pouch, a travel flashlight and extra batteries, a Swiss Army knife with a bottle opener, a medical kit (with first-aid supplies and basic over-the-counter remedies), binoculars, and lots of extra film. If you have the room, try to take any clothes you don't wear as well as extra soap, over-the-counter medicines, etc., to give away. That $1 bottle of aspirin at the discount drugstore could be a godsend for a retired school teacher trying to survive on $10 a month; the blouse that no longer fits might be the perfect gift for the maid at your hotel.

In your carry-on luggage, **pack an extra pair of eyeglasses or contact lenses and enough of any medication** you take to last the entire trip. In luggage to be checked, **never pack prescription drugs or valuables.** To avoid customs delays, carry medications in their original packaging. And don't forget to **carry addresses of offices that handle lost credit cards and refunds of lost traveler's checks.** Check *Fodor's How to Pack* (available in bookstores everywhere) for more tips.

CHECKING LUGGAGE

You are allowed one carry-on bag and one personal article, such as a purse or a laptop computer. Make sure that everything you carry aboard will fit under your seat or in the overhead bin. Get to the gate early, so you can board as soon as possible, before the overhead bins fill up.

If you are flying internationally, note that baggage allowances may be determined not by piece but by weight—generally 88 pounds (40 kilograms) in first class, 66 pounds

(30 kilograms) in business class, and 44 pounds (20 kilograms) in economy.

Airline liability for baggage is limited to $1,250 per person on flights within the United States. On international flights it amounts to $9.07 per pound or $20 per kilogram for checked baggage (roughly $640 per 70-pound bag) and $400 per passenger for unchecked baggage. You can buy additional coverage at check-in for about $10 per $1,000 of coverage, but it excludes a rather extensive list of items, shown on your airline ticket.

Before departure, **itemize your bags' contents** and their worth, and label the bags with your name, address, and phone number. (If you use your home address, cover it so potential thieves can't see it readily.) Inside each bag, **pack a copy of your itinerary.** At check-in, **make sure that each bag is correctly tagged** with the destination airport's three-letter code. If your bags arrive damaged or fail to arrive at all, file a written report with the airline before leaving the airport.

PASSPORTS & VISAS

When traveling internationally, **carry your passport** even if you don't need one (it's always the best form of I.D.) and **make two photocopies of the data page** (one for someone at home and another for you, carried separately from your passport). If you lose your passport, promptly call the nearest embassy or consulate and the local police.

ENTERING CUBA

All foreigners must have passports to enter Cuba. Beyond that, in most cases tourist cards ($20), rather than visas, are all that's required. Most tourist cards are good for 30 days, but in some cases are valid for up to three months. Renewing a 30-day card for an additional month is easy to do (it costs $25).

Visas are required of business travelers, working journalists, and some other visitors. They cost $25 and are valid for 30 days. You must apply for them at your nearest Cuban embassy or consulate (if you're an American, contact the Cuban Interests Section), and they can take up to three weeks

to process. You may extend your visa for stays of up to six months.

PASSPORT OFFICES

The best time to apply for a passport or to renew is in fall and winter. Before any trip, check your passport's expiration date, and, if necessary, renew it as soon as possible.

➤ AUSTRALIAN CITIZENS: **Australian Passport Office** (☎ 131–232, WEB www.dfat.gov.au/passports).

➤ CANADIAN CITIZENS: **Passport Office** (☎ 819/994–3500; 800/567–6868 in Canada, WEB www.dfait-maeci.gc.ca/passport).

➤ NEW ZEALAND CITIZENS: **New Zealand Passport Office** (☎ 04/494–0700, WEB www.passports.govt.nz).

➤ U.K. CITIZENS: **London Passport Office** (☎ 0870/521–0410, WEB www.ukpa.gov.uk) for fees and documentation requirements and to request an emergency passport.

➤ U.S. CITIZENS: **National Passport Information Center** (☎ 900/225–5674; calls are 35¢ per minute for automated service, $1.05 per minute for operator service; WEB www.travel.state.gov/npicinfo.html).

REST ROOMS

All major public areas, from hotels to airports, have facilities, though the more public the area, the less likely they are to be clean. The words for "rest room" are *servicio* and *baño*. "Men" is *caballeros*; "women" is *mujeres* or *damas*.

SAFETY

There have been mixed reports on crime in Cuba. Some of them say that crime against tourists is on the rise, particularly in cities. Take the same precautions you would elsewhere in South America or the Caribbean; **keep a close eye on personal belongings, avoid adorning yourself with expensive jewelry,** and **follow local advice about where it's safe to walk,** particularly at night.

There are increasing numbers of panhandlers, looking for anything from cash to clothing to soap; *jineteros* (hustlers), wanting to serve as your guide or refer you to a casa particular or paladar; and *jineteras* (prostitutes). It's best to decline their services. If you consider the local economic conditions, it shouldn't be hard to remain polite and still keep confrontation to a minimum.

WOMEN IN CUBA

Women traveling alone more often than not say that Cuban men treat them with great respect, but this is a Latin country: expect men to be a bit forward. Also **be aware that some Cubans are on the prowl for foreign mates.** Unless you're truly interested, it's best to avoid lengthy eye contact with the opposite sex. It's probably safer for a woman traveling alone in Cuba than in most countries; still, use the same caution you would at home.

SENIOR-CITIZEN TRAVEL

To qualify for age-related discounts, **mention your senior-citizen status up front** when booking hotel reservations (not when checking out) and before you're seated in restaurants (not when paying the bill). When renting a car, ask about promotional car-rental discounts, which can be cheaper than senior-citizen rates.

➤ EDUCATIONAL PROGRAMS: **Elderhostel** (✉ 11 Ave. de Lafayette, Boston, MA 02111-1746, ☎ 877/426–8056, ℻ 877/426–2166, 🖳 www.elderhostel.org).

SHOPPING

Most people buy rum and cigars, and for good reason—Cuban versions of these products are among the world's finest. But there's much more here: artwork, crafts, CDs, T shirts, coffee-table books, musical instruments, and such traditional offerings as the men's dress shirt, the *guayabera.* ARTEX stores sell all these goods and more, and there's one in practically every Cuban town.

Cuba also has other types of stores (including gift shops in hotels and at museums and other sights), as well as formal state-owned art galleries. Open-air markets and streets where artists and craftsmen sell their wares from small stands are recommended because things are less expensive and the artisans and artists earn much

more. Bargaining with street vendors is acceptable, but keep in mind that they pay $100–$200 per month for a permit to set up their stand.

Note that **if you buy a large painting, get an export permit or an official receipt from a government store** or the work is subject to confiscation upon departure from Cuba. A permit costs $10, and is usually available from the artist. The National Registry of Cultural Goods also sells permits.

Diplotiendas and more abundant Tiendas Panamericanos sell an array of consumer products—from electronic equipment to clothing to personal-hygiene items—for U.S. dollars, though most of the things travelers need are available in the larger hotels, or even gas stations.

➤ EXPORT PERMITS: **National Registry of Cultural Goods** (✉ Calle 17, No. 1009, Vedado, Havana, ☎ no phone).

STUDENTS IN CUBA

Some of Cuba's state agencies run foreign-language and Cuban culture classes, and several Cuban universities offer courses for foreigners or welcome them into their courses. The American Friends Service Committee offers student exchange. The non-profit tour organization, Global Exchange, also offers educational trips—whether you're interested in learning Cuban Spanish or studying Cuban culture.

➤ I.D.s & SERVICES: **Council Travel** (CIEE; ✉ 205 E. 42nd St., 15th floor, New York, NY 10017, ☎ 212/822–2700 or 888/268–6245, ℻ 212/822–2699, 🖳 www.councilexchanges.org) for mail orders only, in the U.S. **Travel Cuts** (✉ 187 College St., Toronto, Ontario M5T 1P7, Canada, ☎ 416/979–2406 or 800/667–2887 in Canada, ℻ 416/979–8167, 🖳 www.travelcuts.com).

➤ TOUR OPERATORS & ORGANIZATIONS: **American Friends Service Committee** (✉ 1501 Cherry St., Philadelphia, PA 92102, ☎ 215/241–7000). **Global Exchange** (✉ 2017 Mission St., No. 303, San Francisco, CA, 94110, ☎ 800/497–1994, 🖳 www.globalexchange.org).

TAXES

The departure tax is $20 (it's payable in U.S. dollars before you board the plane home). No taxes are levied on goods and services. If you buy artwork, however, you need to get a $10 export permit.

TAXIS

Modern, well-maintained tourist taxis with dollar meters congregate in front of hotels, transportation hubs, and major sights. Rates are affordable by North American and European standards, but are expensive compared to the island's other transportation options. Metered cabs from the companies Havanatur, Cubataxi, and Taxi OK charge about $5 for every 10 km (6 mi) traveled. Smaller yellow cabs that park at public areas in Havana and other large cities have dollar meters, but charge about $3 for a 10 km (6 mi) trip. Havana's cute little *coco-taxis*—three-wheeled motorcycles with round, fiberglass shells—don't have meters but charge a little more than the yellow cabs. They are, however, quite dangerous. Unmetered *taxis particulares* (private cabs) aren't supposed to pick up tourists, but they will, and they tend to be inexpensive—determine the fare before you get in. Photogenic *taxis colectivos,* most of which are vintage American cars, aren't permitted to transport tourists, but they often will. Taxi drivers, who earn a monthly wage of $7, survive on tips.

TELEPHONES

Since 1992, Cuban phone service has been improving, thanks to a partial privatization and to joint ventures with foreign investors. Though Cuban homeowners suffer a phone shortage, hotels and other tourist enterprises have lots of the newest equipment. As Cuba has been upgrading its phone system over the last few years, numbers have changed throughout the country. The changes made up to this writing have been incorporated throughout the guide, but be aware that more changes may be imminent.

Making phone calls from hotels can be quite expensive; public ETECSA phones cost considerably less. These phones are abundant and from them you can dial direct to anywhere in the world. Most hotels offer fax service to guests and, sometimes, nonguests, though you can send faxes for less from the local correos. E-mail service and Internet access is scarce and costly.

COUNTRY & AREA CODES

Cuba's country code is 53, and there's direct-dial service to the country from North America and Europe. When calling within the country, dial 0 plus the area code before the number. Area codes vary in length from one to three digits; the length of phone numbers varies from four to seven digits. Some of the more useful city codes are: Bayamo, 23; Camagüey (Santa Lucía), 32; Ciego de Ávila (Cayo Coco, Cayo Guillermo), 33; Cienfuegos, 432; Guantánamo, 21; Havana, 7; Holguín (Guardalavaca), 24; Matanzas, 45; Morón, 335; Pinar del Río, 82; Sancti Spíritus, 41; Santa Clara, 42; Santiago de Cuba, 226; Trinidad, 419; Varadero, 5; and Viñales 5.

DIRECTORY & OPERATOR INFORMATION

The number for local information (in Spanish) is 113. The number for a local operator changes according to where you call from, but is usually 00 or 110. Numbers for international operators vary even more—they can be 180, 112, 0112, etc.—and few operators speak English, so it's best to ask a Cuban to help you.

INTERNATIONAL CALLS

All major hotels offer international phone service at very high rates—the more expensive the hotel, the higher the phone rates—so be sure to check the price beforehand. It's considerably cheaper to dial direct from an ETECSA pay phone.

LOCAL & LONG-DISTANCE CALLS

To make a long-distance call within Cuba, dial 0, the area code, and the number. To make an international call, dial 00 plus the country code, area code, and number. Common country codes are: 1 for the United

States and Canada, 61 for Australia, 64 for New Zealand, and 44 for the United Kingdom.

PHONE CARDS & PUBLIC PHONES

You can buy cards in denominations from $10 to $50 at most hotels, or centrally located *telecorreos* and *centros de llamadas internacionales*. Many phone centers are open 24 hours a day, and abundant blue ETECSA pay phones also accept cards.

WIRELESS PHONES

Cubacel has been offering wireless phone service since 1993 through a joint venture with foreign investors (note that it has agreements with Telcel and Portatel in Mexico, Telecom Personal and TCP in Argentina, Telefonica Moviles in Spain, and Bell Mobility and Telus Mobility in Canada). The network extends to all but the most remote areas and allows for the use of AMPS cell phones (American norm).

Cubacel may be able to activate your own wireless phone for use within Cuba or you can rent one of theirs—an expensive proposition. Security deposits run several hundred dollars (depending on the length of usage), and rental fees are about $7 a day plus a daily $3 activation fee. A 90¢-per-minute air-time fee is charged in addition to long-distance or international fees. Several car-rental agencies include cell phones with the rental of standard or luxury vehicles.

➤ WIRELESS COMPANY: **Cubacel** (✉ Calle 28, No. 510, e/Calle 5 y Calle 7, Miramar, Havana ☎ 7/880–2222; ✉ Aeropuerto Internacional José Martí, ☎ 7/880–0043).

TIME

Havana is in the same time zone as Miami and New York, and is 5 hours behind Britain, 3 hours ahead of Los Angeles, and 14 hours behind Melbourne, Australia. The island switches to daylight saving time from April through October, when it's only 4 hours behind Greenwich mean time.

TIPPING

In hotel restaurants with buffet-style meals, tip the waitstaff $2–$5, depending on the extent of service and the number of people in your party. Elsewhere, tip waiters and waitresses 10%–15% of the check. Tip hotel maids $2 a day and porters $2 a bag. Tips should also be given to museum docents, tour guides, taxi drivers, and anyone who keeps an eye on your rental car for you. For most of these people, $1 is usually enough; if your cab fare comes to more than $10, tip the driver 10%–15% of the total. Cubans who work in the service industry rely heavily on tips to merely subsist; therefore, you may feel better if you err on the generous side. You should also consider tipping people you wouldn't elsewhere, such as receptionists, rental-car agents, public relations people, travel agents—all of whom earn $10–15 a month—and hotel doctors, who earns less than $30.

TOURS & PACKAGES

Because everything is prearranged on a prepackaged tour or independent vacation, you spend less time planning—and often get it all at a good price.

BOOKING WITH AN AGENT

Travel agents are excellent resources. But it's a good idea to collect brochures from several agencies as some agents' suggestions may be influenced by relationships with tour and package firms that reward them for volume sales. If you have a special interest, **find an agent with expertise in that area**; the American Society of Travel Agents (ASTA; ☞ Travel Agencies, *below*) has a database of specialists worldwide.

Make sure your travel agent knows the accommodations and other services of the place being recommended. Ask about the hotel's location, room size, beds, and whether it has a pool, room service, or programs for children, if you care about these. Has your agent been there in person or sent others whom you can contact?

Do some homework on your own, too: local tourism boards can provide information about lesser-known and small-niche operators, some of which may sell only direct.

BUYER BEWARE

Each year consumers are stranded or lose their money when tour operators—even large ones with excellent reputations—go out of business. So **check out the operator.** Ask several travel agents about its reputation, and try to **book with a company that has a consumer-protection program.** (Look for information in the company's brochure.) In the United States, members of the National Tour Association and the United States Tour Operators Association are required to set aside funds to cover your payments and travel arrangements in the event that the company defaults. It's also a good idea to choose a company that participates in the American Society of Travel Agents' Tour Operator Program (TOP); ASTA will act as mediator in any disputes between you and your tour operator.

Remember that the more your package or tour includes the better you can predict the ultimate cost of your vacation. Make sure you know exactly what is covered, and **beware of hidden costs.** Are taxes, tips, and transfers included? Entertainment and excursions? These can add up.

➤ TOUR-OPERATOR RECOMMENDATIONS: **American Society of Travel Agents** (☞ Travel Agencies, *below*). **National Tour Association** (NTA; ⌧ 546 E. Main St., Lexington, KY 40508, ☎ 859/226–4444 or 800/682–8886, WEB www.ntaonline.com). **United States Tour Operators Association** (USTOA; ⌧ 342 Madison Ave., Suite 1522, New York, NY 10173, ☎ 212/599–6599 or 800/468–7862, FAX 212/599–6744, WEB www.ustoa.com).

➤ OPERATORS, AGENCIES, & ORGANIZATIONS: **Caribe Tours** (⌧ 3246 East Gage Ave., Huntington Park, CA 90255, ☎ 562/904–3433). **Caribbean Family & Travel Services** (⌧ 114B Ponce de Léon Blvd., Coral Gables, FL, 33135, ☎ 305/445–8799). **Caribic Vacations** (⌧ 69 Gloucester Ave., Montego Bay, Jamaica, ☎ 876/953–

9878). **Cubanacán Mexico** (⌧ Av. México No. 99, Mexico City, DF Mexico, ☎ 525/574–1523). **Cubanacán Canada** (⌧ 372 Bay St., Suite 1902, Toronto, Canada, ☎ 416/601–0343). **Cubanacán UK** (⌧ Skylines, Suite 49, Limeharbor, Docklands, London, U.K., ☎ 020/7537–7909). **Emely Tours** (⌧ Av. Tiradentes y Roberto Pastoriza, Plaza JR, 2nd floor, Ensanche Naco, Santo Domingo, Dominican Republic, ☎ 809/566–4545). **Global Exchange** (⌧ 2017 Mission St., No. 303, San Francisco, CA, 94110, ☎ 800/497–1994, WEB www.globalexchange.org). **Havanatur UK** (⌧ 3 Wyllyotts Pl., Potters Bar, Hertfordshire EN6 2JD, U.K., ☎ 017/0766–5570). **Instituto Cubano de Amistad** (Cuban Institute of Friendship; ⌧ Calle 17, No. 301, Vedado, Havana, Cuba, ☎ 7/32–8017). **Latin American Travel** (⌧ 7 Buckingham Gate, London SW1E 6JX, U.K., ☎ 020/7630–0070). **Magna Holidays** (⌧ 163 Buttermill Ave., Unit 3, Concord, Ontario L4K 3X8, Canada, ☎ 905/761–7330). **Regent Holidays** (⌧ 6205 Airport Rd., Mississauga, Ontario L4V 1E1, Canada, ☎ 905/673–3343, WEB www.regentholidays.com). **Sol del Caribe** (⌧ 11865 S.W. 26 St., No. B9, Miami, FL 33175, ☎ 305/221–7100). **Wings of the World Travel** (⌧ 1200 William St., No. 706, Buffalo, NY 14240, ☎ 800/465–8687).

TRAIN TRAVEL

Cuba has the Caribbean's only comprehensive passenger rail system. Because they're the island's cheapest form of transportation, trains are popular with the country's impoverished masses. Foreigners, however, pay inflated dollar prices; tickets are sold by the Ferro Cuba/Ladis agency in each station or in a separate building behind Havana's Estación Central. Still, fares are reasonable; the 15-hour, overnight Havana–Santiago train, for example, costs $43 one-way.

When possible, book an *especial* tourist train (with air-conditioning, reclining chairs, and a food car), which moves faster and makes fewer stops. At press time, especiales departed Havana for Santiago daily at 10:40 AM and 7:30 PM, stopping in Santa Clara, Ciego de Ávila, Camagüey, and Holguín. The trip should take 15 hours, but trains often run late, and though they have dining cars, you'll want to pack lots of food and water, just in case.

➤ CONTACTS: **Ferro Cuba/Ladis** (✉ Behind Estación Central, Havana ☎ 7/861–8540 or 7/861–8330). **Information** (✉ ☎ 7/862–1929 for Havana's Estación Central or 7/862–1006 for Estación Coubre).

TRAVEL AGENCIES

A good travel agent puts your needs first. Look for an agency that has been in business at least five years, emphasizes customer service, and has someone on staff who specializes in your destination. In addition, **make sure the agency belongs to a professional trade organization.** The American Society of Travel Agents (ASTA)—the largest and most influential in the field with more than 26,000 members in some 170 countries—maintains and enforces a strict code of ethics and will step in to help mediate any agent-client disputes if necessary. ASTA (whose motto is "Without a travel agent, you're on your own") also maintains a Web site that includes a directory of agents. (If a travel agency is also acting as your tour operator, *see* Buyer Beware *in* Tours & Packages, *above*.)

➤ LOCAL AGENT REFERRALS: **American Society of Travel Agents** (ASTA; ✉ 1101 King St., Suite 200, Alexandria, VA 22314 ☎ 800/965–2782 24-hr hot line, FAX 703/739–7642, WEB www.astanet.com). **Association of British Travel Agents** (✉ 68–71 Newman St., London W1T 3AH, U.K., ☎ 020/7637–2444, FAX 020/7637–0713, WEB www.abtanet.com). **Association of Canadian Travel Agents** (✉ 130 Albert St., Suite 1705, Ottawa, Ontario K1P 5G4, Canada, ☎ 613/237–3657, FAX 613/237–7052, WEB www.acta.net). **Australian Federation of Travel Agents** (✉ Level 3, 309 Pitt St., Sydney NSW 2000, Australia, ☎ 02/9264–3299, FAX 02/9264–1085, WEB www.afta.com.au). **Travel Agents' Association of New Zealand** (✉ Level 5, Paxus House, 79 Boulcott St., Box 1888, Wellington 10033, New Zealand, ☎ 04/499–0104, FAX 04/499–0827, WEB www.taanz.org.nz).

VISITOR INFORMATION

On the island, you can get information at the offices of Infotur, whose staffers answer questions, distribute maps (often free), and sell tickets for Víazul buses. The state-operated tour and travel agencies have desks in the lobbies of most hotels, where representatives can arrange flights, tours, and rental cars.

Internationally, Cuba is usually represented by tourist board offices and branches of state-owned companies—such as Havanatur (a tour operator), Cubanacán (a hotel and tour operator), or Cubana (the national airline). Because the Cuban government has no tourist offices in the United States, one of the best sources of information there is the Center for Cuban Studies, which publishes the bimonthly *Cuba Update*.

➤ TOURIST INFORMATION: **Center for Cuban Studies** (✉ 124 W. 23rd St., New York, NY 10011, ☎ 212/242–0559, WEB www.cubaupdate.org). **Cuban Tourist Board** (✉ 55 Queen St. E, Suite 705, Toronto, Ontario M5C 1R6, Canada,, ☎ 416/362–0700; ✉ Blvd. René Lévesque W, Suite 1105, Montréal, Quebec H37 1V7, Canada, ☎ 514/875–8004; ✉ Goethe 16, 3er piso, Colonia Anzures, Mexico City 06100, DF, Mexico, ☎ 5/250–7974; ✉ 167 High Holborn, London WC1V6PA, U.K., ☎ 44/207–240–2488. **Cubanacán** (☎ 416/601–0346 in Toronto; 207/537–7909 in London; 119/525–574–1523 in Mexico City). **Infotur** (✉ Calle del Obispo, e/Habana y Compostela, Havana, ☎ 7/33–3333; ✉ Simón Bolivar/Desengaño y Maceo/Gutierez, Trinidad, ☎ 419/2149).➤ U.S. GOVERNMENT ADVISORIES: **U.S. Department of State** (✉ Overseas Citizens Services Office, Room 4811 N.S., 2201 C St. NW, Washington, DC 20520, ☎ 202/647–5225 for interactive hot line, WEB http://travel.state.gov/travel/html); enclose a self-addressed, stamped, business-size envelope.

WEB SITES

Do check out the World Wide Web when planning your trip. You'll find everything from weather forecasts to virtual tours of famous cities. Be sure to **visit Fodors.com** (www.fodors. com), a complete travel-planning site. You can research prices and book plane tickets, hotel rooms, rental cars, vacation packages, and more. In addition, you can post your pressing questions in the Travel Talk section. Other planning tools include a currency converter and weather reports, and there are loads of links to travel resources.

For more information specifically on Cuba, there are plenty of options: The tourism ministry's official site is www.cubatravel.cu. The English-language site cubaweb.com has information on travel, history, and culture, plus a variety of links. The Cuba Tourism Directory, www.dtcuba. com/eng/default.asp, is a commercial site for Canadian travelers; www. cubanonet.com is geared more toward American travelers (it also lists casas particulares). Cubalinda, www.cubalinda.com, is a commercial tourism site started by CIA defector Philip Agee. Another decent site with general information and links is www1click2.Cuba.com. For information on private rooms, check out www.casaparticular.com, which books rooms all over the island.

The Cuba Solidarity Site (www.igc.apc.org/cubasoli) works for an end of the U.S. trade and travel embargo. A fun time line of Cuban history is historyofcuba.com, which has wonderful sidebars. The University of Texas site lanic.utexas.edu/la/cb/cuba has links to dozens of sites ranging from academic to commercial. Americans interested in travel to Cuba should check out the U.S. State Department's Cuba site (www.state. gov/www/regions/wha/cuba/travel/index.html) and the U.S. Treasury Department's Cuba site (www.treas.gov/ofac), which fully explains who can travel to Cuba.

WHEN TO GO

The best time to visit, December through April, is also the most popular time. Cuba's weather is at its coolest and driest during these months, yet it's still far warmer than North America and Europe.

In the spring and fall, things slow down. At off-the-track destinations and even some beach resorts, these off-seasons can mean fewer hotel amenities; some hotels may be closed entirely. There are, however, benefits to traveling in the off-seasons: lack of crowds, prices that tumble by up to 25%, and special events (such as Santiago's Carnaval in late July) are among them.

CLIMATE

Average temperatures range from 19°C (67°F) in January to 27°C (81°F) in July. Average humidity is about 80%, but much of the island is blessed by cooling trade winds. The central mountains are probably the coolest regions; temperatures here can dip down to 40°F at night during "cold spells." El Oriente, the country's easternmost portion, broils, especially in summer. In some urban areas, summer heat and humidity mixed with vehicular pollution is an irritating combination—especially for allergy sufferers.

The rainy season runs from May to November; the dry season, from December to April. About 52 inches (132 centimeters) of rain fall on Cuba each year. The north Atlantic coast and the central mountains are wetter than the south coast. Hurricane season runs from June to November, though most hurricanes hit between August and October.

➤ FORECASTS: **Weather Channel Connection** (☎ 900/932–8437), 95¢ per minute from a Touch-Tone phone.

FESTIVALS & SEASONAL EVENTS

➤ DEC.: Havana's **Festival Internacional de Cine Latinoamericano** (International Festival of Latin American Film) held in mid-December, has become one of the hemisphere's great film festivals—blockade or no. The December 17th **Procesión de los Milagros** (Procession of the Miracles) features penitents dragging stones or themselves through the streets of Rincón (outside Havana, near Santiago de las Vegas) to the Santuario de San Lázaro to give thanks to the Santería *orisha* (god) Babalu Aye, patron of lepers, medicine, and the harvest.

➤ JAN.: Havana's **Festival Cabildos** on January 6 features people in costumes dancing through the streets. During Trinidad's (central Cuba) **Festival Cultural,** held the second week of January, there are music, dance, and theater performances as well as art exhibitions.

➤ FEB.: In Havana, February sees the **Festival Nacional de Teatro** (National Theater Festival). **Carnaval,** centered in La Habana Vieja, is a three-week blowout that seems headed for eventual equity with Rio de Janeiro's famous fete. In the first week of February, Camagüey celebrates the **Semana de la Cultura** (Culture Week) with art exhibits, an array of concerts, dance performances, and various other events. The mid-February **Santa Lucía Festival,** at the central-Cuba beach resort, includes music, dance, and other performances.

➤ MARCH: Cárdenas, in western Cuba, celebrates a **Semana de la Cultura** in early March honoring the founding of the city.

➤ APR.: You can get your chops at April's **Festival de Jazz de la Habana.** During the first week of April, Baracoa (eastern Cuba) holds its **Semana de la Cultura** (Culture Week).

➤ MAY: Havana's impressive **Primero de Mayo** celebration, on the first of May, features a procession of more than a million Cubans filing by El Comandante on his reviewing stand in the Plaza de la Revolución.

➤ JUNE: The central Cuban city of Trinidad holds a *procesión* (religious procession) on June 13. The lively **Trinidad Carnaval** happens June 24–29.

➤ JULY: July sees a **Festival de la Guitarra** (Guitar Festival) in Havana. Early in July, Santiago hosts the **Festival de la Cultura Caribeña,** organized by the Casa del Caribe, which features musical and cultural events involving local artists and those from throughout the Caribbean. In western Cuba, mid-July is the time for the **Varadero Carnaval.** Eastern Cuba's biggest annual event is **Santiago's Carnaval,** which takes place in late July. The streets are filled with costumed dancers, musicians, floats, and revelers. In the middle of July, Cienfuegos holds its **Fiesta de los Amigos del Mar** (Friends of the Sea Festival) with a variety of boating competitions and plenty of partying on land.

➤ SEPT.: The **Festival Internacional de Teatro de la Habana** (Havana International Theater Festival) takes place in September.

➤ OCT.: October sees Havana's **Festival Internacional de Balet** (International Ballet Festival).

➤ NOV.: In November, head to Havana for the **Festival de Música Contemporanea** (Contemporary Music Festival).

1 DESTINATION: CUBA

CUBA: A ROMANTIC DRAMA

EVER SINCE CHRISTOPHER Columbus called the largest of the Antilles "the most beautiful thing human eyes ever beheld," everyone who has known Cuba has fallen hopelessly in love with the place. Graham Greene, Ernest Hemingway, Ava Gardner, Winston Churchill, King Edward VIII . . . Cuba has had many passionate admirers. Novelists, in particular, have found Cuba fertile hunting ground for comedy, tragedy, and, above all perhaps, for poiesis—the production of art and emotion. Cuba is consistently moving in a poetic way.

At once the most Spanish country in the Americas and the most Americanized of the Hispanic countries in the New World, Cuba is on the cusp of all things: New World and Old, Atlantic and Caribbean, Gulf of Mexico and Straits of Florida, Uncle Sam and Latin America, animism and Catholicism, Africa and Spain, East and West, and—for the last 40 years—individualism and collectivism, capitalism and socialism. Cuba is romantic and irresistible, it would seem, precisely because it's so conflicted, so paradoxical, so relentlessly ripe with irony, so oxymoronic, so impossible.

The list of Cuba's contradictions is long. One of the most fertile islands in the world, it has historically been plagued by extreme poverty and food shortages, first as a result of sugarcane that dominated the countryside for the enrichment of Spanish, Cuban, and American landowners; then as a result of trade with the Soviet Union; and, today, as a result of the island's own Soviet-style state apparatus. Education is easy to acquire, yet many well-educated people work as hotel doormen because it pays better than the profession for which they trained. Cuba's corps of physicians is among the best in the world, though treatment of patients can be erratic owing to the scarcity of medical supplies (partly as a result of the U.S. embargo) and gasoline.

In one area there is no contradiction: the island's natural beauty is matched by the beauty of its people, a tonic blend of indigenous cultures, former Spanish colonial masters, and West African slaves. A museum of slavery in the Valle de los Ingenios (Valley of the Sugar Mills) celebrates the resilience and courage of Afro-Cubans, just as the mountain camps of *cimarrons* (runaway slaves) are maintained as monuments to the heroic Afro-Cuban resistance during Cuba's independence movements. Cuba—which once was so racially segregated that dictator Fulgencio Batista was denied admittance to Havana's exclusive country and yacht club owing to his cosmopolitan bloodlines—now claims its Afro-Cuban heritage as one of its proudest assets.

Nowhere is the island's heritage better reflected than in its music. Fernando Ortiz, the late, eminent Cuban ethnomusicologist, put it this way: "Cuba's history lies in the aroma of its tobacco and the sweetness of its sugar, but also in the lasciviousness of its music. And in tobacco, sugar and music, black and white have coexisted in the same creative effervescence since the 16th century. . . ." To experience the island's many rhythms—*son, chachacha, guajira, mambo,* to name a few—is to understand Cuba and its people. The tiniest trio in the least famous bar is apt to hit that sweet musical spot that suddenly creates, or releases, emotion. Whether they're performing or listening to jazz tunes, folk songs, or Handel and Prokofiev, Cubans communicate in a way that is moving; it's a sharing of sweetness, an unconditional surrender to what the German philosopher and mathematician Gottfried Wilhelm Leibniz termed "the secret arithmetic of the soul."

Cuba—the real Cuba, not the tourist circuit—and its people will, sooner or later get a grip on your heart. The rank-and-file citizens are gracious and dignified; the children—in national school uniforms, having been sworn in as "pioneers of socialism" at age 6—happy and beautiful; the dancers and musicians joyful and sensual; even the mobs of hitchhikers awaiting transport along the Autopista Central seem peaceful and cheerful. Despite the hustlers and *jiniteras* around tourist hotels,

Che Guevara's ideal of the New Man seems to have had an effect: most Cubans seem more interested in sharing something with you than getting something from you. How the island came to arrive at this state of affairs is a drama that is still unfolding.

The Plots and the Players

For 400 years Spain ruthlessly exploited its "Pearl of the Antilles." Trade monopolies, slavery, and lack of political autonomy caused many to suffer financially, physically, and emotionally. Although Cuba saw several skirmishes for greater freedom (including slave rebellions in 1812, 1841, and 1862), its first great flirtation with independence (and with America) began, ironically, when its economy burgeoned in the 19th century. Though talk of independence often invoked high-minded principles such as self-rule and freedom for all men, it was also linked, in certain quarters, to self-serving issues—including maintaining the system of slavery that was key to Cuba's plantation economy.

Act I: The Ten Years' War
Napoléon's 1808 conquest of the Iberian Peninsula sparked many independence movements in Spain's far-flung colonies. Initially, Cuba's landed aristocracy hesitated to take such bold steps, fearful of losing Spanish support in the event of a major slave revolt such as those that occurred on Sainte-Domingue (Haiti) in the late 18th century. Further, many *peninsulares* (Spaniards) emigrated to Cuba during the Napoleonic Wars, strengthening the bonds with the motherland. In 1817, however, the British began encouraging Spain to abolish its slave trade. Fearful of losing their labor source and their way of life, some land-owning *criollos* (creoles, Cuban-born people of Spanish descent) began to look at the United States as a possible benefactor. Between 1822 and 1861 there were several Cuban missions to America, seeking U.S. support if not outright annexation. (The United States expressed interest in acquiring the island as early as 1808, when President Jefferson tried to buy it from Spain. Subsequent purchase attempts by presidents Monroe, Polk, Pierce, and Buchanan brought the price up to $130 million, but Spain wouldn't sell.) It wasn't until the South lost the American Civil War and slavery was abol-

ished in the United States that Cuban interest in American assistance dissolved. The criollos, once again, turned to Spain for reforms.

The independence movement reached its first nexus in 1868, when Carlos Manuel de Céspedes freed the slaves on his plantation and read his Grito de Yara (a Cuban Declaration of Independence). The Ten Years' War ensued, and with it two of Cuba's great military leaders—the Dominican-born Máximo Gómez and the Cuban mulatto Antonio Maceo—made their names. In February 1878 the Spanish and the Cuban rebels accepted the Peace of El Zanjón. The treaty seemed only to acknowledge that both sides were exhausted, their resources depleted. Its terms were unsatisfactory to many (including Maceo, who fought for another year and never did surrender); the island seemed far from achieving true local autonomy; and although steps were taken to gradually abolish slavery, its complete abolition—a goal for many revolutionaries—had not been realized.

Act II: The Second War of Independence
In 1895 a new independence movement was launched, with the great Cuban writer and patriot José Martí (1853–95) as its chief ideologue and Maceo and Gómez as its top generals. Martí, Cuba's foremost martyr and hero, was first a lyric poet, author of romantic verses such as *El corazón es un loco / Que no sabe de un color / O es su amor de dos colores / O dice que no es amor* (The heart is a madman / Who doesn't know one color / Either his love is of two colors / Or he says it isn't love) and such patriotic lines as *Muro de cuatro siglos, tiranía / Cada vez mas atrás para ir al frente / Bandera de cien años, cada día / mas y mas alta / para alzar la frente* (Wall of four centuries, tyranny / Ever farther back to move ahead / Flag of a hundred years, day by day, ever taller / to stand proud). He also contributed moving lyrics to the ubiquitous song "Guantanamera": *Yo quiero cuando me muera / con patria pero sin amo / poner a mi losa un ramo / de flores, y una bandera* (I want, when I die / with a country but without a master / on my stone a bouquet / of flowers, and a flag).

Martí's long struggle for Cuba's freedom from Spain began with his imprisonment for publishing treasonous material at age 16 and ended with his death in 1895 (he was one of the first to fall in the Second War of Independence). In between, Martí studied law in Madrid; published books of poetry; wrote essays on the future of Latin America; and worked as a journalist in New York and as a reader in a cigar factory in Tampa, Florida, where he launched Cuba's definitive independence movement. Martí was wary of becoming too closely allied with the United States. The quote of his most often heard today is: "I know the Monster, because I have lived in his lair."

Cuba seemed on the verge of achieving its independence in 1898 when the United States, in a display of military power, sent the battleship *Maine* to the island. While in Havana Harbor, the ship was blown up. The flames of public opinion, fanned by Joseph Pulitzer's *New York World* and William Randolph Hearst's *New York Journal,* blamed the Spanish, and demanded war with the cry, "Remember the *Maine,* to hell with Spain!" (Spanish and Cuban history texts maintain that the *Maine* was blown up by U.S. agents to provide a pretext for entering the war. Proponents of this version cite the facts that the explosion blew the hull out, not in, and that there were no officers on board at the time of the blast. The U.S. Navy has since claimed that a defective boiler caused the explosion.) On April 25, 1898, the United States declared war on Spain. American forces took Guam, Puerto Rico, and the Philippines in one day; the Spanish held on to Cuba till July 17. Down came the Spanish flag and up went . . . the Stars and Stripes.

Since its earlier purchase attempts, the United States had made little secret of its interest in acquiring "the key to the New World," a prize of enormous strategic and economic value. As Cuba's Second War of Independence drew to a close, the moment had arrived for the United States to make its move. General Gómez tried to avoid U.S. intervention by asking for arms and ammunition instead of troops. However, the *mambises* (from the Congolese word meaning "despicable"), as the Spanish called the Cuban freedom fighters, could only watch helplessly as their liberation movement was stolen out from under them. In the end, the mambises, after losing more than 300,000 fighters in the struggle begun in 1868, were ordered to turn in their arms and were excluded from the victory parade staged by the U.S. military leaders.

Act III: The Way to Revolution

Martí's fears that the United States would subsume Cuba should the two nations become politically linked proved uncannily prophetic. In 1899 the island became an independent republic under U.S. protection. The 1901 Platt Amendment—accepted begrudgingly by Cuba—stipulated that America could intervene in Cuban affairs if the island's stability was at risk. It also allowed the United States to buy or lease Cuban land on which to build a military outpost (hence, the Guantánamo Naval Base). U.S. military occupation ended in 1902, but U.S. meddling did not. The Platt Amendment was invoked twice during the next 15 years, and U.S. diplomats whispered instructions into the ears of many a Cuban leader right up until Fidel Castro's Revolution in the 1950s. The United States was also heavily involved in the island's economics. By 1958, Wall Street controlled 90% of Cuba's nickel and copper mines; 90% of its sugar, tobacco, and coffee plantations; 80% of its public services; and 50% of its railroads. In addition, Standard Oil's annual profits were greater than all U.S. aid to Latin America combined, while, for good measure, North American sugar markets bought Cuban sugar at abusively low prices.

By the 1950s, average Cubans were in no better shape economically than many of their forebears had been at the beginning of the Wars of Independence. In addition, the American mafia had made Havana its headquarters (Cuba was notorious as the brothel of North America, a free port for gambling, prostitution, and all the pleasures that were illegal to the north). Years of political corruption, civil unrest, and such greedy dictators as Gerardo Machado and Fulgencio Batista had taken their toll. The country was ready for Fidel Castro Ruz and his message.

The early Castro, a romantic Robin Hood figure, miraculously survived the 1953 attack on the Moncada Barracks in eastern

Cuba and his subsequent trial and capture. Upon being released from prison, he went into exile in Mexico. In 1956, he and 81 rebels left Mexico aboard the yacht *Granma*. He lost most of his men after being ambushed by Batista forces in a landing described by Che Guevara as a shipwreck. Castro then organized an improbable guerrilla resistance movement in the highland jungle sanctuary of the Sierra Maestra. He took Havana in January 1959, after dictator Batista fled the country with much of the treasury. During his triumphal address, a white dove landed on his shoulder, an apparently spontaneous event that convinced Cuba's Santería worshippers of Castro's divine right to rule. Now well into his 70s, El Comandante is the planet's last governing socialist, head of a Soviet-style totalitarian regime short on civil liberties but proud of successes in health, education, and culture.

Ernesto "Che" Guevara, an Argentine born into a leftist bourgeois family in 1928, met Castro in Mexico in 1955 and joined the Cuban revolutionary movement. Described by Jean-Paul Sartre as "the most complete human being of our age," Che (the nickname comes from Argentine slang for "pal") was trained as a physician but proved to be an outstanding field commander. Poet, idealist, and philosopher, he seemed the perfect complement to the ever-pragmatic Fidel. The two revolutionaries parted ways only when Castro (for practical reasons) allied Cuba with the Soviet Union, which Guevara considered an imperialist menace no less voracious than America. Obsessively opposed to capitalism, Che believed in the perfectibility of man and strove to create El Hombre Nuevo (the New Man), the true socialist who would work for the common good instead of for personal gain. After his break with the Cuban revolution, Che took up fights in the Congo and Bolivia. On October 9, 1967, he was ambushed, wounded, captured, and executed by Bolivian Army Rangers (allegedly on orders from the CIA). Castro has made his former comrade into a cult figure. Che's likeness is everywhere, from the huge sculpture in Havana's Plaza de la Revolución to the three-peso coin peddled (counter to Che's guiding beliefs) for dollars on the streets. The

motto of the Young Pioneers, the national youth movement, is "Seremos como Che" ("We will be like Che"), a reprise of Castro's farewell speech to his comrade in arms, in which he asked "How do we want our children to be? We want them to be like Che!"

To protect its interests since the Revolution, the United States has compiled a somewhat embarrassing record vis-à-vis Cuba. The 1961 Bay of Pigs Invasion was an outstanding example of American interventionism. As the Cold War drama unfolded, so did the naval blockade, the Cuban missile crisis, the trade embargo, and numerous alleged attempts to assassinate Castro. Though the Cold War has ended, relations between the two countries have hardly warmed up, as evidenced by the 1996 Helms-Burton Act (proposing to penalize businesses and travelers from third countries for trading with or visiting Cuba).

Act IV: Today and Tomorrow

Today Cuba maintains a precarious balance between state-controlled economy, expression, and movement, and the beginnings of such free-market phenomena as the legalization of the dollar and the heavily taxed private restaurants known as *paladares*. That the dollar should be regarded as the salvation of one of the world's last bastions of socialism is yet another Cuban irony.

The lifting of the 40-year blockade, the pacification of the radical right-wing anti-Castro Cubans, and a transition to some form of government acceptable to all sides are urgent priorities as the new millennium begins and Fidel Castro starts his fifth decade of autocratic rule. "Our project," said a prominent Cuban statesman, "is to preserve the basic triumphs of the Revolution—our sovereignty, independence, health care, and education. Everything else is negotiable."

This view is shared by many Cubans and Cubanophiles who, perhaps naive utopians, hope for the best of all worlds in a peaceful future: guaranteed medical care, education, and subsistence in an increasingly democratic society. A difficult act to balance, but for Cuba, master of the impossible, it could all fall into place.

— by George Semler

WHAT'S WHERE

Havana

Slightly more than 2 million people call the nation's capital home. Set on Cuba's northwestern coast, the city is surrounded by the Straits of Florida and Havana Province. It's also divided into 15 municipalities, which themselves often contain various neighborhoods. Some 145 km (90 mi) from Key West (which Cubans call Cayo Hueso, literally Bone Key), Havana is very nearly Cuba's closest point to the United States.

Western Cuba

Western Cuba includes the three provinces of Matanzas, La Habana, and Pinar del Río, as well as the Municipio Especial (Special Municipality) of Isla de la Juventud. Here you'll find everything from wetlands, such as the Ciénaga de Zapata, to the finest tobacco country, such as that in Pinar del Río. The diversity continues with the peaks of the central Cordillera de Guaniguanico, the scrubby woodlands of the Península de Guanahacabibes, and sandy beaches along miles of coast.

Central Cuba

Between the lowlands east of Havana and the mountainous eastern provinces, central Cuba is connected to the rest of the country by a highway that runs the length of the island. Moving eastward, that highway skirts Cienfuegos, a small province surrounding a 19th-century city of the same name, then enters the larger Villa Clara Province near its capital, Santa Clara. Those two provinces, together with Sancti Spíritus, surround the dark green Escambray Mountains, though they consist largely of flat or rolling lowlands covered with sugarcane, tobacco, and pasture. In Sancti Spíritus, the colonial city of Trinidad is nestled between mountains and the pale beaches of the Península de Ancón. Ciego de Ávila Province is known for the beaches of Cayo Coco and Cayo Guillermo, two keys off its north shore. Camagüey Province has a large colonial capital set in an agricultural plain, to the northeast of which is the beach resort of Santa Lucia.

Eastern Cuba

The cradle of revolution, anvil-shape eastern Cuba includes the provinces of Granma, Holguín, Santiago, and Guantánamo. Together with Las Tunas, they once comprised the single province of Oriente. Santiago de Cuba, the region's most important city, lies on the southern coast of the province that shares its name. Far removed from Havana, Santiago has, throughout its history, been influenced by its Caribbean neighbors, as well as by French settlers and Afro-Cuban denizens. Though miles of farmland cover the region, it is also blessed with fabulous beaches, the majestic Sierra Maestra, and the forests surrounding Baracoa.

PLEASURES AND PASTIMES

Beaches

Cuba's 3,735 km (2,319 mi) of coastline are washed by the waters of the Atlantic Ocean to the north, the Caribbean Sea to the south and east, and the Gulf of Mexico's Yucatán Channel to the west. Just 20 km (12 mi) east of Havana are the famous Playas del Este, whose white sands frequently fill up with *habaneros,* as the city's residents are called. In the western provinces you'll also find everything from the lively resort strip of Varadero to the wild, unspoiled Playa María la Gorda. Central Cuba's northern keys (Cayo las Brujas, Cayo Coco, and Cayo Guillermo) have beautiful sandy stretches as well as outstanding fishing and dive sites. Oriente is blessed with a dark-sand coastline in southwest Granma Province, resort towns along Holguín's northern coast, and isolated coastal enclaves surrounding Baracoa in the far reaches of Guantánamo Province.

Dining

A standard Havana wisecrack credits the Revolution's three great triumphs—health, education, and culture—as having been achieved at the expense of breakfast, lunch, and dinner. Food conversations here turn repeatedly to the vicissitudes of supply: 100 heads of garlic for 100 pesos ($5) is a true bargain opportunity; the arrival of friends from the country with a load of *frijoles negros tiernos* (tender black beans) is an event to recount—albeit in whispers as these are black-market black beans. *Res* (beef) and *pernil* (ham) are dollar-store items, until recently off-limits to Cubans and now merely cripplingly expensive. Without a doubt, the combi-

REVOLUTIONARY RECIPES

Pollo al bloqueo (chicken à la blockade) is a popular recipe from the Special Period (the belt-tightening period proclaimed by Castro after trade with and support from the Soviet Union ceased).

Day 1: Skin a chicken, boil it, and make soup from the stock, adding *viandas* (potatoes, tomatoes, carrots, yuca, boniato, tamale, and maybe some pasta, corn, or rice). Day 2: Brown the pieces and parts of the chicken, and serve it in a salsa criolla (onion, tomato, pepper, garlic, salt, and oil). Day 3: Sauté the chicken until it's crackly hard; serve with white rice. Day 4: Crack the chicken bones and suck out the marrow.

In the colonial city of Trinidad, the *pargo* (red snapper) run in the Gulf of Mexico just in time for Mother's Day. Sons and grandsons emerge from restaurants all over town carrying large platters home for a feast of *pargo a la criolla.*

Step 1: Marinate pargo in lemon, onion, garlic, and salt. Step 2: Place in earthenware vessel with a small amount of butter spread over the bottom. Step 3: Cook for three minutes on low heat, turning quickly several times. Step 4: Cover casserole and allow pargo to simmer until done. Step 5: Serve to mother with an exuberant *"felicidades!"* ("congratulations!")

---

nation of food shortages and state-run restaurants has produced some remarkably undistinguished cooking over the past 40 years. But the legalization of the dollar and the opening of privately owned paladares have sparked a renaissance of authentic *cocina criollo*, traditional Cuban home cooking that truly ennobles lowly ingredients.

Pollo (chicken), *puerco* (pork), *camarones* (shrimp), *langosta* (lobster), *pescado* (fish), and to a lesser degree, beef and *cordero* (lamb), are the meat and seafood staples. *Frijoles negros* (black beans), *arroz* (rice), *yuca* (cassava or manioc), *malanga* (sweet potato), *boniato* (yam), and *plátanos* (plantains) are the leading legumes and starches. *Salsa criolla* (onion, tomato, pepper, garlic, salt, and oil), *ajiaco* (aji—a hot, red pepper—yucca, malanga, turnips, and herbs) and *mojo* (garlic, tomato, and pepper) are the main sauces.

The plantain alone has 1,001 preparations in the Cuban kitchen. When ripe, it may be cut diagonally and fried. When green, it can be sliced into *lascas* (thin wafers), fried, and salted to create *mariquitas,* or chopped into thick wedges, pounded, and fried as *plátanos a puñetazos* (punched plantains). Green or mature it may be boiled, mashed with a fork, dressed with olive oil and crisped pork rinds to create *fufú,* or mashed and mixed with *picadillo* (ground meat) and melted cheese for a *pastel de plátano* (plantain pudding)—tropical shepherd's pie.

Moros y cristianos ("Moors and Christians") is a combination of black beans and white rice. *Ropa vieja* (literally, "old clothes") or *aporreado de res* is shredded beef recooked in a criolla sauce. *Arroz congrí* is white rice "with gray," that is, with frijoles negros *dormidos* (literally "put to sleep"—cooked and allowed to stand overnight). *La caldosa,* a universal favorite, is a soup or stew of chicken, onions, garlic, oregano, plantain, squash, yams, carrots, potatoes, malanga, butter, and ham—all left to simmer slowly. Another favorite is cordero *estofado con vegetales* (lamb stew made with malanga, boniato, carrots, onions, garlic, and turnips), though almost any meat may be served *estofado* (stewed). Other common dishes include *chicharrones de puerco* (pork crisps), and *masas de cerdo* (morsels of pork), which is often served in a mojo criollo.

On the island's eastern end, dishes are more Caribbean and less Spanish; they're prepared with more spices and are typically cooked in coconut oil and *lechita* (coconut milk). Eastern dishes include *congrí oriental* (rice and red kidney beans), *bacón* (a plantain tortilla filled with spicy pork), and *tetí* (a small, orange fish caught in the river estuaries between August and December.) Rice is yellow not from saffron but from annatto seeds, also used to color butter. "Indian bananas" are boiled in their salmon-colored skins and dressed with garlic and lime juice.

Desserts include specialties such as *guayaba* (guava paste) or *mermelada de mango* (mango jelly), both often served *con queso* (with cheese). The eastern treat *cucurucho* is made of coconut, sweet orange, papaya, and honey. Of course the island's long cultivation of sugarcane led to its *ron* (rum) industry. Be sure to have a *mojito* (light rum, sugar, mint, and soda; from the verb "mojar," meaning "to moisten, to wet" as in "to whet your whistle") or the classic *daiquiri* (blended light rum, lime, and ice). If you'd like the sugar experience without the kick, have a *guarapo* (cane juice; thought to be an aphrodisiac). Cuba also has several fine beers ranging from light lagers such as Cristal to dark varieties like Hatuey and Mayabe.

Music

Your Cuban journey will no doubt be accompanied by a veritable soundtrack of island music. There are countless genres, from classical to Latin jazz to such hybrids of European and African sounds as *salsa, timba, conga, rumba, bolero, son, danzón, guájira, mambo, nueva, and vieja trova.* And every community seems to have some sort of weekly musical event. On a typical Sunday night in Trinidad, for example (where two music havens—La Casa de la Musica and La Casa de la Trova—are steps from each other), you might encounter a septet led by a man of 70-odd years playing for a crowd of 50-year-olds. Men and women of all ages will no doubt dance with confidence and aplomb.

For another type of experience, try to catch a performance of the Cuban National Symphony in Havana's Amadeu Roldan concert hall. Don't let the youth of the musicians or their seemingly casual attire (white shirts and black bow ties as opposed to the white tie and tails of European symphonies) fool you. These are professional, well-directed musicians who open their hearts and truly communicate with music.

Scuba Diving

Cuban waters hold countless acres of healthy coral reefs and dozens of wrecks, home to hundreds of fish and invertebrate species, and both the water temperature and visibility are excellent. There are at least 100 dive spots that have been explored, and countless more that have yet be discovered. The island's premier diving areas are María la Gorda, Cayo Levisa, Isla de la Juventud, Cayo Largo, Jardines del Rey, Santa Lucía, the coast near Santiago de Cuba, and the isolated archipelago of Jardines de la Reina (Gardens of the Queen). In addition to extensive coral reefs, there are dozens of shipwrecks, most of which lie near Havana, Santa Lucía, or Santiago de Cuba—the *flota hundida* (sunken fleet), near Santiago, has three ships dating from the Spanish American War. In addition to its varied attractions and excellent conditions, Cuba has more than two dozen dive centers, and the cost of boat dives, rentals, instruction, and snorkeling excursions is surprisingly low. There are also six hyperbaric chambers distributed around the country, in case of a diving accident.

FODOR'S CHOICE

Cigar Sights

Fábrica de Tabacos Partagás, Havana. You can smoke, sip coffee or a mojito, or tour the upstairs factory, where 500 people roll cigars for eight hours a day Monday through Saturday.

Vuelta Abajo, Western Cuba. Some 80,000 acres of the finest-quality tobacco are planted annually in this region west and south of Pinar del Río. The best of it is found around San Luis and San Juan y Martínez.

Dining

Antigüedades, Varadero, Western Cuba. With an intimate, antiques-filled dining room and only the freshest of seafood, this restaurant is considered by many to be the best on the Península de Hicacos. $$$$

El Floridita, Havana. On everyone's short list as one of Havana's greatest spots, El Floridita lives up to the advance billing splendidly. The bar is better than the restaurant. $$$–$$$$

El Aljibe, Havana. The breezy Miramar pavilion takes top honors in the criollo cuisine stakes. Leaving Havana without a taste of *pollo Aljibe* is almost as serious an offense as failing to dance or to smoke a Havana cigar. $$–$$$$

Palacio de Valle, Cienfuegos, Central Cuba. Surrounded by this 19th-century mansion's elegant marble columns and sculpted Moorish arches, you can feast on langosta. $$–$$$$

La Guarida, Havana. This funky paladar run by Enrique Nuñez and his wife, Odeysis, is a delight for its decor, its cuisine, and its gracious owners. $$

La Maison, Santiago, Eastern Cuba. Dinner at this elegant establishment in the Vista Alegre neighborhood may well be accompanied by a fashion show. Lunch in the patio and browsing in the on-site boutique are also options. $–$$$

Casa de Don Tomás, Viñales, Western Cuba. If you have to pick a place to go out of your way for, this spot—known for both its fine food and its good music—is it. $

Rumayor, Pinar del Río, Western Cuba. Though state-owned, this restaurant is filled with Afro-Cuban crafts that give it great personality. $

Sol y Son, Trinidad, Central Cuba. This intimate restaurant in the garden patio of a private home is one of the region's best paladares, serving an inventive, eclectic selection of dishes. $

La Campana de Toledo, Camagüey, Central Cuba. Housed in an 18th-century building on Camagüey's timeless Plaza de San Juan, this small restaurant serves food to match its ambience—authentic Cuban. ¢–$

Lodging

Hotel Casa Granda, Santiago, Eastern Cuba. This classic property—with a gracious patio bar, an elegant dining room, and antiques-filled guest rooms—is set right on Parque Céspedes in Santiago's historic district. $$$$

Hotel Nacional, Havana. The memorabilia-filled Nacional, Cuba's great national treasure, retains its glitter no matter how bad times may get (and they're getting better). $$$–$$$$

Hotel Moka, Las Terrazas, Western Cuba. Ecology is the theme at this modern hotel, where a large tree grows up through the center of the reception area and the bar and restaurant seem perched over the valley. $$–$$$

Hostal Valencia, Havana. Although the gracious patio is more reminiscent of Seville and Andalusia, each of the guest rooms is named for a Valencian village, and the restaurant specializes in paella. ¢–$

Convento de Santa Clara, Havana. This former Clarist convent has very few rooms, but if you can get one you'll be sleeping in one of Havana's most picturesque and historic spots. ¢

Faro Luna, Playa Rancho Luna, Central Cuba. Set on a rocky point near the public beach, this hotel has bright, spacious, ocean-view rooms and a dive center whose staffers help you discover just what's in that shimmering sea. ¢

Hotel Castillo, Baracoa, Eastern Cuba. Set in a fort dating from the 18th-century, this hotel offers comfortable rooms that mix antiques with modern facilities and afford views of the town and El Yunque. ¢

Hotel Mascotte, Remedios, Central Cuba. Dating from the late 19th century, this small hotel on an historic plaza offers tranquil, charming accommodations in an equally enchanting town. ¢

Museums and Monuments

Casa Natal de José Martí, Havana. Cuba's *padre de la patria* (father of the nation) was born of Spanish parents in this humble Habana Vieja house on January 28, 1853. The moving displays here convey the esteem in which this poet-patriot is held by Cubans.

Monumento Che Guevara, Santa Clara, Central Cuba. It wasn't until 1997 that the remains of Cuba's great revolutionary were identified; it took another year for them to arrive in Cuba from Bolivia for burial here.

Museo Bacardí, Santiago, Eastern Cuba. Founded in 1898 by the rum-making Bacardí family, this museum fascinates with its collection of indigenous artifacts, colonial items, and 19th- and 20th-century works of art.

Museo Histórico, Trinidad, Central Cuba. A stroll through Trinidad's rambling historic center feels like a trip into the 18th century. The history museum traces the city's development from its founding by Diego Velázquez to the early years of the Revolution.

Museo de la Revolución, Havana. Set in what was once Batista's Palacio Presidencial, this museum has displays that tell the tale of Cuba's Revolution. The Cretin's Corner has some familiar faces.

Natural Wonders

Caleta Buena, Western Cuba. East of Playa Girón is this exquisite limestone *cenote* (sinkhole) and coral cove.

Cayo Coco and Cayo Guillermo, Central Cuba. The white-sand beaches and turquoise sea of these two islands are enough to make them major destinations, but they're are also near an array of legendary fishing and diving spots and are home to an abundance of birds.

Cueva Punta del Este, Western Cuba. This group of caves on Isla de la Juventud has aboriginal paintings of stunning color and originality.

Parque Nacional Turquino, Eastern Cuba. A short hike through the vegetation of this national park in the Sierra Maestra brings you to Castro's camp and headquarters during the Revolution.

Playa Santa Lucía, Central Cuba. Its sands are pale and lovely, and the ocean that washes against them affords excellent diving opportunities.

Sacred Spots

Iglesia y Convento Menor de San Francisco de Asis, Havana. This lovely church has many irresistible features, from its facade and bell tower to its cloister and interior patios. The artwork displayed in the permanent and itinerant collections is excellent.

Iglesia Santo Cristo del Bien Viaje, Havana. A diminutive-yet-weighty character gives this church universal appeal. The square around it and the verdant churchyard all form a compact aesthetic unit.

Necrópolis Cristóbal Colón, Havana. Founded in 1868, the Christopher Columbus Cemetery is a veritable pantheon of monuments commemorating poets, novelists, musicians, soldiers, statesmen, and rank-and-file citizens.

Time-Honored Places and Spaces

Castillo de Jagua, Cienfuegos, Central Cuba. Set above the Bahía de Cienfuegos, this fort was built in 1745 to discourage pirates from trading with locals. It has been refurbished (even the drawbridge works), and has a historical museum, a bar, and a restaurant.

Castillo de San Carlos de la Cabaña, Havana. Every night at 9 sharp, the ceremony of the cannon draws Cubans and visitors alike to this fort. This not-to-miss event is even more enjoyable when followed by dinner at one of the restaurants in the Morro fortress area.

Parque Céspedes, Santiago, Eastern Cuba. Santigueros love to congregate in this historic square, where life continuously unfolds and music always fills the air.

Plaza de Armas, Havana. The most fundamental of Havana squares is surrounded by fascinating buildings, from the Castillo de la Real Fuerza to the Palacio del Segundo Cabo and the Palacio de los Capitanes Generales.

Plaza de la Catedral, Havana. The baroque facade of the Catedral de la Habana is a powerful sight, and the square on which it sits is ringed with other important palaces. The restaurant El Patio has tables here, and the Bodeguita del Medio is right around the corner.

Plaza de San Juan de Dios, Camagüey, Central Cuba. This splendid cobbled square—surrounded by 18th- and 19th-century buildings—is part of the historic district of Cuba's third largest city.

Plaza Vieja, Havana. Plaza Vieja and the buildings around it—particularly the Casa de los Condes de Jaruco, the Casa del Conde de Lombillo, and the Casa de la Hermanas Cárdenas—are all knockouts.

2 HAVANA

In this historic seaport, long known as the "Key to the New World", classic American cars clatter along streets lined with Spanish architecture and pulsating with African and Caribbean rhythms. Old Havana's baroque facades, massive-columned palaces, and lush patios whisper tales of Cuba's colonial past, while Vedado's 20th-century skyscrapers shout dreams of the future. Everywhere, Spanish, African, Caribbean, and American flavors boil in a dynamic and sensual brew.

By George
Semler

I F I GET LOST, LOOK FOR ME IN CUBA. . . " wrote Spanish poet Federico García Lorca. If you visit Havana, you'll soon understand why. Part Cádiz, part Miami, the city is an intoxicating mixture of opulence and decay, Old World and New, socialism and capitalism, Europe, Africa, and America. The Spanish baroque architecture of the 16th- and 17th-century colonial period, the neoclassical dome of the Capitolio (built in 1929 and modeled on the U.S. Capitol), and Vedado's modern glass-and-steel skyscrapers all have stories to tell.

Once-elegant buildings crumble behind Corinthian columns while 1950s Chevrolets and Oldsmobiles overshadow Soviet-made Volgas and Ladas and a new wave of Japanese Hyundais and Nissans. Tiny motor scooter–powered *coco-taxis* and *ciclo-taxis,* bicycle rickshaws for two, roll by. Modern hotel and apartment blocks tower garishly over streets choked with roaring trucks spewing clouds of black fumes. Exhortatory slogans printed in red and black block letters loom alongside bars and cafés where red-hot salsa bands set the city to music. The air is all but asphyxiating, the heat is relentless, and many things are in disrepair; yet all this seems only to add to Havana's rough allure. Graham Greene and Ernest Hemingway drank deeply of it and were inspired; Ava Gardner and Winston Churchill—to name a few—also imbibed and were enchanted.

One of the oldest cities in the Americas, Havana was founded on Cuba's southern coast as San Cristóbal de la Habana in 1514. In 1519 it was moved to its present northwestern location, where a natural harbor, one of the Caribbean's best, made it an ideal maritime hub. For almost 250 years, however, Havana was little more than a staging area for Spanish convoys loaded with New World treasures and bound for Europe. In 1750, Cuba's population numbered only about 150,000, half of whom lived in Havana or in other towns such as Matanzas, Trinidad, Sancti Spíritus, and Santiago de Cuba. The island had a handful of relatively aristocratic *criollo* (descendents of Spanish settlers born in the New World) families but few plantations, and hence, few slaves. Trade with foreigners for the island's few resources was officially banned (though there was a lively smuggling industry), making Cuba seem isolated. In 12 years, all this would change, and Havana, with its great port, would be transformed.

In 1762, Britain's Lord Albemarle conquered Havana during the Seven Years' War. Under his yearlong administration, British merchants flocked to the city. They sold foodstuffs, cloth, horses, agricultural equipment, and thousands of slaves. Though the island was turned back over to the Spanish in 1763 (under the Treaty of Paris and in exchange for Florida), the ties to British markets were already strong. The ports were flung open to trade, and the interior was flung open to development. Before the British arrived, Havana saw half a dozen ships a year, and the average size of Cuba's few plantations was 300 acres; after the British left, about 200 ships called annually in Havana, and the island's ever greater number of plantations grew to an average of 700 acres. By the 19th century, Havana was the Western Hemisphere's busiest commercial center, made fabulously rich by sugar, tobacco, coffee, and rum. Behind such exports was a plantation society run by criollos for their own benefit and that of the *peninsulares* in Spain. The labor force consisted of vast numbers of West African slaves, whose culture, traditions, and blood often mixed with that of the criollos to create a truly Cuban people and heritage.

Cuba's campaign for independence began along with its 19th-century prosperity, and Havana, as the capital, was often in the eye of the storm. During the Ten Years' War (1868–78), Cuba's first attempt to break free of Spain, the city was a haven for conservatives loyal to the mother country. Havana would later became a hotbed of liberalism and the nerve center for phase two of the independence movement—sparked by its native son, the eloquent writer and revolutionary José Martí—which led to the Second War of Independence (1892). In 1898, Havana harbor was the last port of call for the *Maine,* a major U.S. military vessel, which was blown up (depending on whose history books you read) by accident, by Americans, or by pro-annexationist Cubans. This event led to the Spanish-American War, the end of Spanish sovereignty, and the beginning of heavy U.S. involvement in Cuban affairs. Though the 1950s Revolution against dictator Fulgencio Batista began on the eastern end of the island, Fidel Castro's most charismatic moment was his triumphal entry into Havana on January 1, 1959.

Castro's Soviet-style regime improved the quality of life for most Cubans, especially in the areas of education and medicine. But the 1990 collapse of the Soviet Union combined with the long-standing U.S. blockade have caused severe shortages of goods throughout the island. A steady flow of visitors from Canada and Europe (and increasingly, though not always legally, from America) and the state authorization of the U.S. dollar as legal tender have helped to improve matters.

Havana today is a work in progress, rough and real, caught in its own history and struggling toward an uncertain future. Although hundreds of its colonial buildings have been preserved, many more need much more than just another coat of paint. Across from the imposing Capitolio, apartment dwellers can be seen using pulleys to hoist water buckets up from the street because their buildings' pipes no longer function. Ornate baroque entryways are festooned with spiderwebs of loose wires. Impeccably uniformed *pioneros* (schoolchildren) emerge from colonial mansions and one-time luxury hotels—now wryly referred to as *ciudadelas* (citadelles)—that today house dozens of families. Palpably, the determination and openheartedness of the Cuban people have given present-day Havana an undeniable poetic power. Add rum, baseball, tobacco, salsa music, Spanish baroque churches, and antique American *carros,* and you have a tropical metropolis with a unique blend of looks, sounds, aromas, and rhythms.

Pleasures and Pastimes

Architecture

Havana has many outstanding examples of Spanish colonial architecture, particularly those done in the exuberant, early baroque style known as *churrigueresque,* named for Spanish architect José Benito Churriguera. (His highly textured and dramatically sculpted facades, or copies of them, are found throughout the Americas.) Eusebio Leal, the Historiador de la Ciudad (City Historian) and the man in charge of restoration, has become one of Havana's most powerful figures. The UNESCO restoration project currently underway will, over the next decade, transform La Habana Vieja (Old Havana)—a World Heritage Site—into a living museum of colonial architecture.

For now, the contrasts and ironies that history and circumstances have wrought in the city's physiognomy provide a sumptuous visual feast. Dubbed "the city of columns" by Cervantes Prize–winning Cuban novelist Alejo Carpentier, Havana has many, often poor, neighborhoods filled with crumbling houses behind ornate Corinthian columns. As, over the centuries, Havana's wealthy citizens moved westward from

La Habana Vieja through El Vedado to Miramar and beyond, architectural styles evolved. The mansions of the Miramar district are reminiscent of posh American enclaves in Palm Beach or Newport, while El Vedado could have drifted over from Miami.

Beaches

Habaneros (residents of Havana) catch their rays on the Playas del Este, a string of white-sand beaches 20 km (12 mi) east of Havana on the Straits of Florida. The strands themselves are fine, shoaling off into brilliant aquamarine waters over coral reefs; the resorts, however, may disappoint. The western beaches of El Mégano and Santa María del Mar are the best and most popular.

Dining

Shortages of raw materials and a bureaucratized approach to food preparation in state-owned restaurants have produced many a mediocre meal, but, with the privateer restaurants leading the way, Cuban cuisine is coming back. For the best cooking in Havana, seek out the *paladares* (privately owned establishments; the name, which literally means "palates," was cribbed from a popular Brazilian soap opera in which the heroine makes her fortune with a roadside restaurant named "El Paladar de Raquel"). Call ahead to reserve a table if you go to a paladar, and never believe a taxi driver who swears to you that the place is closed; he gets a commission for taking you to the place he is flacking for. The best state-run restaurants are El Abanico de Cristal in the Meliá Cohiba; La Cava de Vinos in the Giraldilla, part of the La Coronela complex way out west on Calle 222 (corner of Calle 37); Chez Emérito in the Hotel Presidente; the Aguiar in the Hotel Nacional; and El Floridita.

Carne de cerdo or *puerco* (pork) and *pollo* (chicken) dishes are common, with *res* (beef), *pargo* (snapper), *cherna* (grouper), *camarones* (shrimp), and *langosta* (lobster) close behind. In the paladares, which can't legally serve beef and lobster, look for *conejo* (rabbit), *cordero* (lamb), and *cangrejo* (crab). Bananas, plantains, and *viandas* (tubers) such as potatoes, yams, and yucca (also known as cassava or manioc) are staples.

Standard criollo dishes include *frijoles negros con arroz* (black beans with rice); pollo *asado en salsa criolla* (grilled in a sauce of tomato, onion, and *ají*—a hot, red pepper); *pierna de puerco asado en su jugo* (roast leg of pork in its own gravy); *aporreado de* res, *aporreado de tasajo*, or *ropa vieja* (different names for shredded beef in salsa criollo); *enchilado de* langosta (stewed in peppers, tomato, onions, and garlic); langosta *a la mariposa* (grilled and served with lemon); *frituras de malanga* (crisp, fried wedges of a tuber that tastes like a tangy potato); and *yuca con mojo* (cassava in salsa criolla).

There are seemingly endless ways to prepare plantains in Cuba, among them *chicharrones de plátano* (finely sliced and salted plantain chips, also known as *mariquitas*); *tostones* (fried chunks of green plantain); and plátanos *a puñetazos* (literally, "punched plantains"; banana or plantain half cooked, taken out, placed under a cloth and hammered flat with a fist before being placed back in the pan to finish browning). Keep your eyes peeled for typical criollo desserts such as *casco de guayaba* (guava paste) or *mermelada de mango* (mango marmalade), both served *con queso* (with cheese).

Wine is increasingly available as proper storage at stable temperatures improves. Vintage Riojas and Ribera de Duero wines show up from time to time, though the price of good wine ($20–$25) compared to a

$1 bottle of local beer is a factor difficult not to keep in mind. Torres wines from Catalonia's Penedès region and from Chile are also frequently available. *Mojitos* (light rum, sugar, mint, lemon juice, and fizzy water) and *daiquirís* (blended light rum, lime, sugar, and crushed ice) are Cuba's most famous rum drinks. Cuban beer includes the standard light lager, Cristal; the slightly more full-bodied Lagarto; the still darker Bucanero (which also comes in a light version); and the darkest brews of all, Hatuey and Mayabe.

Lodging

If you're interested in exploring colonial Havana, the most convenient and aesthetically pleasing place to stay is La Habana Vieja. A dozen hotels and hostels, all part of the Habaguanex chain connected with the city's restoration operation, offer lodging in Old Havana. A stay in one of these places means that your lodging expenses help finance the refurbishment of this neighborhood. Hotels in Centro Habana at the periphery of the old city offer are close to La Habana Vieja as well as to the paladares and attractions of Centro Habana, Vedado, and Miramar.

Many lodgings are concentrated in the Vedado district, where the Hotel Nacional and the Hotel Habana Libre reign supreme. The traditional and elegant Nacional is the city's most historic and emblematic hotel, though it's an hour's walk or a 10-minute taxi ride from La Habana Vieja. The Meliá Cohiba probably has the best services and infrastructure, with the Meliá Habana and the Château Miramar close behind. Many of the top hotels, including the Meliá Cohiba, Meliá Habana, Hotel Nacional, Habana Libre, Parque Central, and Santa Isabel have executive floors with separate check-in facilities and business centers with internet, e-mail, fax, and phone services.

You can save from $75 to $100 a night by staying in a *casa particular* (a private home that rents guest rooms). The opportunity to help individual Cubans directly with U.S. dollars, as well as the chance to live more like a Cuban, makes this an attractive alternative. Specific private accommodations are difficult to recommend (people go in and out of business rapidly as a result of ferocious taxation), but rest assured that arriving in Havana without a reservation and finding acceptable private lodging *in situ* is a sure thing.

Music

Havana is almost literally made of music. Musicians—many of them trained at the Instituto Superior de Arte (ISA)—musicologists, and music lovers are the rule rather than the exception in Cuba. Havana is the main cauldron for what is, along with baseball, the national passion. In the city's plethora of bars, café, patios, restaurants, rooftops, terraces, and clubs, dozens of sounds and rhythms pulsate nearly around the clock: salsa, *guaguancó* (Afro-Cuban percussion), *son* (a style of music usually performed by a trio of singer, guitarist, and percussionist), *timba* (a hot, fast mambo), and *la nueva trova* (guitar-accompanied ballads) are but a few of them. All Havana seems to turn out for these *bailables* (literally, "danceables"), and they come to *move*. In addition, Afro-Cuban music is often performed at the Union de Escritores y Artistas de Cuba (UNEAC) and in the Callejón de Hamel. For jazz, head to the Zorro y el Cuervo and the Jazz Café; for salsa, Casa de la Música and Café Cantante; for boleros, Gato Tuerto and Dos Gardenias. The Sinfónica Nacional—a brilliant young symphony orchestra directed by the equally brilliant and young Iván del Prado—performs in the Teatro Amadeo Roldán.

EXPLORING HAVANA

Set in Havana Province and edged by the Straits of Florida to the north, the city of Havana is officially divided into 15 municipalities, which themselves often contain various neighborhoods. For the purposes of touring the city, it's best to divide it into six main areas. Moving from east to west (and, roughly, from old to new) you'll find La Habana Vieja, with its many historical charms; Centro, with the scenic Paseo de Martí (Prado), the Capitolio, and the 7-km (4-mi) seaside Malecón; Vedado, which is reminiscent of both Manhattan and Miami; and Miramar, with its grand manses. Across Havana Harbor are the fortresses—El Morro and La Cabaña—and the Cristo de la Habana statue as well as the municipality known as Regla and other sights in Eastern Havana.

To see La Habana Vieja and its many colonial palaces and baroque churches at their best, plan to tour on foot. Although you could spend days here, you can see the highlights of Old Havana's southern half on one day, and visit its northern portion on another. Make the fortresses across the bay a side trip from La Habana Vieja, and save the sights farther east and the Playas del Este for another day. Centro Habana also has many historic sights, the Capitolio, Chinatown, and Parque Central among them. A tour of Centro Habana can begin and end at the Hotel Inglaterra and Parque Central. El Malecón, from La Punta all the way to La Chorrera fortress at the mouth of Río Almendares (Almendares River), is an important part of Havana life and a good hour's hike.

Vedado stretches from Calzada de Infanta to the Río Almendares and is difficult to explore on foot. Taxi rides to objectives such as the Museo de Artes Decorativos or UNEAC can be combined with strolls through leafy streets filled with stately mansions. The area around the Hotel Nacional, the Habana Libre, La Rampa (Calle 23), and the Universidad de la Habana teems with humanity of every kind. Miramar, which stretches southwest across the Río Almendares, was the residential area for wealthy Habaneros and foreigners before the Revolution. A tour of its wide, tree-lined avenues is best made by car. A 20-minute drive farther southwest is the Marina Hemingway yacht harbor. (Note that pre- and postrevolutionary street names are often used in the older parts of the city; addresses contain both throughout this chapter).

Great Itineraries

IF YOU HAVE 3 DAYS

In **La Habana Vieja,** do a whirlwind tour of Plaza Vieja, Plaza de la Catedral, and Plaza de Armas, with a stop at La Bodeguita del Medio (or, for better scenery and fewer tourists, El Patio, in front of the cathedral) for a mojito. Take a taxi through the harbor tunnel to the **fortresses.** Have dinner at La Divina Pastora before (or after) the 9 PM cannon blast at the Castillo de San Carlos de la Cabaña. On day two, explore **Centro Habana**; visit the Capitolio, the Fábrica de Tabacos Partagás, and the Parque Central before having a daiquirí at El Floridita. In the afternoon, walk the length of Calle Obispo from El Floridita to Plaza de Armas; stroll the Paseo del Prado or El Malecón. On day three, visit the Universidad de la Habana and the Necrópolis Cristóbal Colón before touring **Vedado**'s impressive town houses and the mansions of Miramar. Dine at El Aljibe, then head for the Tropicana cabaret and its kitsch reviews or Macumba for hot music and incandescent dancing.

IF YOU HAVE 5 DAYS

On the first day, explore the many sights in **La Habana Vieja**'s southern half, starting at the Casa Natal de José Martí and ending at the Plaza Vieja. On day two, take in the Plaza de la Catedral and the Plaza de Armas before wandering along Calle de los Oficios, with its many art galleries. In the early evening, taxi through the harbor tunnel to the **fortresses.** Visit the Museo del Che and the Museo de la Cabaña in the Castillo de San Carlos de la Cabaña, have dinner at La Divina Pastora before or after the 9 PM cannon blast at La Cabaña.

On the third day, head for **Centro** to see the Capitolio, the Fábrica de Tabacos Partagás, the Teatro Nacional García Lorca, the Hotel Inglaterra, and the Parque Central. In the afternoon, after a daiquirí at El Floridita, walk the length of Calle Obispo from El Floridita to Plaza de Armas; stroll the Paseo del Prado or El Malecón. On day four, explore the campus of the Universidad de la Habana and visit the Callejón de Hamel, UNEAC (for an Afro-Cuban performance), and the Necropolis de Colón. On the fifth day, stroll the Paseo del Prado or El Malecón in the morning, then take a taxi tour of **Vedado**'s elegant town houses and the mansions of Miramar. Have dinner at El Aljibe, then take in the floor show at the Tropicana or try Macumba for salsa and dancing.

IF YOU HAVE 7 DAYS
Follow the five-day itinerary. On the sixth day, check out the waterfront crafts market on El Malecón before driving (or hiking) through the lush jungle of the Parque Almendares on the west side of the Río Almendares on the way to the Plaza de la Revolución. From here, drive through the harbor tunnel to **Eastern Havana,** stopping at the fishing village of Cojímar for lunch at Las Terrazas. Visit Hemingway's Finca Vigía in San Francisco de Paula before returning to Havana. Have a late dinner at a paladar in Miramar and continue out to Macumba for some dancing. On day seven, try the beach at Santa Maria del Mar in **Playas del Este.** Come back to Havana for dinner and a music show at Café Cantante or Casa de la Música.

When to Tour

November through May is high season, and temperatures are more moderate than at other times of the year. February is Cuba's coolest month, with temperatures in the 24°C to 26°C (75°F to 79°F) range. Don't rule out a visit during May through October; although this is rainy season and the weather is hot and humid, there are fewer tourists and generally lower rates.

La Habana Vieja

La Habana Vieja is a thick concentration of colonial architecture and humanity—a vibrant wedge of restoration work and tumultuous street life all set to music. Dubbed "Key to the New World" for its strategic position at the confluence of the Atlantic, the Carribbean, and the Gulf of Mexico, Havana was the staging point for the riches shipped back to Spain, and the tremendous wealth of this era is reflected in the plazas and mansions sprinkled throughout the old city. This opulent colonial patrimony also bears witness to the social inequities that led to the Revolution, which, in turn, resulted in the unusual conditions that make present-day Old Havana such a unique blend of colonial splendor and contemporary squalor.

Development of Havana began on the eastern edge nearest the harbor and moved west. Unlike the standard models for Spain's imperial capitals, the city has no main square. Plaza de Armas, as the seat of colonial rule, comes closest to this role historically, though its position on the edge of the bay (and the city) deprives the square of the required centrality. Plaza Vieja (originally called Plaza Nueva) was created as a space for markets and festivities instead of for the military and the gov-

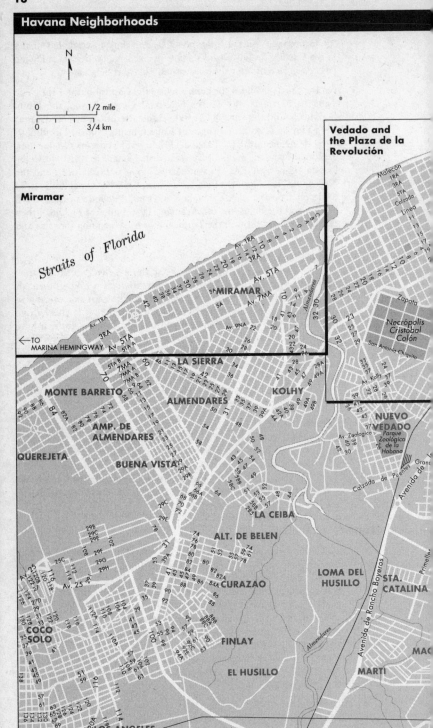

N

| 0 | | 1/2 mile |
| 0 | | 3/4 km |

Vedado and the Plaza de la Revolución

Miramar

Straits of Florida

Malecón
1RA
3RA
5TA
Calzada
Linea
13
15
17

AV. 1RA
3RA

AV. 5TA

3A **MIRAMAR**
AV. 7MA
5A

Almendares

Zapata

Necrópolis Cristóbal Colón
San Antonio Chiquito

AV. 9NA

←TO
MARINA HEMINGWAY
Av. 1RA
3RA
5TA
AV. 51A

AV. Kohly

5TA B
7MA
7MA A
7MA B

LA SIERRA

MONTE BARRETO

ALMENDARES

KOLHY

NUEVO VEDADO
Parque Zoológico de la Habana

Av. Zoológico

AMP. DE ALMENDARES

QUEREJETA

BUENA VISTA

Calzada de Puentes Grandes

Avenida de

LA CEIBA

ALT. DE BELEN

LOMA DEL HUSILLO

STA. CATALINA

CURAZAO

Avenida de Rancho Boyeros

Primelle

AV. 25

COCO SOLO

FINLAY

MAC

Almendares

EL HUSILLO

MARTI

LOS ANGELES

Straits of Florida

La Habana Vieja, Centro Habana, and The Fortresses

Via Monumental
TO
PLAYAS DEL ESTE,
REGLA, GUANABACOA

Caleta de San Lázaro

LA
HABANA
VIEJA

VEDADO

7MA Malecón

Línea

Av. de los Presidentes (G)

23

Calzada de Infanta

Malecón

El Parque
de los
Mártires

Canal de Entrada

Av. del Puerto

CENTRO

Paseo de Martí (Prado)

Parque
Céspedes

Zanja

Parque
Central

Av. Salvador Allende (Carlos III)

Zapata

Padre Varela (Belascoaín)

Zanja

Zapata

Feria de la
Juventud

27
29
31
33
35
37
39

Carlos M. de Céspedes

Av. Simón Bolívar (Reina)

Dragones

Plaza
de la
Revolución

Avenida Carlos

Avenida Rancho Boyeros

Aranguren

Calzada de Ayestarán

Egido

Av. Manglar

Máximo Gómez (Monte)

Desamparado

*Bahía de la
Habana*

ndencia

CERRO

Calzada del Cerro

Calzada de Infanta

Vía Blanca

Ensenada de Atarés

Straits of Florida

ía Blanca

PALATINO

Colz. de Palatino

General Lacret (Dolores)

STA. SUAREZ

Maria Rodríguez

Av. Santa Catalina

Calzada del 10 de Octubre

LUYANO

Calzada de Luyanó

Luyano

Av. Porvenir

Vía Blanca

Central

Calz. de San Miguel del Padrón

JUANELO

JACOMINO

Calzada de Güines

Calzada de Vento

Av. Acosta

VIBORA

amaguey Andres (San Miguel)

LAWTON

Av. de Acosta

General Lacret (Dolores)

Av. Porvenir

MA. CRISTINA

SEVILLANO

ernment. Plaza de San Francisco was Havana's third square, followed by the Plaza de la Catedral, originally known as La Ciénaga (the swamp) for its marshy terrain. La Habana Vieja's fifth square was the Plaza del Santo Cristo.

More than half surrounded by the Bahía de la Habana (Havana Bay), Calle Águila, the only street that begins and ends at the sea (running from the Ensenada de Atares to the Malecón) is officially the western limit of La Habana Vieja, although the true border is Calle de Bélgica (more often known by its old name as Egido), which becomes Monserrate at its center and Avenida de las Misiones at its northern extreme.

La Habana Vieja is composed of a dozen north–south streets intersected by 20 east–west arteries, forming more than 100 surprisingly symmetrical (for 16th-century urban planning) blocks. Innumerable mansions and palaces, nearly two dozen cultural centers and museums, six churches, and five convents are crowded into this 1½-square-mi municipality. Calle Brasil (Teniente Rey) roughly divides La Habana Vieja into a southern sector including Plaza Vieja and Plaza del Santo Cristo, and a northern sector that includes Plaza de Armas, Plaza de San Francisco, and Plaza de la Catedral.

La Habana Vieja Sur

The southern portion of La Habana Vieja is more residential and less monumental than its northern section. Less frequented by tour groups, this is the ideal place to see how Habaneros live. This walk begins at the railroad station and passes some of Havana's oldest (17th-century) structures, many of them brilliantly restored.

Numbers in the text correspond to numbers in the margin and on the Habana Vieja and Centro Habana map.

A GOOD WALK

Starting at the Estación Central de Ferrocarriles (Central Railway Station), walk down to the section of city walls still standing at the corner of Avenida de Bélgica and Desamparados for a look at the layout of early Havana. Across the street to your left is the **Casa Natal de José Martí** ①, the birthplace of Cuba's poet-patriot. Follow Calle Leonor Pérez (Paula) east toward the bay and the **Iglesia y Convento de la Merced** ②, just up from the corner of Calle de Cuba. The **Antigua Iglesia de San Francisco de Paula** ③ stands almost catercorner to La Merced, at the end of Calle de Cuba. From this church, follow Calle Desamparado (Calle San Pedro/Av. del Puerto) along the harbor, and turn left onto Calle Acosta. Follow it to Calle de Cuba to reach the **Iglesia del Espíritu Santo** ④, Havana's oldest church. From here walk north on Calle de Cuba; on your left, in the block between Calle Luz and Calle Sol, you'll see the lovely **Convento de Santa Clara** ⑤. Return to Calle Luz, turn right and walk to the **Antigua Iglesia y Convento de Nuestra Señora de Belén** ⑥, which is between Calle Picota and Calle Compostela.

From Nuestra Señora de Belén, take Compostela north for four blocks to the intersection with Calle Brasil (Teniente Rey) and the art nouveau **Droguería Sarrà** ⑦. Follow Calle Brasil east to the intersection with Calle de Cuba. Look up to see the ornate baroque facades and balconies overhead. Have a look inside the *comedor obrero* (workers' dining room). For less than a penny, yuca con mojo is served with water or raw rum here. Continue along Brasil to Calle San Ignacio and the **Plaza Vieja** ⑧. After exploring this plaza, backtrack along Calle Brasil, take a right onto Calle de Cuba, and follow it to the **Museo Histórico de las Ciencias Carlos J. Finlay** ⑨. After learning a little more about the life and work of this Cuban-born scientist, follow Calle Amargura west for five blocks to the **Iglesia Santo Cristo del Buen Viaje** ⑩.

TIMING

You can march through this walk in about three hours, though you need a full day to truly do it justice. (Wear cool clothing and very comfortable shoes.) If you're short on time, the Casa Natal de José Martí, the Plaza Vieja, and the Iglesia Santo Cristo del Buen Viaje are the must-see sights.

SIGHTS TO SEE

6 **Antigua Iglesia y Convento de Nuestra Señora de Belén.** Havana's first baroque church (1712–18) was originally conceived as a convalescent hospital. The founding Belenistas (members of the Order of Bethlehem) were replaced in 1842 by the Jesuits, who established a school here in 1856. The niche over the main door contains a nativity scene under a fluted conch shell. The figures in the niche are illuminated from behind by an amber reflector that throws extra light on the heads of the saints. (The lighting here is the work of electrical engineer Félix de Noval, who has illuminated many of Havana's monuments.) The convent's Arco de Belén, at the corner of Acosta and Compostela, has long been identified with the neighborhood's Jewish community, which after their 1492 expulsion from Spain became an important presence in Cuba as the Sephardic diaspora spread throughout the Mediterranean and the New World. ⊠ *Calle Compostela y Calle Luz, La Habana Vieja,* ☎ 7/861–7283. ⊡ *$2.* ⊙ *Mon.–Sat. 9–5, Sun. 9–1.*

3 **Antigua Iglesia de San Francisco de Paula.** The restored San Francisco de Paula church stands in a plaza at the edge of the harbor at the southern end of the Alameda de Paula. Built between 1730 and 1745 as part of what was then a hospital for women, its facade is described as "pre-churrigueresque," meaning that it was done prior to the popular exuberant baroque style for which Spanish architect José Benito Churriguera is known. The church fell into disrepair in the 20th century, when the adjoining hospital was moved far from the uproarious port. Restored in early 2001 and filled with Cuban art (including a series of crosses by prominent contemporary painter Zaida del Río), the church is now often used as a concert hall and art gallery. ⊠ *Plazuela de Paula, esquina de Calle San Ignacio, La Habana Vieja,* ☎ 7/54–5339. ⊡ *$2.* ⊙ *Mon.–Sat. 9–5, Sun. 9–1*

★ **1** **Casa Natal de José Martí.** On January 28, 1853, Cuba's *padre de la patria* (father of the nation), José Martí, was born of Spanish parents in this humble house. As a child he prophetically announced "Five generations of slaves must be followed by a generation of martyrs." At age 15 he wrote a newspaper piece judged treasonous by the Spanish governors, and, after time in a Havana prison followed by exile to the Isla de la Juventud, he was exiled to Spain, where he later studied law. Martí then spent 14 years in the United States, working as a newspaper reporter. Three volumes of poetry and several books of essays established him as the most brilliant Latin American writer and political analyst of his day.

Martí's words stirred both moral and financial support for Cuban independence. In mid-April 1895, as part of a revolutionary plan that was months in the making, Martí joined General Máximo Gómez on Santo Domingo (Dominican Republic). The two set out for eastern Cuba, where General Antonio Maceo awaited them. A month later, on May 19, 1895, Martí became one of the first casualties of the Second War of Independence, when he charged, mounted on a white steed, into a Spanish ambush during a battle at Dos Ríos. His lyrics in "Guantanamera," are premonitory: *"Que no me entierran en lo oscuro / a morir como un traidor / yo soy bueno y como bueno / moriré de cara al sol."* ("May they not bury me in darkness / to die like a traitor / I am good, and as a good man / I will die facing the sun.")

22

La Habana Vieja and Centro Habana

LA
HABANA
VIEJA

Vía Monumental

Canal de Entrada

TO →
PLAYAS DEL ESTE,
REGLA, GUANABACOA,
COJIMAR, FINCA VIGÍA,
PARQUE LENIN

El Parque
de los
Martires

Av. del Puerto

Casa
Steinhardt

Genios

Martí (Prado)

Hotel
Caribbean

Teatro
Fausto

Palacio de la
Artesanía

Parque
Céspedes

Casa José
Miguel
Gómez

Chacón

Crafts Market

Antiguo
Casino
Español

Hotel
Sevilla

Tejadillo

La Bodeguita
del Medio

Empedrado

El
Patio

Hotel
Inglaterra

Progreso

O'Reilly

Gran Teatro/
Teatro García Lorca

Floridita

Obispo

Café de Paris

Obrapía

Aguiar

Cuba

San Ignacio

Mercaderes

El Templete

Agromonte

Lamparilla

Hanoi

Amargura

Brasil

(Teniente Rey)

Habana

Oficios

Dragones

Bélgica (Monserrate)

Bernaza

Villegas

Aguacate

Compostela

Muralla

Sol

Santa Clara

Luz

Economía
Cárdenas
Cienfuegos

Apodaca (Somerruelos)

Factoría

Egido

Picota

Acosta

Jesus María

Merced

Damas

Inquisidor

San Pedro

Estación
Central de
Ferrocarriles

Leonor Pérez (Paula)

San Isidro

Restos de la
Muralla

Desamparado

Bahía de la
Habana

Ensenada de Atarés

0   1/4 mile
0   1/4 km

The memorabilia in this museum range from locks of the young Martí's hair to the shackle he wore around his ankle as a prisoner to letters, books, and poetry. Look for the martyr's spurs and ammunition belt, a rare 1893 photograph of Martí with Máximo Gómez in New York, and another of the Manhattan office on Front Street where he worked on the Cuban independentist newspaper *Patria*. ⊠ *Calle Leonor Pérez (Paula) 314, La Habana Vieja,* ☎ *7/861–3778.* ⌑ *$3.* ☉ *Mon.–Sat. 9–5, Sun. 9–1.*

❺ Convento de Santa Clara. It's hard to miss Havana's oldest convent (c. 1638–44), as it's painted a bright, rich yellow and occupies an entire block. It now houses the Centro Nacional de Conservación, Restauración, y Museología (National Center for Conservation, Restoration, and Museum Science) as well as the Residencia Académica (Academic Residence), where small groups and some individuals can stay. It once housed hundreds of nuns and was a refuge for young women with problems that ranged from the routine broken heart to unwanted pregnancies and dowries insufficient for marriage. The *mudéjar* wood-beamed ceilings and the lush courtyard are extraordinary, as is the Salón Plenario, the marble-floored hall used for seminars. The convent regularly hosts art exhibits and concerts and has a small bar and restaurant. ⊠ *Calle de Cuba 610, La Habana Vieja,* ☎ *7/66–9327.* ⌑ *$2.* ☉ *Weekdays 9–5.*

❼ Droguería Sarrà. This art nouveau pharmacy is short on drugs but long on design. Founded by a Catalan apothecary in 1874, it was built in the elaborate modernist style universally favored by 19th-century pharmacies. The carved wooden racks and shelves backed by murals painted on glass are especially ornate, and the ceramic apothecary jars, though probably empty, are colorfully painted. Also known as La Reunión (note the inscription on the wall behind the counter), this pharmacy was a famous meeting place, a sort of informal neighborhood clubhouse. ⊠ *Calle Brasil (Teniente Rey) 251, esquina de Calle Compostela, La Habana Vieja,* ☎ *7/861–0069.* ⌑ *Free.* ☉ *Weekdays 9–5.*

❷ Iglesia y Convento de la Merced. Although it was begun in 1755, this church and convent complex wasn't completed until the 19th century. Hence you can clearly see a progression of architectural styles, particularly in the facade, with its six starchy-white pillars and its combination of late-baroque and early neoclassical elements. Inside are numerous works by 19th-century Cuban painters. ⊠ *Calle de Cuba 806, esquina de Calle de la Merced, La Habana Vieja,* ☎ *7/863–8873.* ⌑ *Free.* ☉ *Mon.–Sat. 9–5, Sun. 9–1.*

❹ Iglesia del Espíritu Santo. Havana's oldest church (c. 1638) was built by Afro-Cubans who were brought to the island as slaves but who later bought their freedom, a common phenomenon in Cuba. Fittingly, today it's the only church in the city authorized to grant political asylum. Its interior has several notable paintings; notice especially the representation of a seated, post-Crucifixion Christ on the right wall. The crypt under the left of the altar contains catacombs, which you can visit with the custodian-guide, who speaks a little English (a $1 tip is appreciated). The three-story belfry to the left of the church is one of La Habana Vieja's tallest towers. ⊠ *Calle Acosta 161, esquina de Calle de Cuba, La Habana Vieja,* ☎ *7/862–3410.* ⌑ *Free.* ☉ *Mon.–Sat. 9–5, Sun. 9–1.*

★ **❿ Iglesia Santo Cristo del Buen Viaje.** Although originally founded in 1640 as the Ermita de Nuestra Señora del Buen Viaje, the present church was built in 1755. The advocation to the *buen viaje* (good voyage) was a result of its popularity among seafarers in need of a patron and a place to pray for protection. The baroque facade is notable for the simplicity of its twin hexagonal towers and the deep flaring arch in its entryway. Traditionally the final stop on the Vía Crucis (Way of the Cross) held during Lent, the church and its plaza have an intimate and informal charm. This is the plaza where Graham Greene's character Wormold (the vacuum-cleaner salesman/secret agent) is "swallowed up among the pimps and lottery sellers of the Havana noon" in *Our Man in Havana*. Don't miss the view from the corner of Amargura: you can see straight down Villegas to the dome of the old Palacio Presidencial (Presidential Palace). ⊠ *Plaza del Cristo, La Habana Vieja,* ☎ *7/863–1767.* ☞ *Free.* ☉ *During Masses (held at 10 and 5).*

NEED A BREAK?	From the Iglesia Santo Cristo del Buen Viaje it's a short walk southwest to the **Hanoi** (Calle Brasil/Teniente Rey y Calle Bernaza, Centro, ☎ 7/867–1029) restaurant, a great place for an eclectic criollo-Vietnamese meal.

---

❾ Museo Histórico de las Ciencias Carlos J. Finlay. This science museum is named in honor of Carlos Juan Finlay (1833–1915), the Cuban physician of Scottish and French descent whose life work on yellow fever conclusively proved, in 1882, that the mosquito of the genus *stegomyia* was the carrier of the disease. Trained at Jefferson Medical College in Philadelphia, Dr. Finlay spent his entire professional life in Havana and was Cuba's chief health officer from 1902 to 1909. The museum contains scientific and medical paraphernalia and Finlay memorabilia. ⊠ *Calle de Cuba 460, La Habana Vieja,* ☎ *7/863–4823.* ☞ *$2.* ☉ *Weekdays 8:30–5, Sat. 9–3.*

★ ❽ Plaza Vieja. What is now called the Old Square was originally Plaza Nueva (New Square), built as a popular alternative to Plaza de Armas, the military and government nerve center. Later called Plaza del Mercado (Market Square) as Havana's commercial hub, Plaza Vieja was the site of executions, processions, bullfights, and fiestas—all witnessed by Havana's wealthiest citizens, who looked on from their balconies. The original Carrara marble fountain surrounded by four dolphins was demolished in the 1930s when President Gerardo Machado (1871–1939) built an underground parking lot here. Today the square's surrounding structures vary wildly in condition, though all of them are noteworthy. Don't miss the splendid view west down Calle Brasil (Teniente Rey) to the Capitolio.

The impressive mansion on the square's southwestern corner is the **Casa de los Condes de Jaruco** (1733–37), seat of the Fondo Cubano de Bienes Culturales (BFC; Cuba's version of the National Endowment for the Arts). Its lush main patio is surrounded by massive, yet delicate, pillars. Look for the ceramic tiles along the main stairway and the second-floor stained-glass windows. You can linger in the tearoom, the boutique, or at one of the art exhibitions frequently held here. To your left as you exit is the interesting 1762 Elias Durnford painting titled *A View of the Market Place in the City of the Havana* [sic].

On the square's southeastern corner, the **Palacio Viena Hotel** (also known as the Palacio Cueto) is a 1906 art-nouveau gem that was occupied by several dozen families after the Revolution. The intense floral relief sculpture and stained-glass windows are still intact, if a little sooty, on all five stories. At this writing, restoration of this spectacular building was slated to be complete by late 2002.

On the square's western edge is the 1752 **Casa de Juan Rico de Mata** (Calle Mercaderes 307), now housing the Fototeca de Cuba. The building, together with the towers on the corner beyond it, will someday be a magnificent hotel. The **Casa de las Hermanas Cárdenas** (Calle San Ignacio 352), on the square's eastern side, was once used by Havana's first Philharmonic society. It's now home to the Centro de Desarrollo de Artes Visuales (Center for the Development of Visual Arts), which hosts temporary exhibits. In the 18th-century **Casa del Conde San Estéban de Cañongo** (Calle San Ignacio 356) you'll find the Artesanías para Turismo workshop, where you can watch artisans assemble crafts that are for sale. While wandering along San Ignacio, notice the faded VAPORES CUBA–ESPAÑA (STEAMBOATS CUBA–SPAIN) sign on the wall inside the entryway of **No. 358**. The 18th-century **Casa del Conde de Lombillo** (Calle San Ignacio 364; not to be confused with the Conde de Lombillo house in the Plaza de la Catedral) has lovely original murals in amber hues with faded blue and green floral motifs decorating its facade. Look carefully; the murals appear to represent scenes of early Havana. The restoration of the 17th-century **Colegio del Santo Angel** (Calle Brasil/Teniente Rey 56, esquina de Calle San Ignacio) was completed in late 2001. It was originally the house of Susana Benitez de Parejo, a wealthy young widow who departed for Spain in the mid-19th century; it was later used as an orphanage for boys under 12 years of age and then as a music conservatory until it collapsed in 1993, leaving only the facade standing. Now housing an excellent restaurant and 11 luxury apartments, this is one of the finest triumphs of the restoration work in Plaza Vieja.

La Habana Vieja Norte

This walk through the most popular and best restored of La Habana Vieja's sights stays close to the Bahía de la Habana and the harbor (except for a probe down Calle Obispo). For the most part, it also stays above Calle Brasil (Teniente Rey), which divides La Habana Vieja into its northern and southern sectors. All the streets in La Habana Vieja merit a careful perusal; this route takes you to the key spots.

Numbers in the text correspond to numbers in the margin and on the Habana Vieja and Centro Habana map.

A GOOD WALK

Begin at the Plaza de San Francisco and the lovely **Iglesia y Convento Menor de San Francisco de Asís** ⑪, across from the Sierra Maestra boat terminal. After looking through the church and convent, walk out to Avenida del Puerto (Calle Desamparado/San Pedro) and head south to reach the **Fundación Destilera Havana Club** ⑫, a replica of a rum distillery. Return to the Plaza de San Francisco and walk north along Calle de los Oficios to the corner of Calle Obrapía. Turn left and walk two blocks to No. 158 and the **Casa de la Obrapía** ⑬, one of La Habana Vieja's most beautiful colonial houses. Backtrack to Calle Mercaderes, and turn left toward Calle Obispo. The **Maqueta de la Habana Vieja** ⑭ is No. 111. Continue to Calle Obispo, where a right turn leads into the **Plaza de Armas** ⑮. After browsing through some bookstalls, you can visit several important structures on or near the plaza, including the **Palacio de los Capitanes Generales** ⑯, **El Templete** ⑰, and the **Castillo de la Real Fuerza** ⑱. From the Plaza de Armas follow Calle Obispo one block west to the Hotel Ambos Mundos, where Ernest Hemingway once lived. After exploring Calle Obispo, head for Calle San Ignacio and go north. Cross Calle O'Reilly and proceed to the **Plaza de la Catedral** ⑲, where you'll find the **Catedral de la Habana** ⑳ and a cluster of graceful buildings. If you feel like shopping, visit the Mercado de Arte y de Artesanía, a crafts market near the cathedral on Calle Empedrado.

From the Plaza de la Catedral, take a few steps up Calle San Ignacio to the **Centro Wifredo Lam** ㉑, an arts center named for the painter considered to be the Cuban Picasso, in the Casa del Obispo Peñalver. Return to Calle Empedrado and turn right. You'll see the always booming Bodeguita del Medio; next door is the **Fundación Alejo Carpentier** ㉒. After touring the house of Cuba's Cervantes Prize–winning novelist, head to Calle de Cuba and turn right. Four blocks north, in the Plazuela de la Maestranza, is the late 18th-century Palacio Pedrosa, which now houses the Palacio de la Artesanía. In its graceful patio you'll find a bar, a cigar store, and a shop with a vast selection of Cuban music. Upstairs, textiles and *guayaberas* (classic Cuban shirts) are for sale. Calle de Cuba leads north past the Hostal San Miguel and La Cabaña restaurant to the **Museo de la Música** ㉓, in the elaborate, early 20th-century Casa Pérez de la Riva.

TIMING

This walk will take several hours (or days, if you have them), particularly if you linger in the museums and galleries along the way. Taxis are readily available along the northern (harbor) edge of the Old City, a block above the Plaza de la Catedral.

SIGHTS TO SEE

⑬ Casa de la Obrapía. This house is named for the *obra pía* (pious work) with orphans that was carried out here in colonial times. Its elaborately wrought baroque doorway is thought to have been carved in Cádiz around 1686. The architecure of the interior patio is based on North African *fondouks* (inns) and, later, of Spanish *corralas* (patios). There's much to see here: arches of different sizes and shapes, vases decorated with paintings by Spanish painter Ignacio Zuloaga, and a collection of Alejo Carpentier artifacts (including the car he used in Paris). ✉ *Calle Obrapía 158, La Habana Vieja,* ☎ *7/861–3097.* ▣ *Donation suggested.* ☉ *Tues.–Sat. 9:30–4:30, Sun. 9:30–12:30.*

⑱ Castillo de la Real Fuerza. Constructed in 1558 by order of Spanish King Felipe II three years after an earlier fortress was destroyed by the French pirate Jacques de Sores, this classic, moat-enclosed fortress was the residence of the local military commanders until 1762. The tower, added in 1632, is topped by the famous Giraldilla (Weathervane), a nod to the one atop the Giralda minaret in Seville, the city whose Casa de Contratación (House of Trade) oversaw financial and shipping operations between Spain and its territories in the Americas. Havana's favorite symbol—it's even on the Havana Club rum label— the Giraldilla honors Doña Inés de Bobadilla, Cuba's lone woman governor, who replaced her husband, Hernando de Soto, when he left to conquer Florida (and search for the Fountain of Youth) in 1539. De Soto and his expedition went on to explore much of North America and were among the first white men to cross the Mississippi River. He died in 1542, but Doña Inés spent years scanning the horizon, awaiting his return. The current Giraldilla is a copy of an earlier bronze one toppled by a hurricane and now on display in the Museo de la Ciudad de La Habana. In addition to absorbing the fort's historical ambience, you can visit its museum devoted to ceramics, shop in its gift store, or have a drink in its El Globo bar. ✉ *Plaza de Armas, e/Calle O'Reilly y Av. del Puerto (Calle Desamparado/San Pedro), La Habana Vieja,* ☎ *7/861–6130.* ▣ *$2.* ☉ *Weekdays 9–5.*

★ ⑳ Catedral de la Habana. Cuba's Cervantes Prize–winning novelist, Alejo Carpentier, may have borrowed from St. Augustine when he described the city's cathedral as "music made into stone", but the words— like the bells in the structure they describe—ring true and clear. Work on the church was begun by the Jesuits in 1748, who weren't around to see it finished in 1777 (King Carlos III of Spain expelled them from Cuba in 1767). The facade is simultaneously intimate and imposing, and one of the two towers is visibly larger, creating an asymmetry that seems totally natural. The two bells in the taller, thicker tower are said to have been cast with gold and silver mixed into the bronze, giving them their sweet tone. In *Our Man in Havana,* Graham Greene describes the statue of Columbus that once stood in the square as looking "as though it had been formed through the centuries under water, like a coral reef, by the action of insects." This is, in fact, exactly the case: coral, cut and hauled from the edge of the sea by slaves, was used to build many of Havana's churches. Look carefully and you'll see fossils of marine flora and fauna in the stone of the cathedral. ⊠ *Plaza de la Catedral, La Habana Vieja,* ☏ *7/861–5213.* ☉ *Weekdays 9–11 and 2:30–6; mass Tues. and Thurs. at 8 AM, Sun. at 10:30 AM.*

㉑ **Centro Wifredo Lam.** Dedicated to and named for the great Cuban surrealist painter known as the Cuban Picasso, this gallery and museum is just behind the Catedral de la Habana in the elegant, 18th-century Casa del Obispo Peñalver. Along with a permanent exhibit of Lam's lithographs and etchings, the center hosts temporary shows with works by contemporary Cuban and South American artists. Lam, born in 1902, studied in Spain and fought with the Republic against Franco. He later fled to France, where he was influenced by Pablo Picasso, Georges Braque, and the poet André Breton, among others. He returned to Cuba to support the Revolution, and later returned to Paris, where he died in 1982. His best works hang in the Cuban collection of Havana's Museo de Bellas Artes. ⊠ *Calle San Ignacio 22, esquina de Calle Empedrado, La Habana Vieja,* ☏ *7/861–2096.* ▣ *$3.* ☉ *Mon.–Sat. 10–5.*

㉒ **Fundación Alejo Carpentier.** The house where Cuba's greatest novelist, essayist, musicologist, poet, and all-purpose literato set his most famous work, *El Siglo de las Luces* (The Century of the Lights), is now open as a museum, lecture hall, research facility, library, and cultural center. Alejo Carpentier (1904–80) began as a journalist and professor of music history at Havana's National Conservatory, and went on to publish *La Musica en Cuba* (Music in Cuba), *El Arpa y la Sombra* (The Harp and the Shadow), as well as musical scores, librettos, and poetry. The house itself, the Casa de la Condesa de la Reunión, was built in 1809 and renovated in 1878. Classified as Cuban baroque, the building is trimmed in pastel "Havana blue" and has a simple facade and a graceful interior patio with painted ceramic tiles. The collection of Carpentier memorabilia includes his Olympia typewriter, the text he was working on the day before he died, American scholar Sally Harvey's study entitled *Carpentier's Proustian Fiction,* an interesting engraving of 18th-century Havana, and various manuscripts. ⊠ *Calle Empedrado 215, e/Calle de Cuba y Calle San Ignacio, La Habana Vieja,* ☏ *7/861–3667.* ▣ *$2.* ☉ *Mon.–Sat. 9–5.*

⑫ **Fundación Destilera Havana Club.** A stop here provides a look at the insides of a rum distillery—including a model *central* (sugar mill) with miniature steam engines—as well as the chance to taste *añejo* (aged rum) and to enter a raffle for a 12-year-old bottle of rum. The Casa del Conde de la Mortera, an elegant 18th-century mansion, offers an interesting look into Cuba's sugar industry and the craftsmen (such as the coopers, or barrel makers) who were a part of it. The Casa del Ron sells rum on the premises. There's also a café-restaurant and the Casa del Habano for tobacco enthusiasts. ⊠ *Calle San Pedro 262, esquina de Calle Sol y Av. del Puerto (Calle Desamparado/San Pedro), La Habana Vieja,* ☏ *7/862–1825.* ▣ *$5.* ☉ *Mon.–Sat. 9–5, Sun. 10–4.*

★ ⑪ **Iglesia y Convento Menor de San Francisco de Asis.** The Latin inscription over the main door of this church and convent dedicated to St. Francis reads: NON EST IN TOTO SANCTIOR ORBE LOCUS (THERE IS NO HOLIER PLACE ON EARTH). As it's now a museum and concert hall, it may no longer be earth's holiest place, but it certainly is one of the loveliest. Built in the 16th century, in 1730 it was restored in a baroque style, resulting in a richly adorned facade with fluted conchlike tympanums over the doors and windows. Just inside the door you'll see tombs beneath a glass floor panel. (Churches were used as cemeteries until Bishop Espada founded what is now the Necrópolis Cristóbal Colón in 1868, a detail all Cubans seem to know and cherish). Note also the 19th-century grandfather clock made by Tiffany. The rooms to the right of the nave house archaeological finds and art exhibits.

Precisely 117 steps lead to the top of the 141-m (463-ft) tower, the tallest in Havana. Your climb (and your well-spent payment of an extra dollar) are rewarded by an excellent view of La Habana Vieja and the harbor. You can also get a close-up look at the fossilized imprints in the *arrecife* (reef coral) stone used to build this and many other Havana churches. On your way down, notice the ceiling vault over the last set of stairs. Concerts are usually held in the main nave at 6 PM on Saturday and 11 AM on Sunday (check the schedule at the entrance). The Philadelphia Boys Choir—directed by Dr. Robert Hamilton—performed here in May 1999, filling the church with admirers. One of them, Grupo Moncada leader Jorge Gomez, later confessed that "the tears just kept coming. I couldn't stop!" ⊠ *Plaza de San Francisco, La Habana Vieja,* ☎ 7/861–3312. ⊡ *$3 (not including $1 bell-tower fee).* ☉ *Weekdays 9–12:30 and 5–8.*

⓮ **Maqueta de la Habana Vieja.** This scale model of La Habana Vieja is a very handy way to get a feel for the lay of the land. The lighting effects that simulate sunset and sunrise are beautiful, and the extra dollar that buys an explanation from one of the attendants is well spent. ⊠ *Calle Mercaderes 114, La Habana Vieja,* ☎ 7/861–8166. ⊡ *$1.* ☉ *Mon.–Sat. 10–5.*

㉓ **Museo de la Música.** This museum is housed in the early 19th-century Casa de Pérez de la Riva, a white, ornately decorated structure overlooking the harbor. You can browse through its collection of Cuban musical instruments, as well as the sheet music and recordings for sale in its store. The wide range of West African percussion instruments is especially interesting. ⊠ *Calle Capdevila (Cárcel) 1, La Habana Vieja.* ☎ 7/861–9846. ⊡ *$2.* ☉ *Tues.–Sat. 9–5, Sun. 8–noon.*

⓰ **Palacio de los Capitanes Generales.** At the western end of the Plaza de Armas is the former residence of the men who governed Cuba. A succession of some five dozen Spanish captain-generals (also called governors) lived here until 1898, and the U.S. governor called it home prior to the Revolution. The wooden "paving" on the plaza in front of it was installed on the orders of a 17th-century captain-general, who wanted to muffle the clatter of horses and carriages so he could enjoy his naps undisturbed. Today the palace contains the **Museo de la Ciudad de la Habana,** with such unique treasures as a throne room built for the King of Spain (but never used); the original Giraldilla weathervane that once topped the tower of the Castillo de la Real Fuerza; and a cannon made of leather. Groups of pioneros often gather in the gallery here for art history classes, and you can buy art books in the on-site shop. Concerts are often held in the bougainvillea-draped, palm-shaded patio. Inside it to the right is a plaque dated 1557; it commemorates the death of Doña Maria de Cepeda y Nieto, who was felled by a stray shot while praying in what was then Parroquia Mayor, Havana's main parish church. The tomb in the pit to the left holds the remains of several graves discovered in the church cemetery. ⊠ *Plaza de Armas, Calle Tacón, e/Calle Obispo y Calle O'Reilly, La Habana Vieja,* ☎ 7/861–5779. ⊡ *$3.* ☉ *Tues.–Sat. 9:30–6:30, Sun. 9–1.*

★ ⓲ **Plaza de Armas.** So called for its use as a drill field by colonial troops, this plaza was the city's administrative center and command post almost from the beginning. The statue in the center is of Manuel de Céspedes, hero of the Ten Years' War, Cuba's first struggle for independence from Spain. Today, this is the city's most literary square; an army of erudite secondhand booksellers encircles it during the day.

As home to the UNESCO Cultural Library and the Instituto Cubano del Libro (Cuban Book Institute), the **Palacio del Segundo Cabo** (☏ 7/862–8091), on the square's northwestern corner, is a haven for literati of every spot and stripe. They come for lectures and readings, to buy books in the on-site shops, and to see films and art exhibitions. Nearby is the Palacio de los Capitanes Generales, across from which are El Templete and the Castillo de la Real Fuerza. Note that there are often concerts in the plaza on Sunday evenings—events not to be missed.

★ ⓳ **Plaza de la Catedral.** The square that surrounds and is named for the Catedral de la Habana is one of La Habana Vieja's most beautiful spots. In addition to the cathedral, you'll find several elegant mansions that once housed the city's aristocrats.

The **Casa de los Marqueses de Aguas Claras** (1751–75), in the square's northwestern corner, was built by Antonio Ponce de León, the first Marquis of Aguas Claras and a descendent of the discoverer of Florida, Juan de Ponce de León. Today the building contains El Patio Colonial, a restaurant whose tables fill a verdant interior courtyard as well as the upper floors. On the square's western edge is the 19th-century **Casa de Baños** (Bath House), which was built on the spot where an *aljibe* (cistern) was constructed in 1587. It served as the main municipal water supply as well as a public bathing house. The narrow cul-de-sac next to the Casa de Baños is the Callejón del Chorro (Alley of the Water Fountain), named for an aqueduct that ended here in Havana's early days.

Directly across the square from the cathedral is the **Museo de Arte Colonial** (✉ Calle San Ignacio 61, ☏ 7/862–6440), with its rich collection of colonial objects ranging from violins to chamber pots. It's in the Casa de Luis Chacón—also known as Casa del Conde de Bayona after the son-in-law of the original owner—which dates from the 17th century and which saw its first restoration in 1720. A small theater here, La Salita, often has plays and monologues. The museum is open Tuesday–Saturday 10–6 and Sunday 9–1; admission is $3. Wander along the square's eastern edge for a look at the early 18th-century **Casa de Lombillo,** the site of Cuba's first post office. A letter drop in the shape of a Greek tragedy mask grimaces from the wall to the right of the main door. Its inscriptions reads: CORRESPONDENCIA INTERIOR Y PENINSULAR. In the old days, it seems, you could plop both local and international ("peninsular" mail was being sent to the Iberian Peninsula or Spain) letters in one slot. The building is now home to an education museum, with displays honoring a 1961 campaign in which students and teachers took to the hills to spread literacy.

NEED A BREAK?   For a longer and seated perusal of the cathedral, try **El Patio** in the Plaza de la Catedral. Around the corner on Calle Empedrado is **La Bodeguita del Medio,** where you can sip a mojito and take in the Hemingway vibe. The upstairs bar is usually less crowded.

⓲ **El Templete.** This neoclassical, faux-Doric temple was built in 1828 on the site where the city's first mass and its first *cabildo* (city council) meeting were held. The cabildo took place under a massive *ceiba* (kapok) tree, which was felled by a 19th-century hurricane. The present tree—

A LANDMARK STROLL

Calle Obispo is arguably La Habana Vieja's most exciting street: a sweep back and forth along it—say, from the Plaza de Armas to Calle Monserrate and the Plaza de Albear—will take you past two dozen landmarks as well as cafés, restaurants, and shops. At the corner of Calle de los Oficios on the Plaza de Armas, the restaurant La Mina has a lovely patio and is a good place for lunch. Next door, at No. 109, is La Casa del Agua also known as La Tinaja (The Amphora), where fresh filtered water—all you can drink for 10¢—has been served since the late 18th century. The balustrade-enclosed openings in the sidewalk mark the early 16th-century water and sewage systems in front of No. 119, Havana's oldest house, which was built in 1570 and is now the headquarters for city historian Eusebio Leal.

On the corner of Calle Mercaderes is the Hotel Ambos Mundos, site of Hemingway's first Havana pied-à-terre. Across the street is the Universidad de la Habana's original bell, all that remains here since the university was moved to Vedado. Beside the Ambos Mundos is the Farmacia-Droguería Taquechel, marked by a brass vial and snake symbolizing the pharmacist's trade of concocting remedies of snake oils and the like. The *raiz de España* underneath refers to a root-based Spanish remedy. Next is the Panadería San José, with a spectacular ceramic mural of an overloaded slave and his jauntily dressed master on the upper part of its facade. Beyond this is the Quitrín, an excellent guayabera and textile shop in a series of buildings that ranges in style from art nouveau to Spanish Renaissance to colonial to eclectic.

On the corner of Calle San Ignacio is the Café Paris, always hot and hopping. The huge neoclassical columns of the Ministerio de Finanzas y Precios, formerly the Banco Nacional de Cuba, are next on the left at No. 211. The 13-ton safe door inside once protected Cuba's gold reserves. At No. 252 you'll see the Hotel Florida's immense marble doorway and mahogany door, with its mermaid doorknocker. The lobby bar is a good place for a break. A few steps beyond the hotel is the Johnson Drugstore/Droguería Johnson (the name appears in both languages), with its 100-foot wooden counter and elaborate marble column. Across the street is the neoclassical facade of what was once the Trust Company of Cuba, while farther along, at No. 305, is yet another immense 20th-century building with giant columns, making it easier to understand why Calle Obispo was known as the Wall Street of Havana.

At No. 316 is the bar-café La Lluvia de Oro (The Golden Rain), a mythological reference redolent of Gustav Klimt's erotic painting *Danae,* especially in the evening when red-hot groups play here and Cuban couples lay down blistering rumba, timba, and salsa moves. At No. 360, the Longina music and instrument shop, with a lovely etched-glass door, sells Cuba's best exports. The corner park at Obispo and Aguacate marks the spot where a building collapsed. At No. 411, the crafts store of the Asociación Cubana de Artesanos y Artistas sits behind two iron columns that date from 1894. No. 525 and No. 526 house Havana's two most important bookstores: La Moderna Poesía and the Ateneo Cervantes, also known as La Internacional. On Plaza Albear—dedicated to the designer of Havana's first municipal water system, Francisco de Albear—is the restaurant Gentiluomo (which serves a creditable bruschetta). At the corner of Avenida Bélgica (Monserrate), El Floridita is a always tempting place for peerless frozen daiquirís.

planted in the little patio in front of El Templete in 1959, the year of
the Revolution—is honored each November 19, the day celebrating Havana's founding. It's said that if you walk three times around the tree
and toss a coin toward it, you'll be granted a wish—provided, of course,
that you keep your wish secret. El Templete is also the site of a triptych
by French painter Jean-Baptiste Vermay portraying the first mass, the
first cabildo, and the municipal personalities who participated in the
building's opening ceremonies. It's also home to the ashes of the painter
and his wife, who—along with 8,000 other Habaneros—were victims
of the 1833 cholera epidemic. ⊠ *Plaza de Armas, La Habana Vieja,* ☎
7/862–1021. ⊙ *Weekdays 9–11 and 2:30–6.*

The Fortresses and Monuments

Havana's great *fortalezas* (fortresses; also referred to as *castillos,* or
castles) are reminders of Spain's mighty presence. Monuments testi-
fying to Cuba's struggles for independence surround these forts, and
museums have long since replaced barracks within their massive, time-
worn walls. Sunsets and the *cañonazo de las nueve* (9 PM cannon blast)
at the Castillo de San Carlos de la Cabaña are timeless events beloved
by Cubans. You can join them and then enjoy a meal at the nearby XII
Apóstoles or La Divina Pastora restaurants. Locals also like to picnic
and party in the park around El Cristo de la Habana.

*Numbers in the text correspond to numbers in the margin and on the
Habana Vieja and Centro Habana map.*

A Good Tour

Begin at the remnants of the **Cárcel de la Habana** ㉔, just off the Paseo
de Martí (Prado) and across from the **Monumento Máximo Gómez** ㉕,
honoring the great military hero of Cuba's wars of independence.
North along the paseo is another monument, the **Estudiantes de Medicina** ㉖, commemorating the execution of a group of medical students
by the Spanish in 1871 (one of many events leading to the Ten Years'
War). Just across Avenida del Puerto (Calle Desamparado/San Pedro),
at the beginning of the Malecón, is the 16th-century **Castillo de San
Salvador de la Punta** ㉗, a stalwart reminder of Spain's control of the
island. From here, take a taxi through the tunnel to the other side of
the bay and the mighty **Castillo de los Tres Reyes del Morro** ㉘, or El
Morro. From here head east to the **Castillo de San Carlos de la
Cabaña** ㉙. A way beyond this fort is **El Cristo de la Habana** ㉚, a giant
statue of Christ overlooking the harbor.

TIMING

Touring the monuments and fortresses on both sides of the harbor can
easily fill an afternoon. Although ferries regularly cross the bay to the
eastern Havana municipalities of Regla and Casa Blanca, the lines for
them are long. If you haven't rented a car, your best bet is to hire a
taxi for the duration of the tour. Just be sure to agree upon a price before setting off.

Sights to See

㉔ **Cárcel de la Habana.** A fragment of this 19th-century jail has been preserved as the Cárcel José Martí, commemorating the national hero's
1869–70 incarceration here as an adolescent advocate of and activist
for independence. It contains four cells and a chapel presently used for
concerts and art exhibits. ⊠ *Av. de los Estudiantes, e/Paseo de Martí
(Prado) y Calle Agramonte (Zulueta), Centro,* ☎ *no phone.* ▦ *$2.* ⊙
Tues.–Sat. 10–6, Sun. 9–1.

★ ♺ ㉙ **Castillo de San Carlos de la Cabaña (La Cabaña).** In 1762 Lord Albemarle took El Morro for the English after a 44-day siege. A year later,

Carlos III recovered Cuba in exchange for Florida and promptly ordered the construction of what was then the largest fort in the Americas. Sprawling across the hill east of El Morro, the fortress was named for the Spanish king and for the typical Cuban cabanas or *bohíos* (cabins) that once occupied the site. With the capacity to house 1,000 troops, this immense bastion was said to be so big that Carlos was given a telescope with which to admire it from Madrid.

The infamous Foso de los Laureles (Graveyard of the Laurels) was the execution wall where hundreds died during the wars of independence. The 9 PM *ceremonia del cañonazo* (ceremony of the cannon shot) is a must-see event filled with nostalgia and mystery. First, a lamplighter lights the gas lanterns. Then, a crier (a recruit with a voice so good he's been signed on permanently even though his military service ended years ago) begins an eery plainsong chant that reverberates throughout the fortress and, when the wind is right, across the bay to La Punta: *"Silencio; ha llegado la noche / Las luces están encendidas / Nuestro cañon se llama Capitolino / A las nueve sonará"* ("Silence; night has fallen / The lanterns are lit / Our cannon is named Capitolino / At nine it will sound"). Finally, a detail of some half-dozen soldiers dressed in scarlet, 18th-century uniforms marches in and loads and fires the cannon, which makes a deafening noise (cover your ears).

La Cabaña's two museums are of moderate interest. The Museo de la Cabaña documents Cuba's military history, and the Museo del Che is dedicated to the life of Ernesto "Che" Guevara, who ranks alongside José Martí as one of Cuba's national martyrs. ⊠ *Carretera de la Cabaña, Las Fortalezas,* ☎ 7/862–4092. ☞ *$3.* ⊙ *Daily 10 AM–11 PM.*

⑳ **Castillo de San Salvador de la Punta (La Punta).** On a point (hence, the name) directly across from El Morro, La Punta took 11 years to build (1589–1600), under the supervision of the same Italian military engineer—Juan Bautista Antonelli—responsible for its sister fortress. The two forts are so close, it's said that voice communication is possible in calm weather. In the early 17th century a heavy chain was stretched between them, sealing the port at night and during attacks. Today the fortress has an even more romantic role in the city's unfolding drama: it's a favorite spot for lovers. ⊠ *Paseo de Martí (Prado) y Av. del Puerto (Calle Desamparado/San Pedro), Las Fortalezas,* ☎ *no phone.* ☞ *Free.* ⊙ *Daily 10–10.*

★ ⓒ ㉘ **Castillo de los Tres Reyes del Morro (El Morro).** Begun in 1589, Havana's landmark fort is named for the Reyes Magos—the Magi or Three Kings of Bethlehem, who are the patrons of its chapel—and for the fact that it occupies a *morro* (promontory) at the harbor entrance. It and its sister fort across the way, La Punta, made Havana the safest port in the Americas at a time when both pirates and imperialists helped themselves to whatever could be had. Built into cliffs, El Morro was furnished with a battery of 12 cannons christened La Batería de los Doce Apóstoles (The Battery of the Twelve Apostles) facing the sea and another dozen, called Las Pastoras (The Shepherdesses) nearer the ramparts. The active lighthouse flashes its beam over Havana every 15 seconds. Inside the castle, across a moat and drawbridge, are stables, the chapel, dungeons, and a wine cellar. You'll also find the fortified vaults, which contain the Museo del Morro, with displays on the fortress itself; the Museo de la Navegación, with navigation and seafaring artifacts; and the Museo de Piratas, with exhibits and bits of folklore on pirates. The armory displays weapons from around the world. ⊠ *Carretera de la Cabaña, Las Fortalezas,* ☎ 7/862–0617. ☞ *$3.* ⊙ *Tues.–Sat. 10–6, Sun. 9–1.*

🖑 ㉚ **El Cristo de La Habana.** Sometimes referred to as El Cristo de Casa Blanca for the eastern Havana municipality above which it stands, the 18-m (59-ft) Carrara-marble colossus by Cuban sculptress Jilma Madera is said to be the largest open-air sculpture ever created by a woman. It was unveiled in 1958, a year before the Revolution and a year after the student assault on Fulgencio Batista's Palacio Presidencial. It's said that Batista's wife, praying for her husband to escape the shoot-out alive, vowed to erect a statue of Christ like that in Rio de Janeiro, Brazil, if her prayers were answered. Batista survived, and the statue was built while he tortured and murdered political opponents—especially students—with renewed brutality. For this reason, there's a certain official coldness toward the site. Certainly the sculpture itself is less interesting than the views (from its base) of the harbor and La Habana Vieja and the ambience of the park—a popular local picnic spot—that surrounds it. ⊠ *Carretera de Casa Blanca, Casablanca,* ☎ *no phone.* 🎟 *Free.* ☉ *Daily 10–10.*

㉖ **Estudiantes de Medicina.** A fragment of Havana's early ramparts commemorates the spot where eight medical students were unjustly executed for independence activism by the Spanish governors in 1871. At night the monument is beautifully illuminated, the work of the electrical engineer Félix de la Noval. You'll see amber light representing rifle fire; it can't, however, extinguish the white light (against the wall), which symbolizes the ideals of independence. ⊠ *Paseo de Martí (Prado) y Av. del Puerto (Calle Desamparado/San Pedro), Centro.*

㉕ **Monumento Máximo Gómez.** This bronze equestrian monument honors the great military leader of Cuba's 19th-century wars of independence. It was erected in 1935 in modern Havana's most pivotal location—in an important traffic circle and at the entrance to the tunnel leading to the fortresses across the harbor. The Dominican-born General Gómez led the *mambises* (a term used by the Spanish for Cuban rebels) in the Ten Years' War, refused to surrender when an unsatisfactory treaty was signed in 1878, left the island, and returned with José Martí almost 20 years later to continue the fight in the 1895 Second War of Independence. Martí died in the opening battle; fellow general Antonio Maceo fell in December of 1895, but Gómez survived. ⊠ *Av. del Puerto (Calle Desamparado/San Pedro), e/Calle Agramonte (Zulueta) y Av. de las Misiones (Bélgica/Edigio/Monserrate), Centro.*

Centro Habana

The Centro Habana neighborhood has a little something for everyone. History buffs will appreciate its eclectic mixture of monuments and monumental architecture from the 17th through the 20th centuries. Art lovers will enjoy its Museo Nacional de Bellas Artes. Connoisseurs of all things Cuban will appreciate its offerings of cigars, rum, and Revolution.

Numbers in the text correspond to numbers in the margin and on the Habana Vieja and Centro Habana map.

A Good Walk

Begin at the 17th-century **Iglesia del Santo Angel Custodio** ㉛. Across Avenida de la Misiones (Bélgica/Edigio/Monserrate) is the former Palacio Presidencial, which now houses the **Museo de la Revolución** ㉜ on Calle Refugio. Behind the museum to the south is the **Memorial Granma** ㉝. From here you can follow Calle Agramonte (Zulueta) south two blocks and take Calle Ánimas west one block to the **Paseo de Martí (Prado)** and its attractions or you can stay on the tour, following Avenida de las Misiones south to the **Museo Nacional de Bel-**

las Artes–Colección Cubana ㉞, the **Edificio Bacardí** ㉟, the **Museo Nacional de Bellas Artes–Colección de Arte Universal** ㊱, and the **Parque
Central** ㊲.

From the park, follow Calle San Martín (San José) to the **Capitolio** ㊳.
Behind it, on Calle Industria, is the **Fábrica de Tabacos Partagás** ㊴,
where cigars are still made by hand. Just south of here, at the **Asociación
Cultural Yoruba de Cuba** ㊵, you can learn about African deities. Across
the Parque de la Fraternidad Americana and Avenida Simón Bolívar
(Reina) is the **Palacio de Aldama** ㊶, once owned by a prominent member of the Havana *zacarocracia* (sugar aristocracy or sugar barons) who
fought for Cuba's independence.

TIMING

Paseo de Martí (Prado) aside, you can walk this tour in a couple of
hours. But walking isn't all you'll be doing, so budget a half to a full
day. You can easily spend an hour in the Museo de la Revolución; two
hours would seriously short-change the Museo Nacional de Bellas
Artes Cuban Collection; the Collection of Universal Art is another two-
hour visit; and you'll need at least an hour, if not two, in the Fábrica
de Tabacos Partagás. A promenade slightly off the path and along the
Paseo de Martí (Prado) is a chance to take Havana's pulse—something
you shouldn't rush.

Sights to See

㊵ **Asociación Cultural Yoruba de Cuba.** The Asociación Cultural Yoruba
provides a close look at African culture. The bigger-than-life *orishas*
(Yoruban deities) on display are all identified and explained in English,
French, and Spanish. The entry fee is steep compared with those of
other museums, but paying it makes you an association member—hence,
you'll be invited to all lectures and dance and music events. The association is near the Parque de la Fraternidad Americana, a shady space around
a sacred ceiba tree planted in 1928 with soil from each of the free countries of the Americas. ⊠ *Paseo de Martí (Prado) 615, e/Calle Montes y
Calle Dragones, Centro,* ☎ *7/863–5953.* 🖃 *$10.* ☉ *Mon.–Sat. 9–5.*

㊳ **Capitolio.** Modeled after Washington, D.C.'s domed Capitol, Havana's
Capitolio was built in 1929 and is rich in iconography. The statue to
the left of the entrance stairway represents Work (considered a mas-
culine ethic); that on the right is of Virtue (a perceived feminine attribute).
Some 30 bas-reliefs on the main door depict events in Cuba's history.
The giant main hall is called the Salon de los Pasos Perdidos (Hall of
the Lost Steps), allegedly for the fading reverberations of footsteps. It's
dominated by the gigantic bronze statue of Minerva (once known as
La República). Set into the floor at her feet is a diamond (presently a
fake) from which all distances on the island are measured. The former
Senate Chamber is at the end of the right-hand corridor; the one-time
Chamber of Representatives is on the far left. The on-site restaurant,
El Salón de los Escudos, serves a reasonable lunch; the Café Mirador
offers lighter fare. ⊠ *Paseo de Martí (Prado), Centro,* ☎ *7/862–6536.*
🖃 *$3.* ☉ *Tues.–Sun. 10–5.*

㉟ **Edificio Bacardí.** Built in 1930, the former Bacardí rum headquarters
(the family elected not to brave the Revolution and now makes rum
in Puerto Rico) is an art deco outburst best admired from the roof of
the Hotel Plaza across the street. Its terra-cotta facade is covered with
nymphs, sylphs, salamanders, and undines; its bell tower is capped with
a brass, winged bat you'll recognize from the Bacardí rum label (or
from the coat of arms of the House of Aragón, a clue to the family's
Catalonian heritage). ⊠ *Calle San Juan de Dios 202, esquina de Av.
de la Bélgica (Monserrate), Centro.*

★ ㊴ **Fábrica de Tabacos Partagás.** Tobacco is a fundamental part of Cuban life, and a look inside this cigar factory, which is also known as La Casa del Habano, is a must—despite the high entry fee and the pricey cigars. The store itself has more than $1 million of tobacco on sale and an inner sanctum sanctorum where you can smoke and sip coffee or a mojito. The upstairs factory has been in operation since 1845 and employs 500 people, who roll cigars for eight hours a day Monday through Saturday. When the *lector* isn't entertaining these artisans by reading a newspaper or a novel, Cuban music is piped into the rooms and 500 voices sing along, often drowning out the speakers on the crescendoes.

The operation is divided into seven departments: *despalillo* (stripping the central nerve from the tobacco leaf); *liga* (mixing leaves into combinations appropriate for making a cigar); *la galera* (the gallery) or *departamento de torcido* (rolling—literally, twisting—department), where some 260 workers actually craft cigars; *escogida* (choosing aesthetically matching cigars for presentation in the box); *anillado* (placing the paper rings on the cigars); *adorno de caja* (decorating the cedar boxes); and *embalaje* (wrapping for shipping). Depending on the quality of the cigar, from the majestic Monte Cristo A on down, each roller is expected to meet a daily quota of anywhere from 60 to 250 cigars (the average is about 170). Look for the older woman in the liga department who works with a giant stogie dangling from her lips. Seek out la galera's Alfredo Pérez (he sits in the back row, in an aisle seat in front of the air shaft), the top gun who rolls three times his quota daily. ✉ *Calle Industria 520, Centro,* ☎ *7/33–8060.* 🎫 *$10.* ☾ *Store: Mon.– Sat. 9–5. Factory visits: 10 and 4.*

㉛ **Iglesia del Santo Angel Custodio.** This prim little white church is a required visit for literature buffs hot on the trail of scenes from the novel by Cirilo Villaverde (1812–1894), *Cecilia Valdés (o la Loma del Angel).* The novel's bloody denouement takes place on the steps here during a marriage scene straight out of Racine. A plaque on a wall across from the church door lauds Villaverde's portrait of 19th-century Cuban life. Villaverde, in fact, made literary history with the stark social realism with which he portrayed the inhuman treatment of slaves in his novel. (One scene, for example, depicts plantation owners complaining bitterly about their foreman whipping slaves so early in the morning that the screaming and the crack of the lash disturbs their morning slumber.) The neo-Gothic church is, indeed, on La Loma del Angel (The Hillside of the Angel). With its pure, vertical lines, it's markedly different from La Habana Vieja's hulking baroque structures. Originally erected in 1690 and rebuilt in 1866, Santo Angel del Custodio was the site of the baptisms of both José Martí and Félix Varela, the priest, patriot, and educator credited with having "first taught Cubans to think." Martí, Varela, and Villaverde were all key contributors to the cause of Cuban independence. *Calle Compostela 1, esquina de Calle Cuarteles, Centro,* ☎ *no phone.* 🎫 *Free.* ☾ *Daily 10–10.*

★ ✋ ㉝ **Memorial *Granma*.** A glass enclosure behind the Museo de la Revolución shelters the *Granma*, the yacht that transported Castro and 81 guerrillas back to Cuba from exile in Mexico in 1956. Bought from an American, the 38-ft craft designed to carry 25 (presumably unarmed) passengers nearly foundered during the weeklong crossing. It eventually ran aground at Oriente Province in eastern Cuba, but it was two days behind schedule. The saga gets worse: Castro's forces were ambushed and only 16 survived, including Fidel, Che, Raúl Castro, and Camilo Cienfuegos. The park around the yacht is filled with military curios: tanks, jeeps, the delivery truck used in the 1957 assault on the

Palacio Presidencial, and a turbine from a U-2 spy plane allegedly downed during the 1962 Cuban Missile Crisis. ⊠ *Calle Colón, e/Av. de la Bélgica (Misiones/Edigio/Monserrate) y Calle Agramonte (Zulueta), Centro,* ☏ 7/862–4091. ⊡ *$3 (for memorial and Museo de la Revolución).* ⊙ *Tues.–Sun. 10–5.*

③④ **Museo Nacional de Bellas Artes–Colección Cubana.** Havana's fine-arts museum occupies two separate buildings, each of which deserves careful exploration. The original location on Calle Trocadero, finished in 1954, occupies the site of what was once a market. Designed by Alfonso Rodríguez Pichardo, the building, a compact prism with a large central courtyard, seems to breathe light. It now contains a varied and exciting Cuban collection. The third floor has 16th- to 19th-century colonial religious paintings, portraits, landscapes, and street scenes. Rooms 3 and 4 follow the 1927–1938 beginning and consolidation of Cuban modern art. On the second floor, in rooms 5–8, are works by artists from the 1950s–1990s. The power, color density, and intensity of Cuban painting is extraordinary, as is the rush through 500 years of history—from Armando Menocal's chained Columbus embarking for Spain in 1493 to Servando Cabrera Moreno's *Guernica*-like depiction of the 1961 Bay of Pigs Invasion and beyond to more contemporary pieces. Paintings to look for include the sensual *El Rapto de las Mulatas* by Carlos Enríquez, *Gitana Tropical* (sometimes known as the "Cuban Mona Lisa") by Victor Manuel Garcia, *Maternidad* by Wifredo Lam, *Recibido en Mal Estado* by Zaida del Río, and *Mundo Sonádo* by Tonel (Antonio Eligio Fernandez). ⊠ *Calle Trocadero, e/Av. de la Bélgica (Misiones/Egido/Monserrate) y Calle Agramonte (Zulueta), Centro,* ☏ 7/861–3856. ⊡ *$5.* ⊙ *Tues.–Sun. 10–6, Sun. 9–1.*

③⑥ **Museo Nacional de Bellas Artes–Colección de Arte Universal.** The collection is housed in the splendid Centro Asturiano finished in 1928 (in answer to the Centro Gallego across the Parque Central), a building designed by Spanish architect Manuel del Busto, as dazzling as the collection it contains. Its sweeping stairway was inspired by the Paris Opera House, and its immense stained-glass window alludes to the discovery of America. The collection ranges from Roman, Greek, and Egyptian ceramics and statuary to European art from the Italian, German, Flemish, Dutch, Spanish, French, and British schools. In addition there are rooms devoted to the art of the United States, as well as displays of Asian, Mexican, Antillean, and South American works. Works by Joseph Turner, Sir Joshua Reynolds, Francisco José de Goya, Bartolomé Esteban Murillo, Zurbarán, Brueghel, Canaletto, Peter Paul Rubens, Velázquez, Sorolla, and Zuloaga, among others, are displayed here. ⊠ *Calle Trocadero, e/Av. de la Bélgica (Misiones/Egido/Monserrate) y Calle Agramonte (Zulueta), Centro,* ☏ 7/861–3856. ⊡ *$5.* ⊙ *Tues.–Sat. 10–6, Sun. 9–1.*

★ ③② **Museo de la Revolución.** Batista's Palacio Presidencial, unsuccessfully attacked by students on March 13, 1957, was converted into the Museum of the Revolution after Castro's 1959 victory. The Russian tank outside was used in the Bay of Pigs Invasion. The marble staircase and the magnificent upstairs ceiling mural tell one story while galleries, with displays of items from colonial times to the present, tell another; the contrast is effective. Photographs of tortured revolutionaries, maps tracing the progress of the war, the bloodstained uniforms of rebels who fell in the 1953 Santiago de Cuba Moncada Barracks attack, and photos of Fidel and Che complete a comprehensive tour of the Revolution's history. Don't miss Cretin's Corner for a look at some familiar faces. ⊠ *Calle Refugio 1, Centro,* ☏ 7/862–4092. ⊡ *$3 (for museum and Memorial Granma).* ⊙ *Tues.–Sun. 10–5.*

④ Palacio de Aldama. Just past the Parque de la Fraternidad Americana's southwest corner is this Italianate mansion built in 1840 by the Spanish merchant Domingo de Aldama. His son, Miguel de Aldama, worked for Cuban autonomy from Spain until his palace was sacked by the Spanish authorities in 1869. Don Miguel fled to the United States, where he continued his work as an activist for Cuban independence until his death in 1888. The building isn't open to visitors, but the massive columns and monumental size of the place are striking proof of the economic power of the 19th-century Cuban sugar barons, dubbed the *zacarocracia* by Cuban journalists and historians. ⊠ *Av. Simón Bolívar (Reina) 1, Centro.*

③⑦ Parque Central. Across from the Hotel de Inglaterra and the Gran Teatro de la Habana, this park has always been a hub of Havana social activity. Centered around a statue of (who else?) José Martí and shaded by royal palms and almond trees, this is *the* place for heated debates on Cuba's national passion—baseball. The Hotel Plaza is on the park's northern end. On its southern end, notice the opulent 1885 Centro Asturiano, now the home of the Museo de Bellas Artes and its Arte Universal collection. The Teatro Payret, built in 1878, on Paseo de Martí (Prado) across from the Capitolio, is now a cinema.

NEED A BREAK?   Centro is full of classic Havana haunts. If you're not staying at the **Hotel Inglaterra** (Paseo de Martí/Prado 416, ☏ 7/860–8595), its rooftop terrace restaurant is a good excuse to stop by. A plaque to the right of the hotel commemorates victims of the wars of independence who traditionally rallied at the nearby Acera del Louvre (Sidewalk of the Louvre). The ground-floor Gran Café del Louvre is a well-known saloon and café—long a Havana nerve center.

OFF THE BEATEN PATH   **PASEO DE MARTÍ (PRADO) –** The shady, tree-lined Paseo de Martí, generally known as Paseo del Prado, is favored by Habaneros for strolls and encounters of all kinds. It's lined with 19th- and 20th-century architecture, such as the 1914 **Antiguo Casino Español** (No. 306, esquina de Calle Ánimas, ☏ 7/862–5781)—once a den of iniquity known worldwide and now the Palacio de Matrimonios (Marriage Palace), where couples from all over Cuba come to be married (and photographed) in elegant Old World–style rooms. The **Hotel Sevilla**, a slightly ramshackle but charming building, is to the right on Trocadero. North toward the bay you'll see the **Casa José Miguel Gómez,** also known as the Casa del Científico, a good budget hotel, across from the Sevilla. The **Teatro Fausto,** at the corner of Colón, is both a cinema and theater venue. The **Hotel Caribbean,** at No. 164, overlooks rampant lions on each of the four corners of the intersection of Calle Colón and Paseo de Martí. The **Casa Steinhardt,** at No. 120, is another elegant facade. If you continue all the way to the harbor, you'll come to La Punta.

Vedado and Beyond

In colonial days this area was placed off-limits—that is, *vedado* ("vetoed," or forbidden)—to provide jungly protection from the pirates that attacked Havana from the west. Trespassers, whether friend or foe, faced a stiff penalty: loss of an arm or a leg. The forest has long been replaced by fast-moving traffic, skyscrapers, and wide streets, but the name remains. Although a walk through this neighborhood involves long distances and won't be as pleasant as one through La Habana Vieja, don't veto it entirely—there are plenty of leafy-green side streets and noteworthy sights.

Vedado is a good area from which to wander west along the water-front Malecón to the fortress-restaurant Santa Dorotea de Luna de la Chorrera, at the mouth of the Río Almendares. From here you can either tour the forest—the Parque de Almendares on the west side of the river—or continue southwest on a drive through the Miramar district, with its beautiful mansions, famous hotels, good restaurants, and legendary nightclubs. Vedado is also a good jumping-off point for the Necrópolis Cristóbal Colón, Havana's showcase cemetery crammed with heroes, legends, and elaborate memorials. The monolithic Plaza de la Revolución, farther south, is another short taxi hop from Vedado.

Numbers in the text correspond to numbers in the margin and on the Vedado and the Plaza de la Revolución map.

A Good Tour

At the Plaza Mella, next to the Hotel Colina, climb the famous 100-step Escalinata to the seated figure of Alma Mater at the **Universidad de la Habana** ㊷ on La Colina (The Hill). From here you can head northeast and slightly off the tour to the **Callejón de Hamel,** an Afro-Cuban street project, or you can wander northwest through the shady university courtyard to the **Parque Coppelia** ㊸. From the park, take Calle 21 southwest three blocks, turn right onto Calle H, and follow it to Calle 17 and the **Union Nacional de Escritores y Artistas de Cuba (UNEAC)** ㊹. From UNEAC to the **Museo de Artes Decorativos** ㊺ it's just a three-block walk west on Calle 17. From here either grab a cab or walk nine blocks back east on Calle 17 and turn right onto Calle N. At Calle 21 (two blocks south) turn left into the Hotel Nacional, an excellent place for a swim or a mojito. From here you have two choices: head west along **El Malecón** ㊻ on foot or by taxi and then take a ride through **Miramar** ㊼ to see, among other sights, the Instituto Superior de Arte (ISA) and the Acuario Nacional, or hop a cab south to the **Necrópolis Cristóbal Colón** ㊽. From the cemetery, it's a short taxi ride east to the **Plaza de la Revolución** ㊾.

TIMING

You can follow the walk through Vedado in about three hours. Promenading along the Malecón from La Punta to Santa Dorotea de Luna de la Chorrera takes one to two hours. A car tour of Miramar can be done in an hour if you don't make any stops. Add another hour each for visits to the Museo de Artes Decorativos, the ISA, and the aquarium. A tour of the Necrópolis Cristóbal Colón is at least a two-hour affair, as is the exploration of the Plaza de la Revolución.

Sights to See

OFF THE
BEATEN PATH

CALLEJÓN DE HAMEL – This neighborhood project, directed by and featuring the painting (note the vivid street murals) and sculpture of Salvador Gonzalez Escalona, is an ongoing Afro-Cuban educational and artistic event. There's always something happening here: a performance by the youth club on the third Saturday of each month, theatrical events on the fourth Thursday, music shows on the last Friday. The outstanding Afro-Cuban music and theater ensemble Clave y Guanguancó regularly performs here. ⊠ *Off Calle San Lázaro, e/Calle Ánimas and Calle Soledad, Centro,* ☏ *7/878–1661.* ☉ *Daily 9 AM–midnight.*

㊻ **El Malecón.** Havana's famous Malecón (Sea Wall) runs west for 7 km (4 mi) from La Punta (where it's also known as Avenida Antonio Maceo) and the harbor's entrance to the Santa Dorotea de Luna de la Chorrera fortress, near the mouth of the Río Almendares. Although it was designed in 1857 by a Cuban engineer, it wasn't built until 1902, thanks, in part, to the American capital that flowed to the island after the Spanish-American War. Once an opulent promenade flanked by

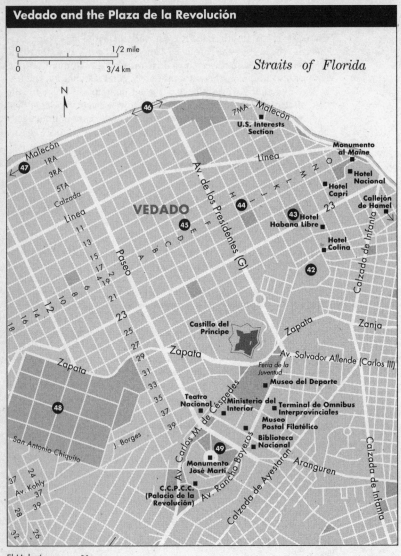

Straits of Florida

0 ——— 1/2 mile
0 ——— 3/4 km

N

Malecón

7MA

U.S. Interests Section

Línea

Monumento al *Maine*

Malecón

1RA
3RA
5TA
Calzada

Hotel Nacional

Hotel Capri

23

Callejón de Hamel

Línea

VEDADO

Av. de los Presidentes (G)

Hotel Habana Libre

Paseo

11
13
15
17
19
21
23
25
27
29
31
33
35
37
39

Hotel Colina

Castillo del Príncipe

Zapata

Zanja

Calzada de Infanta

Zapata

Av. Salvador Allende (Carlos III)

Feria de la Juventud

Museo del Deporte

Teatro Nacional

Ministerio del Interior

Terminal de Omnibus Interprovinciales

Museo Postal Filatélico

Biblioteca Nacional

Monumento José Martí

Av. Carlos M. de Céspedes

C.C.P.C.C. (Palacio de la Revolución)

Av. Rancho Boyeros

Aranguren

Calzada de Ayestarán

Calzada de Infanta

San Antonio Chiquito

J. Borges

Zapata

Av. Kohly

24
37
37
28
39
32
26

brightly painted houses, the Malecón today is dark and dilapidated, the houses crumbling, and the wide limestone walkway broken and eroded. Yet it still has its charms. As it faces north, it offers spectacular views of both sunrise and sunset—perhaps accounting for the belief that there's not a single habanero who hasn't professed love eternal here at one time or another. Crashing waves and the rainbows created from their spray and the sun adds to the Malecón's magic.

As you walk, look for rectangles carved into the stone. These were once (and are still used as) sea baths, which fill at high tide and allowed people to splash about, safe from both currents and sharks. Just west of the Hotel Nacional you'll come to **Monumento al *Maine,*** honoring the 260 American sailors killed in the 1898 explosion of that U.S. warship, which was visiting Havana in a display of American might. Although the Spanish did all they could to immediately help the seamen, American officials and the press accused them of destroying the vessel. Cuban and Spanish historians believe that the explosion was deliberately planned by the Americans to justify U.S. intervention in the ongoing Second War of Independence. American historians maintain that the explosion was either accidental or provoked by Cuban annexationists. Though the explosion appears to have happened *inside* the vessel, as clearly indicated by the outward eruption of the steel hull, no definitive proof has ever been etablished. The event did, in any case, lead to what the United States calls the Spanish-American War (for Cubans this was the final stage of their War of Independence, which began in 1868) followed by a period of heavy U.S. involvement in Cuban affairs. A plaque dedicated by the Castro government here reads: TO THE VICTIMS OF THE *MAINE,* WHO WERE SACRIFICED BY IMPERIALIST VORACITY IN ITS EAGERNESS TO SEIZE THE ISLAND OF CUBA.

Farther along, where Calle L runs into the Malecón, is the **U.S. Interests Section,** the de facto embassy. Until the Elián crisis, a giant billboard facing it depicted a Cuban soldier shaking a rifle at Uncle Sam (who peers across from Florida), with the Cuban soldier shouting: *"Señores Imperialistas: No les tenemos absolutamente ningún miedo"* ("Señores Imperialists: We are not in the least bit afraid of you"). During the long battle over Elián's "kidnapping" by his Miami relatives and the long process of his repatriation (upon which, for once, the governments of Cuba and the United States wholeheartedly agreed), an entire stage, theater, and propaganda venue was built here to host massive rallies demanding Elián's return and generally whipping Cuban nationalism up to a pearly froth. What you now see here is an elongated outdoor stage with an elaborate lighting and sound system called Forum Anti-Imperialista José Martí.

When you reach the **Santa Dorotea de Luna de la Chorrera (La Chorrera)** fortress—built in 1643 and named for the wife of Governor Alvaro de Luna and for the Río Almendares, or *chorrera* (stream)—be sure to stop in its restaurant for a meal or a mojito.

47 **Miramar.** At the beginning of the 20th century, Cuban magnates and American businessmen built their houses in this neighborhood, which begins west of the tunnel under the Río Almendares and ends at the Río Jaimanitas. Unless you're eager for some long-distance hiking, it's best to tour this part of town by rental car or taxi. Public transport here is scarce, as indicated by the mobs of schoolchildren *pidiendo botellas* (hitchhiking; literally "asking for bottles," as in favors or baby bottles).

In the **Museo del Ministerio del Interior** (⊠ Av. 5 y Calle 14, Miramar, ☎ 7/33–2112, ⊡ $3, ☉ Tues.–Fri. 8:30–5) you can see displays with hard evidence of the 40 years of CIA efforts to eliminate Fidel

Castro. The **Parque Emiliano Zapata** (⊠ Av. 5, e/Calle 24 y Calle 26, Miramar) is dedicated to the Mexican revolutionary agrarian reformist Emiliano Zapata (1889–1919). Look for the John Lennon bronze seated on a bench. The Iglesia de Santa Rita, overlooking the park, is notable for its tower and for the sculpture of Santa Rita (by Rita Longa, whose work adorns the entrance to the Museo Nacional de Bellas Artes–Colección Cubana) just inside to the left. With sensuous lips, smooth features, and graceful curves, the work was branded as too erotic to display by the early 20th-century chaplain, and the sculpture was hidden away until the mid-1990s.

At the **Acuario Nacional** (⊠ Calle 60 y Av. 1, Miramar, ☎ 7/33–1321, ☞ $3, ⊙ Tues.–Sat. 2–6) you can learn about many of Cuba's 900 species of fish. The weekend dolphin shows are also very popular. The **Museo de la Alfabetización** (⊠ Calle 31 y Av. 100, Marianao, ☎ 7/260–8054, ☞ $3, ⊙ weekdays 8–5) is dedicated to the literacy crusade of 1961, during which students and teachers took to the countryside to teach illiterate peasants to read and write.

Built on the site of the pre-Revolutionary Country Club of Havana, which was so exclusive that dictator Fulgencio Batista was denied a membership, the **Instituto Superior de Arte** (ISA; ⊠ Calle 120, e/Av. 9 y Av. 13, Cubanacán/Playa, ☎ 7/208–9771, ☞ $3, ⊙ weekdays 8–5), is the country's top art school, with separate pavilions for dance, art, music, and drama. Considered Cuba's best example of post-Revolutionary architecture, its redbrick halls and pavilions are covered with Catalan vaults and cupola skylights. From the 800 students in 39 specialties have come some of Cuba's finest artists and musicians. Zaida del Río studied here, as did Emmy-winner Chucho Valdés. Many of the little trios performing all around Havana have ISA students in their ranks.

Jaimanitas is a sweet little fishing village composed of wooden houses built of tongue-and-groove boarding and painted in pastels. Fresh fish and a friendly atmosphere make this a good place to visit. The mouth of the Río Jaimanitas marks the western end of town; the Club Habana is at the eastern edge. Miramar ends at the **Marina Hemingway**, a yachting facility just across the Río Jaimanitas. Unless you want to see some yachts or arrange a fishing trip, there's not much to see here but modern hotel complexes and the marina itself.

㊺ **Museo de Artes Decorativos.** The house containing this museum was built in 1927 and owned by José Gómez Mena, one of Cuba's wealthiest aristocrats. The collection is a staggering display of treasure and taste: antique furniture; Aubusson rugs; a Louis XVI *secrétaire*; Ming vases; paintings by Tocqué, Nattier, and Largillière. Don't miss the upstairs bathroom or the gardens with the giant bronze dogs guarding the door to what was called El Jardín de Noche (The Night Garden), a terrace dance floor. ⊠ *Calle 17, No. 502, e/Calle D y Calle E, Vedado,* ☎ *7/830–9848.* ☞ *$3.* ⊙ *Mon.–Sat. 11–6:30.*

★ ㊸ ㊽ **Necrópolis Cristóbal Colón.** The Christopher Columbus Cemetery sprawls behind a huge ceremonial arch and is a repository for a great deal more than just the deceased. Founded in 1868 by Bishop Espada, it's a veritable pantheon of monuments commemorating poets, novelists, musicians, soldiers, statesmen, and rank-and-file citizens. Cuban novelist Cirilo Villaverde and Cervantes-laureate Alejo Carpentier are here, as are the martyrs of the *Granma* yacht landing and the students killed in the 1957 assault on the Palacio Presidencial. This is also a place full of extraordinary legends, some of them macabre. You can learn all about them on a guided tour (highly recommended; you can arrange

CUBA'S ORGANIC REVOLUTION

When the United States blockaded Cuba in 1961, the Soviet Union was Castro's only trade-partner option. As the island's economy progressively fell apart, Soviet aid became Cuba's daily bread. In 1989, however, the Berlin Wall and the Soviet Union both collapsed. Cuba's economy went from bad to worse, and its shelves were left bare. Castro declared a "Special Period in Time of Peace" and called for belt-tightening austerity and Revolutionary sacrifice.

Life during the Special Period, especially after June 1992 when the supply of oil ceased, has included electricity blackouts, stopped machinery, crops rotting in the fields, and hotel and restaurant closures. Once the only country in the Americas to have eliminated hunger, Cuba became malnourished.

For centuries, Cuba was reliant on food imports, as the nation's agriculture was dominated by the export crop of sugarcane. After the 1959 Revolution, dependence on the Soviet Union led to mechanization and the use of chemical insecticides and fertilizers. Upon the collapse of the Soviet bloc, Cuba was left without either subsidies for agricultural chemicals or food shipments. To make matters worse, the years of insecticide use had caused a dearth of natural insect predators as well as the development of new "super-pests" resistant to chemicals. Further, the quality of the soil had deteriorated owing to over-irrigation and the heavy use of both pesticides and chemical fertilizers.

Over the last decade, Cuba has had a surprising agricultural revolution. The nation has turned to organic farming, using natural fertilizers and creative pest-management strategies and practicing such soil conservation techniques as crop rotation. The oxen you may see plowing the fields are actually a sign of progress, not penury.

More than 200 enterprises around Cuba are now run by university-educated agronomists. East Havana's Rotonda de Agricultura Organopónica, is a thriving plantation of lettuce, chard, Chinese cabbage, celery, parsley, spinach, and spring onions. Year-round watering and the use of biofertilizers (animal manure, bat guano, and organic material created by the cultivation of earthworms) have replaced much needed nitrogen in the soil and enabled crops to grow more rapidly. Instead of using chemical fertilizers to combat plant pests, farmers now use other insects as well as bacteria and fungal diseases. Oxen are used for plowing because they provide natural fertilizer instead of petroleum-based air pollution.

California's Institute for Food and Development Policy (Food First) works with both the Cuban Association for Organic Farming and with the Advanced Institute for Agricultural Sciences of Havana. They're watching carefully as Cuban agronomists establish what may well be a world model for agriculture in the future. (Further reading: *The Greening of Cuba: A National Experiment in Organic Agriculture,* by Peter Rosset and Medea Benjamin.)

for one in English for a $2 fee at the hut just inside the grounds to the right). Be sure to ask about the story of La Milagrosa (The Miraculous). ⊠ *Calle Zapata y Calle 12, Vedado,* ☎ *7/832–1050.* 🖾 *$2.* ⊙ *Mon.–Sat. 9–5, Sun. 8–noon.*

🐚 ㊽ **Parque Coppelia.** Named for the 1870 ballet by the French composer Léo Délibes, this Vedado park and its ice-cream emporium are Havana institutions. The *Star Wars*–type flying saucer in the middle of the square was the Revolution's answer to the many ice-cream parlors, that, prior to 1959, were highly discriminatory. This state-owned establishment serves more than 25,000 customers daily—the only requirement is that they be Cuban. (Note that non-Cuban visitors not part of a tour group and possessing good Spanish-language skills have been known to secure one of the four-scoop bowls despite the taboo and the long lines). The parlor once offered a legendary number of flavors, but after the Special Period (the national emergency declared upon the collapse of the Soviet Union, after which Cuba suffered severe shortages of everything from fuel to food) supplies became scarce, and a flavor a day became the rule.

🐚 ㊾ **Plaza de la Revolución.** This plaza in upper Vedado may seem grandiose and soulless, but it has several monuments with a lot of heart. Since the Revolutionary victory of 1959, it has been the official parade ground for events ranging from the annual May Day celebration to the 1998 visit of Pope John Paul II. A political, administrative, and cultural hub, the square is surrounded by army, police, Communist Party, and other ministries. Castro's whereabouts, always a mystery, include visits to these government centers, though he's just as likely to be coaching the national baseball team, resting in one of his many secret Havana residences, or off fishing on the Península de Zapata. The highlight is the **Museo Memorial José Martí** in the plaza's center. It consists of a massive granite sculpture of the national hero—in a seated, contemplative pose—on a 30-m (98-ft) base and a 139-m (456-ft) tower constructed of marble from La Isla de la Juventud (where Castro was imprisoned for his attack on the Moncada Barracks). The museum contains first editions of Martí's works, drawings, maps, and other memorabilia. Also on display are the original plans for both the monument and the square. ⊠ ☎ *7/882–0906.* 🖾 *$5 museum entry fee, $5 extra for photos, $5 entry fee to tower observation deck.* ⊙ *Tues.–Sat. 10–6, Sun. 10–2.*

It's hard to miss the giant etching of Che Guevara on the **Ministerio del Interior** (Ministry of the Interior) at the plaza's northwestern edge. It bears the words HASTA LA VICTORIA SIEMPRE (ALWAYS ONWARD TO VICTORY). Just east of Che, you'll find the outstanding **Museo Postal/Filatélico** (Postal Museum; ☎ 7/870–5193, 🖾 $2, ⊙ weekdays 9–4) on the ground floor of the Ministerio de Comunicaciones (Communications Ministry). Still farther east of Che is the **Biblioteca Nacional José Martí,** which, with 2 million volumes, is Cuba's largest library. Two blocks up along Avenida de la Independencia (Rancho Boyos), you can get an interesting look at the achievements of Cuban athletes over the past 40 years in the **Museo del Deporte** (☎ 7/881–4696, 🖾 $1, ⊙ Tues.–Sun. 10–5). On the square's western edge, across Avenida Carlos Manual de Céspedes, is the **Teatro Nacional,** Cuba's most important theater.

㊹ **Union Nacional de Escritores y Artistas de Cuba (UNEAC).** Occupying what was once the Casa Juan Gelats, one of Vedado's finest early 20th-century mansions, the National Union of Writers and Artists is the site of cinematic events; lectures and prose and poetry readings; and, on Wednesday and Saturday, Afro-Cuban performances. The bar and restaurant serve good criollo fare. The building across Calle H from this one is an important UNEAC annex. ⊠ *Calle 17 y Calle H, Vedado,* ☎ *7/832–2211.* ▧ *$3.* ☉ *Open daily 9* AM*–midnight.*

NEED A
BREAK? Made famous in the days when Batista still ruled the nation and gangsters like Meyer Lansky ruled its casinos, the **Hotel Nacional** (Calle O y Calle 21, Vedado, ☎ 7/33–3564 through 7/33–3567) is still very much a center of activity. You can have a meal or a mojito in the outstanding Aguiar restaurant here or refresh yourself with a dip in the pool.

㊷ Universidad de la Habana. The University of Havana was originally founded in 1728 behind the Palacio de los Capitanes Generales on Calle Obispo. The present Vedado campus was built early in the 19th century and modeled after New York City's Columbia University. Its 100-step Escalinata leads to the *Alma Mater,* a statue that welcomes students to the halls of higher learning and has been a gathering spot for demonstrations and rallies ever since 1928, when student leader Julio Antonio Mella led uprisings against the brutal dictator, General Gerardo Machado. (Mella, the founder of Cuba's Communist Party, whose ashes rest in the monumental sculpture at the foot of the Escalinata, was assassinated by Machado agents in Mexico in 1929.) It was here that thousands—including Fidel, who gave a three-hour speech—welcomed the national baseball team back from the United States after their victory over the Baltimore Orioles in May 1999. The courtyard is generally a peaceful place, shaded by luxuriant *jagüe* trees, which are often referred to as "the trees that walk" or "the trees of a thousand feet," owing to their multiple trunks and roots. The tank at the back of the courtyard was captured (for a while) by students in a pitched battle with Batista forces in the early 1950s.

Eastern Havana

Havana's eastern reaches have several interesting sights. The **Regla** neighborhood has strong Afro-Cuban traditions, and nearby **Guanabacoa** is known for its excellent museum dedicated to Santería, an Afro-Cuban religion. You can visit both municipalities as an extension of your tour of the fortresses or on a separate side trip. Transportation to and around them can be a combination of ferries or launches, taxis, trains, and walks.

Hemingway fans must make the trip to the small fishing village of **Cojimar**—home to Gregorio Fuentes, Hemingway's friend and boatman—and **Finca Vigía,** Hemingway's home in San Francisco de Paula. Drive along the Carretera Central 13 km (8 mi) southeast of Havana to San Francisco de Paula, spend a few hours looking through Hemingway's house, preserved exactly as it was the day he left it, never to return. Afterward, drive up to Cojímar on the Circunvalación (Ring Road) for lunch at one of Papa's favorite haunts, La Terraza, overlooking the mouth of the river Cojímar.

You could spend your life in the **Parque Lenin,** a sprawling, Soviet-style amusement park 20 km (12 mi) southeast of Havana. To drive out to it, have a look, and drive back is only a two-hour proposition. If your time is limited, this is one eastern excursion you can skip.

Sights to See

Cojímar. The fishing village Hemingway described in *The Old Man and the Sea* is modeled after this sleepy maritime hamlet where the author's wooden sportfishing craft, *El Pilar,* was berthed. El Torreón, the small fortress built here after the English used Cojímar as a landing point in their 1762 attack on Havana, is the site of a Hemingway bust made of brass boat propellers donated by Cojímar fishermen.

Wander around town; Gregorio Fuentes—Hemingway's skipper and pal from 1935 to 1960—once lived at Calle Pezuela 209. Gregorio provided Hemingway with a great deal of inspiration. The writer, having based the novel on the then thirtysomething Gregorio, was at a loss for a title until Gregorio shrugged and commented that, as far as he could tell, it was just about *"un viejo y el mar"* ("an old man and the sea").

NEED A
BREAK?
    Cojímar would merit a visit even without its literary significance as home of **La Terraza** (Calle Real y Candelaria, Cojímar, ☎ 7/55–9232). From the opening *curaçao*—a frozen daiquirí made with a blue bitter-orange liqueur—and *majuas* (tiny deep-fried fish) through the *ranchito de mariscos* (fish, lobster, and shrimp stewed in tomato, onion, and peppers), everything is very good here. The graceful mahogany bar dangerously dignifies the act of drinking, and the Hemingway memorabilia aren't overdone.

★ ☾ **Finca Vigía.** Even those convinced that they've outgrown their thirst for Hemingway will feel a flutter of youthful romanticism on a visit to Finca Vigía (Lookout Farm), the American Nobel Prize–winner's home from 1939 to 1961. The excellent guides will show you his weight charts—faithfully kept on the bathroom wall and never varying much from 242.5 pounds—a first edition of Kenneth Tynan's *Bull Fever* by the toilet; the lizard preserved in formaldehyde and honored for having "died well" in a battle with one of Hemingway's five dozen cats; the pool where Ava Gardner swam naked; Hemingway's favorite chair (ask about what happened to people who dared sit in it); his sleek powerboat, *El Pilar*; and much, much more. ⊠ *San Francisco de Paula*, ☎ *7/91–0809.* ☜ *$3.* ☾ *Mon.–Sat. 9–4, Sun. 9–12:30.*

Guanabacoa. Once a small sugar and tobacco center, Guanabacoa is inhabited primarily by the descendents of slaves who worked the fields here. Though the town, which is full of colonial treasures, is now part of sprawling Havana, its old Afro-Cuban traditions and religions have been kept alive. The **Museo Histórico Municipal de Guanabacoa** (⊠ Calle Martí 108, ☎ 7/97–9117, ☜ $2, ☾ Mon. and Wed.–Sat. 8–6, Sun. 9–1), installed in a handsome colonial mansion, exhibits a comprehensive history of Guanabacoa, with emphasis on its ethnic and religious traditions. For a deeper understanding of Santería as well as of the Palo Monte and Abakua sects that have been so important in Afro-Cuban sociology and history, this is an important visit.

☾ **Parque Lenin.** This vast amusement park was popular with Cubans before the 1992 collapse of the Soviet Union. The penury of the Special Period, however, has caused the carousels and other fairground attractions to be shut down. Developed on what was once a farming estate 20 km (12 mi) southwest of Havana, the 745-hectare (1,841-acre) park contains rolling meadows, small lakes, and woodlands. Look for the Monumento Lenin, a mammoth granite sculpture of the Russian Revolutionary. The Monumento a Celia Sánchez has photographs and portraits of Cuba's unofficial First Lady. The park's offerings also include art galleries, ceramics workshops, and a movie theater. Horseback riding, boating, and swimming are options here as well. You can have a good meal in Las Ruinas and stay overnight in the comfortable motel. ⊠ *Carretera de la Presa*, ☎ *7/44–2721.* ☜ *$3.* ☾ *Daily 9–12 noon.*

★ **Regla.** Probably named for a West African Yoruba deity, this seafarers' and fishermen's enclave retains a rough vitality. Originally a camp for black slaves—especially of the Ibibio, Bantu, and Yoruba tribes—Regla's Afro-Cuban roots are strong.

CELIA SÁNCHEZ

Fidel Castro's secretary, confidante, and lover, Celia Mandu-ley Sánchez, was Cuba's unofficial First Lady and, as stated on her monument in Manzanillo, LA MAS HERMOSA Y AUTÓCTONA FLOR DE LA REVOLUCIÓN (THE MOST BEAUTIFUL AND INDIGENOUS FLOWER OF THE REVOLUTION). The two were inseparable from their meeting in 1957 till her death of cancer in 1980.

Before becoming involved in the resistance against Fulgencio Batista, Sánchez worked as a teacher. Ever the idealist, she was a José Martí disciple; in 1952 she climbed Pico Turquino to erect a bust of the national hero there. After joining the 26th of July Movement (named for the 1953 attack on Santiago's Moncada Barracks), Sánchez again climbed Cuba's highest mountain, this time with Castro and a CBS news crew for an interview with him next to Martí's bust.

Sánchez worked as Castro's logistics, propaganda, and espionage chief in the lowlands around Manzanillo while he held out in the Sierra Maestra. Later, she shared his command cabin on a ridge west of Pico Turqino. Without her efforts, it's difficult to imagine Castro's mountain-based guerrilla movement gaining political strength. Sánchez was El Commandante's "eyes and ears," and the only person who could tell him things he didn't like to hear. Her death deprived him of a link with reality—his own and Cuba's.

The waterfront **Iglesia de Nuestra Señora de Regla,** the first stop as you leave the ferry, was built in 1810. It's famous as the home of La Virgen de Regla (The Black Virgin of Regla), a black Madonna who cradles a white infant. Identified with Yemayá, the Yoruban orisha of the sea, the Virgin is the patron saint of motherhood and of sailors. On September 8 both Catholic and Santería celebrations honor her. There's a procession through the streets to the wailing of dirge music. The faithful also fill the church—dressed in their finest and wearing something blue, the color of the sea and of Yemayá—waiting their turn to touch the virgin or their favorite icons and crucifixes in side chapels. At the water's edge, women standing ankle-deep in the harbor's oily waters sing or pray to Yemayá, sometimes tossing in a coin or launching offerings of flowers, oranges, or melons. A branch of the Museo Municipal de Regla, just to the right of the church, has a display of Afro-Cuban orishas. There's also a shrine to Yemayá in the entryway of a private house, two doors up at No. 15.

There are several points of interest on or just off Calle Martí, among them the **Plaza Antonio Maceo,** with its monument to La Maternidad (Motherhood), another Yemayá reference. The statue of Antonio Maceo, the great general of Cuba's War of Independence, stands at the far end of the square.

Behind the Maceo statue in the Plaza Antonio Maceo is the **Taller Antonio Canet** (⊠ Calle de Facciolo 167, esquina de Calle Maceo, ☎ 7/97–6989, 🖾 donations suggested, ☉ Mon.–Sat. 9–5). This studio and gallery offers an interesting look at the work of Cuba's master print-maker and graphic designer, particularly his woodcut and linocut engravings for an edition of Cirilo Villaverde's major 19th-century novel

Cecilia Valdés. The building in which the gallery is set is also called the Eduardo Facciolo House. Known as "the first martyr of Cuban journalism," Facciolo was executed at the age of 23 (in 1852) by the Spanish for publishing an article in *La Voz del Pueblo Cubano* (The Voice of the Cuban People) criticizing the imperial power for brutal policies in Cuba.

The **Museo Municipal de Regla** (✉ Calle Martí 158, ☎ 7/97–6989, 🎫 $2, ⏱ Mon. and Wed.–Sat. 9:30–6, Sun. 9–1) offers insight into Regla's history. During the Revolution, this area was a rebel stronghold known as La Sierra Chiquita (The Little Sierra; as opposed to the Sierra Maestra where Fidel and his forces operated). Close to but outside of and largely separate from Havana, Regla was a convenient place for clandestine activity. Photographs of the Regla heroes and heroines (such as Lidia Doce) who were tortured and murdered by the Batista regime line the walls. Also on display is a copy of the first edition of Eduardo Facciolo's *La Voz del Pueblo Cubana,* dated June 13, 1852.

Calle Martí is also home to **Plaza del Ayuntamiento,** Regla's central square. Here you might find an impromptu street party breaking out, with a beer wagon selling 5¢ glasses of draft. Note the floral and fluted columns on the facade of the former theater on the corner at No. 410. Around the square are monuments to heroes of the struggle for independence: Comandante Miguel Coyula (1876–1948), José Martí, and Eduardo Facciolo.

BEACHES

The Playas del Este (Eastern Beaches) are just 20–30 minutes from Havana on the coast road, La Vía Blanca, to Varadero. Full of sun worshipers and local flavor, these sands have an atmosphere like that of a daytime disco by the sea. Although a morning of basking in the sun is conceivable, it's really more of a full-day operation. Take Vía Monumental toward Cojímar; 1 km (½ mi) beyond the second Cojímar exit, Vía Blanca splits off to the beaches.

Bacuranao is 18 km (11 mi) east of Havana. Beneath the waters off this small, white-sand cove are coral reefs and an 18th-century Spanish galleon, making this a popular scuba-diving spot. Look for the Villa Bacuranao, a bustling bar-disco that also has inexpensive cabins to rent. Two kilometers (1 mile) east of Bacuranao is **Playa Tarará,** a small stretch of white sand that's home to the 50-berth Marina Tarará/Club Nautico, site of the Old Man and the Sea Fishing Tournament every July. You can arrange boat rentals, yacht cruises, and diving or snorkeling excursions here.

Just 2 km (1 mi) east of Playa Tarará is **Playa El Mégano,** a quiet stretch of sand. El Mégano is really considered a western extension of the main beach, **Playa de Santa María,** which runs east to the mouth of the Río Itabo. Just beyond the mouth of the Río Itabo is the dune-flanked **Playa Boca Ciega.** If you head farther east from Playa Boca Ciega, you'll come to **Playa Guanabo,** second loveliest of the Playas del Este (after the Playa de Santa María) and a popular spot for surfcasters and joggers.

Santa Cruz del Norte, 10 km (6 mi) east of Playa Guanabo, is an industrial town that's home to Cuba's greatest distillery, the Ronería Santa Cruz, where the ubiquitous Havana Club rum is made. Don't let the offshore oil rigs or the less than pristine waters here deter you from continuing. Just 3 km (2 mi) east of Santa Cruz is **Playa Jibacoa,** the best and least spoiled of all of the beaches near Havana. Nestled between headlands at the mouth of the Río Jibacoa, its white sands are backed by cliffs that overlook crystal-clear, aquamarine waters. Divers will appreciate the coral reefs here, while terrestrial types can follow hiking trails from the beach into the back country. The Breezes Hotel here is one of the finest beach hotels in Cuba.

DINING

Although Havana may not, for the moment, offer a head-spinning number of irresistible gastronomical options, things are improving. And there *are* ways to have a good meal. Stick with the top paladares as much as possible. These privately owned establishments are, by law, only allowed a maximum of 12 seats and can only be staffed by family members. The food is usually fresh, authentic, and inexpensive. Although there are regulations on what can be served (lobster, shrimp, and beef are officially forbidden at paladares), the owners are infinitely resourceful, often serving lamb instead of beef, or crab instead of lobster. The paladares have a cozy, clandestine atmosphere, and the tastes and aromas are the best Havana has to offer. The Vedado, Miramar, and Playa districts are prime paladar habitat, as the Habaguanex chain has squeezed nearly all of them out of La Habana Vieja. Centro Habana has the most famous of all, La Guarida.

State-owned establishments, with a few exceptions (such as El Aljibe), are mediocre at best. However, they're often in settings you may find hard to resist, despite the overpriced and uninteresting fare. Some hotel restaurants (not the cafeterias or buffets) are noteworthy, especially the Abanico de Cristal in the Meliá Cohiba, the Chez Emérito in the Hotel Presidente, and the Aguiar in the Hotel Nacional. Two caveats: beware of elegant but empty establishments, and opt for simple criollo fare over sophisticated or "international" creations unless you are in the top hotels.

For the moment, consider the U.S. dollar the most reliable form of payment in Cuba. Credit cards *not* affiliated with U.S. banks or companies can generate *pesos convertibles* (convertible pesos) in ATM machines. These are interchangeable with U.S. dollars. Credit cards not affiliated with U.S. banks are also accepted in government restaurants and hotels, though never in paladares. Don't be alarmed if a menu offers a salad for what appears to be $100; one line through the letter "S" is the symbol for pesos, two lines through the letter is the symbol for U.S. dollars. Hence, that salad actually costs 100 pesos, or $5. For price categories, *see* the chart *under* Dining *in* Smart Travel Tips A to Z.

La Habana Vieja

$$–$$$$ ✕ **La Paella.** Set in the charming Hostal Valencia, this restaurant specializes in paella, just as its name suggests, and has won high praise for its Valencian dishes. In keeping with the cuisine, the large, airy dining room has a terra-cotta floor and traditional Spanish furnishings. Reservations are a good idea. ✉ *Calle de los Oficios 53, esquina de Calle Obrapía, La Habana Vieja,* ☎ *7/57–103. MC, V. No dinner Sun.*

$$–$$$ ✕ **Don Giovanni.** It's named not for Mozart's *Don Giovanni*—based on the Spanish legend of Don Juan—but rather for military engineer Juan Bautista Antonelli, designer of Havana's 16th-century fortresses. The staff is elegant and pleasant, as is the setting in a stately mansion surrounding a leafy patio. The view of the harbor and El Morro from the upper floor is one of the best things about the place. The menu offers both passable Italian fare (the pizzas are noteworthy) and simple criollo dishes. ✉ *Calle Tacón 4, La Habana Vieja,* ☎ *7/861–2183. MC, V.*

\$\$–\$\$\$ ✕ **Al Medina.** This restaurant is part of an Arabic cultural center with the city's only mosque and an oasislike courtyard that hosts arts-and-crafts shows and sales. The eclectic menu offers both Moroccan and criollo fare, ranging from couscous and lamb dishes to criollo standards such as roast chicken or pork and black beans with rice. ⊠ *Calle de los Oficios 12, La Habana Vieja,* ☎ 7/863–0862. *MC, V.*

\$\$–\$\$\$ ✕ **El Patio.** It might be hard to pick a spot here: tables are either out
★ on the Plaza de la Catedral or in the namesake patio of the colonial house in which the restaurant is set. The criollo menu is complete, and although the food and service fall short of the spectacular settings, the prices are reasonable and the quality is good. ⊠ *Plaza de la Catedral 54, La Habana Vieja,* ☎ 7/861–8504. *MC, V.*

\$–\$\$\$\$ ✕ **La Bodeguita del Medio.** Havana's best-known bar-restaurant is a great place to hoist one for Hemingway, despite the steep, \$6 mojitos. The downstairs bar is always packed with tourists looking expectantly toward the door as if Papa himself were about to swagger in and belly up to the bar. If you decide to dine here, ask for a seat on the airy upstairs terrace. The criollo fare is unjustifiably famous, and the expensive dishes aren't any better than the cheap ones. Best bets are *picadillo a la habanera* (ground beef with onions, garlic, tomatoes, and olives) and *aporreado de tasajo* (shredded beef in criollo sauce). ⊠ *Calle Empedrado 207, La Habana Vieja,* ☎ 7/862–4498. *MC, V.*

\$–\$\$\$\$ ✕ **Café del Oriente.** Try for the upstairs corner table, which overlooks the Plaza de San Francisco and has a view of the Sierra Maestra boat terminal, the Iglesia y Convento Menor de San Francisco de Asís, and the Lonja del Comercio (Commerce Exchange) across the way. The food is overpriced and only fair, but as the restaurant is relatively new, perhaps the criollo and international cuisine will improve with time. ⊠ *Calle de los Oficios 112, La Habana Vieja,* ☎ 7/66–6686. *MC, V.*

\$–\$\$\$ ✕ **Café el Mercurio.** If you're peckish before or around sunrise, this is a good place to come. It's named for Mercury—the god of commerce, whose likeness sits atop the Lonja del Comercio building in which it's set—and is open around the clock every day. Its specialties are unusual for Cuba: omelets, sandwiches, and salads. ⊠ *Plaza de San Francisco de Asís, La Habana Vieja,* ☎ 7/66–6188. *MC, V.*

\$–\$\$ ✕ **El Mesón de la Flota.** Opened on the site of a warehouse that was frequented by Spanish sailors in colonial times, this little hideaway serves such creditable Spanish specialties as *tortilla de patata* (potato omelet) and *gambas al ajillo* (shrimp sautéed in garlic). The flamenco performances (nightly at 9) provide a bracing shot of atmosphere. ⊠ *Calle Mercaderes 257, e/Calle Amargura y Calle Brasil (Teniente Rey), La Habana Vieja,* ☎ 7/863–3838. *MC, V.*

\$–\$\$ ✕ **Vuelta Abajo.** An elegant, intimate spot in the Hostal Conde de Villanueva, this restaurant specializes in dishes from Vuelta Abajo, Cuba's best tobacco-growing region. Try the pollo *yumurino* (in a criollo sauce). ⊠ *Calle Mercaderes 202, La Habana Vieja,* ☎ 7/862–9682. *MC, V.*

\$ ✕ **La Moneda Cubana.** The quarters at this friendly, inexpensive paladar are tight, but the brothers Pérez Alonso take good care of their guests. Criollo specialties include *chuletas de puerco* (fried pork cutlets), *lomo ahumado* (smoked pork loin), pargo *a la plancha* (grilled and served with garlic and ají), and the standard side orders of *banana frita* (fried plantain) and frijoles negros. ⊠ *Calle San Ignacio 77, La Habana Vieja,* ☎ 7/867–3852. *No credit cards.*

The Fortresses

\$\$–\$\$\$\$ ✕ **Bar el Mirador.** This little annex to La Divina Pastora offers terrific city views and the same menu as the main restaurant next door. A breezy terrace makes it one of Havana's romantic getaways. Standard criollo dishes—plátanos a puñetazos, frijoles negros, ropa vieja—are available along with international specialties. ⊠ *Parque Histórico Militar Morro–Cabaña, Las Fortalezas,* ☎ *7/860–8341. MC, V.*

$$–$$$$ ✕ **La Divina Pastora.** Although prices are on the high side, the romantic location makes them worth it. Tucked into the berth of the sailing ship *El Galeón* at the foot of El Morro, this restaurant offers splendid views over Havana and is a good spot for dinner after the cañonazo at La Cabaña. Your best bet is lobster; kept alive in an on-site tank, it's guaranteed to be fresh. ⊠ *Parque Historico Militar Morro–Cabaña, Las Fortalezas,* ☎ *7/860–8341. MC, V.*

Centro Habana

$$–$$$$ ✕ **El Floridita.** The 16 varieties of daiquirí at this famous (albeit over-
★ priced) bar-restaurant are nonpareil however they're made: with or without sugar, frozen, shaken, stirred. The ever-present mariquitas are way better than potato chips, and the appetizers are, well, appetizing. Try the *crepas de espinacas* (spinach crepes) or the frogs' legs soufflé. The bar has some *marcha* (movement) and excitement; in the restaurant beyond, things slow down and prices go up. Dress warmly, as the air-conditioning is chilling. ⊠ *Calle Obispo 557, Centro,* ☎ *7/867–1301 or 7/867–1300. MC, V.*

$$ ✕ **La Guarida.** Enrique Nuñez and his wife, Odeysis, have transformed
★ their early 20th-century town house into a fine paladar. It's so photogenic that scenes in *Fresa y Chocolate* (*Strawberry and Chocolate*) were filmed here. The three-floor climb up the squalid but picturesque stairway generates an appetite-enhancing adrenline. The daily special is never what Enrique and Odeysis need to get rid of, but what they hope will make you happiest. Look for cherna *compuesta a lo caimanero* (with coconut and spices) or conejo *al aceite de oliva con caponata* (cooked in olive oil with a sauce of aubergines, peppers, and onion). On Sunday the restaurant opens only for brunch from noon to 4. ⊠ *Calle Concordia 418, e/Calle Gervasio y Calle Escobar, Centro,* ☎ *7/863–7351. Reservations essential. No credit cards. No lunch Sat.*

$–$$$$ ✕ **La Terraza.** In the terrace grill-saloon of the Hotel Inglaterra, you can dine on criollo and international fare that's less pretentious and of a better quality than at many of Havana's more opulent restaurants. Try the pollo en salsa criolla or, if it's available, the grilled lobster. The views over the Parque Central, the Teatro Nacional, and the Centro Gallego next door are memorable. ⊠ *Paseo de Martí (Prado) 416, Centro,* ☎ *7/860–8595. MC, V. No lunch.*

$–$$$ ✕ **Castillo del Farnés.** Notable as Fidel Castro's favorite hangout when he was a student, and the place where he and Che celebrated victory on January 9, 1959, this modest bar-restaurant is a good choice for a meal or a drink. You'll pay a little extra for the historical rush (which seems counterrevolutionary), but the shrimp dishes are good, and the Spanish and criollo cuisine is acceptable. ⊠ *Av. de la Bélgica (Misiones/Edigio/Monserrate) 361, Centro,* ☎ *7/33–8694 or 7/57–1030. MC, V.*

$ ✕ **Hanoi.** Also known as Casa de la Parra (House of the Grape Arbor), this simple restaurant specializes in criollo and Vietnamese food, an unlikely combination until you remember that any foe of Uncle Sam's is a friend of Fidel's. The varied menu includes such dishes as arroz *Vietnamita* (with chicken, chorizo, and shrimp) and *boniato cocido* (boiled yam). ⊠ *Calle Brasil (Teniente Rey) y Calle Bernaza, Centro,* ☎ *7/867–1029. MC, V.*

¢–$ ✕ **Tien-Tan.** Its name means "heaven's temple" in Mandarin, and it has
★ enough worshipers that you'll be lucky to find a spot inside. No matter, though, as there are tables outside as well—all the better for watch-

52

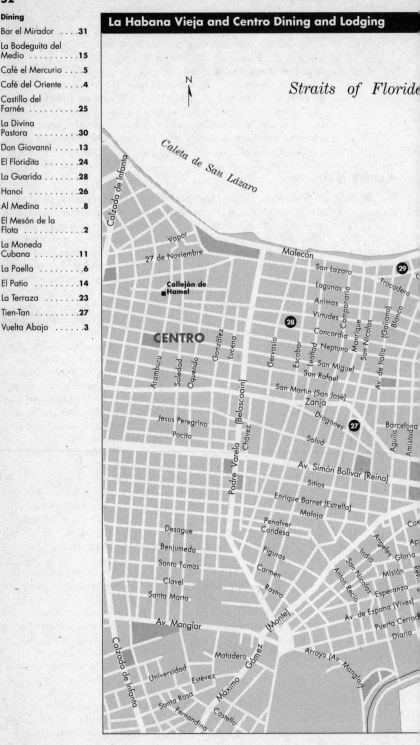

La Habana Vieja and Centro Dining and Lodging

Straits of Floride

N

Caleta de San Lázaro

Calzada de Infanta

Vapor

27 de Noviembre

Callejón de
Hamel

CENTRO

Malecón

San Lázaro

Lagunas

Animas

Virtudes

28

Concordia

Neptuno

San Miguel

San Rafael

San Martin (San José)

Zanja

Dragones

27

Salud

Av. Simón Bolívar (Reina)

Sitios

Enrique Barnet (Estrella)

Maloja

Penalver

Condesa

Figuras

Carmen

Rastro

Av. Manglar

Matadero

Arroyo (Av. Manglar)

Puerta Cerrada

Diaria

Desague

Benjumeda

Santo Tomas

Clavel

Santa Marta

Calzada de Infanta

Universidad

Estévez

Santa Rosa

Fernandina

Castello

Máximo

Gómez

(Monte)

Av. de Espana (Vives)

Esperanza

Misión

Antón Recio

San Nicolás

Indio

Angeles

Gloria

Aguila

Amistad

Barcelona

29

Trocadero

Blanco

Av. de Italia (Galiano)

San Nicolás

Manrique

Campanario

Lealtad

Escobar

Gervasio

Lucena

González

Oquendo

Soledad

Aramburu

Padre Varela (Belascoain)

Chávez

Jesus Peregrino

Pocito

Jesus Peregrino

ing passersby on Chinatown's wildest street. The fresh vegetables, tasty seafood, and lamb brochettes come at prices that (almost) make you plead to pay more. Certain dishes (such as the crispy duck) must be ordered in advance. ⊠ *Calle Cuchillo 17, e/Calle Zanja y Calle San Nicolas, Centro,* ☎ *7/861–5478. No credit cards.*

Vedado

$$$–$$$$ ✕ **El Abanico de Cristal.** One of Havana's best restaurants specializes in
★   historic recipes used by the colonial Spanish and Cuban elite. Gazpacho laced with morsels of lobster is prepared as well here as in any of Spain's leading kitchens. *Fideuá,* a paella made with vermicelli noodles, is an eastern Spanish specialty, and the conejo *ahumado al aroma de comino* (smoked with cumin seed) is from Al-Andalus, the 8th- to 15th-century Moorish empire on the Iberian Peninsula. The wine list's fine selections include varieties from Castile's Ribera de Duero region, as well as Riojas and wines from Catalonia's Penedès. ⊠ *Hotel Meliá Cohiba, Calle Paseo, e/Calle 1 y Calle 3, Vedado,* ☎ *7/33–3636, MC, V.*

$$$–$$$$ ✕ **Aguiar.** For decades, the elegant dining room in the Hotel Nacional has been one of the city's premier establishments. Despite the tableside shrimp-and-rum flambé performances, which are always entertaining, the atmosphere is generally subdued—even when the place is full. The wine list is excellent, though pricey. ⊠ *Calle O y Calle 21, Vedado,* ☎ *7/33–3564. MC, V.*

$$–$$$ ✕ **La Terraza Florentina.** The Italian restaurant in the Hotel Capri was probably what drew the mob to this Havana address in the first place. Lots of good pasta and other Italian specialties—particularly the shrimp pasta in a garlic sauce—at more than acceptable prices make this 18th-floor dining room overlooking the Malecón hard to resist. The wine list has some excellent Italian vintages. ⊠ *Calle 21, e/Calle N y Calle O, Vedado,* ☎ *7/33–3747 or 7/33–3748. MC, V.*

$$ ✕ **Aries.** Mirtha and Luis Soteras run a very tight ship. Service at their
★   paladar—in a house that dates from 1925—is bright and quick, and dishes are prepared using traditional Cuban recipes. *Ajiaco* (a savory stew), *tamal* (dishes based on sweet corn), frituras de malanga, and ropa vieja *de carnero* (shredded lamb) are just a few of the criollo specialties. The *enchilado de cangrejo* (crab stew) is the star offering. Your meal may well be accompanied by Cuban music from the good old, bad old days of the 1950s and 1960s. ⊠ *Av. Universidad 456 (bajo), e/Calle J y Calle K, Vedado,* ☎ *7/832–4118. No credit cards. No lunch.*

$–$$$$ ✕ **El Gato Tuerto.** This café-restaurant serves a first-rate onion soup; the ropa vieja, presented elegantly on a huge plate with mint and parsley garnishes, is also excellent. The specialty, however, is *solomillo a la pimienta sobre piperrada* (pepper steak on piperade). Downstairs, in the cabaret, performances continue until the sun rises over the Malecón. ⊠ *Calle O, e/Calle 17 y Calle 19, Vedado,* ☎ *7/55–2696. MC, V.*

$–$$ ✕ **Le Chansonnier.** Founded by a waiter from the original Paris Chansonnier, this friendly paladar is very much like a French bistro. In a stately house near the Alliance Française, you can feast on such Franco-European staples as lamb chops, duck, and rabbit as well as criollo fare from tostones (fried plantain) to frijoles negros. ⊠ *Calle J, No. 257 e/Linea y Calle 15, Vedado,* ☎ *7/832–1576. No credit cards.*

$ ✕ **La Casa.** Explain to your cabbie that this paladar is on Vedado's
★   western edge—east of the Río Almendares in Nuevo Vedado—and insist that he get you here, as the food is sensational. The opening round of *pica-pica* (assorted tapas) secures a stellar rating, as do such entrées as *filete de pescado almendrina* (grilled red snapper with almonds) and *brochetas de pollo con champiñon* (chicken brochettes with mushrooms). The wine list features several good Riojas (Faustino VII and Marqués

de Cáceres) and whites from Chile and the Catalan Penedés region. ⊠ *Calle 30, No. 865, e/Av. 26 y Calle 41, Nuevo Vedado,* ☎ *7/881–7000. Reservations essential. No credit cards.*

Miramar

$$$–$$$$ ✕ **Don Cangrejo.** Shrimp, crab, lobster, grouper, snapper—every type of seafood available in the Antilles seems to find its way through this bustling kitchen. The ambience is relaxed, and the service is quick and friendly. Look for the specialty steak Neptuno, a surf and turf consisting of beef and lobster. ⊠ *Av. 1, e/Calle 16 y Calle 18, Miramar,* ☎ *7/204–4169. MC, V.*

$$$–$$$$ ✕ **Ranchón.** This Miramar standby is noteworthy for its open-air atmosphere and its bargain-price specials. Chef Juan Luis Rosales's strong suits are grilled lobster and roast pork or chicken (occasionally he also finds some lamb). The wine list is only mediocre; stick with beer, which accompanies Cuban food extremely well. ⊠ *Av. 5, esquina de Calle 16, Miramar,* ☎ *7/204–1185. MC, V.*

$$–$$$$ ✕ **El Aljibe.** The criollo fare here is reasonably priced and served
★ gracefully, and the place is always filled to the brim with clued-in diners (including such celebrities as Omar Linares, Cuba's finest baseball player), who appear to be having the time of their lives. The roast chicken served in bitter-orange, lemon, and chicken juices sauce is the house dish, at once dark and tangy. And, oh yes, the *oferta* (plate of appetizers, black beans and rice, chicken Aljibe, and tostones) is an all-you-can-eat special. ⊠ *Av. 7, e/Calle 24 y Calle 26, Miramar,* ☎ *7/204–1584. MC, V.*

$$–$$$$ ✕ **Cava de Vinos.** It's a long way from the Malecón, but this wine cel-
★ lar and restaurant is in the same complex as the sizzling Macumba dance and music club, which means yours can be an evening of wining, dining, *and* dancing. Choose from the menu's Cuban and international dishes as well as from one of the finest wine selections in the Antilles. ⊠ *La Giraldilla, Calle 222, esquina de Calle 37, La Coronela/La Lisa,* ☎ *7/33–0568. MC, V.*

$$–$$$$ ✕ **Tocororo.** Depending on who you read, this is either the Caribbean's best restaurant or its worst. It may not be European perfect, but it's Cuban pluperfect. Don't hesitate to come here for good, although somewhat overpriced, criollo fare. ⊠ *Calle 18 y Calle 3, Miramar,* ☎ *7/204–2209. MC, V.*

$$–$$$ ✕ **La Fontana.** Chef Ernesto Blanco blends the aromas and flavors of
★ Moorish and Sephardic cooking with those of Cuba (and elsewhere in the Caribbean), Spain, and Africa. The result is some of Havana's most inventive cuisine. At this friendly, graceful garden restaurant, you can order such appetizers as tostones *rellenos* (stuffed with ropa vieja, guacamole, or diced ham) and such main dishes as *emperador al ajillo* (swordfish with garlic flambéed in aged rum). ⊠ *Calle 3, No. 305, esquina de Calle 46, Miramar,* ☎ *7/202–8337. No credit cards.*

$$–$$$ ✕ **Villa Esperanza.** Wine flows freely at this diminutive villa run by
★ Hubert Corrales and Manolo Arceo. The tables are invariably filled with interesting people who seem to enjoy the funky decor and classic Cuban music as well as the food. Keep your eyes peeled for *crema africana* (deconstructed black beans with cumin, garlic, rice, and laurel); plátanos *ochún* (with honey, garlic, and hot pepper); and sweet-and-sour red snapper or chicken, prepared either with honey or oranges. ⊠ *Calle 16, No. 105, e/Av. 1 y Av. 3, Miramar,* ☎ *7/202–4361. No credit cards. Closed Thurs. No lunch.*

$–$$$ ✕ **Dos Gardenias.** This restored colonial mansion is filled with various restaurants, all of which offer solid international and criollo dishes at reasonable prices. The downstairs Fonda de Maravillas, a garden

Vedado and Miramar Dining and Lodging

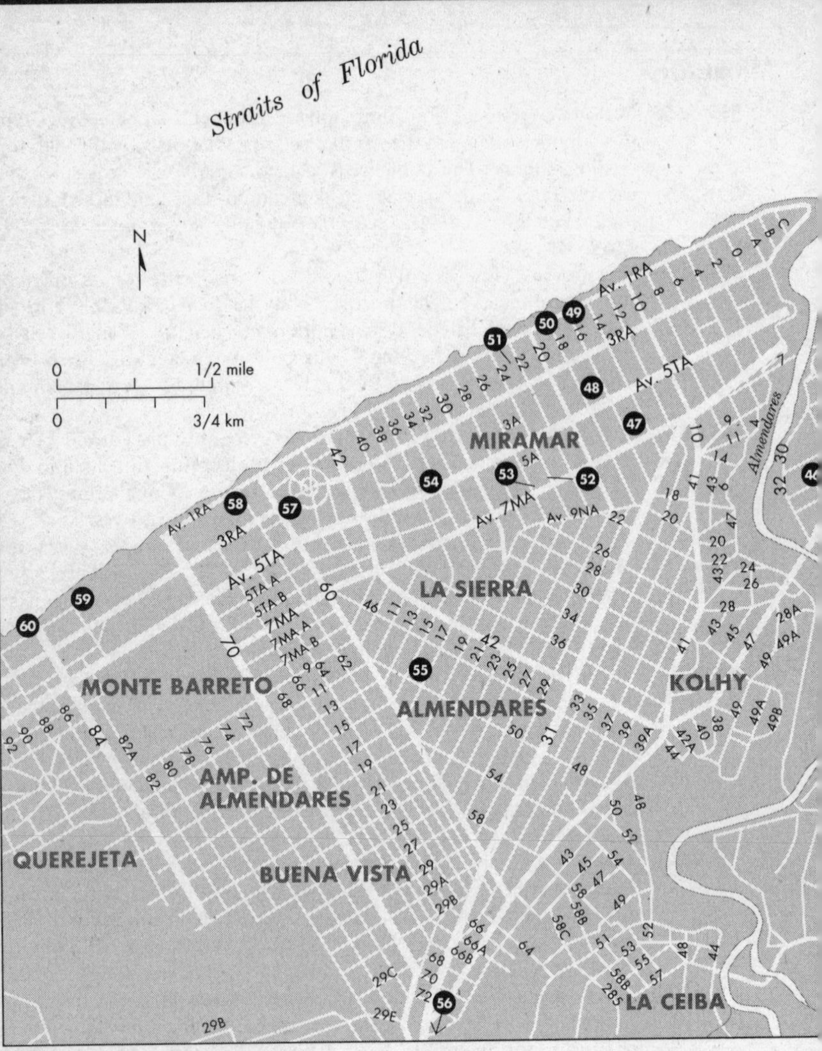

Straits of Florida
N
0 1/2 mile
0 3/4 km
MIRAMAR
LA SIERRA
MONTE BARRETO
ALMENDARES
KOLHY
AMP. DE ALMENDARES
QUEREJETA
BUENA VISTA
LA CEIBA
Av. 1RA
3RA
Av. 5TA
5TA A
5TA B
7MA
7MA A
7MA B
Av. 7MA
Av. 9NA
Almendares

Dining

- El Abanico de Cristal **44**
- Aguiar **40**
- El Aljibe **53**
- Aries **36**
- La Casa **46**
- Cava de Vinos. . . . **56**
- Le Chansonnier . . . **42**
- La Cocina de Lilliam. **55**
- Don Cangrejo **50**
- Dos Gardenias . . . **52**
- La Fontana **57**
- El Gato Tuerto **41**
- Ranchón **47**
- La Terraza Florentina **39**
- Tocororo **48**
- Villa Esperanza . . . **49**
- Vistamar **51**

Lodging

- Chateau Miramar **58**
- Habana Riviera . . . **45**
- Hotel Capri **39**
- Hotel Colina **35**
- Hotel Comodoro . . **60**
- Hotel Habana Libre. **37**
- Hotel Meliá Cohiba **44**
- Hotel Meliá Habana **59**
- Hotel Mirazul **54**
- Hotel Nacional . . . **40**
- Hotel Presidente. . . **43**
- Hotel Victoria **38**

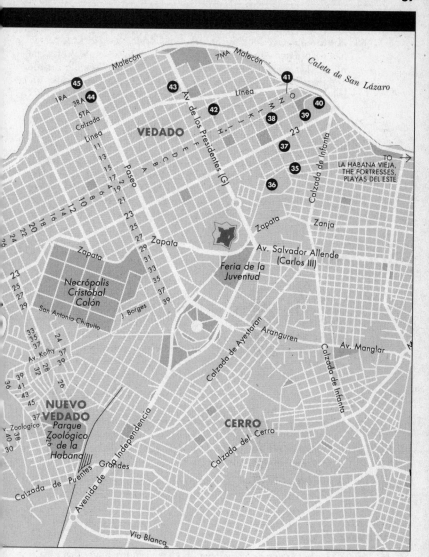

enclave, is particularly good. ⊠ *Av. 7 y Calle 26, Miramar,* ☎ *7/204–2353. MC, V.*

$$ ✕ **Vistamar.** Overlooking the Straits of Florida, this cozy little paladar has, as its name suggests, fine views—well, at sunset any way (at night, it's blacker than Hades out there). The fresh pargo al ajillo is good, and there's also first-rate salad and creditably prepared tostones and frijoles negros dormidos. ⊠ *Av. 1, No. 2206, e/Calle 22 y Calle 24, Miramar,* ☎ *7/203–8328. No credit cards. No lunch.*

$–$$ ✕ **La Cocina de Lilliam.** In terms of polish and glamor, this lovely gar-
★   den restaurant is positively European. No detail has been overlooked— from the etched glass in the hand-carved wooden doors to the heavy plates and weighty silverware. The *garbanzos fritos* (fried garbanzos) are excellent, as are the *guisado de cordero* (lamb stew) and ropa vieja. The wine list is strong on Torres products from Catalonia (a Coronas tempranillo) and Chile (Casillero del Diablo white). ⊠ *Calle 48, No. 1311, e/Calle 13 y Calle 15, Playa,* ☎ *7/209–6514. No credit cards. No lunch.*

LODGING

Let your interests dictate where you stay. If you love history and architecture, pick a hotel in La Habana Vieja or Centro. If you like to play until the wee hours, Vedado offers a Manhattan atmosphere with plenty of nightlife. If you seek peaceful sea breezes, consider staying in Miramar. If you can't decide, head for the Hotel Nacional: it's set in an early 20th-century Vedado enclave that's close to all the nighttime action, yet offers the peace and quiet of gardens and a waterfront location just a 10-minute taxi ride from La Habana Vieja.

Lodging in private houses is highly recommended but difficult to arrange in advance. Any taxi driver can take you directly to a friend or family member with rooms to rent, but you should check the place out carefully before making a deal. Since laws in Cuba change overnight, the rental of private rooms, now legal, could be illegal by tomorrow. Ask at the airport hotel reservation desk.

Nearly all the government-operated hotels take credit cards as long as they aren't affiliated with U.S. banks or companies. For price categories, *see* the chart *under* Lodging *in* Smart Travel Tips A to Z.

La Habana Vieja

$$–$$$$ 🖼 **Hostal Conde de Villanueva.** In a 19th-century house that once belonged to a Spanish financier, this is a far cry from your typical hostel. It was designed as a cigar-aficionado enclave, and there's an on-site smoke shop and cigar club with leather chairs and cigar-related memorabilia as well as lockers for important guests. The theme throughout is a nod to the Vuelta Abajo, the western Cuba region where the world's finest leaves grow. The restaurant, Vuelta Abajo, specializes in country cooking from Pinar del Río and Viñales. Rooms are impeccable, comfortable, and spacious; the central Habana Vieja location is ideal. ⊠ *Calle Mercaderes 202, La Habana Vieja,* ☎ *7/862–9293,* FAX *7/862–9682,* WEB *www.hostalcondedevillanueva.cu. 9 rooms. Restaurant, bar, air-conditioning, minibars. MC, V.*

$$–$$$ 🖼 **Hotel Santa Isabel.** This 17th-century building is so stately that the Counts of Santovenia made it their home until 1867, when it became one of Habana Vieja's most elegant hotels. Rooms have Spanish colonial furniture and contemporary works by Cuban artists like Zaida del Río. Most rooms overlook the Plaza de Armas, though some have port views. Despite its many comforts and its lush interior patio, the Santa

Isabel has a chilly (and empty) feel. At this writing, plans were on the table to build a pool overlooking the harbor; such a feature may help bring the hotel back to life. ⊠ *Plaza de Armas, Calle Baratillo 9, La Habana Vieja,* ☎ *7/33–8201,* FAX *7/33–8391,* WEB *www. hotelsantaisabel.cu. 17 rooms, 10 suites. Restaurant, bar, air-conditioning, minibars, business services. MC, V.*

$$ 🏨 **Hostal del Tejadillo.** Just a block from the harbor, a few steps from
★ the cathedral, and very near Plaza de la Catedral, this 18th-century mansion has an ideal location. Although rooms are equipped with many modern amenities, they're more like those in a private colonial estate than a hotel. Decorative details include Spanish ceramic tiles, wrought-iron grates, and lathed-wood trim. ⊠ *Calle Tejadillo 12, La Habana Vieja,* ☎ *7/863–7283,* FAX *7/863–8830,* WEB *www.hostaldeltejadillo.cu. 28 rooms, 2 suites, 2 minisuites. Breakfast room, snack bar, air-conditioning, minibars, shop. MC, V.*

$–$$ 🏨 **Hotel Ambos Mundos.** Hemingway stayed here in 1928 on his first
★ trip to Havana; he went on to make it his hideaway before moving to Finca Vigía in 1939. Room 511 is kept as it was in 1938, when Hemingway lived here while writing *For Whom the Bell Tolls.* In one of the magazine articles collected here, you can read Hemingway's description of the sun rising over eastern Havana "to wake you up fresh, no matter where you've been the night before." Rooms are small but cozy, and the hotel is equipped for everything from meetings to honeymoons. ⊠ *Calle Obispo 153, La Habana Vieja,* ☎ *7/860–9529,* FAX *7/860–9532,* WEB *www.hotelambosmundos.cu. 52 rooms, 3 suites. Restaurant, 2 bars, air-conditioning, minibars, baby-sitting, meeting room. MC, V.*

$–$$ 🏨 **Hotel Florida.** Joaquín Gómez, a wealthy merchant, built this man-
★ sion in 1835. It later served as a bank and has now been lavishly restored and transformed into a hotel under the supervision of Habaguanex, the government consortium that's developing and restoring Habana Vieja. Geared for business travelers, guest rooms and facilities (including the communications network) are outstanding. ⊠ *Calle Obispo 252, La Habana Vieja,* ☎ *7/862–4127,* FAX *7/862–4117,* WEB *www.hotelflorida.cu. 21 rooms, 4 suites. Restaurant, bar, air-conditioning, minibars, meeting room, parking (fee). MC, V.*

$ 🏨 **Hostal El Comendador.** Before becoming the home of Don Pedro Re-
★ galado Pedroso y Zayas in 1801, this building—one of the earliest in the original town of San Cristóbal de La Habana—served as a cabildo, a jailhouse, a butcher shop, and then a fish market. It's now an intimate hotel overlooking Havana's harbor. Rooms are tastefully restored and have the full complement of modern amenities. ⊠ *Calle Obrapía 55, La Habana Vieja,* ☎ *7/867–1037,* FAX *7/860–5620,* WEB *www.hostalelcomendador.cu. 14 rooms. Breakfast room, bar, snack bar, wine shop, air-conditioning, minibars, shop. MC, V.*

$ 🏨 **Hostal San Miguel.** Carrara-marble floors, intricate plaster carvings,
★ and rich woodwork make this one of Habaguanex's best La Habana Vieja restoration projects. Built in the mid-19th century, the house was bought in 1923 by Antonio San Miguel, a well-to-do journalist who financed some of the building's eclectic architectural details. The belle-epoque decor, the creature comforts, and the modern facilities guarantee your stay here will be pleasant. The third-floor terrace offers a panoramic view of El Morro fortress and sweeping seascapes. ⊠ *Calle de Cuba 52, La Habana Vieja,* ☎ *7/862–7656,* FAX *7/863–4088,* WEB *www.hostalsanmiguel.cu. 10 rooms. Breakfast room, terrace, bar, air-conditioning, minibars, meeting room. MC, V.*

¢–$ 🏨 **Hostal Valencia.** Although the bougainvillea-draped central patio
★ is more reminiscent of Seville and Andalusia, the theme at this restored 18th-century mansion is really Valencia. Each room is named for a Valencian village or town; request the Morella Room, which has a pri-

vate rooftop patio. Ceiling fans keep the air moving, but the lack of air-conditioning can be a problem. Following the eastern Spanish theme, the on-site restaurant is known (and named) for its paella. ⊠ *Calle de los Oficios 53, esquina de Calle Obrapía, La Habana Vieja,* ☎ *7/867–1037,* FAX *7/860–5620,* WEB *www.hostalvalencia.cu. 12 rooms. Restaurant, bar, shop. MC, V.*

¢ ★ 🏨 **Convento de Santa Clara.** Although this beautiful 17th-century building, a former convent, is officially a Residencia Académica for students, the management accepts other guests if there's space. Rooms, some of which are dormitory style, have wood-beam ceilings and overhead fans; the lack of air-conditioning, TVs, and other modern amenities is offset by the Habana Vieja location, the elegantly authentic atmosphere, and the reasonable rates. As the convent is also a gallery, its doors are patrolled at all hours. ⊠ *Calle de Cuba 610, La Habana Vieja,* ☎ *7/861–3335,* FAX *7/33–5696,* WEB *www.cuba.tc/conventodesantaclara. 9 rooms (2 doubles, 3 triples, 3 quadruples, and a room for 6). Restaurant, bar. No credit cards.*

¢ 🏨 **El Mesón de la Flota.** Named for a *mesón* (tavern) frequented by Spanish sailors in colonial times, this hotel in the heart of the Old City has five rooms with every modern amenity and spotless bathrooms. The bar's nightly flamenco performances are worth a look, and the restaurant's Spanish cooking offers respite from Antillean fare. ⊠ *Calle Mercaderes 257, e/Calle Amargura y Calle Brasil (Teniente Rey), La Habana Vieja,* ☎ *7/863–3838,* FAX *7/862–9281,* WEB *www.cuba.tc/ mesondelaflota. 5 rooms. Restaurant, bar, air-conditioning. MC, V.*

Centro Habana

$$$–$$$$ 🏨 **Parque Central.** Part of the Dutch Golden Tulip chain, this hotel, which is right on the park for which it is named, offers modern creature comforts as well as a convenient location. It may not be as charming as other area hotels, but it has spacious, well-equipped rooms. The pool area, bar, and restaurant are lively. There's also an on-site cigar shop and club. ⊠ *Calle Neptuno, e/Paseo de Martí (Prado) y Calle Agramonte (Zulueta), Centro,* ☎ *7/860–6627,* FAX *7/860–6630,* WEB *www. goldentuliphotels.nl/gtparquecentral. 281 rooms. Restaurant, bar, airconditioning, minibars, pool. MC, V.*

$$$ 🏨 **Hotel Sevilla.** The setting for several episodes in Graham Greene's *Our Man in Havana,* this hotel is right on the edge of La Habana Vieja. Although it has a pleasant, clublike atmosphere and an appealing garden surrounding its swimming pool, its rooms are small and disappointing. The view from the rooftop restaurant is better than the food. ⊠ *Calle Trocadero 55, Centro,* ☎ *7/860–8560,* FAX *7/860–8582,* WEB *www.accor.com/hotelsevilla. 182 rooms. Restaurant, bar, air-conditioning, minibars, pool. MC, V.*

$–$$ ★ 🏨 **Hotel Inglaterra.** In 1958, when Graham Greene last visited Havana, he stayed at this landmark hotel. Its interior seems gloomy at first, but give your eyes a chance to adjust, as there's much to admire: photographs of old Havana, intricate Andalusian tiles, the shield of Spain's Catholic Kings behind the bar. Rooms are gloomy as well, but they seem more "real" than those in the glass-and-steel high-rises. The ground-floor Gran Café del Louvre is a great people-watching spot, the roof terrace restaurant has nonpareil views, and all the sights of Centro and La Habana Vieja are a short walk away. ⊠ *Paseo de Martí (Prado) 416, Centro,* ☎ *7/860–8595,* FAX *7/33–8254,* WEB *www.hotelinglaterra.cu. 83 rooms. Restaurant, bar, air-conditioning, shop, cabaret, parking (fee). MC, V.*

$–$$ 🏨 **Hotel Plaza.** There's something charming about the Plaza, despite its cavernous, tourist-packed hallway. Although its rooms aren't very distinguished, the early 20th-century Spanish architecture has inspiring overtones of pre–Civil War Madrid. This hotel is no Madrid Ritz, but with its full range of services and facilities it will do in early 21st-century Havana. A stay here gets you pool privileges at the Hotel Sevilla. ⊠ *Calle Agramonte (Zulueta) 267, Centro,* ☎ *7/860–8583,* FAX *7/860–8591,* WEB *www.hotelplaza.cu. 188 rooms. Restaurant, bar, air-conditioning, billiards, cabaret. MC, V.*

¢–$ 🏨 **Hotel Deauville.** Most people agree that the building in which this hotel is set is Havana's second ugliest structure (the Russian Embassy, ironically, is considered the ugliest). A stay here, however, means you won't spend much time looking at it; indeed, the views (of the city and the Straits of Florida) *from* it are terrific. It's such a good deal, the clientele is usually an interesting collection of students, professors, and the occasional writer. What's more, its disco is one of the city's hottest. ⊠ *Av. Italia (Galiano) 1, Centro,* ☎ *7/33–8812,* FAX *7/33–8148,* WEB *www. horizontes.cu/hoteldeauville. 144 rooms. Restaurant, bar, air-conditioning, pool, cabaret. MC, V.*

¢ 🏨 **Casa del Científico.** Once the residence of Cuba's second president, José Miguel Gómez—known as *El Tiburón* (The Shark)—this charming old house near the Museo de Bellas Artes has a grandiose marble stairway and a tile-and-mahogany–lined dining room. Rooms come in a variety of prices and configurations (with bath and without), but the best is the top-floor suite for two (additional beds $11 each). ⊠ *Paseo de Martí (Prado) 212, Centro,* ☎ *7/862–4511,* FAX *7/860–0167,* WEB *www.casadelcientifico.cu. 10 rooms, 6 share bath; 1 suite. Restaurant, air-conditioning. MC, V.*

¢ 🏨 **Hotel Caribbean.** Don't expect too much from this budget option on the border of La Habana Vieja and Centro. Although it's no Shangri-la, its rooms have air-conditioning, TVs, and baths. Top-floor rooms are the best. ⊠ *Paseo de Martí (Prado) 164, Centro,* ☎ *7/860–8241,* FAX *7/866–9479,* WEB *www.horizontes.cu/hotelcaribbean. 40 rooms. Restaurant, coffee shop, air-conditioning. MC, V.*

Vedado

$$$–$$$$ 🏨 **Hotel Habana Libre.** Originally the Havana Hilton, this high-rise monster is, at least, easy to find. Rooms are functional and modern; some offer astounding sea views. The restaurants and bars are always abuzz, and Cuba's best musicians play at the rooftop Turqino disco (the vistas from here are stunning, especially at dawn). The location puts you in the municipal nerve center: Calle 23 (La Rampa) slopes right down to the Malecón, Parque Coppelia's ice-cream emporium is just across the way, and the Universidad de la Habana is a five-minute walk east. ⊠ *Calle 23 (La Rampa) y Calle L, Vedado,* ☎ *7/33–4011,* FAX *7/33–3141,* WEB *www.solmelia.com. 547 rooms. 3 restaurants, 3 bars, air-conditioning, minibars, pool, shops, dance club, parking (fee). MC, V.*

$$$–$$$$ 🏨 **Hotel Meliá Cohiba.** This mammoth glass-and-steel hotel looms over the western end of the Malecón and has very little to do with the Havana of baroque churches and colonial palaces. It does a superb job of providing efficient service and support for executives on the move. The staff—from the bellhops and busboys to the receptionists and concierges—is highly professional, and everything in the place functions impeccably. All the hotel's restaurants are top-notch. ⊠ *Calle Paseo, e/Calle 1 y Calle 3, Vedado,* ☎ *7/33–3636,* FAX *7/33–4555,* WEB *www.solmelia.com. 342 rooms, 120 suites. 4 restaurants, 3 bars, air-conditioning, room service, pool, shops, cabaret, parking (fee). MC, V.*

$$$–$$$$ 🏨 **Hotel Nacional.** Officially the Hotel Nacional de Cuba, this elegant
★ establishment recalls another era. Filled with memorabilia of such famous (and infamous) guests as Winston Churchill, Ava Gardner, Frank

Sinatra, and Meyer Lansky, the Nacional still buzzes. Although rooms are disappointing and the service is only fair, the Vista al Golfo (Gulf View) bar is a great place for a mojito, as is the patio with its gracious columns. Invariably there's a hot trio playing son, the perfect accompaniment to the movements of visitors from all over the world as they wander in and out of this national monument. ⊠ *Calle O y Calle 21, Vedado,* ☎ *7/33–3564 through 7/33–3567,* FAX *7/33–5054,* WEB *www. hotelnacionaldecuba.com. 434 rooms, 16 suites. 2 restaurants, 2 bars, air-conditioning, minibars, 2 pools, cabaret, parking (fee). MC, V.*

$$$–$$$$ 🏨 **Hotel Presidente.** If the shady lobby bar and a beverage don't soothe your weary traveler's soul, then head immediately to your comfortable, well-appointed room overlooking the pool and the Straits of Florida beyond. The restaurant, Chez Emérito, has a good wine list and unusual offerings ranging from frogs' legs from the Zapata wetlands to lamb chops. The breakfast room next to the pool is bright and cheery, and breakfast is generous, enough to get you through to a late dinner in a nearby paladar. ⊠ *Av. de los Presidentes y Calzada (Av. 7), Vedado,* ☎ *7/55–1801,* FAX *7/33–3753,* WEB *www.hotelesc.com/hotelpresidente. 142 rooms. 2 restaurants, bar, air-conditioning, minibars, pool, parking (fee). MC, V.*

$$ 🏨 **Habana Riviera.** Although it's large, impersonal, *and* inefficient, the Riviera is home to El Palacio de la Salsa, one of Havana's best music venues. The top groups all perform here, and the place turns into a disco the moment they stop. If you end up staying here, take comfort in the fact that Esther Williams and Ginger Rogers once splashed about in the pool and the notion that your bed is crawling distance from one of the city's hottest dance floors. ⊠ *Calle Paseo y Malecón, Vedado,* ☎ *7/33–4051,* FAX *7/33–3739,* WEB *www.habana.riviera.cu. 330 rooms. 2 restaurants, 2 bars, air-conditioning, minibars, pool, shops, dance club, parking (fee). MC, V.*

$ 🏨 **Hotel Victoria.** Just a few blocks from the Malecón, this hotel may be modest but it has much to recommend it. It's one of Vedado's few intimate establishments. Rooms are small but well equipped, the restaurant is passable, and you can't help but make a new friend or two at the pocket-size swimming pool. The Victoria's clientele tends to return faithfully, so reserve well in advance. ⊠ *Calle 19, No. 101, esquina de Calle M, Vedado,* ☎ *7/33–3510,* FAX *7/33–3109,* WEB *www.hotel-victoria.cubaweb.cu. 31 rooms. Restaurant, bar, air-conditioning, pool. MC, V.*

¢–$$ 🏨 **Hotel Capri.** At first glance, this high-rise doesn't seem very distinguished. But look again and you'll understand why this was once the mob's favorite Havana hangout. Rooms are spacious and tastefully decorated, and the service is more personal than that at the Capri's more famous neighbors. You can bask in the afternoon sun beside the attractive rooftop pool, have a dinner of decent Italian fare at La Terraza Florentina, and end the day dancing to hot salsa at the Salon Rojo disco. ⊠ *Calle 21, e/Calle N y Calle O, Vedado,* ☎ *7/33–4504,* FAX *7/ 33–3750,* WEB *www.horizontes.capri.cu. 183 rooms, 12 suites, 10 triples, 10 duplexes. 2 restaurants, 2 bars, breakfast room, air-conditioning, minibars, pool, shops, dance club, parking (fee). MC, V.*

¢   🏨 **Hotel Colina.** Set on and named for the famous hill occupied by the Universidad de la Habana, the Colina has a down-at-the-heel 1950's charm and a drop or two of student (read: revolutionary) chic that seems to attract a predominately French clientele. Rooms are small and humbly furnished, but you can't beat the atmosphere and convenient location. ⊠ *Calle L, No. 501, esquina de Calle 27, Vedado,* ☎ *7/832– 3535,* FAX *7/33–4071,* WEB *www.horizontes.cu/hotelcolina. 75 rooms. Restaurant, bar, air-conditioning. MC, V.*

Miramar

$$$$ ☐ **Hotel Meliá Habana.** Despite this hotel's immensity, the staff succeeds in making you feel as if they know you're here and care how you're getting along. The decor is minimalist (bordering on sterile), but rooms are clean and well maintained. The various swimming pools (the view of the Gulf of Mexico is terrific from the ocean-side pool) and the private beach make this a refreshing place to unwind after a few hours of sightseeing. ☒ *Av. 3, e/Calle 76 y Calle 80, Miramar,* ☎ *7/204–8500,* FAX *7/204–9505,* WEB *www.solmelia.com. 405 rooms, 4 suites. 3 restaurants, 2 bars, air-conditioning, minibars, 3 pools, beach, shops, cabaret, parking (fee). MC, V.*

$$ ☐ **Château Miramar.** If you're looking for a small, intimate Miramar hotel, this is a viable option. Although its rooms have a somewhat antiseptic decor, the place is so close to the Gulf of Mexico that sea spray reaches the windows; rooms on the gulf side have wonderful terraces overlooking the water. ☒ *Av. 1 y Calle 62, Miramar,* ☎ *7/204–1952,* FAX *7/204–0224,* WEB *www.cubanacan.com/chateaumiramar. 41 rooms, 9 suites. Restaurant, bar, air-conditioning, minibars, pool, parking (fee). MC, V.*

$$ ☐ **Hotel Comodoro.** Although popular with package tours, the Comodoro isn't as impersonal as you might expect from a hotel with a thousand or so guests. Quarters here are in modern rooms or condominium bungalows, and there's a private beach as well as a pool. Its amenities and location are both a blessing and a curse: you may be tempted to stay on the grounds—remaining cool, comfortable, and collected—rather than taking yet another taxi to Habana Vieja or Vedado. If that's your inclination, you might as well be in Miami or Acapulco. ☒ *Av. 1 y Calle 84, Miramar,* ☎ *7/204–5551,* FAX *7/204–2028,* WEB *www.hotelcomodoro.cu. 257 rooms, 301 bungalows. 3 restaurants, 2 bars, air-conditioning, minibars, pool, beach, shops, dance club, parking (fee). MC, V.*

¢ ☐ **Hotel Mirazul.** "Mirazul" means "blue view," an appropriate name for this hotel. It's in a stately, blue, early 20th-century *palacete* (town house) once owned by the heirs of the Partagás cigar dynasty. Each room has a different shape and decor; all are equipped with everything from cable TV to air-conditioning. The bathrooms deserve rave reviews for their original design. Although this hotel is far from La Habana Vieja, its rates are reasonable for the level of comfort it offers. ☒ *Av. 5, e/Calle 36 y Calle 40, Miramar,* ☎ *7/204–0088,* FAX *7/204–0045,* WEB *www. hotelmirazul.cu. 45 rooms. Restaurant, bar, air-conditioning, minibars, pool. MC, V.*

Playas del Este and Jibacoa

$–$$$ ☐ **Hotel Atlántico.** It won't take your breath away, but this modern hotel has acceptably furnished and equipped bungalows, and it's on a beach less than 20 minutes from the city. Request a room with an Atlantic view. ☒ *Av. Las Terrazas, Playa Santa María del Mar,* ☎ *7/97–1085,* FAX *7/880–3911,* WEB *www.horizontes.cu/aparthotelatlantico. 92 bungalows. Restaurant, bar, air-conditioning, pool, beach, dance club. MC, V. All-inclusive.*

$–$$ ☐ **Hotel Breezes Jibacoa.** This modern glass-and-steel marvel opened in late 2000 and quickly became one of Cuba's top beach resorts because of its postmodern design and first-rate service. The all-inclusive plan here turns out to be penny-wise though somewhat confining. The staff members are helpful, intelligent, and cheerful, and the beaches are impeccable. ☒ *Playa Arroyo Bermejo, Santa Cruz del Norte,* ☎ *692/85122,* FAX *692/85150. 250 rooms,* WEB *www.breezesjibacoa.cu. Restaurant, bar, air-conditioning, pool, hot tub, horseback riding,* *beach, dive shop, snorkeling, boating, dance club. MC, V. All-inclusive*

$–$$$ 🏨 **Villa Megano.** Just a few minutes' walk from the beach, this hotel is generally considered one of the best in the Playas del Este. The bungalow-style quarters stretch up a hill behind the reception and pool area. The modern structure is no design triumph, but the staff is friendly and helpful, and downtown Havana is 15 minutes away. ✉ *Carretera Vía Blanca, Km 22.5, Playa Santa María del Mar,* ☎ 7/97–1610, FAX 7/97–1624, WEB *www.horizontes.cu/villamegano. 73 bungalows. Restaurant, bar, air-conditioning, pool, dance club. MC, V. All-inclusive.*

NIGHTLIFE AND THE ARTS

Music is a Cuban passion rivaled only by baseball and the Revolution itself. *Everyone* here knows who El Médico de la Salsa (The Salsa Doctor) is and what type of music he plays. The Van Van, Beny Moré, and Compay Segundo are all celebrities on the order of Frank Sinatra, the Beatles, or Elvis. Caribbean, Spanish, African, and American rhythms have been combined to create more than three dozen musical styles, which are themselves evolving into still more varieties. To experience the music is to learn about it, and Havana offers plenty of opportunities for both. The city also has splashy cabaret revues as well as jazz haunts and cafés that offer quieter entertainment.

Dance performances—from traditional ballet to traditional Afro-Cuban—are also options. If your Spanish is good, you'll appreciate the active film, theater, and literary scenes. You don't need any Spanish to enjoy the art exhibited in Havana's many galleries. Attire at theaters and other venues ranges from cocktail dresses and jackets and ties to blue jeans and shorts. Tickets are nearly always available (check with your hotel concierge) at box offices and are very inexpensive by European or North American standards.

Cartelera, a Spanish-English weekly published by the Instituto Cubano del Libro and usually available free at major hotels, lists concerts, plays, and other artistic events. *Opciones* is another bilingual weekly publication with cultural listings. The *Programación Cultural,* published monthly in Spanish by the Oficina del Historiador de la Ciudad (Office of the City Historian), has what is probably the most complete schedule of events. Ask for a copy at Museo de la Ciudad in the Plaza de Armas.

Nightlife

Bars and Cafés
Azotea de Dulce Maria (Calle San Ignacio 78, La Habana Vieja, ☎ 7/867–1837). If it's Monday night, don't miss the *descarga* (jam session) from 9:30 on. The $5 entrance fee includes a mojito.
Bar Dos Hermanos (✉ Av. del Puerto/Calle Desamparado/San Pedro y Calle Sol, La Habana Vieja, ☎ 7/861–7845). At what was once a Hemingway haunt, you can drink with the locals and get the feel of life along the wharf.
Café Cantante "Mi Habana" (✉ Calle Paseo y Calle 39, Vedado, ☎ 7/33–5713). On the upper edge of Vedado, near the Plaza de la Revolución, this café often has live music and dance or comedy shows.
Café O'Reilly (✉ Calle O'Reilly 203, e/Calle de Cuba y Calle San Ignacio, La Habana Vieja, ☎ 7/862–0613). Here you can take a seat on a New Orleans–like, wrought-iron balcony that overlooks the street for people-watching all day and all night.
Café Paris (✉ Calle San Ignacio 22, esquina de Calle Obispo, La Ha-

bana Vieja, ☎ no phone). You're usually entertained by one of the city's excellent trios at this 24-hour standby. No matter how many times you have heard "Guantanamera," these performers always give it new meaning.

Café Taberna (Calle Brasil/Teniente Rey, esquina de Calle Mercaderes, La Habana Vieja, ☎ 7/861–1637). Founded in 1772, this café was restored in mid-2001 and now offers live music and dancing from 8 to midnight.

La Columnata Egipciana (✉ Calle Mercaderes 109, La Habana Vieja, ☎ 7/862–0216). This hot spot has Buena Vista Social Club look-alikes playing hot salsa around the clock.

El Gato Tuerto (✉ Calle O, e/Calle 17 y Calle 19, Vedado, ☎ 7/66–2224). Just steps from the Hotel Nacional, the Gato Tuerto offers music (boleros) downstairs and an upstairs restaurant open until dawn.

La Lluvia de Oro (✉ Calle Obispo 316, esquina de Calle Aguiar, La Habana Vieja, ☎ 7/862–9870). Open around the clock, this bar-café often has live music and is always full of life. It's a good starting point for a night on the town.

Monserrate (✉ Av. de la Bélgica/Misiones/Edigio/Monserrate, esquina de Calle Obrapía, La Habana Vieja, ☎ 7/860–9751). Just across from Fidel's student-days hangout, the Castillo del Farnés, this place hops 24 hours a day, usually to the tune of a hot trio.

El Patio (✉ Plaza de la Catedral, Calle San Ignacio 54, La Habana Vieja, ☎ 7/861–8511). You'll be hard-pressed to avoid stopping here at least once during your stay. The flow of human scenery through the square is endless.

Piano Bar La Torre (✉ Calle 17, e/Calle M y Calle N, Vedado, ☎ 7/832–5650). Come for the giddy views and the fabulous music. Depending on the crowd, you may want to stay till the wee hours—possibly even till sunrise.

El Polvorín (✉ Carretera de la Cabaña, Las Fortalezas, ☎ 7/863–8295). Tucked in El Morro castle, this little-known place has good dance music and views over the harbor. It's a good spot for an evening away from downtown Havana's rush.

Taberna del Galeón (✉ Plaza de Armas, Calle Obispo y Calle Baratillo, La Habana Vieja, ☎ 7/33–8061). Just off the eastern corner of the Plaza de Armas is this store where you can sample shots of rum. Afterward, head to the upstairs bar for some punch made with rum, coffee, and mint.

Cabarets

La Cecilia (✉ Av. 5, e/Calle 110 y Calle 112, Miramar, ☎ 7/204–1562). Here, a feather-clad chorus dances to incandescent salsa. The place goes disco between and after performances.

Habana Café (✉ Hotel Meliá Cohiba, Calle Paseo, e/Calle 1 y Calle 3, Miramar, ☎ 7/33–3636). The show in the Hotel Meliá Cohiba is a torrid mix of live music and dance performances and red-hot dancing, with patrons and professional dancers joining the fray.

Parisien Café (✉ Hotel Nacional, Calle O y Calle 21, Vedado, ☎ 7/33–3564). The Hotel Nacional is always at the center of things, so it's no surprise that the nightly performance in its café is a winner. The wild show is followed by equally wild dancing by the audience. The cover charge is $30.

Tropicana (✉ Calle 72, e/Calle 43 y Calle 45, Marianao, ☎ 7/267–1717). Havana's most famous floor show is in a district just south of Miramar. Reserve a table (this place fills up fast), a bottle of Havana Club, and a bucket of ice, and you're set for the night. More than 200 gorgeous dancers picked from Cuba's many dance troupes are guaranteed to get your attention. The cover ($40–$70 per person, depending on seating and including a drink) is astronomical for Cuba, but the lush, outdoor venue is unforgettable. Shows are held Tuesday–Sunday at 9 PM, and when they finish, the place becomes a disco.

Dance Clubs and Discos

Club Ipanema (✉ Hotel Copacabana, Av. 1, e/Calle 44 y Calle 46, Miramar, ☎ 7/204–1037). This hot dance club in the Hotel Copacabana has an open bar (all you can drink for a $5 cover) on Monday and Tuesday. It's open nightly until 4 AM.

Palacio de la Salsa (✉ Habana Riviera, Calle Paseo, Vedado, ☎ 7/33–4051). As its name suggests, this establishment in the Habana Riviera hotel is *the* place for salsa. Big bands, from Los Van Van (they've been together for 30-odd years, and they're still hot) to the Grupo Moncada, drive audiences mad here nightly. Don't let the steep (for Cuba) $20 cover charge prevent you from spending a night on the town here.

Río Club (✉ Calle A, e/Calle 3 y Calle 5, Miramar, ☎ 7/209–3389). Just across the Río Almendares is this torrid dance club—beloved by Cubans and filled with action of every kind.

Sala Macumba Habana (✉ La Giraldilla, Calle 222, esquina de Calle 37, La Coronela/La Lisa, ☎ 7/33–0568). The hottest spot in town at this writing, the Macumba offers live performances followed by ardent dancing.

Salon Rojo (✉ Hotel Capri, Calle 21, e/Calle N y Calle O, Vedado, ☎ 7/33–3747). At this hot spot in the Hotel Capri, live musical entertainment and spectacle alternates with disco and participation.

Jazz Clubs

Jazz Café (✉ Galerías de Paseo, Calle Paseo y Calle 1, Vedado, ☎ 7/862–6401). This is Havana's *other* jazz place, and a good one it is. The many jam sessions and the introduction of new jazz groups mean there's lots of improvisation and hot young musicians.

Jazz Club La Zorra y el Cuervo (✉ Calle 23/La Rampa, e/Calle N y Calle O, Vedado, ☎ 7/66–2402). An Afro-Cuban hook makes the tunes at the city's premier jazz venue unique. Unlike most of Havana's music venues, the sounds here make you snap your fingers and shake your head instead of everything else.

The Arts

Dance, Music, and Theater

Live Cuban music and dance performances are regularly held in the city's many cultural centers. Some of these centers also host more traditional music and dance shows as well as literary events, plays, and art exhibits. At UNEAC, for example, you can find everything from lectures to performances of Santería rituals. The Palacio del Segundo Cabo in the Plaza de Armas is another literary and artistic hub.

If your Spanish is good, try to take in a play. These are held not only in theaters and cultural centers but also in such surprising venues as the Museo de la Ciudad in the Palacio de los Capitanes Generales, the Casa Natal de José Martí, and the Museo de Arte Colonial.

Havana teems with dancers. Drop by the Escuela Provincial de Ballet (Provincial Ballet School) at Calle L and Calle 19 and have a look at the 220 little swans that Silvia María Rodriguez is training. Each year 45 of 800 9-year-old applicants begin working here. After five years, some 15 of them (and those chosen from the six other provincial schools) make it to the new Escuela Nacional de Ballet (National Ballet School) at Calle Prado y Calle Trocadero, currently run by Marta Ulloa under the supervision of the Ballet Nacional de Cuba's director and prima ballerina, Alicia Alonso. Other large dance troupes include Christi Dominguez's Compañia de Ballet de la Television Cubana (Ballet Company of the Cuban Television Network), the Compañia de Dansa Contemporánea de Cuba (Cuban Contemporary Dance Company), and the Ballet Nacional Folklórico (National Folklore Ballet). Reinaldo Suarez's Danz-Art and Regla Salvent's Compañia de Dansa del Cuerpo Armónico are among the city's many small ensembles, along with Marianela Bovan's Danza Abierta and Rosario Cárdenas's Danza Combinatoria.

CULTURAL CENTERS

Casa de África (⊠ Calle Obrapía 157, e/Calle Mercaderes y Calle San Ignacio, La Habana Vieja, ☎ 7/861–5798). As its name suggests, this center specializes in Afro-Cuban music.

Casa de la Amistad (⊠ Calle Paseo 406, esquina de Calle 17, Vedado, ☎ 7/830–3114). Come any day but Monday (when it's closed) to hear groups that perform Afro-Cuban and other traditional music.

Casa de la Comedia (⊠ Calle Justiz 18, esquina de Calle Baratillo, La Habana Vieja, ☎ 7/863–9282). This center has a full and ever-changing roster of events, including Cuban music shows, that take place weekdays from 9 to 1.

Casa de la Cultura Julián del Casal (⊠ Calle Aguiar 509, e/Calle Amargura y Calle Brasil/Teniente Rey, La Habana Vieja, ☎ 7/863–4860). One of the most active and authentic of the ubiquitous Casas de Cultura hosts everything from big bands to Cuban trios to solo singer-songwriters.

Casa 10 de Octubre (⊠ Calzada de Luyanó 361, Luyanó, ☎ 7/99–0653). Just south of La Habana Vieja, this center hosts authentic performances of trova and other types of traditional Cuban music.

Casa de la Trova (⊠ Calle San Lázaro 661, e/Calle Gervasio y Calle Padre Varela/Belascoaín, Centro, ☎ 7/879–3373). This is a good place to hear traditional Cuban music.

Delirio Habanero (⊠ Calle Paseo y Calle 39, Vedado, ☎ 7/33–5713). Not many visitors know about this hot spot, despite the fact that it's a great place to hear Cuban musicians work their magic. Reservations are essential on weekends.

Dos Gardenias (⊠ Av. 7 y Calle 26, Mindanao, ☎ 7/204–2353). There's almost always some type of musical event at this complex. The Bar la Tarde is open from 8:30 to 11:30; Salon Boleros operates from 11:15 on; and Jardin del Humor Dos Gardenias has comedy shows Wednesday through Sunday.

THEATERS

Gran Teatro de la Habana (⊠ Paseo de Martí/Prado 458, e/Calle San Rafael y Calle San Martín/San José, Centro, ☎ 7/862–9473). Also known as the Teatro García Lorca, this theater has a spectacular baroque facade with white marble angels dancing gracefully on its four corner towers. It's a beautiful place to see operas, jazz shows, symphony performances, and plays. In addition, the National Ballet performs here under the direction of Alicia Alonso, who is now in her 80s but is still Cuba's honorary prima ballerina. There are two theaters here: the Sala García Lorca and the Sala Antonin Artaud, which is known for its avant-garde theater productions.

Teatro Amadeo Roldán (⊠ Calzada, e/Calle D y Calle E, Vedado, ☎ 7/832–1168). This is the home of the Sinfónica Nacional (National Symphony), which is currently directed by the young Iván del Prado and which is much better than the ages and outfits of the musicians (who look for all the world like a high school band) would suggest. Listen to them deal with with Handel's *Water Music* or Prokofiev's 7th, especially the allegro movements.

Teatro Nacional (⊠ Plaza de la Revolución, Calle Paseo y Av. Carlos Manuel de Céspedes, Vedado, ☎ 7/879–6011). Cuba's most important theater is used for classical music and ballet performances, as well as for contemporary theater and dance productions.

Teatro Julio Antonio Mella (⊠ Calle Línea/Calle 7, No. 657, esquina de Calle A, Vedado, ☎ 7/38–6961). The home of the Danza Contemporánea de Cuba is the standard venue for contemporary theater as well as for dance.

Teatro Trianon (⊠ Calle Línea/Calle 7, e/Calle Paseo y Calle A, Vedado, ☎ 7/831–3611). This theater stages plays by contemporary playwrights.

Film

For a small, blockaded country, Cuba has a surprisingly prestigious film industry. Camilo Vives, director of the Instituto Cubano de Arte e Industria Cinematográficos (ICAIC; Cuban Institute of Art and Cinematography) predicts that Cuban filmmakers will continue to coproduce (with countries such as Spain) four or five films a year. Cubans love the cinema, and if your Spanish is good you can join them for a night at the movies. Cubans love American movies, and somehow (pirated, smuggled, loaned) such films always get here, though they're nearly always dubbed in Spanish.

Cine Charles Chaplin (⊠ Calle 23/La Rampa, e/Calle 10 y Calle 12, Vedado, ☎ 7/831–1101). This extremely large movie house shows pictures at 5 PM and 8 PM every day but Tuesday.

Cine Payret (⊠ Paseo de Martí/Prado 513, Centro, ☎ 7/863–3163). American films, nearly always Westerns, start playing at 12:30 PM here.

Cine Yara (⊠ Calle 23/La Rampa y Calle L, Vedado, ☎ 7/832–9430). Near the Parque Coppelia and its famous ice-cream shop, Cine Yara is a great favorite. It opens its doors at 12:30 PM.

ICAIC (⊠ Calle 23/La Rampa 1155, e/Calle 10 y Calle 12, Vedado, ☎ 7/55–2854). The Cuban film industry's central nervous system often shows advance screenings of new Cuban releases.

La Rampa (⊠ Calle 23/La Rampa y Calle O, Vedado, ☎ 7/878–6146). La Rampa starts showing movies at 4:30 PM.

La Riviera (⊠ Calle 23/La Rampa y Calle H, Vedado, ☎ 7/830–9564). Here the Cuban and international films start rolling at 4:30 PM.

Painting and Sculpture

Carmen Montilla (⊠ Calle de los Oficios 162, La Habana Vieja, ☎ 7/33–8768). A $3 admission gets you in to see this patio's sculptures and other objets d'art by Cuban and international artists. It's open Tuesday–Saturday 10–5 and Sunday 9–1.

Centro de Desarrollo de las Artes Visuales (⊠ Plaza Vieja, Calle San Ignacio 352, La Habana Vieja, ☎ 7/862–6295). The emphasis here is on contemporary and conceptual art by Cuban and other Latin American artists. Admission is $3, and the center is open Tuesday–Saturday 10–5.

Galería–Estudio Yanes (⊠ Calle Obrapía y Calle San Ignacio, La Habana Vieja, ☎ 7/862–6195). You can stop by Tuesday–Sunday 10–5 (admission is free) to see the permanent collection of works by resident artists Orlando Yanes and his wife, Casiguaya, as well as temporary exhibits of pieces by other Cubans.

Galería Haydee Santamaría (⊠ Calle G, e/Av. 3 y Av. 5, Vedado, ☎ 7/832–4653). Named for a fallen heroine of the 1953 attack on the Moncada Barracks, this gallery shows prints, drawings, graphics, and photographs from Cuba and throughout Latin America. It's open Monday–Saturday 10–4; admission is free.

Galería Horacio Ruiz (⊠ Palacio del Segundo Cabo, Plaza de Armas, Calle Tacón 4, La Habana Vieja, ☎ 7/832–4653). You can drop by Monday–Saturday 10–4 to see (and, perhaps, buy) leather goods, glassware, drawings, and prints made by Cuban craftspeople and artists. Admission is free.

Galería los Oficios–Nelson Dominguez (⊠ Calle de los Oficios 166, La Habana Vieja, ☎ 7/33–9804). The sculptures and paintings of Nelson Dominguez and other artists are shown in a lovely 17th-century colonial mansion and patio weekdays 10–5 and Saturday 9–2. There's no admission fee.

Galería Roberto Diago. (⊠ Plaza Vieja, Calle Muralla 107, La Habana Vieja, ☎ 7/862–3577). The patio here is as fantastic as the Afro-Cuban art. It's open Monday–Saturday 10–5 and Sunday 9–2. Admission is $3.

Galería Victor Manuel (⊠ Plaza de la Catedral, Calle San Ignacio 56, La Habana Vieja, ☎ 7/861–2955). This gallery with works by Latin American artists is almost an inevitable stop on a trip to the Plaza de la Catedral. It's open daily 9–9, and a $2 admission fee is charged.

Taller Experimental de la Gráfica (⊠ Callejón del Chorro 62, La Habana Vieja, ☎ 7/862–0979). If you find yourself in the Plaza de la Catedral on a weekday or Saturday 10–4, head for this gallery (there's no admission fee) in a nearby alleyway for a look at graphic works by a wide range of artists, all of them Cuban.

Terracota 4 Galería-Estudio (⊠ Calle Mercaderes 156, La Habana Vieja, ☎ 7/66–9417). This gallery specializes in ceramic and terra-cotta artwork and crafts. It's open daily 10–6; admission is free.

OUTDOOR ACTIVITIES AND SPORTS

Participant Sports

Boating, Fishing, and Scuba Diving

Marina Hemingway (⊠ Calle 248 y Av. 5, Santa Fé, Jaimanitas/Playa, ☎ 7/204–1149), home of the Ernest Hemingway International Marlin Tournament each May–June, can help you to arrange fishing, yachting, diving, and snorkeling trips—regardless of your level of skill or your budget. Scuba diving costs $30 per dive (there are discounts if you book multiple dives), and snorkeling excursions go for $20. A four-hour, deep-sea fishing outing in the Gulf Stream will cost about $250 (per boat load). Yacht rentals range from $250–$300 a day to $2,000–$3,000 a week.

July sees the Old Man and the Sea Fishing Tournament. The staff at the **Marina Tarará/Club Naútica** (⊠ Calle 5, e/Calle 2 y Calle Cobre, Tarará, Playas del Este, ☎ 7/97–1462) can fill you in on this competition. They also charter boats and run diving, snorkeling, and deep-sea fishing excursions in the Gulf Stream.

Golf

The **Club de Golf Habana** (⊠ Carretera de Vento, Km 8, Capdevila/Boyeros, ☎ 7/45–4578) is a 15-minute (and roughly $15) taxi ride south of downtown Havana. Though a little rough, the course offers a good walk in the sun, and the swimming pool and Hoyo 19 bar are both good places to relax after a round. Greens fees are $20 for 9 holes, $30 for 18 holes. A top set of clubs rents for $10, and caddies cost $10 for 9 holes, $15 for 18 holes. If you'd like to play, call ahead to be sure there's not a tournament on.

Hiking and Horseback Riding

Cubans favor the Parque Escaleras de Jaruco, 25 km (15 mi) east of La Habana, for hiking or horseback-riding outings. Well-marked trails of varying degrees of difficulty and length wind through the park's rolling hills and along its limestone cliffs, which are full of caves and underground streams. It makes a good day trip from the city, particularly if you stop at one of the Playas del Este on the way back. From Havana, take the Autopista Nacional 15 km (9 mi) east to the turnoff for Tapaste and Jaruco. The park is 6 km (4 mi) west of Jaruco village.

Running

Although the air quality can be poor, the Malecón is a picturesque place to jog, for the human as well as for the marine scenery. The **Estadio Juan Abrahantes** (⊠ Calle Zapata y Calle G/Av. de los Presidentes, Vedado, ☎ 7/878–6959), just south of the university, has a well-groomed track-and-field complex that's open to serious runners (call ahead for details). There are places to run (there's a $2 locker fee) at the **Ciudad Deportivo** (⊠ Av. de la Independencia/Rancho Boyeros y Vía Blanca, Palatino, ☎ 7/40–3302).

Swimming

Pools are everywhere in Havana; even the elegant Hotel Nacional allows nonguests to use its two swimming pools for a $5 fee. The **Complejo Panamericano** (⊠ Av. Monumental, Km 4.5, Villa Panamericana, ☎ 7/95–4221), which is 2 km (1 mi) east of Havana on the road to Cojímar, has the city's best Olympic pool. You can swim here for a $5 fee.

Although you'll see residents swimming off the Malecón, it's not recommended that you join them: the water quality is poor to poisonous. If you really want a beach, head to the Playas del Este.

Tennis (And More)

The **Canchas de Tenis** (⊠ Av. Monumental, Km 4.5, Villa Panamericana, ☎ 7/95–1561) at the all-purpose Complejo Panamericano—a sports complex on the way to Cojímar and Playas del Este—are some of the best tennis courts around.

Club Havana (⊠ Av. 5 y Calles 188–192, Flores, Playa, ☎ 7/204–5700) is the country club that was once so exclusive that even President Fulgencio Batista was denied membership (he didn't meet the racial standards). "The Club" is still private and exclusive, but if you're polite and ask nicely, the management may be able to arrange a day pass. In addition to a match on one of the four tennis courts (both clay and hard courts are available), a game of squash, a swim in the pool, a windsurfing excursion along the private beach, a massage, or some time in a sauna are also possibilities. A pass costs $10 weekdays, $15 weekends; getting a massage, indulging in a sauna, or using the tennis and squash courts will cost you $2 (each) extra. Windsurfers rent for $5 an hour.

Spectator Sports

Baseball

Cuba, a recognized baseball power, has teams capable of beating Major League U.S. clubs, as the Cuban National Team's 12–5 victory over the Baltimore Orioles (in Baltimore) amply demonstrated in May 1999. To watch Cubans play baseball is to see poetry and passion in motion. Top league teams play from December through June in the 60,000-seat **Estadio Latinoamericano** (⊠ Calle Zequeira 312, Cerro, ☎ 7/870–6576). Games are usually held Tuesday–Thursday at 8 PM, Saturday at 1:30 and 8, and Sunday at 1:30. Tickets are cheap. You may be able to catch a baseball game at the Universidad de la Habana's **Estadio Juan Abrahantes** (⊠ Calle Zapata y Calle G/Av. de los Presidentes, Vedado, ☎ 7/878–6959).

Boxing

To watch young boxers being developed in what is pound-for-pound and citizen-for-citizen the world's leading pugilistic power, stop in at **Gimnasio de Boxeo Rafael Trejo** (⊠ Calle de Cuba 815, La Habana Vieja, ☎ 7/862–0266). Catch boxing matches in town at the **Sala Polivalente Kid Chocolate** (⊠ Paseo de Martí/Prado y Calle Brasil/Teniente Rey, La Habana Vieja, ☎ 7/861–1547).

Pelota

For Basque pelota in its various forms (*pala, remonte,* or jai alai), the **Canchas de Pelota Vasca y Patinódromo Raul Díaz Arguelles** (⊠ Av. 26 y Av. de la Independencia, Nuevo Vedado, ☎ 7/881–9700) is the only game in town.

SHOPPING

Until very recently, shopping lists in Cuba were short: *puros habanos* (cigars) and rum. Since the Cuban government's decision to permit the free circulation of the U.S. dollar as legal tender, things have changed somewhat—such international chain stores as Benetton have even opened.

Look for *muñequitas,* little dolls representing orishas. Handmade goods—from wood and leather items to terra-cotta pieces—cinema posters and other graphics, musical instruments, and photographs from the Revolutionary period also make interesting buys. The light-cotton men's shirt known as the *guayabera* is Cuba's national garment, worn by everyone from taxi drivers to El Comandante himself. Practical (side pockets) and elegant (embroidered), the guayabera is worn loose (not tucked in) for coolness, and is considered flattering to middle-age figures.

The state agencies ARTEX and Fondo de Bienes Culturales have shops throughout Havana that sell postcards, books, CD's, cassettes, rum, cigars, and crafts. *La Habana: Touristic and Commercial Guide,* a booklet published by Infotur, lists the locations of the city's many Tiendas Panamericanas, which sell toiletries and other basic items.

Bargaining is expected, but unlike shopkeepers in other countries where this is true, Cubans ask very low prices to begin with and don't move far. It generally feels better to pay the extra dollar or two. At this juncture, it means a lot more in Cuban hands than in yours.

Note: owing to the trade embargo, if you're caught bringing Cuban goods into the United States, customs could confiscate them, and you could be subject to penalties. Even Americans who are visiting Cuba with either a general or specific license or on a fully hosted basis are subject to strict limitations on the total amount they're allowed to spend daily—for hotels, meals, transportation, and Cuban goods—and customs officials may ask to see receipts. For more information, *see* Americans and Cuba *in* Smart Travel Tips A to Z.

Areas and Markets

The Plaza de Armas, the Plaza de la Catedral, and the Plaza Vieja are rich in shops and vendors selling crafts. The excellent and eclectic **Mercado de Arte y de Artesanía la Ataraya** (Av. 1, e/Av. D y Av. E, Vedado) on the Malécon is open every day but Wednesday from 9 AM to dusk. At the end of Calle Empedrado, near the Catedral de la Habana and along the Parque Luz Caballero, is the **Mercado de Arte y de Artesanía de la Catedral** (⊠ Calle Tacón, La Habana Vieja), a street market choked with paintings and crafts. It's open Monday–Saturday 10–7.

Specialty Shops

Cigars

Cuba is, of course, *the* place for cigars. The best leaves are grown here, and the world's most skilled artisans roll them into the finest of stogies. In Havana, a box of Monte Cristo A's sells for $500; the same box costs roughly $700 in Canada and as much as $900 in, say, Belgium. Never buy from the many street *jineteros* (hustlers), whose cigars are invariably of inferior quality but dressed up to look like top Cohibas or Romeo y Julietas.

The many locations of the ubiquitous tobacco emporium, **Casa del Tabaco** (⊠ Av. 5, No. 1407, Miramar, ☎ 7/209–4040; ⊠ Calle Obispo, esquina de Calle Bernaza, La Habana Vieja, ☎ 7/863–1242; ⊠ Marina Hemingway, Calle 248 y Av. 5, Jaimanitas/Playa, ☎ 7/33–1154), make shopping for tobacco convenient. At the fascinating **Fábrica de Tabacos Partagás** (⊠ Calle Industria 520, Centro, ☎ 7/33–8060), also known as the Casa del Habano, you can see how cigars are made by hand as well as shop for them. Note, however, that the tobacco sold here can be found elsewhere at better prices. The **Palacio del Tabaco** (⊠ Calle Agramonte/Zulueta 106, La Habana Vieja, ☎ 7/862–0001) is another good bet for cigars.

Clothing

For guayaberas, check out hotel shops, open-air markets, and Cuban department stores (which price things in pesos, though they accept dollars) along Calle San Rafael or Avenida de Italia (Galiano) in Vedado.

Acuario (⊠ Calle San Rafael 102, Centro, ☎ 7/33–8431) has a good selection of guayaberas. For women's clothing, including lovely dresses by Verano, as well as guayaberas with the coveted Pepe Antonio label, head for **La Flora** (⊠ Av. 11, esquina de Calle 6, Mindanao, ☎ 7/202–3522). At **Quitrín** (⊠ Calle Obispo, esquina de San Ignacio, La Habana Vieja, ☎ 7/862–0810) off-the-rack guayaberas sell for $40, and tailor-made ones cost up to $45.

At **La Maison** (⊠ Calle 16, No. 701, esquina de Av. 7, Miramar, ☎ 7/204–1541) the evening fashion shows will knock your eyes out—more for the human display than for the textiles—and the luxury clothing is on sale duty free. The guayaberas here are the cheapest you'll find anywhere. **Salon Galiano** (⊠ Av. de Italia/Galiano 480, Centro, ☎ 7/863–1861) has a good guayabera stock.

Graphics

Centro del Desarollo de los Artes Visuales (⊠ Casa de las Hermanas Cárdenas, Plaza Vieja, La Habana Vieja, ☎ 7/862–3533) sells posters and art books. In the Casa de Juan Rico de Mata, **Fototeca de Cuba** (⊠ Plaza Vieja, Calle Mercaderes 307, La Habana Vieja, ☎ 7/862–2876) purveys photographs from the Revolutionary period. **Galería Exposición** (⊠ Manzana de Gómez, Calle San Rafael, Centro, ☎ 7/863–8364) has prints by Cuba's best artists, and famous Revolutionary pictures and posters.

Handicrafts

In the Plaza Vieja, behind the facade with the murals, is the **Casa del Conde de Lombillo** (⊠ Calle San Ignacio 364, La Habana Vieja, ☎ 7/33–1884), where you can watch artisans make muñequitas. **La Casona** (⊠ Plaza Vieja, Calle San Ignacio y Calle Muralla, La Habana Vieja, ☎ 7/33–8005) sells a variety of crafts. For tobacco, rum, Cuban music, and all manner of crafts, don't miss the **Palacio de la Artesanía** (⊠ Calle de Cuba 10, La Habana Vieja, ☎ 7/33–8072). In addition, the colonial architecture here is superb, and the mojitos are first-rate.

Rum

You'll find rum in the Casas del Ron at tourist attractions all over town—from the Castillo de la Real Fuerza to El Morro across the bay. The **Taverna del Galeón** (⊠ Calle Baratillo, esquina de Calle Obispo, La Habana Vieja, ☎ 7/33–8476), at the eastern corner of Plaza de Armas, offers free tastings of everything from Pinar del Río's Guayabito to Caribbean Club's Ron Mulata. La Taverna stocks Cuban rums of every description and even "Cuban" wines such as the dry white San Cristóbal made by Italian oenologists from Chilean grapes.

Musical Instruments

Longina (⊠ Calle Obispo 360, La Habana Vieja, ☎ 7/862–8371) sells an excellent selection of music and Cuban musical instruments. Music and musical instruments can be purchased at the **Casa de la Música** (⊠ Calle 20, No. 3309, Vedado, ☎ 7/204–0447). As its name suggests, the **Musica e Instrumentos Musicales** (⊠ Calle 18, No. 509, Vedado, ☎ 7/204–1212) sells music and instruments.

HAVANA A TO Z

To research prices, get advice from other travelers, and book travel arrangements, visit www.fodors.com.

ADDRESSES

The streets in La Habana Vieja and Centro have been, in European fashion, given such poetic names as Amargura (Bitterness), Esperanza (Hope), or Ánimas (Souls). Note that some streets have pre- and postrevolutionary names; both are often cited on maps and in this chapter. The Vedado and Miramar districts have a New York City–style grid plan with intersecting numbered and lettered streets and avenues. As the scheme of lettering and numbering varies in these two areas, addresses routinely include district names to help avoid confusion. Throughout the city, addresses are also frequently cited as street names with numbers and/or locations, as in: "Calle Concordia, e/Calle Gervasio y Calle Escobar" or "Calle de los Oficios 53, esquina de Obrapía." It's helpful to know the following terms and abbreviations: "e/" is *entre* (between); *esquina de* (sometimes seen as "esq. de") is "corner of"; and *y* is "and."

AIR TRAVEL

AIRPORTS

The Aeropuerto Internacional José Martí is a modern glass and steel facility 17 km (10 mi) south of Havana (via the Plaza de la Revolución and Avenida de la Independencia/Avenida Rancho Boyeros). The nearby Terminal Aerocaribbean serves domestic flights and those throughout the Caribbean. The Aeropuerto Nacional, 1 km (½ mi) south of the international airport, serves domestic flights only.

➤ AIRPORT INFORMATION: **Aeropuerto Internacional José Martí** (☎ 7/33–5666, 7/266–3133, or 7/266–4644). **Aeropuerto Nacional** (☎ 7/45–1853). **Terminal Aerocaribbean** (☎ 7/45–3013).

CARRIERS

Principal international carriers serving José Martí include Aerocaribbean, Aeroflot, Air France, Cubana de Aviación, Iberia, and Mexicana.

➤ AIRLINES: **Aerocaribbean** (☎ 7/33–5520). **Aeroflot** (☎ 7/33–5432). **Air France** (☎ 7/66–2644). **Cubana de Aviación** (☎ 7/33–4949). **Iberia** (☎ 7/33–5041). **Mexicana** (☎ 7/33–3531).

TRANSFERS

Taxis or rental cars are currently the only means of transport to and from the airports. The fare from either airport to town is about $20.

BOAT AND FERRY TRAVEL

The *lanchita de Regla* is a little launch that crosses the harbor to the town of Regla. For 20¢ each way, you get a ride across the bay and a walk through one of Havana's most interesting neighborhoods. Try to travel during nonpeak hours; during rush hours the crush on the ferry can be as bad as on a bus. Also, opt for a spot by the door, for air and the views. The boat departs from the dock at the harbor end of Calle Luz every 30 minutes.

BUS TRAVEL

Havana's famous *camellos* (so-named for their humped, camel-like shape) are little more than huge tractor trailers. Lines for these 300-passenger buses are often hundreds of people long, folks are packed onto them like sardines in a can, and onboard temperatures are all but life-threatening. In addition, you need exact change (10 céntimos) to board, and most Cubans tell tales (no doubt true) of pickpockets and lost watches and jewelry. If, however, you want to experience Cuba the way Cubans do, by all means, hop a camello. The *omnibus,* a smaller local bus, is another a good way to get either crushed or to work up a major sweat. For bus travel to other parts of the island, contact the bus company Víazul.

➤ BUS INFORMATION: **Víazul** (⊠ Calle 26 y Av. Zoológico, Nuevo Vedado, ☎ 7/881–1108).

CAR RENTAL

Car rentals in Cuba are expensive ($500–$600 a week), and the car you reserve may or may not be available when you arrive to pick it up. Be prepared to leave a deposit of $500 or more. Reliable agencies include: Cubacar, which has offices in the Hotel Meliá Cohiba and other major hotels; Havanautos, which has offices at the airport and major hotels; Panautos, which has offices all over Havana; Transautos, which has an office in the Hotel Capri; and Transgaviota, which rents cars with or without a driver.

➤ LOCAL AGENCIES: **Cubacar** (⊠ Calle 1, esquina de Av. 64, Vedado, ☎ 7/33–2277). **Havanautos** (⊠ Aeropuerto José Martí ☎ 7/33–5215 to Terminal 2, 7/330–5197 to Terminal 3). **Panautos** (⊠ Calle Línea/Calle 7 y Malecón, Vedado, ☎ 7/55–3255). **Transautos** (⊠ Hotel Capri, Calle 21, e/Calle N y Calle O, Vedado ☎ 7/33–4038). **Transgaviota** (⊠ Av. del Puerto/Calle Desamparado/San Pedro 102, La Habana Vieja, ☎ 7/33–0742).

CAR TRAVEL

Driving in Havana and its environs isn't as daunting as you might think; there are relatively few cars on the roads, and most drivers are aren't overly aggressive. Remain alert and flexible and watch out for bicycles, ciclo-taxis, and coco-taxis—not to mention pedestrians looking for *botellas* (rides). Road surfaces are uneven, so if you drive, keep your eyes glued to the pavement. Cubans beep their horns often, though rarely in a belligerent way; this is a courteous way to let other drivers know you're coming through.

To travel from Havana to Cojímar, Playas del Este, Matanzas, and eastern Cuba take the tunnel under the harbor over to the Vía Monumental and proceed due east to the Vía Blanca. To reach Pinar del Río (west), pick up Avenida de la Independencia (Rancho Boyeros) at the Plaza de la Revolución and follow it south to the Autopista Central. Turns are marked, but only once. Outside of Havana expect few road markings. Get the best map you can, and be prepared to ask for directions.

Cubalse—which owns gas stations and tow trucks—is the company to call when you need a tow. You could also try for a tow truck from the Municipal Ciudad de la Habana.

➤ CONTACTS: **Cubalse** (☎ 7/33–6558). **Municipal Ciudad de la Habana** (☎ 7/40–3793).

GASOLINE

Gasoline prices are about double those in North America (though probably comparable to those in the United Kingdom). Other chains include Cupet-Cemex (Cuba-Petroleo) and Oro Negro.

➤ SERVICE STATIONS: **Cupet-Cimex** (✉ Calle Paseo y Malecón, Vedado, ☎ 7/33–3027; ✉ Calle L y Calle 17, Vedado, ☎ 7/33–4587; ✉ Calle 31 y Calle 18, Miramar, ☎ 7/204–0520; ✉ Calle 41 y Calle 72, Mindanao, ☎ 7/33–4587). **Oro Negro** (✉ Av. 7 y Calle 2, Miramar, ☎ 7/204–1906; ✉ Av. 5 y Calle 120, Coco Solo, ☎ 7/33–6149; ✉ Av. 13 y Calle 84, Almendares, ☎ 7/204–1938).

PARKING

Parking isn't generally a problem in Havana as there are still relatively few automobiles circulating. Even around Plaza de las Armas or Plaza de San Francisco de Asís it's usually possible to find parking places. You will, however, encounter freelance parking attendants who will keep an eye on your car for a dollar up front, a bargain automobile security system.

EMBASSIES

Americans in serious trouble can contact the U.S. Special Interests Section, although given its mission in Cuba (to protect U.S. interests, not U.S. citizens flouting the embargo), don't expect them to roll out the carpet. Of course, all of this may change in the near future.

➤ CANADA: **Canada** (✉ Calle 30, No. 518, Miramar, ☎ 7/204–2517 or 7/204–2516).

➤ UNITED KINGDOM: **United Kingdom** (✉ Calle 34, Nos. 702–704, Miramar, ☎ 7/204–1771 or 7/204–1772).

➤ UNITED STATES: **U.S. Special Interests Section** (✉ Calzada, e/Calle L y Calle M, Vedado, ☎ 7/33–3551 or 7/33–4401).

EMERGENCIES

The Clinica Central de Atención a Extranjeros Cira García, just across the Río Almendares and in a district near Miramar, is dedicated to medical care for foreigners. Considered the best hospital in Havana, the clinic handles emergencies expertly and pleasantly and expects payment in dollars. Servimed Internacional, part of the Clinica Cira García, is the pharmacy to use; it's open 24 hours a day.

Asistur specializes in helping tourists in trouble. Its staff can handle anything from insurance claims and lost luggage to repatriation of the deceased.

➤ CONTACTS: **Ambulance** (☎ 7/40–5093). **Asistur** (✉ Paseo de Martí/Prado 254, Centro, ☎ 7/862–5519). **Clinica Central de Atención a Extranjeros Cira García** (✉ Calle 20, No. 4101, Mindanao, ☎ 7/204–2811). **Fire** (☎ 115). **Police** (☎ 116). **Servimed Internacional** (✉ Av. 41, esquina de Calle 20, Mindanao, ☎ 7/204–2051).

HEALTH

Locals call the *almacigo* tree the "tourist tree" owing to its red, peeling bark (and its bulging trunk), a nod to Cuba's greatest health risk: the Caribbean sun. Use plenty of sunscreen. Make sure that fruit is thoroughly washed and/or peeled before eating it. Although Cuban lobsters are beyond reproach, clams and mussels are suspect. Bottled water is a good idea in Havana and elsewhere on the island.

Cuban physicians are well trained and numerous. Though health care is free for Cubans, visitors are required to pay (in dollars) for medicines and services.

Official figures on AIDS place Cuba among the world's least affected countries, but the recent boom in sexual tourism and prostitution makes Cuba a potential high-risk zone. Bring your own protection; Cuba's Chinese-made condoms are notoriously crude and cumbersome, and higher-quality imported condoms are sold at extortionist prices.

MAIL AND SHIPPING
Letters and postcards to North America and Europe cost less than $1. Most hotels have letter boxes and sell stamps, as post offices are scarce. The best one is in La Habana Vieja's Plaza de San Francisco de Asís. In Vedado there's one at the corner of Calle 23 (La Rampa) and Calle 12. At this writting, letters were known to take three to four weeks to reach destinations outside Cuba. In Havana, DHL is the company to turn to for fast, efficient deliveries.
➤ COURIER SERVICES: **DHL** (✉ Calle 26, esquina de Av. 1, Miramar, ☎ 7/204–1578 or 7/204–1876).

MONEY MATTERS
CURRENCY EXCHANGE
Automatic teller machines (ATMs) are your best bet for currency exchange, conveniently generating convertible pesos provided you have a non-U.S. credit card. The airport has ATMs. For in-town currency transactions, the Hotel Nacional has a money exchange office that handles travelers checks, credit cards, and currency quickly and flawlessly. The Banco Popular de Ahorro has ATMs in Vedado at Calle 23 y Calle J, Calle 23 y Calle Montero Sánchez, and Calle 23 y Calle P. In La Habana Vieja, look for ATMs at Calle de Cuba y Calle O'Reilly, Calle de Cuba y Calle Brasil (Teniente Rey), Calle Amargura y Calle Mercaderes, and Calle O'Reilly y Calle Compostela.

REST ROOMS
The most reliable rest rooms are in good hotels. No one minds if you choose to use one and you're not a guest of the hotel.

SAFETY
Muggings and petty crime are rare in Cuba, though not unheard-of. Although official policies have eased up on the persecution of gays and lesbians, same-sex couples should still be discreet in public.

LOCAL SCAMS
La lechera (the milk lady) works the Parque Central and across from El Floridita with consummate aplomb. She rushes up to you—and bear in mind that you may be giddy from a frozen daiquirí or two—and asks you to buy milk for her child, claiming that she's a *maestra* (a schoolteacher). When you agree to help out (who could say no?), she escorts you to a dollar store across the way, where it becomes apparent that the milk—*lots* of it—is all packaged up and ready to go. As la lechera disappears around the corner with her milk (almost certainly headed for the store's back door to collect her cut from the ruse), you learn that you're $29.50 in debt. Just say no; it's not about milk.

WOMEN IN HAVANA
Women traveling alone can expect to get plenty of attention, though no dangerous hassling. Even so, walking alone through unlit Centro Habana would be a bad idea.

TAXIS

Taxis, which have meters, are inexpensive by European or North American standards. You can grab them from in front of hotels (though be prepared for price gouging from these cabbies more than others), hail them on the streets, or call them. Official taxis are often Hyundais, Mercedes, or Russian-made Ladas. Around Parque Central you may still find American-made 1950s vehicles. *Cuentapropistas* (privateers) offer their services everywhere, especially along Calle 23 (La Rampa) in Vedado. Ciclo-taxis (bicycle rickshaws) are breezy, slow, offer a scenic ride, and cost about the same as auto taxis. Coco-taxis (motor scooter–powered conveyances) are another option. Always negotiate the price or make sure the meter is on before you get in any type of cab. The fare from Vedado to La Habana Vieja is about $5; from Miramar it's about $8.

➤ LOCAL COMPANIES: **Fenix** (☎ 7/863–9720). **Gaviota** (☎ 7/33–1730). **Micar** (☎ 7/204–2444). **Panataxi** (☎ 7/55–5555). **Taxis OK** (☎ 7/204–9518). **Transgaviota** (☎ 7/267–2727). **Transtur** (☎ 7/33–5543). **Turistaxi** (☎ 7/33–5539).

TELEPHONES

The area code for Havana is 7. Plan to have some problems communicating electronically with the outside world during your stay in Cuba. Direct-dial phones work well in most hotel rooms, but the rates are beyond scandalous (around $10 per minute for international calls). The cheapest way to make local and long-distance calls is from public phone booths, using a prepaid $10 or $20 phone card. You can buy them in hotels, tourist shops, and at the Intertel booths around town (there's one at the corner of Calle 23/La Rampa and Calle N in Vedado, about midway between the Hotel Habana Libre and the Hotel Nacional).

TOURS

Cubatur, one of Cuba's top travel agencies, has very professional staffs, who can help you make arrangements for anything from a guided tour to a table at the Tropicana. The agency's office in the Hotel Nacional is a good place to know about. Havanatur, an agency with offices in many of Havana's top hotels, can arrange cultural and ecological tours as well as excursions to beaches. The staff does it all—from car rentals to plane tickets. Paradiso is a small company that offers cultural tours and guided excursions of all kinds. Other agencies include Amistur, Cubanacán, and Rumbos.

The Vaivén is a tourist bus (with a guide) that passes Havana's most important sights, from El Morro to the Palacio de Convenciones. It circulates every 35 minutes, has 23 stops (including the Hotel Nacional, the Hotel Habana Libre, El Capitolio, and the Necrópolis de Cristóbal Colón), and operates 8:45 AM–10 PM. You can buy tickets at Rumbos agencies.

➤ TOUR CONTACTS: **Amistur Cuba** (✉ Calle Paseo, 406, e/Calle 17 y Calle 19, Vedado, ☎ 7/66–2374). **Cubanacán** (✉ Calle 146 y Calle 9, Miramar, ☎ 7/208–6044). **Cubatur** (✉ Calle F, No. 157, e/Calle 9 y Calzada, Vedado, ☎ 7/33–4155). **Havanatur** (✉ Calle 2, No. 17, e/Av. 1 y Av. 3, Miramar, ☎ 7/204–2161). **Paradiso** (✉ Calle 19, No. 560, esquina de Calle C, Vedado, ☎ 7/832–9538). **Rumbos** (✉ Calle 23/La Rampa y Calle P, Vedado, ☎ 7/33–4634 or 7/66–9713 for Vaivén bus information).

VISITOR INFORMATION

Cuba Autrement can recommend lodging in private homes and provide cultural and general information. Infotur has several convenient locations. It's a little far from the center of town, but the Oficina de

Turismo de La Habana/El Palacio del Turismo is a good place to get your bearings. Although Roots & Culture caters primarily to French tourists, the staff is eager to advise visitors from anywhere on private lodging options, paladares, and cultural events.

➤ Tourist Information: **Cuba Autrement** (✉ Lonja del Comercio, Plaza de San Francisco de Asís, La Habana Vieja, ☎ 7/66–9874). **Infotur** (✉ Calle Obispo 63, esquina de Calle San Ignacio, La Habana Vieja, ☎ 7/863–6884; (✉ Calle Obispo 521, e/Calle Bernaza y Calle Villegas, La Habana Vieja, ☎ 7/33–3333; ✉ Av. 5 y Calle 112, Miramar, ☎ 7/204–7036); (✉ Av. Las Terrazas, e/Calle 10 y Calle 11, Playas del Este, ☎ 7/96–1111). **Oficina de Turismo de La Habana/El Palacio del Turismo** (✉ Calle 28, No. 303, e/Av. 3 y Av. 5, Miramar, ☎ 7/204–0624). **Roots & Culture** (✉ Hotel Colina, Calle L, No. 502, esquina de Calle 27, Vedado, ☎ 7/55–4005).

3 WESTERN CUBA

From the remote strands of María la Gorda
to Varadero's smooth white beaches;
from the southern Archipiélago de los
Canarreos to the vertebral Cordillera de
Guaniguanico—western Cuba holds a wide
range of geographical treasures. The Valle
de Viñales and its limestone hillocks, Vuelta
Abajo and its tobacco plantations, and the
wetlands of the Península de Zapata are
quintessential Cuban destinations.

By George
Semler

W **ESTERN CUBA'S THREE PROVINCES** of Matanzas, Havana (outside the capital), and Pinar del Río, along with the Municipio Especial (Special Municipality) Isla de la Juventud, offer attractions that range from the tobacco plantations of Viñales to the cosmopolitan beaches of Varadero to the wilds of crocodile country on the Península de Zapata. In addition, pristine beaches and nonpareil diving opportunities can be found off—among other spots—Cayo Levisa, the Península de Guanahacabibes, and Cayo Largo.

En route west to Pinar del Río Province, the province of Havana offers little in the way of distraction. Pinar del Río is Cuba's prime tobacco-growing country; there's a cigar-rolling factory to visit and numerous plantations to explore. The Valle de Viñales (Viñales Valley) and the curious *mogotes* (hillocks) form some of Cuba's most spectacular countryside. These freestanding limestone formations from the Jurassic era are surrounded by *hoyos* (holes), valleys or depressions filled with rich red soil ideal for the cultivation of tobacco. Far to the west, the Península de Guanahacabibes is a UNESCO-classified nature preserve on the Straits of Yucatán and a haven for nearly every kind of wildlife in the Antilles.

Matanzas Province stretches east and south of its eponymous capital city, traditionally dubbed the "Athens of Cuba" for its artistic and literary prestige. Just west of the city, the Valle de Yumurí, drained by the Río Yumurí (Yumurí River), is a rich basin of sugarcane plantations surrounded by rolling hills. To the east of the city is Cuba's premier beach resort—Varadero, a sandy paradise studded with hotels. On the slender Península de Hicacos, Varadero has two yacht marinas, a golf course, several discotheques and cabarets, and miles of silver sands. The town of Cárdenas, just east of Varadero, is known for its horse-drawn carriages. The Península de Zapata is an ornithologist's and bonefisherman's paradise, while the eastern coastline offers sandy beaches, limestone sinkholes filled with brightly colored fish, and Playa Girón.

The Isla de la Juventud is the largest island in the Archipiélago de los Canarreos, south of the Cuban mainland. Known for the diving off Punta Francés, the former Isle of Pines is the site of the Presidio Modelo (Model Jail), where Castro penned his famous "La Historia me Absolverá" speech and spent 18 months for his part in the Moncada attack.

Pleasures and Pastimes

Beaches
The beaches throughout Matanzas, Havana, and Pinar del Río provinces and in the Archipiélago de Canarreos vary from virtual outdoor discotheques to vast strands all but devoid of human life. Varadero has gorgeous but well-populated beaches; Cayo Levisa, Playa María la Gorda, and the Isla de la Juventud's Playa Larga are among the wildest. Cayo Coco is nearly all white-sand beach.

Dining
Dining in the provincial capitals and towns is spotty; some places are acceptable while others seem fortunate to be able to provide nourishment at all. Pinar del Río and Cárdenas, for example, have no acceptable restaurants. Varadero has several good Italian, Chinese, criollo, and international options, though buffets in hotels tend to be mediocre. Look for local staples, such as crocodile tail (said to be an aphrodisiac) at Guamá, roast pork on the Isla de la Juventud, and lobster at María la Gorda.

Reservations aren't necessary, except in Varadero—especially at the Mansión Xanadú and Antigüedades. Tipping is important to Cubans; an extra dollar here or there is much appreciated. Credit cards *not* affiliated with U.S. banks or companies are accepted in most government restaurants and hotels, though never in *paladares* (privately owned restaurants). For price categories, *see* the chart *under* Dining *in* Smart Travel Tips A to Z.

Lodging

There are luxury hotels in Varadero and Cayo Largo, charming hotels around Viñales, modern accommodations at María la Gorda, and ecologically engineered hotels in the reserve around Soroa. Lodging on the Península de Zapata ranges from the simple farm *bohíos* (thatch-roof cabins) at the Batey de Pedro to the fading beach hotels around Playa Girón. In towns and cities outside Havana, rooms are available in *casas particulares* (private houses), though quarters may be cramped. Nearly all government-operated hotels take credit cards *not* affiliated with U.S. banks or companies. For price categories, *see* the chart *under* Lodging *in* Smart Travel Tips A to Z.

Scuba Diving and Snorkeling

Cuba is gaining recognition as one of the Caribbean's great diving and snorkeling destinations, with sunken Spanish galleons to explore as well as such aquatic life that includes 900 species—from rays and barracudas to triggerfish. The diving on the south coast is considered better than that on the north coast, although the latter also has some excellent spots, particularly along the 40-km-long (25-mi-long) reef off Santa Lucía. Other top destinations include the Archipiélago de los Colorados to the north at Cayo Levisa, the Isla de la Juventud to the south, and María la Gorda at the island's western tip.

Exploring Western Cuba

Caves, beaches, mountain waterfalls, underwater reefs and galleons, and flora and fauna—from hummingbirds to whale sharks—are all present in western Cuba. Pinar del Río's *vegas* (tobacco fields), the mogotes of Viñales, the Robinson Crusoe-esque simplicity of Cayo Levisa's virgin beaches, the faded glory of the city of Matanzas, and Varadero's long strand are all worlds unto themselves. The swampy Península de Zapata, with its crabs and crocodiles, and the dive sites near María la Gorda and the Isla de la Juventud offer even more variety.

Numbers in the text correspond to numbers in the margin and the Western Cuba map.

Great Itineraries

IF YOU HAVE 3 DAYS

Head west to **Pinar del Río** ④, stopping briefly at the cigar factory for a look at this unique Cuban craft. Continue on to the ☒ **Valle de Viñales** ② for a night at the Hotel Los Jazmines. The next day, after exploring the caves and tobacco fields around Viñales, take the scenic northern coastal route from **Cayo Levisa** ③ back to Havana or drive through Pinar del Río along the central Autopista Nacional, with a lunch stop at the Hotel Moka near the biosphere reserve of ☒ **Soroa** ①. On day three drive through **Matanzas** ⑩, stopping to see the town center, to **Varadero** ⑪ for an evening *mojito* (a Cuban cocktail of rum, mint, sugar, and soda) at the Mansión Xanadú, the old du Pont mansion.

IF YOU HAVE 5 DAYS

Follow the first day of the itinerary above. On the second day, after exploring the caves and the tobacco fields around Viñales, follow the northern shore from **Cayo Levisa** ③ through the tiny port of Santa Lucía and the town of Mantua to ⚇ **María la Gorda** ⑥ for a night at Villa María la Gorda on the Bahía de Corrientes. On the third day, after exploring (if you get the required permit and start early enough) the Península de Guanahacabibes, drive back through the Vuelta Abajo tobacco country around **San Juan y Martínez** ⑤, stopping at San Luis to visit the Robaina vega. Continue through Pinar del Río along the central Autopista Nacional and spend a night at the Hotel Moka near ⚇ **Soroa** ①. On the fourth day, drive east past Havana for a stop at **Matanzas** ⑩ and on to **Varadero** ⑪ for an evening mojito at the Mansión Xanadú, the old du Pont mansion. Spend the fifth morning on the beach before exploring **Cárdenas** ⑫ on the way to the **Península de Zapata** ⑬ and **Playa Girón** ⑭.

When to Tour Western Cuba

La Seca is the February to April dry period in Cuba's western and central zones; with temperatures down to 25°–27°C (77°–81°F) and rains scarce, this is a good time to go. Peak vacation times in spots such as Cayo Largo and Varadero fall during Christmas and Easter breaks, when package-tour groups fly in from all over the world. If wild parties are what you're looking for, this is the time to come. If not, visit in November, early December, or early May. Reserve early for Easter and Christmas.

PINAR DEL RÍO PROVINCE

Settled during the early 18th century (relatively late in the Spanish colonial era) and dubbed La Cenicienta, or Cinderella, for its reputation as a newcomer and for its poverty and good-heartedness, the province forms either the head of the crocodile or the tail of the shark, depending on which view of the Cuban mainland's shape you prefer. Once the home of the Guanahatabey aboriginal people, the region was taken over by the Ciboney in their flight from the Taíno civilization that dominated until the arrival of the Spanish.

Tobacco, sugar, and coffee plantations have been rival influences in what traditionally has been one of Cuba's most backward regions. Famous as the producer of the world's finest tobacco leaves, the typical *pinareño* (native of Pinar del Río) is the straw-hatted, oxen-driving *guajiro* (peasant) with a drooping mustache and a home-rolled cigar clenched between his teeth. Pinareños are known as noble and simple citizens with an extraordinary capacity for hard work and generosity. Be prepared to be invited into homes for anything from sweet black coffee to black beans and rice.

The province's spine is the Cordillera de Guaniguanico, a mountain range divided by the Río San Diego into the western Sierra de los Órganos and the eastern Sierra del Rosario, with its highest point at Pan de Guajaibón. The Valle de Viñales is Pinar del Río's most scenic tobacco country, but the best leaves are grown in Vuelta Abajo (literally, "turn down"—so called, according to one theory, for its location southwest of the provincial capital). In addition to Vuelta Abajo's tobacco farms, the pine-forested mountain retreat around Las Terrazas and Soroa, the hillocked Valle de Viñales, the beaches at María la Gorda, and the nature preserve on the Península de Guanahacabibes are the province's main attractions.

Soroa and Environs

❶ *75 km (47 mi) southwest of Havana.*

Known for its orchid garden and its 30-m (99-ft) waterfall, El Salto, Soroa has been dubbed "the Rainbow of Cuba" for the rainbow that

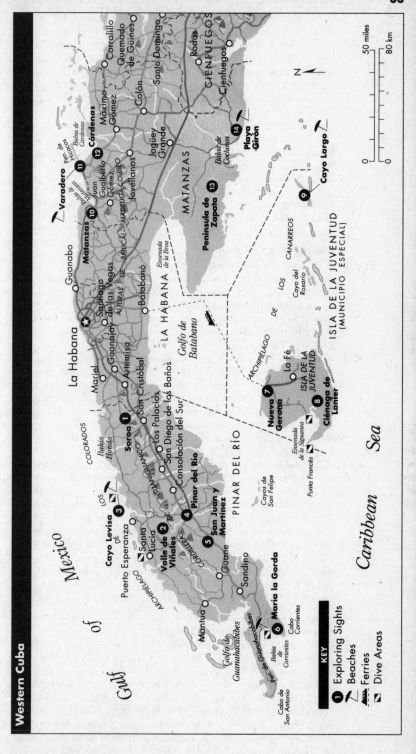

sometimes hovers over the falls. The area is a good place to take a walk in the woods or a tour of the agricultural community of Las Terrazas, 17 km (11 mi) east of Soroa and part of a biosphere reserve established by UNESCO in 1985. You can have lunch or spend a night at the ecological retreat Hotel Moka in Las Terrazas. Named for the terraced forests that were originally carved into the slopes as a coffee plantation, the *terrazas* are now tiers of workers' living quarters. Coming from Havana, you will reach Las Terrazas and the Hotel Moka first, just over the border in Pinar del Río Province. After leaving the Autopista Nacional at the well-marked turnoff at Km 51, pass through the toll gate 4 km (2½ mi) north and continue into the park, which originally was used as coffee plantations by French settlers who had come from Haiti at the end of the 18th century. Soroa can be reached via the mountain road through the reserve or from the autopista turnoff at Km 80. Guided tours of Soroa's orchid garden, the **Orquideario Soroa** (☎ 82/78–555 to Soroa nature park) are available 10–5:30 daily, except Fridays, and cost $3 (not including tips for tour guides).

Dining and Lodging

$ ✗ **El Castillo de las Nubes.** Overlooking the village of Soroa and the palm-canopied valley, this restaurant—appropriately christened Castle in the Clouds—occupies an unusual Spanish-style stone structure. It specializes in Cuban chicken and meat dishes, but the views far outshine the fare; on clear days you can see the Isla de la Juventud more than 100 km (62 mi) to the south. ⊠ *Soroa–Autopista Rd., Soroa,* ☎ *85/1531. No credit cards.*

¢–$ ✗ **El Salto.** Named for the *salto* (waterfall) in a nearby river, this little cluster of tables under a roof supported by the branches of *palmas barrigonas* (pot-bellied palms) specializes in simple Cuban fare featuring chicken. There's always a good trio playing bolero and *son* (a versatile dance rhythm that originated in the eastern cities). The house drink, the daiquirí *cascada,* is made of various colors of alcohol, in honor of Soroa's nickname, Rainbow of Cuba. ⊠ *Carretera de Soroa, Km 8, Candelaria.* ☎ *85/2122. No credit cards.*

$–$$ ✗🏠 **Hotel Moka.** The fine restaurant, the ecological theme, and the
★   comfortable all-but-outdoor rooms with floor-to-ceiling glass doors that lead to terraces make this hotel worth seeking out. An immense tree stands in the reception area, escaping overhead through four skylights. The bar and restaurant ($–$$) seem suspended over the valley's edge. The *aporreado de res* (shredded beef in *criollo,* or creole, sauce) and the *masas de cerdo* (pork fillets) are excellent, as is the specialty *pargo relleno de camarones* (red snapper stuffed with shrimp). The wine list is respectable, if pricey compared to the alternative: the light lager Cristal. ⊠ *Las Terrazas,* ☎ *85/827–8600 or 7/24–3739 and 7/24–3740 in Havana,* FAX *85/827–8605. 27 rooms. Restaurant, bar, pool, free parking. MC, V.*

Outdoor Activities and Sports

Exploring the Sierra del Rosario can provide a day or two of exercise and fresh air. Guides are available for nature hikes ($3 per hour per person, three people maximum). From Las Terrazas, the trails called La Delicias and La Serafina are the two most beautiful, each about 4 km (2½ mi) or two hours long. El Salto, the waterfall, is accessed from Soroa via a concrete stairway leading down from the well-marked Bar Edén. The so-called Baños Romanos (Roman Baths) are below the falls. You can hire hiking guides in Las Terrazas at **Hotel Moka** (☎ 85/827–8600). To arrange guided hikes in Soroa, contact the **Villa Soroa** (⊠ Carretera de Soroa, Km 8, Candelaria, ☎ 85/2111).

Shopping

The Las Terrazas **community center** has several crafts stores to visit. In the center's **Taller de Alberto**, handcrafted hardwood spoons and ladles are the specialty. At the **Taller de Fibras**, a women's cooperative, you can buy straw hats, baskets, and other handicrafts. There are also several artists' studios with works generally related to natural themes.

Valle de Viñales

❷ *212 km (131 mi) southwest of Havana, 137 km (82 mi) west of Soroa, 26 km (16 mi) north of Pinar del Río.*

The valley is justly ranked among Cuba's most beautiful landscapes, an expanse of lush green studded with the famous mogotes—freestanding, flat-topped, sheer-sided rock formations. Don't fail to stop at the Hotel Los Jazmines for a breathtaking view over the valley; immense mogotes tower over deep green vegas that stretch into the distance and are backed by the Sierra de los Órganos (so called for the peaks' resemblance to the pipes of an organ). The mogotes are the remains of the limestone *meseta*, or plateau, that rose from the sea some 160 million years ago to form the Cordillera de Guaniguanico. Subsequent erosion left a karstic terrain replete with sinks, ravines, underground streams, and hoyos—rich depressions of red soil ideal for cultivating tobacco. The hidden canyons and natural tunnels leading into them provided shelter for pre-Columbian peoples and later for communities of *cimarrones* (runaway slaves).

The valley's flora includes many unique treasures: the underbrush, ferns, and rare cork palms on the mogotes; the silk-cotton tree, *Ceiba pentandra*; the royal palm; the caiman oak; and the mariposa, Cuba's national flower. Fauna includes the world's smallest hummingbird, the *zunzuncito*, as well as various snails native to the mogotes.

The town of Viñales itself is a national monument, a charming rural collection of small houses shaded by pine trees. The de rigueur José Martí monument in the main square is surrounded by graceful wooden houses. The **Museo Municipal Adela Azcuy** displays objects and photographs on local history, including a bronze bust of Captain Adela Azcuy herself—a top-ranked woman warrior who fought for Cuba's independence. ⊠ *Calle Salvador Cisnero s/n, Viñales,* ☎ *8/1029.* ⊠ *$3.* ☉ *Tues.–Sat. 8–5, Sun. 8–noon.*

La Casa del Veguero, just south of Viñales and well marked, is a typical tobacco farmer's bungalow and drying shed with a restaurant and souvenir store. El Niño, the much-photographed *veguero* (farmer), and his beautiful daughter, La Flaca (the Skinny One), are celebrities here, and their farm seems like the Garden of Eden. **Cuevas de Viñales,** a grotto 4 km (2½ mi) north of Viñales, doubles as a disco and concert venue at night. The 140-m (462-ft) tunnel piercing the mogote opens onto a replica of a cimarron campsite and the outdoor bohío-style restaurant El Palanque de los Cimarrones. The **Cueva del Indio,** about 6 km (4 mi) north of Viñales, is named for the aboriginal Guanahatabey who once lived here. It has a 1½-km (1-mi) underground river, a third of which is illuminated. After a 255-m (842-ft) walk through the high-ceilinged grotto, a small boat takes you another 300 m (990 ft) past stalagmites shaped like a champagne bottle, a skull, a crocodile, a sea horse, and the *Niña, Pinta,* and *Santa María*. Admission to the cave, open daily 9–5, is $3.

At Dos Hermanas Mogote, 5 km (3 mi) west of Viñales, Diego Rivera disciple Leovigildo González (or the 25 farmers he directed) painted the immense **Mural de la Prehistoria**—200×300 m (660×990 ft)—between 1959 and 1962. Commissioned by Fidel Castro, the painting depicts the evolutionary process in the Sierra de los Órganos. Admission is $1; it's open daily 9–5. The on-site restaurant serves a roast pig dish that's worth the trip on its own.

Dining and Lodging

$ ✕ **Casa de Don Tomás.** The excellent local cuisine, the setting inside
★ Viñales's oldest house (circa 1822), and the charming service make this place memorable. And the trio here sings so well it can be hard to swallow because of the lump in your throat. The *delicias de Don Tomás* (a concoction of ham, pork, chicken, lobster, and sausage) is a favorite, as is the *tasajo a lo guajiro* (shredded beef in a criollo sauce). ⊠ *Calle Salvador Cisneros 141, Viñales,* ☎ *8/93–6300. MC, V.*

¢–$ ✕🔲 **Hotel Los Jazmines.** The views from this hotel up the valley through
★ the limestone hillocks of Viñales are spectacular. Rooms are tastefully decorated with rattan furniture and floral prints. The best are in the old part of the hotel, near the pool—an Olympic-size expanse on the edge of a terrace. The restaurant ($$–$$$) is better than average, and the management offers day hikes and excursions throughout western Cuba. ⊠ *Carretera de Viñales, Km 25,* ☎ *8/93–6205 or 7/33–4042 in Havana,* 🆇 *8/93–6069 or 7/33–3722 in Havana. 14 rooms, 16 bungalows. Restaurant, bar, pool, hiking, free parking. MC, V.*

¢ ✕🔲 **La Ermita.** Sunrises and sunsets viewed from this quiet spot are
★ unforgettable. Thousands of roosters crow for a good hour at first light. Riding and hiking excursions around the valley or diving off Cayo Levisa are the main diversions here. The restaurant ($$) serves passable fare (breakfast is excellent), and the staff is attentive. Be sure to take a walk through the dirt roads between La Ermita and the center of Viñales to see how the locals really live. ⊠ *Carretera La Ermita, Km 2,* ☎ *8/ 93–6071,* 🆇 *8/93–6091. 62 rooms. Restaurant, bar, air-conditioning, pool, hiking, horseback riding, free parking,. MC, V.*

Cayo Levisa

❸ *110 km (68 mi) west of Havana, 52 km (32 mi) north of Viñales.*

The Archipiélago de los Colorados that runs along Cuba's northern coast begins at Cayo Paraíso just west of Las Pozas and continues to the island's western tip. Cayo Paraíso was a famous Hemingway haunt, a spot he visited frequently with his fishing boat *El Pilar*. A plaque erected near the wooden dock at Cayo Paraíso by the provincial authorities on the 90th anniversary of his birth immortalizes Hemingway's love for this pristine spot, which, in fact he named (old navigational charts identify it as Cayo Megano).

Cayo Levisa is the next key to the west. Easily visible 5 km (3 mi) offshore, it has 4 km (2 mi) of white-sand beaches along its northern edge and offers excellent diving and snorkeling. Lobsters and black coral are the main aquatic attractions. Cayo Levisa is, at a distance of 140 km (87 mi), the Antilles' closest point to Key West, and for this reason you need a passport to embark. The boat leaves at 11 AM and 6 PM from the coast guard station at Palma Rubia, and leaves Cayo Levisa at 10 AM and 5 PM for the run in to Palma Rubia. Boat fare is $10 per passenger one-way, $19 round-trip, with a cocktail included. To get to the boat landing, turn north off the northern-coast circuit just after the town of Las Cadenas.

Dining and Lodging

¢–$ ✕🔲 **Villa Cayo Levisa.** This simple tourist resort and dive center offers cabins on the beach and a variety of water sports. The restaurant

($) serves passable Cuban specialties, fresh-caught lobster and pargo foremost among them. The bar is a lively spot after hours, and in the true castaway spirit you'll meet all of your fellow guests; Spain and Italy are especially well represented in summer. This is a good place if what you're seeking is a very quiet time. Bring insect repellent. ⊠ *Cayo Levisa,* ☎ *8/66–6075 or 7/33–5030 in Havana,* FAX *7/66–6075. 20 bungalows. Restaurant, bar, air-conditioning, beach, dive shop, dock, snorkeling, surfing, windsurfing, boating, waterskiing, shop. MC, V.*

Pinar del Río

❹ *178 km (110 mi) southwest of Havana, 26 km (16 mi) south of Viñales.*

Named for the stands of pine trees that once shaded the banks of the Río Guamá, this has been Cuba's tobacco city since its first land grants were allocated in 1544. Viñales and Vuelta Abajo were the island's great tobacco plantations, and Pinar del Río prospered as the tobacco market town and manufacturing center, even after the rest of the island turned almost exclusively to the cultivation and export of sugarcane.

Today the city (population 125,000) is distinguished by little more than its cigar factory, a distillery that produces *guayabita* (a brandy-like liqueur made from sugarcane and guava), and its many fluted-columned and pillared porches in pastels that seem to reflect the red soil of the surrounding vegas. Pinar del Río doesn't have the atmosphere of Viñales, but a short layover here would provide a sampling of life in what is probably the most provincial of Cuba's provincial cities, an opportunity to drop in on Cuba au naturel.

The **Fábrica de Tabacos Francisco Donatien** offers a more intimate visit than some of the major Havana cigar factories. You might even hear the *lector* (reader) entertain the cigar rollers with newspaper articles from *Granma* or novels. ⊠ *Calle Antonio Maceo 157,* ☎ *82/77–3424.* ⌑ *$3.* ☉ *Weekdays 7–5, Sat. 8–noon.*

The **Casa del Habano** is the place to buy tobacco, offering a wide selection of products from the $15 machine-made wonders to the $500 Pyramides. Some of the wood-and-leather cigar boxes and cases are also interesting. ⊠ *Calle Antonio Maceo 162,* ☎ *82/77–2244.* ⌑ *$3.* ☉ *Weekdays 7–5, Sat. 8–noon.*

The **Fábrica de Bebidas Guayabita** offers tours and tastes of the traditional rum-and-guava brew flavored with wild berries that grow exclusively in Pinar del Río Province. ⊠ *Calle Isabel Rubio 189,* ☎ *82/77–2966.* ⌑ *$3.* ☉ *Weekdays 9–5.*

Pinar del Río has its own **Museo Histórico Provincial** tracing local history. ⊠ *Calle Martí 58,* ☎ *82/4300.* ⌑ *$3.* ☉ *Mon.–Sat. 9–5, Sun. 9–1.*

Pinar del Río's **Casa de Cultura** is open during concerts and other events, usually in the evening. ⊠ *Calle Máximo Gómez 108,* ☎ *82/77–9923.* ⌑ *$3.*

Dining

$ ✕ **Rumayor.** This Afro-Cuban crafts center, dance venue, and restau-
★ rant just outside of town is highly acclaimed. The decor at the restaurant—which is famed for its pollo *ahumado* (smoked)—is basic bohío style, with wood beams and a cane roof. The bar and cabaret are the city's top nightspots. Keep your eyes peeled for the Arrieta sisters, Irma and Yordanka, two of the best dancers. ⊠ *Carretera Viñales, Km 2,* ☎ *82/63007. MC, V.*

CIGAR SOCIETY

Early chronicles tell us that Taíno Indians were found puffing on twisted bunches of what they called *cohiba* (tobacco) when Christopher Columbus came ashore in early December 1492. Five hundred years later, some 60 million cigars, known as *habanos* or *puros*, are consumed annually worldwide; Cubans are estimated to smoke some 250 million domestically. International journals and magazines such as *Cigar Aficionado* and *European Cigar Cult Journal* keep the faithful informed on every aspect of the Cuban cigar, and conventions such as early 1999's Habanos 2000 bring together eminent cigar lovers, merchants, and producers from around the world.

Tobacco was found to have narcotic or soothing qualities from the start, and became popular in Spain by the late 16th century. By 1717, cigars made with Cuban tobacco were manufactured in Sevilla; the British and French brought the habit home from the Peninsular campaign of the early 19th century. By the middle of that century, tobacco was Cuba's main export, with more than 1,000 cigar factories on the island.

Cigars come in a bewildering range of brands, lengths, widths (ring gauges), and shapes. The Cohiba brand is generally understood to be the best cigar in the world, though Upmann, Partagás, Romeo y Julieta, and Montecristo are among the elite brands. The newest addition to this group, Vegas Robaina, honors nonpareil *veguero* (tobacco grower) Don Alejandro Robaina.

The worldwide fascination with Cuban cigars is difficult to calibrate or comprehend. Every detail of the growing and rolling process is of vital interest to cigar worshipers—from soil composition in the Vuelta Abajo region of Pinar del Río Province and the amount and timing of the rainfall to the training and selection of cigar rollers, or *torcedores,* in the top cigar factories of Havana. Though legend has it that the national treasure was "rolled on the dusky thighs of Cuban maidens," the fact is that, although women sorted the leaves holding the bunches across their laps, only men were employed to roll cigars until after the Revolution.

Ideally, the story of a cigar begins in the *vegas* (fields) of Vuelta Abajo, 200 km (124 mi) southwest of Havana—preferably those of Don Alejandro Robaina, now nearly 80 years old, a veguero whose tobacco leaves have been identified by connoisseurs as the best in the world. Planted in late October and harvested by hand 120 days later, tobacco leaves are hung to dry in sheds for 45 to 60 days. Sorted, selected, and left to ferment for up to three months, they are then fermented again to remove more tar and nicotine before being sent to cigar factories. There the leaves may be left to mature for as long as two years before passing through the factory's six stages: *despalillo* (stripping out veins), *liga* (bunching filler, wrapper, and binder leaves), *galera* (the "galley," where artisans roll the cigars), *escogida* (selecting uniformly colored cigars), *anillado* (placing on of paper rings), and *adorno de caja* (boxing).

Cigar factories are a fundamental part of Cuban life. One of the best to visit is Havana's Partagás factory. It houses hundreds of workers, most of them seated in long rows at old-fashioned wooden school benches in the galera section. When lectors aren't reading to the workers from newspapers or novels, Cuban music soothes and entertains these artisans as they concentrate on their craft, the windows rattling as dozens of singing voices drown out the recording on the crescendos.

San Juan y Martínez

⑤ *23 km (14 mi) southwest of Pinar del Río, 209 km (130 mi) southwest of Havana.*

The finest-quality tobacco leaves come from Vuelta Abajo—the region southwest of Pinar del Río city—thanks to a combination of abundant rainfall throughout the year (except during the growing season). And although the countryside here is relatively drab, it's the mecca *puro* (cigar) purists must visit. Some 80,000 acres of tobacco are planted annually in the province, and the best of it is found around San Luis and San Juan y Martínez.

The main street in San Juan y Martínez is lined with the provincial pastel-color, columned houses. Other than a café or two and the odd paladar, this sleepy tobacco town has little to offer. A visit to a tobacco farm is the main reason for lingering in Vuelta Abajo. Drop in at any plantation and the farmers will show you the crops, techniques, and drying barns, and possibly invite you for lunch.

Vega Robaina. Don Alejandro Robaina has become a celebrity since 1997, when his Vega Robaina cigar label was launched. He credits his acclaimed tobacco leaves to the Atlantic freshness of the Vuelta Abajo microclimate, the limestone soil, and the know-how acquired over six generations. Don Alejando welcomes visitors interested in learning more about the cultivation of tobacco. To find Vega Robaina, take the main road west from Pinar del Río 12 km (7 mi) to the left turn for San Luis. Turn left again 3 km (2 km) later at the VIETNAM HEROICO sign. The next few roads are dirt: take the first left, the first right, the next right at the tiny Iglesia de Dios and continue for a kilometer to a black barn, where a left will take you right up to Don Alejando's place. ⊠ *Calle Antonio Maceo 162,* ☎ *no phone.* ✉ *$5 suggested donation.* ☉ *Mon.–Sat. 9–5.*

María la Gorda

⑥ *123 km (74 mi) southwest of San Juan y Martínez, 150 km (93 mi) southwest of Pinar del Río, 328 km (203 mi) southwest of Havana.*

Named for a voluptuous young woman who was allegedly captured by pirates and returned to this westernmost Cuban point only to set up a brothel, María la Gorda is on the Bahía de Corrientes, 2½ to 3 hours from Pinar del Río over difficult road. The small, quiet beaches and clear water make the trip worthwhile, as does the chance to encounter boar, deer, crocodiles, wildcats—though you're more likely to see Cuba's ubiquitous land-crab population headed for the seashore to lay eggs.

The flat, scrub-forested Península de Guanahacabibes was the final refuge for Cuba's Ciboney aboriginals fleeing first the Taíno Indians and then the Spanish conquerors of the late 15th and 16th centuries. The Bahía de Corrientes has some excellent virgin beaches, and the 90-km-long (56-mi-long), 30-km-wide (19-mi-wide) peninsula is known for certain species of birds found only here—notably, the tiny zunzuncito and the *torcaza*.

At the end of the road from Pinar del Río, the village of La Bajada lies at a junction: the road to the left heads to Playa María la Gorda (14 km/9 mi south), the one to the right takes you into the **Parque Nacional Península de Guanahacabibes** (Villa María la Gorda for information and permits; ⊠ Bahía de Corrientes, ☎ 82/78131). Permits ($10 per person) to enter the park, a UNESCO Biosphere Reserve, must be obtained to clear the military checkpoint at La Bajada. The drive out to

Cuba's western tip at Cabo de San Antonio, 54 km (33 mi) over a rough dirt track, is a long haul to undertake, unless you're eager to explore the wilderness. If you go, a cooler and a few sandwiches are advised.

Dining and Lodging

¢ ✕▥ **Villa María la Gorda.** This crack diving center attracts an interesting clientele, by no means all divers. The cabins and rooms are comfortable, and the restaurant's buffet fare ($$) improves vastly when someone catches a fresh pargo. Frank Cabrera and his dive school organize some of the best dives in the hemisphere—from the beginners' one-day "baptism" ($48) to the 5-day package ($175) to the 20-day program ($560), with equipment rental included. The hotel also serves as bar, disco, and general headquarters for the entire peninsula. Permits for the Parque Nacional Península de Guanahacabibes must be obtained here before driving the 2½ hours out to Cuba's western tip, a gruelling trip over rough roads only recommended for the geographically obsessed. ✉ Bahía de Corrientes, ☎ 82/78131, FAX 82/78077. 40 units. Restaurant, bar, air-conditioning, beach, dive shop, dock, snorkeling, windsurfing, boating, waterskiing, free parking. MC, V.

Outdoor Activities and Sports

Run by the Villa María la Gorda hotel, the **Centro Internacional de Buceo María la Gorda** (María La Gorda International Dive Center; ✉ Bahía de Corrientes, ☎ 82/78131) has half a dozen dive masters and programs ranging from initiation dives to 20-dive packages. The proximity of the prime diving areas just 200 m (656 ft) out, the sunlit underwater caves, the variety of fish, and the abundance of black coral 15 m (50 ft) down all conspire to make this an extraordinary place to dive.

ARCHIPIÉLAGO DE LOS CANARREOS

Of Cuba's 4,000 islands, most of them specks, the largest is the main island in the Archipiélago de Canarreos, the Isla de la Juventud (Isle of Youth). Nearly due south of Havana in the Golfo de Batabanó, it was previously called La Isla de los Piños (Isle of Pines) for the native pine forest that once covered it. The roughly circular, 50-km-diameter (31-mi-diameter) island was originally a destination for exiles and later the cite of a prison (Fidel Castro was jailed here for 18 months after the July 26, 1953, assault on the Moncada Barracks in eastern Cuba). After the Revolution, Castro's Third World experiment in education and field work, known as the Youth Brigades, was based here—hence the island's name change.

Isla de la Juventud is a special municipality (as opposed to a full-fledged province) and has little to offer outside of abundant grapefruit orchards, its quirky nature, and excellent dive opportunities. Nueva Gerona, the only important town, is where some 30,000 of the archipelago's 70,000 residents live.

Isla de la Juventud

Flat, scrubby, and—except for its subaquatic marvels—geographically undistinguished, the island was a pirate refuge for centuries after Columbus discovered it in 1494. In the 19th century, the Spanish sent exiles here. Later that century, emigrants from the Cayman Islands started a British colony here, leaving some native English-speakers even today around the town of Cocodrilo on the south coast. Americans colonized the island in the early 20th century, thinking it could become another state; the Mafia considered making it an insular gambling paradise in the 1940s. Finally, after the Revolution, Castro established his experimental, international student community—a plan to combine work and study and, in the process, convert the island into a citrus power. The experiment fell apart during the Special Period in the 1990s; most of the boarding schools are now in ruins.

Nueva Gerona

❼ *170 km (105 mi) south of Havana.*

This sleepy town barely merits a browse, although its pillars and columns and horses with buggies make it seem refreshingly stuck in the flow of history. The main street, Calle 39 (Calle Martí), will take you past the restaurants El Cochinito and El Corderito—"the piglet" and "the lamb," respectively. If you walk to Nueva Gerona's **ferry terminal** (✉ Calle 31, e/Calle 22 y Calle 24, ☎ 61/24406) on the Río Las Casas, you can see *El Pinero,* the boat that ferried Castro to freedom in 1955 after his prison sojourn.

At the **Museo de la Lucha Clandestina** (Museum of the Clandestine Struggle), you can view exhibits relating to the Movimiento 26 de Julio—the date of the attack, in 1953, on the Moncada Barracks and the name of Castro's revolutionary movement. ✉ *Calle 45, esquina de Calle 24,* ☎ *61/2400.* ✑ *$2.* ⊘ *Tues.–Sat. 9–5, Sun. 8–noon.*

Five kilometers (3 miles) east of Nueva Gerona is the area's most popular sight, the **Presidio Modelo** (Model Prison), built in 1926–31 by the dictator Gerado Machado. Modeled on the famous penitentiary in Joliet, Illinois, the presidio facilitated constant surveillance of up to 6,000 prisoners. The doorless cells in the four circular, five-tier buildings were crammed with inmates and overseen from central watchtowers. The fifth block, where prisoners weren't allowed to speak, housed *el comedor de tres mil silencios* (the dining hall of 3,000 silences). German and Japanese prisoners of war were held here during World War II, and, most famously, Fidel Castro, his brother Raúl, and 24 fellow rebels were jailed here from October 1953 to May 1955 after the attack on the Moncada Barracks. Celebrity inmates, Castro and company were housed in the prison infirmary; their bunks are still in place, with photographs of each prisoner on the wall over the bed. Castro penned his now famous "La Historia me Absolverá" ("History Will Absolve Me")—the defense speech for his trial for the Moncada attack and a manifesto of the cause against the dictator Fulgencio Batista—at the Presidio Modelo, which has been a museum since 1967. ✉ *Carretera Playa Bibijagua (Calle 32 leaving Nueva Gerona), Km 5,* ☎ *61/7564.* ✑ *$2.* ⊘ *Tues.–Sat. 9–5, Sun. 9–1.*

DINING AND LODGING

¢–$ ✕ **El Cochinito.** At first glance, this simple restaurant is too fly-infested and generally under-maintained to think about dining in. However, the locals choose it over the other options in town for a reason: the pork specialties such as *chicharrónes de cerdo* (pork crisp), *masas* (pork loin), and *cochinillo asado* (roast pig) are delicious. ✉ *Calle 39, esquina de Calle 24,* ☎ *61/22809. No credit cards.*

¢ ▦ **Villa Gaviota.** The Gaviota's swimming pool, a cool spot above the Río Las Casas, is where all the island inhabitants want to be on weekends. The rooms here, in modern pastel-painted units, are passable at best. South 2 km (1 mi) from Nueva Gerona, this is a handy base from which to explore the town. ✉ *Autopista Nueva Gerona–La Fé, Km 2,* ☎ *61/23290,* ⊠ *61/24486. 20 rooms. Restaurant, bar, air-conditioning, pool, free parking. MC, V.*

Ciénaga de Lanier and Environs

❽ *30 km (19 mi) south of Nueva Gerona.*

Outside of Nueva Gerona, the Isla de la Juventud's other major attraction is its swampland. But a visit is a long and somewhat costly undertaking, involving guides ($15–$20, not including tips), permits ($10), entry fees ($1 for the crocodile farm), a rental car or taxi ($70), and a full-day round-trip from Nueva Gerona. (Permits can be acquired at the Colony Puerto Sol or the Villa Gaviota hotels.) The crocodile farm, 30 km (19 mi) south of Nueva Gerona, is of moderate interest.

★   The **Cueva Punta del Este** (Colony Puerto Sol, ⊠ Carretera de Siguanea, Km 42, ☎ 61/98181; Villa Gaviota, ⊠ Autopista Nueva Gerona–La Fé, Km 2, ☎ 61/23290), 55 km (34 mi) southeast of Nueva Gerona, is actually a series of caves famous for their paintings. As the year proceeds, the sunlight that beams into the caves illuminates different parts of the aboriginal paintings, which date from around 800 BC. The Colony Puerto Sol and Villa Gaviota hotels arrange guides and all details of visits to the site.

LODGING

¢   ☎ **Colony Puerto Sol.** This remote resort 42 km (26 mi) southwest of Nueva Gerona on the Bahía de Siguanea takes full care of its captive audience in every way, from the *pineritos* (the classic Isla de la Juventud cocktail of white rum, grapefruit juice, and ice) to the sailing, swimming, and boogying programs. The island's best hotel is also a haven for divers and snorkelers. The Mojito Bar at the end of the long dock is spectacular in the evening as the sun sets. ⊠ *Carretera de Siguanea, Km 42, ☎ 61/98181, FAX 61/26120. 68 rooms, 9 suites. Restaurant, bar, pool, dive shop, dock, boating, fishing, free parking. MC, V.*

BEACHES

On the Isla de la Juventud's south shore is the seemingly endless **Playa Larga** (Long Beach), well worth a stop for its natural splendor. You may even want to spend a day hiking west to Cocodrilo and Caleta Grande, where descendants of the Cayman Islands still speak a melodic Caribbeanized English. At **Punta Francés,** no fewer than 56 dive sites—with such evocative names as Tunnel of Love and Secret Passage—let you explore the coral reefs, varied fauna, and sunken galleons. The best way to access Punta Francés is via boat from the Colony Puerto Sol.

Cayo Largo

❾   *177 km (110 mi) southeast of Havana, 120 km (74 mi) east of the Isla de la Juventud.*

Popular with Canadian and Italian tour groups that often fly in directly, Cayo Largo is an ideal spot for a carefree vacation, though contact with Cuban life and culture is very limited. The island is also considerably more expensive than the mainland; expect to pay double normal Cuban prices for everything from diving excursions to dinner. On the other hand, the pristine beaches and seductive aquamarine waters are boon and balm to the weary soul.

From Combinado on the island's northwestern tip, around the small elbow called Cocodrilo that juts out from the island's southwest shore, and up the 20-km (12-mi) straightaway, a series of hotels offer activities of every kind. **Playa Sirena** is a superb 3-km (2-mi) white-sand strand. A 10-minute ferry from Combinado goes out to the sliver of a peninsula off Cayo Largo's western tip in the morning and returns in the evening. Boat trips from Playa Sirena to nearby keys such as Cayo Rico and Cayo Iguana are available, along with a full range of water sports including diving and windsurfing. Ferries to Playa Sirena leave the pier at Isla del Sol at 8:30 and 10:30 AM and 2:30 PM, returning at 1:30, 3, and 5 PM. The one-way fare is $3 per person. Day-trip packages from Havana and Varadero include the 40-minute flight, half a day and lunch on Playa Sirena, snorkeling the offshore reef, and a visit to Cayo Iguana. For a taste of the best of Cayo Largo without fully renouncing the experience of Cuba, such a package may be the best of all worlds.

Dining and Lodging

$$–$$$$ ✕ **Taberna del Pirata.** Lobster is the specialty here, along with other
★ criollo recipes featuring fresh fish. It's more than the beach shack it may seem at first sight, with respectable fare and a good wine list. ⊠ *Playa Sirena,* ☎ *45/26786. MC, V.*

$–$$ ✕⌸ **Villa Capricho.** This is a well-equipped spot with bungalows that try hard to seem rustic and South Sea–like, but, in the end, don't succeed. The Marlín Azul (Blue Marlin) restaurant ($$–$$$$), which specializes in seafood, is one of Cayo Largo's better options. ⊠ *Playa Lindamar,* ☎ *45/48111,* ⅌ *45/48160. 60 bungalows. Restaurant, bar, pool, dock, free parking. MC, V.*

$–$$$ ⌸ **Pelícano Hotel.** In some ways, this rambling complex of Mexican-style bungalows and outbuildings epitomizes all that's wrong with Cayo Largo's tourism program, though the beach facing this spot is a cut above those farther east. Relentlessly modern, the Pelícano offers everything from basketball to diving to windsurfing. ⊠ *Playa Lindamar,* ☎ *45/48333,* ⅌ *45/48166. 212 rooms, 110 bungalows, 2 suites. 4 restaurants, café, piano bar, air-conditioning, pool, basketball, health club, beach, dive shop, snorkeling, windsurfing, dry cleaning, free parking. MC, V.*

$–$$ ⌸ **Isla del Sur.** Along the strip of resorts and hotels in Cocodrilo, this is one of the better choices. All rooms have patios facing the sea. A circular swimming pool in the center of the complex gives it a Venice-like, swim-home-for-cocktails feel. Evening entertainment is varied and constant here. ⊠ *Playa Lindamar,* ☎ *45/48111,* ⅌ *45/48201. 59 rooms. Restaurant, bar, air-conditioning, pool, beauty salon, travel services, free parking. MC, V.*

MATANZAS PROVINCE

Formerly Cuba's sugarcane-producing heartland, Matanzas Province offers a variety of attractions. The city of Matanzas, with its immense deepwater harbor, was a sugar- and slave-trading port of great importance during colonial times. Alternately dubbed the Athens of Cuba for its traditional cultural vigor and the Cuban Venice for its two rivers and many bridges, Matanzas is worthy of more attention than it usually gets. Varadero has more than four dozen major hotels along the slender Península de Hicacos, between the Atlantic Ocean and the Bahía de Cárdenas. The city of Cárdenas has a character and charm all its own, while the Península de Zapata, beginning with the crocodile farm at Guamá and ending at the Bahía de Cochinos (Bay of Pigs) and the fascinating Museo Playa Girón, is an engaging combination of flora, fauna, and history.

Matanzas

❿ *100 km (62 mi) east of Havana.*

Matanzas, which means "killings" or "slaughters," was Cuba's early livestock abattoir and exporter of meat to Spain. (An alternate story attributes the name to an ambush and murder of Spanish shipwreck victims by local natives.) Despite its rather gruesome name, the city has a charm that makes it well worth investigating. The San Juan and Yumurí rivers cut through its center and empty into the vast Bahía de Matanzas, still an important sugar port. The typical provincial faded-pastel facades of elegant houses with fluted columns are found scattered throughout the town center and along the rivers.

To reach Matanzas, take the wide and quick Vía Blanca (White Way), which runs 100 km (62 mi) east from Havana and then another 40 km (25 mi) on to Varadero. With views of the coast and the Valle de Yumurí, the Vía Blanca is one of Cuba's finest highways. The *Hershey Train*—a four-hour run from the Casablanca district across Havana harbor—is the other classic way to visit Matanzas. Including lunch at La Viña, a quick tour of central Matanzas could take two to four hours, plenty of time to get the feel of this once-opulent 19th-century town.

The sky-blue **Hershey railway station** (⊠ Calle 67/San Blas y Calle 155/ San Alejandro, ☎ 45/24–7254) is a picturesque little depot. Once the property of Pennsylvania-based chocolate barons, the railway was built to haul sugarcane but eventually added passenger service. Now its quaint electric engine pulls two passenger cars with wooden benches into this station, which is in the Reparto Versailles, a district settled by French-Haitian refugees during the 19th century.

The **Iglesia de San Pedro Apóstol** (⊠ Calle 57 y Calle 270) was built in 1870 by architect Daniel Delaglio, who also designed Matanzas's emblematic Teatro Sauto. The church's neoclassical symmetry is broken by a jumble of towers, turrets, domes, and cupolas. The bright yellow interior has rich, fluted columns behind the main altar.

Over the Yumurí estuary is the ornate **Puente Concordia,** with its four carved columns at either end. Built in 1878, this bridge is one of the most striking pieces of Matanzas architecture.

The powder-blue building originally called the Palacio Junco is now the **Museo Histórico Provincial.** It houses artifacts, photographs, and memorabilia chronicling the sugar and slave industries. ⊠ *Calle 272 y Calle 79,* ☎ *45/24–3195.* ⊡ *$2.* ☉ *Mon.–Sat. 9–5, Sun. 9–1.*

The marble statue of an independence fighter known as *El Soldado Desconocido* (The Unknown Soldier) sits at the center of the **Plaza de la Vigía,** just south of the intersection of Calle 272 and Calle 83. On the plaza, the Teatro Sauto (☎ 45/24–2721) is one of Cuba's finest and best-preserved neoclassical structures. Also known as the Teatro Antillano, or Theater of the Antilles, it was built in 1863 at the peak of the city's prosperity. Tours of the triple-tier interior, with its carved wood and frescoes, cost $2 a person.

The **Galería de Arte Provincial** shows local painters, sculptors, and *orisha* (Santería deity) artisans. ⊠ *Calle 272,* ☎ *45/24–9142.* ⊡ *$2.* ☉ *Mon.–Sat. 9–5.*

Some of the brightest sights in Matanzas are the restored frescoes at the **Catedral de San Carlos.** ⊠ *Calle Milanés y Calle 282,* ☎ *45/24–8342.* ☉ *Weekdays 9–noon and 3–5, Sun. 9–noon.*

The **Parque de la Libertad,** a leafy square bordered by Calles 79, 83, 290, and 288 contains a bronze of José Martí and a dramatic sculpture of a screaming, bare-breasted woman representing Cuba breaking free from her chains. The **Museo Farmacéutico Triolet** (⊠ Calle Milanés, esquina de Calle Santa Teresa, ☎ 45/24–3179), the main sight on the Parque de la Libertad, is a perfectly preserved 19th-century pharmacy. Established in 1882 by Ernesto Triolet and his son-in-law, Juan Fermín de Figueroa, the pharmacy finally closed in 1964. It specialized in *medecina verde* (natural medicine), and its porcelain jars, great cauldron, giant amphora for medicinal wine, prescription file, and pharmaceutical instruments are impressively displayed. Don't miss the bronze crocodile used to compress and calibrate the corks that, before the screw-top, sealed vials. The museum, which charges $2, is open Monday through Saturday 10 to 6 and Sunday 9 to 1.

Dining and Lodging

$ ✕ **Café Atenas.** On the Plaza de la Vigía, this friendly little patio café is near the city's major cultural treasures. Although it may seem less than a full-fledged restaurant, its sandwiches and tapas are delicious, and its setting—shaded by bougainvillea, grapevine, and ceiba trees—is magical. ⊠ *Calle 272, esquina de Calle 83,* ☎ *45/24–5493. No credit cards.*

¢ 🏨 **Hotel Louvre.** This cold-water (as of this writing, anyway) spot is a risky recommendation. It's such a classic place—in all its decaying splendor—that it's worth a try, and may well have been restored and rehabilitated by the time you arrive. With four antiques-appointed bedrooms over the town's central square, the Louvre is the very essence of Old Matanzas. A romantic (if somewhat harrowing) adventure would include the four-hour Hershey Train to Matanzas, a night at the Louvre, and a performance at the Teatro Sauto. ⊠ *Calle Milanés 47,* ☎ *45/24–4074. 17 rooms. Restaurant, bar, free parking. No credit cards.*

Nightlife and the Arts

With two locations, the **Casa de la Trova** is the main musical venue in Matanzas (which is known for the Afro-Cuban music of Santería). If you're lucky, you might catch Los Muñequitos, considered Cuba's top rumba combo. Performances are held Saturday afternoon and every evening. ⊠ *Calle 83 y Calle 304,* ☎ *45/24–2891;* ⊠ *Calle 272 y Calle 121,* ☎ *45/24–4129.*

The **Centro Nocturno** (⊠ Calle 83 y Calle 268, ☎ 45/24–2969) features musicians and a dance troupe. **Sala de Conciertos José White** (⊠ Plaza de la Libertad, ☎ 45/26–0153) stages jazz, dance, and classical music shows. The famous and ornate **Teatro Sauto** (⊠ Plaza de la Vigía, ☎ 45/24–2721) hosts folkloric performances as well as plays.

Outdoor Activities and Sports

Matanzas is a big baseball town, with a top first-division team called Los Henequeros (named after the fiber used in making rope, a local product). Games are held in the 30,000-seat **Victoria a Girón** stadium (⊠ Av. Martín Dihigo s/n, ☎ 45/24–8813 or 45/25–3551 to Infotur for game times) from October to March. The stadium occupies the site of Cuba's first baseball field, built in 1874.

Varadero

⓫ *140 km (87 mi) east of Havana.*

Depending on your tastes and ambitions, Varadero is either a tropical paradise or a tourist inferno, but the fact remains: its beaches are excellent and its offerings rival those of similar resort areas anywhere in the world. It's also a good base for excursions to Matanzas, Cárdenas, Cienfuegos, Trinidad, and the Península de Zapata.

This narrow peninsula—really an elongated island separated from the mainland by the Laguna Paso Malo—is 18½ km (11 mi) long and is edged by white-sand beaches and clear waters in mesmerizing blues, greens, and aquamarines. At an average width of 700 m (770 yards), Varadero extends northeast to Punta Hicacos, Cuba's northernmost point. Laid out in three longitudinal avenues intersected by 69 cross streets, Varadero is easy to navigate. The town itself, a modest village of some 15,000 inhabitants, is now nearly lost amid the maze of hotels.

Originally inhabited by Taíno aboriginals, Varadero was settled by the Spanish in the late 16th century. In the late 19th century, families from Cárdenas began to build summer houses here. In 1883 the first town council established a plan for building baths and recreational facili-

SANTERÍA: A BLEND OF BELIEFS

It seems another of Cuba's many ironies that a colony of the Spain that expelled its Jewish and Islamic communities in 1492 should prove such fertile ground for Santería, the marriage of West African animism and Spanish Catholicism. Throw in official Soviet-style atheism after 1959 and Pope John Paul II's moving visit in 1998, and the result is an extraordinary and exemplary degree of tolerance and spiritual eclecticism.

Santería is a fusion of Catholicism with, principally, the religion of the West African Yoruba tribe. Prohibited from practicing their religion in Cuba by their Spanish colonial masters, slaves superposed their pantheon of gods and goddesses over Christian saints. Any detail, be it a color or a characteristic, sufficed to identify an *orisha*, or Santería deity, with a Christian saint. Thus, for example, Ochún, the Venus-like goddess of freshwater, is associated with Cuba's patron saint La Virgen de la Caridad del Cobre (The Virgin of Charity of Copper). A beautiful mulatto, she's a symbol of sensuality, femininity, and love; wife of Orula; lover of Chango; and identified with the color yellow or gold. Chango—god of war, thunder, and fire—is associated with Santa Barbara. He is identified with the color red, and is avid for wealth and women. Yemayá is the black goddess of the sea who symbolizes life; she is also the patron saint of sailors, associated with the Virgen de Regla, and identified by the color blue. Obatalá is Zeus, associated with the Virgen de la Merced and white, and respected by all the other orishas. The Yoruba religion has more than 400 orishas, of which some 40 have become part of Cuban Santería.

Throughout Cuban history, the Catholic church's presence has been discreet. During the Wars of Independence, the church sided with the Spanish, thus losing the little influence it had acquired. In 1959, most of the clergy fled with the wealthy Cubans to whom they had primarily administered, and the spiritual life of the island was left in the hands of Soviet-style dialectical materialism and Santería. Today in Cuba there are an estimated 10,000 *babalaos* (Santería priests), compared with some 300 Catholic priests.

Santería ceremonies build to sensorial crescendos of color, music (especially percussion), and a mixture of tobacco and incense. Devotees go into trancelike states of ecstasy, during which they're considered to be possessed by orishas and endowed with their powers. Even Fidel Castro, despite early efforts to suppress Santería, received the King of the Yorubas in 1986 and became a devotee of Obatalá on a trip to West Africa in the '70s. Castro may even owe his long tenure in power to the strength of Santería; the white dove that perched on his shoulder during his January 8, 1959, nationally televised victory speech is considered by *santeros* (believers of Santería) to be a symbol of prosperity, a sign sent to announce the chosen leader.

ties. The Varadero Hotel opened in 1915, and in 1926 the du Pont de Nemours family—powerful American industrialists whose early fortune was made in gunpowder—bought most of the peninsula and built a large estate complete with a golf course. Other wealthy *norteamericanos* followed, including Al Capone.

By the 1950s, numerous hotels were under construction; they followed the example of the Hotel Internacional, a quintessential den of iniquity complete with a casino, mobsters, and abundant available women. After 1959, the Revolution declared the elitist enclave public property and rank-and-file Cubans were allowed on the beach. Varadero then became a favorite Russian resort, where Eastern European tourists frolicked in the sun and guzzled mojitos right under Uncle Sam's nose.

The du Pont mansion, **Mansión Xanadú,** was christened after a verse from the Samuel Taylor Coleridge poem *Kubla Khan* ("In Xanadu did Kubla Khan / A stately pleasure dome decree"). With six rooms for rent, it's by far Varadero's top lodging choice, though you need to secure reservations many months in advance. The restaurant and top-floor terrace and bar offer a nonpareil place for an evening mojito. Even if you're not staying at the Mansión Xanadú, a visit will help you understand the level of luxury the du Ponts established here. Such is the legend of the du Pont villa that Cubanas celebrating their 15th birthdays—the age considered the beginning of young womanhood—still come, sometimes from Havana or even farther away, to pose for photographs on the marble stairway dressed in antique ball gowns.

Parque Josone (⊠ Av. 1 y Calle 56, ☎ 5/66–2740), a municipal park that once was the home of a wealthy sugar-mill owner, is a tranquil spot with swans and flamingos, rowboats for rent ($2), three restaurants, and various open-air bars. Admission is $5.

The **Museo Municipal** is housed in Varadero's prettiest early 20th-century summer house, built entirely of wood and painted sky-blue with white trim. Photographs of early Varadero and of Che and Fidel "taking" the Hotel Internacional after the Revolution are among the memorabilia. ⊠ *Calle 57, esquina de Av. Playa,* ☎ 5/61–3189. ☜ *$2.* ☼ *Tues.–Sat. 9–6, Sun. 9–noon.*

☾ The **Delfinarium** has a troupe of acrobatic dolphins to admire (and, for an extra fee of $60, to swim with) near the peninsula's eastern end. ⊠ *Punta Rincón Francés,* ☎ 5/66–8031. ☜ *$10.* ☼ *Performances daily at 11, 2:30, and 4:30.*

The **Cueva de Ambrosio** contains some 72 aboriginal drawings thought to be more than 3,000 years old. Entering the cave, which is lit by sun that comes in through an opening in the ceiling, requires a 300-m (990-ft) walk through dense jungle. ⊠ *Punta Rincón Francés.* ☜ *$2.* ☼ *Mon.–Sat. 9–5.*

Dining and Lodging

$$$$ ✕ **Antigüedades.** Next to the entrance of the Parque Josone, this ro-
★ mantic spot is a jumble of antique artifacts and furniture. The fare is fresh seafood, including lobster and shrimp. There's no menu: the waiter recites what the last fishing boat brought in and tells you what he recommends. ⊠ *Av. 1 y Calle 59, Parque Josone,* ☎ 5/66–7329. *Reservations essential. MC, V.*

$$–$$$$ ✕ **Albacora.** This excellent seafood restaurant is named for the albacore, or long-fin, tuna, which has darker meat than the bonito and—as served here with a lemon-based sauce—is exquisite. But Albacora is more than a one-trick pony; it serves other seafood specialties, from

lobster to crab to calamari. ✉ *Calle 60, esquina de Calle Mar,* ☎ *5/ 61–3650. MC, V.*

$$–$$$$ ✕ **El Mesón del Quijote.** Cuban and international specialties are pre-
★ pared here—from paella to *fabada marinera* (seafood bean stew)—and
the creative chef adds extraordinarily innovative touches. It's open non-
stop from noon to midnight. ✉ *Carretera de las Américas,* ☎ *5/66–
7796. MC, V.*

$–$$ ✕ **El Bodegón Criollo.** First-rate Cuban cooking is served in this Varadero takeoff on Havana's Bodeguita del Medio—the famous Hem-
ingway haunt—graffiti included. The food is carefully prepared, the
prices are more than reasonable, and the musical trio is one of the reasons diners linger late into the evening. ✉ *Av. de la Playa y Calle 40,*
☎ *5/66–7784. MC, V.*

$$$ ✕⌂ **Mansión Xanadú.** The old du Pont mansion offers only half a dozen
★ rooms. If you can't get a reservation, stop by to ask whether someone
hasn't shown up, as this noble villa, product of a millionaire's fancy,
is truly elegant. The upper-story restaurant ($$–$$$$, reservations essential) is one of the peninsula's prettiest places to dine, even if the food
is a bit overpriced and below par. Don't expect too much; just enjoy
the views and the experience of living it up like a du Pont. ✉ *Av. de
las Américas,* ☎ *5/66–7600,* ℻ *5/66–7625. 6 rooms. Restaurant, bar,
free parking. MC, V.*

$$$$ ⌂ **Sol Elite Palmeras.** You'll find everything you might need at this well-
equipped, well-organized complex run by Spain's Grupo Sol. The
lobby is a split-level jungle, with the noise of commerce competing with
the racket of birdsong. Most of the well-furnished rooms have views
of the Atlantic; the bougainvillea-covered bungalows have pretty terraces (bring mosquito repellent). The restaurants offer cuisine ranging
from criollo to Italian to Chinese. ✉ *Autopista del Sur,* ☎ *5/66–7009,*
℻ *5/66–7008,* 🌐 *www.solmeliacuba.com. 375 rooms, 32 suites, 200
bungalows. 4 restaurants, bar, pool, hair salon, massage, beach, dive
shop, dock, snorkeling, windsurfing, boating, jet skiing, parasailing,
waterskiing, fishing, free parking. MC, V.*

$$$ ⌂ **Breezes Varadero.** There's no need to ever leave the grounds of this
★ complex, 3 km (2 mi) east of Varadero village. A Cuban–Jamaican joint
venture, the hotel has everything you could want, including some of
Varadero's prettiest rooms and one of the area's better buffets. The dive
programs and training courses are considered among the best on the
peninsula. ✉ *Av. de las Américas, Km 3,* ☎ *5/66–7030,* ℻ *5/66–7005.
270 rooms. 3 restaurants, bar, pool, beach, dive shop, dock, snorkel-
ing, surfing, windsurfing, boating, jet skiing, parasailing, waterskiing,
free parking. MC, V. All-inclusive.*

$$$ ⌂ **Meliá Las Américas.** One of Varadero's top four hotels has a hub-
like vitality, set as it is between the Meliá Varadero, the Varadero golf
course, the old du Pont mansion, and the Plaza América shopping mall.
Rooms are modern and colorful, and the restaurants offer barbecue,
paella, and international cuisine. ✉ *Playa de las Américas, Autopista
del Sur, Km 7,* ☎ *5/66–7600,* ℻ *5/66–7625,* 🌐 *www.solmeliacuba.com.
220 rooms, 114 suites, 12 duplex honeymoon suites. 5 restaurants, bar,
2 pools, tennis court, volleyball, beach, snorkeling, surfing, windsurfing, boating, free parking. MC, V. All-inclusive.*

$$$ ⌂ **Meliá Varadero.** This was the first luxury hotel to go up in Varadero,
★ and it remains at the top of the growing heap. Its six wings fan out
from a lush circular atrium, and the quality of its rooms and restau-
rants doesn't disappoint. Each room has a balcony, the best with
sweeping ocean views. More than any other hotel in Varadero, this one
attempts to bring Cuban culture to the Hicacos Peninsula. It's one of
the sites of Havana's December international film festival, and the Na-
tional Ballet of Cuba as well as leading musical performers and per-

sonalities appear here regularly. ⊠ *Playa de las Américas, Carretera de las Morlas,* ☎ *5/66–7013,* FAX *5/66–7012,* WEB *www.solmeliacuba.com. 490 rooms, 7 suites. 5 restaurants, bar, 2 pools, beach, dive shop, dock, snorkeling, surfing, windsurfing, boating, jet skiing, waterskiing, free parking. MC, V. All-inclusive.*

$$$ 🖭 **Paradisus Varadero.** With lots of faux-marble and trompe l'oeil
★ effects, this all-suite spa hotel has a playful Mediterranean feel, putting it a far cry above the Soviet-style behemoths that once passed for hotels. Its eight restaurants—possibly a Varadero record—serve a variety of cuisines. Spa treatments include mud baths and massages. ⊠ *Punta Rincón Francés,* ☎ *5/66–8700,* FAX *5/66–8705,* WEB *www. solmeliacuba.com. 408 junior suites, 12 suites. 8 restaurants, bar, 2 pools, massage, sauna, spa, steam room, tennis court, beach, meeting rooms, free parking. MC, V. All-inclusive.*

Nightlife and the Arts

NIGHTLIFE

Many hotels in Varadero have dance clubs, but there are a few standouts. The $10 cover charge at the torrid disco **La Bamba** (⊠ Av. de las Américas, ☎ 5/66–7560) gets you access to an open bar and revelers surrounded by music videos dancing into the night. At the **Cabaret Continental** (⊠ Hotel Varadero International, Av. de las Américas, ☎ 5/66–7038) you pay $25 or $40 (with dinner) to see Varadero's best Tropicana-style cabaret show at 10 PM; afterward you can dance till dawn. The **Cueva del Pirata** (⊠ Autopista del Sur, Km 11, ☎ 5/61–3829) is an underground cave where, for $10, you can see an Afro-Cuban review and then dance afterward.

Disco Kastillito (⊠ Av. de la Playa y Calle 49, ☎ 5/66–3888) offers fashion shows and dancing for $5. **Havana Club** (⊠ Av. de las Américas, ☎ 5/66–7500) is a good standby club; the cover is $10. **Mambo Club** (⊠ Carretera de las Morlas, Km 14, ☎ 5/66–8565) is one of several Varadero establishments where $10 gets you access to an open bar. You can drink all you like at **El Palacio de la Rumba** (⊠ Av. de las Américas, Km 4.5, ☎ 5/66–8210) after paying the $10 cover.

THE ARTS

The **Casa de la Cultura** (⊠ Av. 1 y Calle 49, ☎ 5/66–3311) hosts concerts and Afro-Cuban dance performances; admission is $5. The various restaurants of **Parque Josone** (⊠ Av. 1 y Calle 56, ☎ 5/66–2740), which charges $5 admission, have concerts. Also in the park is the Rincón de los Enamorados (Lovers' Corner), featuring classical music.

Outdoor Activities and Sports

Arrangements for water sports can be made through hotels. Nonguests can use many of the hotel tennis courts for a $2–$3 an hour fee.

FISHING

Marina Chapelin (⊠ Autopista del Sur, Km 13, ☎ 5/66–7550 or 5/66–7800) can arrange fishing trips. Excursions cost from $150 to $350, depending on the size of your party and what you're looking for.

GOLF

At the 18-hole **Varadero Golf Club** (⊠ Av. de las Américas, ☎ 5/66–7788) the greens fee is $60; for a round of twilight golf (after 5:30), the fee is $20. Carts, clubs, and caddies are available for $10 each.

SCUBA DIVING

Scuba Barracuda (⊠ Av. 1 y Calle 58, ☎ 5/66–3481) can arrange day or night dives, cave explorations, certification courses, and equipment rental. It also offers snorkeling equipment and guided excursions for $35.

Varadero Dining and Lodging

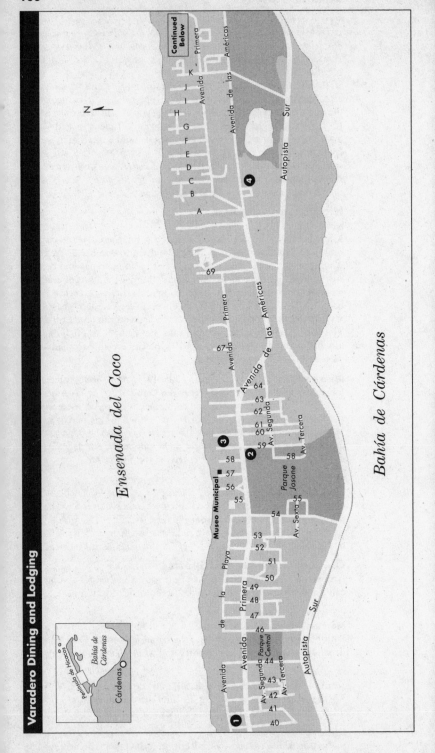

Ensenada del Coco

Bahía de Cárdenas

Peninsula de Hicacos

Bahía de Cárdenas

Cárdenas

Museo Municipal

Continued Below

Avenida Primera

Avenida de las Américas

Autopista Sur

Avenida Primera

Avenida de las Américas

Av. Segunda

Av. Tercera

Parque Josone

Av. Sexta

Avenida de la Playa

Avenida Primera

Parque Central

Av. Segunda

Av. Tercera

Autopista Sur

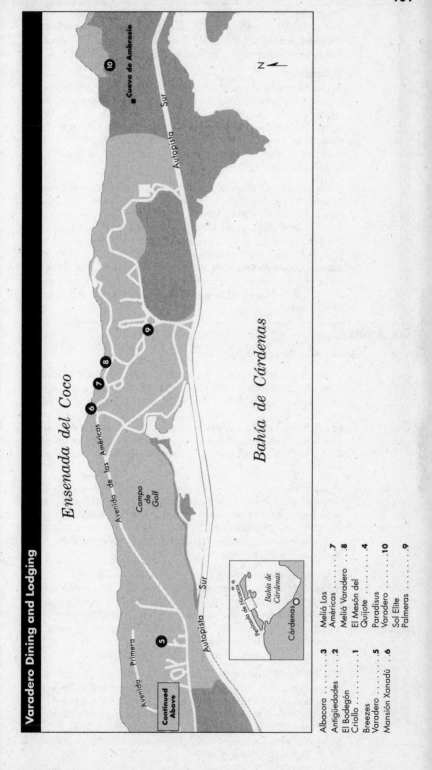

Ensenada del Coco

Bahía de Cárdenas

Cueva de Ambrosio

N

Autopista Sur

Campo de Golf

Avenida de las Américas

Avenida Primera

Continued Above

Autopista Sur

Península de Hicacos

Bahía de Cárdenas

Cárdenas

Albacora **3**
Antigüedades **2**
El Bodegón
Criollo **1**
Breezes
Varadero **5**
Mansión Xanadú . .**6**

Meliá Las
Américas **7**
Meliá Varadero . .**8**
El Mesón del
Quijote **4**
Paradisus
Varadero **10**
Sol Elite
Palmeras **9**

SKYDIVING

Just west of the bridge into Varadero, the **Centro Internacional de Paracaidismo** (⊠ Vía Blanca, ☎ 5/66–7256) offers skydiving training and tandem jumps with a professional instructor for $135.

Shopping

Varadero is well supplied with souvenir shops and arts and crafts goods. Most hotels have gift shops and souvenir emporiums. **ARTEX** (⊠ Av. 1 y Calle 61, ☎ 5/66–7189) sells tapes, CDs, and books. For cigars, visit the **Casa del Habano** (⊠ Av. 1 y Calle 61, ☎ 5/66–7843). **Casa de las Orishas** (⊠ Av. 1, e/Calle 33 y Calle 34, ☎ 5/61–3663) sells beads, weavings, carvings, and leather goods based on Afro-Cuban and Santería themes.

While wandering through Varadero, look for the **Centro Comercial Caimán** (⊠ Av. 1, e/Calle 61 y Calle 62, ☎ 5/66–7692), a cluster of shops. The center's **Max Music** (☎ 5/66–7692) has Varadero's best selection of Cuban music. **Librería Hanoi** (⊠ Av. 1 y Calle 44, ☎ 5/66–8917) is strong in the usual sociopolitical tracts approved by the regime. It also has a good collection of paperbacks in English. At the **Taller y Tienda de Cerámica** (⊠ Av. 1 y Calle 59, ☎ 5/66–3810) you can watch potters at work and buy original pieces. Believe it or not, there's a **United Colors of Benetton** (⊠ Av. 1 y Calle 39, ☎ 5/66–5334) in Varadero.

Cárdenas

⑫ *10 km (6 mi) east of Varadero.*

Although Cárdenas has become famous as the home of Elián González, it's traditionally known for its horse-drawn *caletas* (carts), for its many bicycles, for its crab fishery, and for being the first town in Cuba to raise the national flag. This event, much revered by Cubans, occurred in 1850 after a mercenary force of Kentuckians and Mississippians led by a Venezuelan named Narciso López briefly captured Cárdenas from the Spanish, hoping to provoke a national uprising that failed to materialize.

A gigantic stone crab marks the town line as you approach from Varadero; sculptures of a bicycle and a caleta mark the other end of town. With barely a car in the streets, there's a dramatic simplicity to what lies in between. Cárdenas merits a two- or three-hour visit; the dining and lodging are so superior 10 minutes away in Varadero that trying to do either here isn't advised.

You can sightsee in one of the horse-drawn carriages ($1) that wait for hire in the central **Parque Colón,** which also has the oldest statue of Columbus in the New World (erected in 1858). On the park, the mid-19th-century **Catedral de la Inmaculada Concepción** is known for its stained-glass windows, best admired from inside. To enter, walk around the church to the back door at Number 359. Don't miss the tiny chapel in the conical tower at the northeast corner.

Inspired by the battle to repatriate Elián González, the 7-year-old rescued off the coast of Florida in 1999, the **Museo a la Batalla de Ideas** is a history of Cuba's battle for independence. Everything from the two English cannonballs fired in 1756 to the cross given to Elián by Reverend John Brown Campbell traces Cuba's struggle to achieve and maintain its national sovereignty. ⊠ *Av. José Martí 523, ☎ 5/52–1056.* ☞ *$2. ☉ Mon. –Sat. 10–6, Sun. 9–1.*

The neoclassical **Casa Natal de José Antonio Echeverría,** now the municipal museum, is named for a student leader murdered by Fulgencio

Batista's forces in 1957 and is also known as Museo de la Lucha Estudiantil (Museum of the Student Struggle). Built in 1873, the two-story town house has a lovely hand-carved wooden spiral staircase. Its top floor is filled with Echeverría memorabilia along with photographs and documents of other local Revolutionary heroes. Ask about the machine-gun barrel upstairs if you favor gory stories. ⊠ *Calle Genes 240,* ☎ *5/52–4145.* ⊑ *$2.* ☉ *Tues.–Sat. 10–6, Sun. 8–2.*

At this writing, the **Museo Oscar María de Rojas** was closed for renovations. When it's open, however, it's worth a visit for its veritable potpourri of bugs, butterflies, *polymitas* (snails with multicolored shells), and even two fleas in nuptial dress. In addition, there are the usual photographs of Cárdenas heroes of the wars of independence and the Revolution as well as a baroque, 19th-century, horse-drawn hearse. ⊠ *Calle Calzada 4,* ☎ *5/52–4126.* ⊑ *$1.* ☉ *Tues.–Sat. 9–6, Sun. 9–1.*

Península de Zapata

⑬ *100 km (62 mi) southwest of Cárdenas, 190 km (118 mi) southeast of Havana.*

The Península de Zapata, so called for its slipper-shape outline, is also known as La Ciénaga de Zapata (the Swamp of Zapata). Home to Cuba's largest wetland and wildlife sanctuary, the peninsula backs onto the Bahía de los Cochinos (Bay of Pigs), named for the *cochinos cimarrones* (free-range or runaway pigs) that Spanish colonists lost or deliberately stocked in the Zapata swamps during the 16th century. The Bay of Pigs, known to Cubans as Playa Girón, was the goal of the failed 1961 invasion executed by Cuban exiles with the backing and training of the U.S. Central Intelligence Agency.

During the Bay of Pigs Invasion, Castro had his headquarters near the village of Australia in a sugar mill, part of which is now the **Museo de la Comandancia.** It houses photographs and memorabilia from what the Cubans refer to as La Victoria. Turn-of-the century locomotives still haul sugarcane in and out of the giant mill. The museum is open Monday through Saturday 8 to 5 and Sunday 8 to 1; admission is $2.

The **Finca Fiesta Campesina** (⊠ Off Autopista Nacional at Km 142; ☎ 59/2825 to restaurant) is a hotel, farm, and museum showcasing Cuban flora and fauna, from the *manjuarí,* the island's most primitive form of aquatic life, to the *jutía,* a weasel-like tree rat much prized for guajiro stews. There's also a palm-tree climber who can, with lightning speed, scale a 30-m (99-ft) palm using a system of spike-free loops and stirrups. The restaurant here serves creditable criolla cuisine.

From the wooden walkways of **La Boca de Guamá,** south of the town of Australia, you can observe some 3,000 crocodiles. Custodian Emilio Hernández will relate how Celia Sánchez, Castro's most intimate companion and adviser, was determined to restore the failing crocodile population. He'll also fill you in on some facts: these naturally aggressive creatures can jump 1 m (3 ft) high and run as fast as a horse for 80 m (264 ft), reaching speeds of up to 60 kph (37 mph). There's also a restaurant on the premises. ⊠ *Carretera 3-1-16, Km 19,* ☎ *59/2808.* ⊑ *$3.*

La Laguna del Tesoro (Treasure Lagoon) is where, according to legend, Taíno aboriginals dumped gold and other loot to hide it from the Spanish. No treasure has been found, although Taíno relics have been recovered from the lake and contributed to the **Museo Guamá,** a replica of a Taíno village. It also has figures—created by the famous Cuban sculptor Rita Longa—of Taínos going about their daily business.

At the head of the Bahía de los Cochinos is **Playa Larga** (Long Beach), important chiefly as the jumping off point for the Parque Nacional Ciénaga de Zapata.

La Cueva de los Peces (Cave of the Fish), 17 km (10 mi) south of Playa Larga, is a 61-m-deep (201-ft-deep) sinkhole filled with multicolored fish that come in through a subterranean passage. Diving through the banks of fish and the lush subaquatic vegetation is superb. **La Casa del Pescador** (☎ 59/5567) is a small but decent restaurant next to the cenote.

You can access the **Parque Nacional Ciénaga de Zapata** (Zapata Wetlands National Park), the largest of Cuba's six national parks and biosphere reserves, via Playa Larga, where a checkpoint allows cars through only with a guide and permit. Bird-watching platforms on the way out to Las Salinas offer a chance to see 18 of Cuba's 22 endemic species, including the red, white, and blue *tocororo*—Cuba's national bird—and the *siju platanero* (Cuban pygmy owl). Other activities include a drive and walk into Santo Tomás; a boat and/or tarpon-fishing excursion down the Río Hatiguanico; and a bonefishing trip to the flats around the boat landing at Salinas. Try to get local biologist and bird magnet Frank Medina from the park headquarters to accompany you on a trip. ⊠ *Playa Larga, Km 15, Carretera 3-1-16, south of Australia,* ☎ *59/7249.* ⊡ *$10 entry permit; $25 guide fee; $130 bonefishing permit and guide fee.* ☉ *Daily 8–5.*

Dining and Lodging

$ ✕ **La Boca.** The country criollo cooking is acceptable enough to make you overlook the busloads of travelers on package tours. Roast crocodile tail is the specialty; it's believed to be an aphrodisiac. The chicken in criollo sauce is standard fare, as is the *pargo* (red snapper). ⊠ *Carretera 3-1-16, Km 19 south of Australia,* ☎ *59/2808. No credit cards.*

¢ ✕▥ **Batey de Don Pedro.** A dozen bohíos, somewhat primitively equipped, are surrounded by a full complement of farm animals at this rustic refuge from the cane fields. A cow being milked a few feet from your window is apt to be your wake-up call. It's the perfect base camp for bird-watching or fishing expeditions. The excellent Cuban home cooking in the on-site restaurant ($–$$) is also boon in these parts. The *frituras de yuca* (fried yucca), *tasajo* (shredded beef), and the mango sauce with cheese are classics. ⊠ *Finca Fiesta Campesina–Australia, off Autopista Nacional at Km 142,* ☎ *59/2825. 8 2-person cabins, 2 4-person cabins. Restaurant. MC, V.*

¢ ▥ **Villa Guamá.** Once a Castro bass-fishing refuge (Bohío 33 was El Comandante's), this odd hideaway spread over 12 little islands in the Laguna del Tesoro has bohíos with good screens and adequate comforts—though the mosquitoes can be fierce. A 15-minute boat ride to headquarters, which is on stilts, is followed by a canoe ride to the guest cabins. You must canoe in to the main lodge for meals. This is an interesting place, but unless you long to try the bass fishing, steer clear. ⊠ *Laguna del Tesoro,* ☎ *59/2979,* ℻ *59/5551. 50 cabins. Restaurant, 3 bars, dance club. MC, V.*

¢ ▥ **Villa Playa Larga.** Cabins dot the lawns and bougainvillea-filled gardens here, and there's also a good beach. It's a sound base for bird-watching treks to the Zapata wetlands, bonefishing excursions to the Laguna de las Salinas, or dives to black coral formations. ⊠ *Playa Larga,* ☎ *59/7294,* ℻ *59/7219. 64 rooms. Restaurant, bar, cafeteria, air-conditioning, kitchenettes, pool, beach, dive shop, windsurfing, nightclub, free parking. MC, V.*

Playa Girón

⑭ *125 km (78 mi) south of Varadero.*

Playa Girón is the beach and town on the Bahía de Cochinos where much of the bungled CIA-backed Bay of Pigs Invasion on April 17, 1961, took place. More than 1,100 men of the 1,300 Cuban exiles who made up the landing force were captured, with more than 110 killed. (Five minutes in close contact with the mosquitoes of the Zapata swamp will explain a lot about this fracas.) In December 1962, most of the prisoners were returned to the United States in exchange for a ransom of $53 million in medical supplies. Even today, La Victoria is one of Cuba's great rallying points and sources of pride.

Today some 400 people live in sleepy Playa Girón village, in the middle of which stands a billboard that reads: *PLAYA GIRÓN—LA PRIMERA DERROTA DEL IMPERIALISMO NORTEAMERICANO EN AMÉRICA LATINA* (Playa Girón—the first defeat of U.S. imperialism in Latin America). Along the road between La Boca de Guamá and Playa Girón, you'll also see concrete slabs commemorating Cuban defenders who fell in the invasion.

★ The **Museo Playa Girón** has a photographic history of the social conditions that provoked the Revolution, the counterrevolutionary events after 1959 leading up to the Bay of Pigs Invasion, and the story of the invasion itself. ⊠ *Carretera 3-1-16,* ☎ *59/4122.* ⌷ *$2.* ⊘ *Daily 8–5.*

★ At **Caleta Buena,** 9 km (6 mi) east of Playa Girón, the sea has formed a series of natural pools by entering through underwater caves. The bottom of sponge and coral is a polychromatic marvel, as are the many tropical fish. A 25-m (83-ft) tunnel through the limestone leads out to the sea, for well-prepared and -equipped divers. The on-site restaurant is open until 5 and specializes in shrimp and lobster. If you're having lunch here (the buffet is $10), the $12 admission is waived. A two-hour visit from 3 to 5 costs $6. In spring, be prepared for the dead land crabs that cover the roads, and the accompanying vultures. ⊠ *Carretera 3-1-16,* ☎ *59/5589.* ⌷ *$6–$12; equipment rental for snorkeling, $3; diving, $25.* ⊘ *Daily 10–5.*

Dining and Lodging

$–$$ ✕ **Punta Perdíz.** This boat-shape hulk is the area's best restaurant, with fine views over the water from its upper deck. Fresh shrimp, pargo, and lobster dominate the menu, with *pollo relleno de camarones* (chicken stuffed with shrimp) and *grillada de Montemar* (a mixed grill of red snapper, shrimp, and lobster) leading the way. ⊠ *Carretera Playa Larga–Playa Girón, Km 52,* ☎ *59/5567. MC, V.*

¢ ⊡ **Villa Playa Girón.** Despite the kidney-shape pool and the acceptable buffets, this is a place to stay only if you've failed to make reservations elsewhere (or if you want to visit the noteworthy Museo Playa Girón). The excursions the hotel organizes are its best feature. ⊠ *Playa Girón,* ☎ *5/94110,* ⅢX *5/94117. 228 rooms. Restaurant, bar, air-conditioning, pool, beach, dive shop, dance club, shop, free parking. MC, V. All-inclusive.*

WESTERN CUBA A TO Z

To research prices, get advice from other travelers, and book travel arrangements, visit www.fodors.com.

AIR TRAVEL

International flights go directly to Varadero and Cayo Largo from Canada, Mexico, and Europe, though most flights connect in Havana or Varadero. Outside of Havana, Varadero is the point best connected to the rest of Cuba by air. Cayo Largo is connected by domestic flights to Varadero, the Isla de la Juventud, and other points on the mainland.

AIRPORTS

Nueva Gerona's Aeropuerto Rafael Cabrera is 15 km (9 mi) south of town. The Pinar del Río airport, Aeropuerto Álvaro Barba, is 2 km (1 mi) north of town. The airport serving Varadero—Aeropuerto Juan Gualberto Gómez—is 16 km (10 mi) west of the peninsula.
➤ AIRPORT INFORMATION: **Aeropuerto Álvaro Barba** (☎ 82/63248). **Aeropuerto Juan Gualberto Gómez** (☎ 56/63016 or 56/53612). **Aeropuerto Rafael Cabrera** (☎ 61/22690).

CARRIERS

Cubana de Aviación flights to Nueva Gerona depart from Havana at 7:15 AM and 7:55 PM daily, and at 9:30 AM Monday and Friday. From the Nueva Gerona airport, return flights leave at 8:15 AM and 8:55 PM. Aerocaribbean operates charter flights from Havana and Varadero to Nueva Gerona and Cayo Largo. Aerotaxi has service from Havana to Cayo Largo, Pinar del Río, and Trinidad. Cayo Largo is connected by domestic flights to Havana, Cienfuegos, and Santiago de Cuba via Aerocaribbean, Aerotaxi, and Cubana de Aviación. Round-trip air fare from Havana to Nueva Gerona, Varadero, or Cayo Largo runs $48; it costs about $90 to fly from Havana to Santiago.
➤ AIRLINES AND CONTACTS: **Aerocaribbean** (☎ 61/22690). **Aerotaxi** (☎ 7/66–7540). **Cubana de Aviación** (☎ 7/33–4949).

BOAT AND FERRY TRAVEL

Ferries to Isla de la Juventud depart from Surgidero de Batabanó, 70 km (43 mi) south of Havana, at 10 AM and arrive in Nueva Gerona's terminal on the Río Las Casas at 3. Hydrofoil connections aboard the Russian-built *Kometa* are far faster, leaving Surgidero de Batabanó at 7 AM and 4 PM for the two-hour trip. The regular ferry costs $8 one-way; the hydrofoil costs $12.

BUS TRAVEL

Bus service to western Cuba from other parts of the mainland is available, but generally not recommended. Buses between the Varadero station and Havana's Terminal Ómnibus, however, are quick and frequent. Elsewhere, bus travel is slow and hot, though rock-bottom cheap. Connections are sporadic to remote areas.
➤ BUS INFORMATION: **Varadero station** (✉ Autopista Sur y Calle 36, ☎ 5/61–4886).

CAR RENTAL

Outside Varadero and Nueva Gerona, car rentals are difficult to arrange. They're available in Pinar del Río, Varadero, and Nueva Gerona through Havanautos. In Playa Girón, Transauto has an office across from the Villa Playa Girón. Costs run about $70 a day.
➤ LOCAL AGENCIES: **Havanautos** (✉ Hotel Pinar del Río, Calle Martí, Pinar del Río, ☎ 82/78015; ✉ Av. 1, e/Calle 55 y Calle 56, Varadero, ☎ 5/66–7094; ✉ Aeropuerto Juan Gualberto Gómez, ☎ 5/66–7333; ✉ Servi-Cupet, Calle 39 y Calle 32, Nueva Gerona, ☎ 61/24432; ✉ Villa Gaviota, Autopista Nueva Gerona–La Fé, Km 2, ☎ 61/3256). **Transauto** (✉ Carretera 3-1-16, ☎ 59/4144).

CAR TRAVEL

The Autopista Nacional, a multilane central artery designated A-1, connects all points in western Cuba. For speed and safety, this is undoubtedly the best route to take, although the Carretera Central (Central Highway)—a standard two-lane highway that traverses the

Cuban mainland from one end to the other—is more scenic, winding through little towns and villages. The road to take between Havana, Matanzas, and Varadero is the Vía Blanca, a four-lane freeway in even better condition than the A-1. The Carretera 3-1-16 (also known as Carretera de la Ciéaga de Zapata) that connects the Autopista Nacional A-1 at Australia with Playa Girón and Cienfuegos is only good as far as Caleta Buena. To reach Cienfuegos, resist the temptation to push through to Jaragán and go back around through Playa Girón and Abreus.

Provincial roads in western Cuba are usually in fair to good condition, though even the Autopista Nacional, the island's greatest freeway, has occasional heaves and holes and should never be driven at high speeds. Stray animals, horse-drawn carts, hitchhikers, and (on the Península de Zapata) migratory crabs are the worst driving hazards. There are no toll roads.

GASOLINE

Gasoline availability is generally good at the Servi-Cupet stations. Payment is in U.S. dollars only. Western Cuba, at this writing, had 16 stations distributed around Matanzas, Habana, and Pinar del Río provinces. The only ones *not* to pass without filling up are at the town of Isabel Rubio in western Pinar del Río province and at Australia, the turnoff for the Península de Zapata.

EMERGENCIES

There are hospitals and pharmacies in Matanzas, Nueva Gerona, the Península de Zapata, Pinar del Río, Varadero, and Viñales. For scuba-diving emergencies, the Hospital Julio María Aristegui Villamil in Cárdenas has a decompression chamber in its Centro Médico Sub Acuática. The María la Gorda International Dive Center also has hyperbaric chambers.

➤ HOSPITALS: **Clínica Internacional** (✉ Av. 1, esquina de Calle 61, Varadero, ☎ 5/66–7710). **Hospital Heroes de Baire** (✉ Calle 18, esquina de Calle 41, Nueva Gerona, ☎ 61/23012). **Hospital Juan Ramón Tabranis** (✉ Calle Santa Rita s/n, Matanzas, ☎ 52/24–7011). **Hospital Julio María Aristegui Villamil** (✉ Carretera Varadero, Km 7, Cárdenas, ☎ 5/52–2114). **Hospital Playa Girón** (✉ Gran Parque Montemar, Península de Zapata, ☎ 59/4196). **Hospital Playa Larga** (✉ Gran Parque Montemar, Península de Zapata, ☎ 59/7116). **Hospital Policlínico** (✉ Calle Salvador Cisnero s/n, Viñales, ☎ 8/93245 or 8/93245). **Hospital Quirúrgico** (✉ Calle Isabel Rubio, or Carretera de Viñales s/n, Pinar del Río, ☎ 82/4443).

➤ PHARMACIES: **Matanzas Pharmacy** (✉ Calle 81, esquina de Calle 284). **Nueva Gerona Pharmacy** (✉ Calle 39, esquina de Calle 24, ☎ 61/2–1532). **Playa Girón Pharmacy** (✉ Carretera 3-1-16). **Pinar del Río Pharmacy** (✉ Calle Isabel Rubio, esquina de Calle Martí). **Varadero Pharmacy** (✉ Av. Primera, esquina de Calle 28, ☎ 5/66–2772). **Viñales Pharmacy** (✉ Calle Salvador Cisnero, ☎ 8/93–1690).

➤ POLICE: **Matanzas** (☎ 116). **Nueva Gerona** (☎ 116). **Península de Zapata** (☎ 59/5107). **Pinar del Río** (☎ 82/2525). **Varadero** (☎ 115). **Viñales** (☎ 8/93124).

➤ SCUBA-DIVING EMERGENCIES: **Centro Médico Sub Acuática** (✉ Hospital Julio María Aristegui Villamil, Carretera Varadero, Km 7, Cárdenas, ☎ 5/52–2114). **Centro Internacional de Buceo María la Gorda** (✉ Bahía de Corrientes, Pinar del Río, ☎ 82/78131).

HEALTH

Always drink bottled water. Avoid unpeeled, unwashed fruit and uncooked vegetables, fish, and shellfish. Otherwise, mosquitoes and the tropical sun are the main threats; bring repellents and lotions. There are no poisonous snakes; scorpion bites cause nausea and fever but are not fatal. Crocodiles are aggressive; don't go wading in swampy areas. If pursued by a crocodile (which is unlikely), remember they can't make sharp turns but are frighteningly fast in a straight line.

MAIL AND SHIPPING

In Pinar del Río, the main post office is at the corner of avenidas Martí and Isabel Rubio. There's another post office in the Hotel Pinar del Río. In Viñales, the post office is 100 m (330 ft) west of Hotel San Vicente (Carretera de Puerta Esperanza, Km 32). In Matanzas, it's 50 m (165 ft) north of Palacio Junco, on Calle 272 at Calle 79. Varadero has two post offices, one at the gatehouse at the junction of Avenida 1 and Avenida de las Américas, the other on Avenida Playa between Calles 39 and 40. Nueva Gerona's post office is at the corner of Calles 39 and 18.

MONEY MATTERS

ATM machines in shopping centers such as Varadero's Plaza America generate pesos convertibles, which are equivalent to and as good as U.S. dollars. Credit cards not issued by American banks are widely accepted in Varadero, less so in more remote areas. All hotels provide exchange and banking services.

SAFETY

Street crime in western Cuba is far less of a problem than in most parts of the world. Gay and lesbian travelers would be wise to be discreet, as attitudes toward same-sex lovers—though difficult to predict—tend to be informed by a combination of machismo and early postrevolutionary puritanism about gays.

TAXIS

A taxi between Havana and Matanazas takes an hour and costs $75, or whatever you can negotiate. Try for $25; it's only 100 km (62 mi). Taxis around western Cuba are generally available between major points, though rates can be extortionate.

Most drivers will ask for about a dollar a kilometer for travel within a city or town or small area. In Pinar del Río, tourist taxis can be arranged at the Hotel Pinar del Río. In Varadero, taxis wait outside the Hotel Cuatro Palmas; the fare from one end of the peninsula to the other shouldn't exceed $5. In Matanzas, taxis are available at the Plaza de la Vigía.

In Nueva Gerona, taxis gather at the corner of Calles 32 and 39, while horse-drawn buggies wait at the ferry terminal; the fare for a buggy to a hotel should be about $2. In Cárdenas, which has few cars, a horse-drawn carriage is the way to go.

TELEPHONES

To call western Cuba from abroad, dial the international access number, then 53 (Cuba's country code), then the area code, then the local number. Area codes in the region are: 5 for Cárdenas and Cayo Largo; 7 for Havana; 61 for Isla de la Juventud; 84 for María la Gorda; 52 for Matanzas; 82 for Pinar del Río; 59 for Playa Girón and Playa Larga; 85 for Soroa and Las Terrazas; 5 for Varadero; and 8 for Viñales, Cayo Levisa, San Diego de los Baños, and San Juan y Martínez. In addition, for all Matanzas numbers, you must dial 24 after the 52 local code.

Rates for calls on direct-dial hotel phones are very expensive ($7–$10 a minute for calls abroad); your best bet is to buy a phone card and use a public phone. For calls within Cuba, these cards will hold up well;

a $10 card could last for weeks if used carefully. For calls to Europe or the United States, a $10 card is worth about six minutes. ETECSA (Empresa de Telecomunicaciones de Cuba) booths and hotel receptions sell cards, though they're often out of them. Cellular phones can be rented in Havana or Varadero from Cubacel for a $200 dollar deposit, a daily charge of $7, plus 90¢ a minute for local calls, more for international calls. Prepaid card is the way to go.

For local calls, dial the four-to-six-digit number. For long-distance calls within Cuba, dial 0 then the provincial code and local number. For international calls from Cuba, dial 119 then the country code, city code, and local number you want. For the international operator, dial 0, wait for the higher tone, then dial 9. For information dial 113. For operator-assisted calls to the United States, dial 66/1212.

TOURS

Havanatur, which has several locations in Havana and elsewhere in Cuba, can provide guides. Tour & Travel organizes day excursions to Soroa, Viñales, Pinar del Río, Cárdenas, and Matanzas from either Varadero or Havana.

▶ TOUR CONTACTS: **Havanatur** (✉ Calle 2, No. 17, e/Av. 1 y Av. 3, Miramar, ☎ 7/24–2161). **Tour & Travel** (✉ Av. de la Playa 3606, e/Calle 36 y Calle 37, Varadero, ☎ 5/66–7026).

TRAIN TRAVEL

Train service around western Cuba connects—albeit erratically—Pinar del Río, Matanzas, and Varadero with Havana. Train passage must be purchased in dollars at the Ladis office outside Havana's railroad station. For railroad information, call the offices located at Av. de Bélgica and Calle Arsenal.

A trip on the famous electric *Hershey Train* from Havana's Casablanca district to Matanzas is a four-hour rattle through the scenic Valle de Yumurí. Trains depart from Havana at 4:35 and 9:25 AM and at 3:45 and 8:55 PM; they leave Matanzas at 3:55 and 10:20 AM and at 2:55 and 9:19 PM. The 9:25 AM train from Havana is the suggested trip, though this means your only viable train back leaves Matanzas at 9:19 PM and gets into Havana after 1 AM.

▶ CONTACT: **Ladis** (✉ Calle Arsenal y Calle Cienfuegos, ☎ 7/61–4259).

VISITOR INFORMATION

Infotur has offices in Havana and Matanzas. Look for Cubatur and Havanatur offices in the main hotels of the major towns and cities in western Cuba, both of which serve as de facto tourist-information offices. Publicitur publishes and distributes tourist literature. Asistur offers emergency services from legal advice to medical assistance to banking.

▶ TOURIST INFORMATION: **Asistur** (✉ Calle 23, No. 101, e/Av. 1 y Av. 3, Havana, ☎ 7/33–7277; ✉ Paseo de Martí/Prado 212, Havana, ☎ 7/33–8227). **Cubatur** (✉ Calle 33, Varadero, ☎ 5/66–7269). **Infotur** (✉ Calle Matanzas, esquina de Calle Santa Teresa, Matanzas, ☎ 52/25–3551). **Publicitur** (✉ Calle 19, No. 60, e/ Calle M y Calle N, Vedado, Havana, ☎ 7/55–2835).

4 CENTRAL CUBA

Cuba's geographic heart pounds with the timeless rhythms of Afro-Cuban music, of turquoise waves crashing on white-sand beaches, and of life unfolding in splendid colonial cities. Its coral reefs are awash in color, its mangrove swamps attract flamingos by the thousands, and its lush mountain valleys are filled with birdsong of all types.

By David
Dudenhoefer

NVITING BEACHES BORDER CENTRAL CUBA to the north and south. In between are varied landscapes—from mountains to mangroves—dotted with historic cities. Unlike that of many Caribbean islands, Cuba's early history centered on life in cities, and scattered across this region are three of the nation's seven original "villas"—Trinidad, Sancti Spíritus, and Camagüey—as well as the colonial town of Remedios. In each, time-worn churches and mansions line cobbled streets and tidy parks; in the verdant countryside beyond, old farmhouses overlook sugar plantations, royal palms tower over pastures populated by the people's cattle, and children in red-and-white uniforms play outside one-room schoolhouses.

Central Cuba's history contains many a tale of conquest. Its earliest inhabitants were the Taíno Indians, who island-hopped their way through the Caribbean from South America, arriving on Cuba about 200 years before the Spanish and overrunning the earlier Ciboney Indians, who had settled farther west. The Taíno developed rather sophisticated agricultural techniques, introducing such mainstays as *yuca* (manioc or cassava), potatoes, corn, tobacco, and cotton. Archaeological evidence suggests that they were also potters, weavers, hunters, and fishermen who plied the waters in powerful canoes. By the time Columbus arrived on the island in 1492, however, the Taínos were being challenged by the Caribs, a warlike South American Indian group. The Caribs never actually settled on Cuba, and although they began the conquest of the Taíno, they left its eventual completion—and the island's settlement—to the Spanish.

The conquest of goods led to central Cuba's first period of prosperity. Spanish law mandated that all commerce be conducted with colonial authorities. Such a monopoly drove prices up and left many *criollos* (Cuban-born Spaniards) at odds with Spain. In the mid-16th century, buccaneers (loyal to European nations other than Spain) and pirates (loyal to no one but themselves) attacked ships and sold their plunder on black markets. For many central Cuban residents, smuggling became a highly lucrative profession.

Even after the liberalization of trade, many central Cuban families retained a philosophical distance from Spain. During the wars for independence that wracked the country in the second half of the 19th century, Camagüey was a hotbed of rebellion; the Spanish army even built a coast-to-coast barrier, La Trocha (consisting of fences, embankments, and watchtowers), through the middle of Ciego de Ávila to keep eastern rebels out of the west. Much later, central Cuba's topography made it key in the Revolution. The Sierra de Escambray (Escambray Mountain range) was the haunt of Castro's guerrillas, and rebel leader Che Guevara dealt a decisive blow to Fulgencio Batista's troops in Santa Clara, where his remains rest today.

The Sierra de Escambray, which rises from the provinces of Villa Clara, Cienfuegos, and Sancti Spíritus, has played an economic as well as a political role in the region. In addition to luxuriant forests and waterfalls, its upper slopes are covered with coffee farms; the rolling lowlands surrounding it are fertile grounds for sugar and tobacco. To the east, the land flattens in the provinces of Ciego de Ávila and Camagüey, which are almost completely covered with pasture.

Central Cuba's northern and southern coasts have many beautiful stretches of sand. The beach count leaps dramatically when you include the hundreds of *cayos* (keys) that flank the shores. More and more visitors are discovering the northern cayos, collectively called the Jardines

Central Cuba

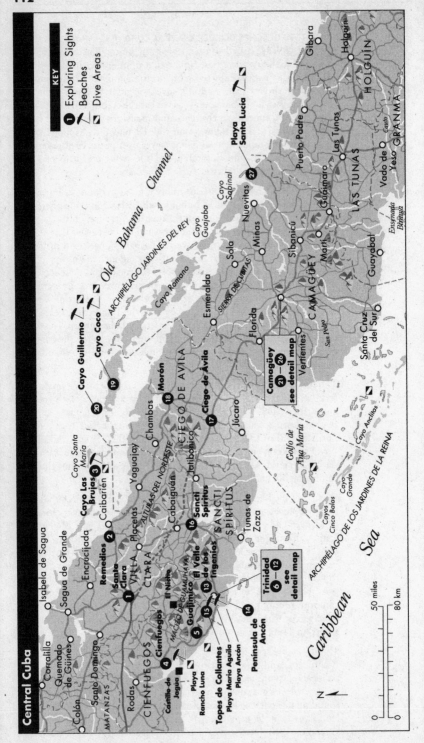

KEY
- **1** Exploring Sights
- Beaches
- Dive Areas

del Rey (Gardens of the King). In the south, the less accessible archipelago known as the Jardines de la Reina (Gardens of the Queen) is visited only by diving excursions.

Pleasures and Pastimes

Beaches
Each central province has a bit of shore, and some of the beaches are lovely: turquoise shallows and powdered ivory sands shaded by coconut palms. Cienfuegos has two small strands just south of it and two more along the road that connects it to Trinidad, 15 km (9 mi) to the east. South of Trinidad are the sand-skirted Península de Ancón and the off-shore isle of Cayo Blanco. Central Cuba's best beaches, however, are on its northern keys—Villa Clara's tranquil Cayo Las Brujas and Ciego de Ávila's more developed Cayo Coco and Cayo Guillermo—and around Santa Lucía, northeast of Camagüey. Most of these beaches offer excellent (and affordable) sportfishing and diving opportunities.

Colonial Architecture
Several cities have histories that date from the arrival of the Spanish. Trinidad, the best preserved of these communities, has block upon block of cobbled streets lined with 18th- and 19th-century structures. Remedios is a similar time capsule, though on a smaller scale and with a fraction of the tourists. Sancti Spíritus also has a small, though nicely restored, colonial center, and though Cienfuegos is a younger city, it has some splendid 19th- and early 20th-century architecture. The biggest of the region's colonial cities is Camagüey, which has an extensive historical center with an eclectic mix of buildings.

Dining
As is true all over Cuba, *puerco* (pork)—prepared the usual variety of ways—figures largely on the region's menus. *Carne de res* (beef) is also common, as are *pollo* (chicken) and *cordero* (lamb). Entrées often come with the traditional *arroz congrí* (fried white rice with beans and pork), which is sometimes called *moros y cristianos* (Moors and Christians). Restaurants in coastal cities and resorts have plenty of seafood on their menus, especially *langosta* (lobster), which abound in the reefs. Because commercial fishing is controlled by the government, however, seafood isn't always as fresh as you might think, even on the coast.

Restaurants are scarce outside Trinidad and Cienfuegos, though every town has a few *paladares* (private eateries), and many *casas particulares* (Cuban homes whose owners have been allowed to rent out rooms) have permits to serve food. Most large beach resorts are all-inclusive, but food quality varies. Reservations are rarely necessary, and though there's no tipping policy per se, most travelers feel better if they tip as many people as possible—in and out of restaurants—as Cubans earn starvation wages. The U.S. dollar is the most reliable form of payment, but credit cards *not* affiliated with U.S. banks or companies are accepted in all government restaurants and hotels, though never in paladares or casas particulares. For price categories, *see* the chart *under* Dining *in* Smart Travel Tips A to Z.

Lodging
Accommodations range from massive, modern beach resorts to historic in-town hotels, and most are on the low end of the price scale. Rare is the double that costs more than $100; in fact, many hotels charge between $30 and $50 for doubles; lodging in casas particulares runs $15 to $25. The facilities vary accordingly, but even the casas particulares have private baths, air-conditioning, hot water, and in-room phones. Credit cards *not* affiliated with U.S. banks or companies are

WHERE CUBA'S WILD THINGS ARE

Cuba may not be famous for its flora and fauna, but it's actually home to an impressive array of wildlife: from massive kapok trees to delicate orchids; from dinosaurian crocodiles to elegant flamingos. Flowering trees light up verdant landscapes, mornings begin with bird choruses, and flower gardens are frequented by countless colorful butterflies and the flitting, iridescent Cuban emerald hummingbird. Just offshore, aquamarine waters hold the living kaleidoscope of the coral reef—Cuba's richest and most extensive ecosystem.

The country's biological diversity is a result of its tropical location, varied environments—savannas, swamps, mountains, mangrove estuaries—its proximity to two continents, and the role islands play in the development of new species. Cuba may lack many of the animals found on the tropical mainland (no monkeys, no toucans, and thankfully, no poisonous snakes), but it has creatures that exist nowhere else. The local living spectrum ranges from albino salamanders that are found in only a few caves, to the pan-tropical coconut palm, which is as common in the Indian Ocean as it is in the Caribbean.

Among the island's rarer creatures are the world's smallest bird (bee hummingbird), frog (Cuban pygmy frog), and mammal (a tiny species of shrew called the *almiquí*). The only one of these animals you're likely to see is the bee hummingbird, known locally as the *zunzuncito*, the male of which weighs a mere 2 grams (0.12 ounce) and stands only 4 centimeters (1½ inches) tall. Head for the Península de Zapata for a glimpse of this diminutive bird. The island's more conspicuous species include the elegant royal palm, Cuba's national tree, and the greater-Antillean grackle—an abundant black bird that makes a lot of noise.

The biggest draws for most nature lovers are Cuba's 388 bird species, 74 of which are indigenous. Some of the more striking ones are the Cuban parrot, Cuban parakeet, Cuban red-bellied woodpecker, and the mountain-dwelling Cuban trogon. The trogon, or *tocorro*, was named the national bird because its colors— red, white, and blue—match those of the flag. Cuba is also home to birds with a wider distribution—the crested caracara, the great lizard cuckoo, and the flamingos that nest here by the thousands—and is visited every winter by more than 150 northern species. Other native species include the Cuban crocodile, various colorful anole lizard species, and the *jutía*—a cat-size rodent that's related to the guinea pig.

Travelers interested in tropical nature usually head for the swampy Península de Zapata or the Sierra del Escambray and the Sierra Maestra. Nowhere on the Cuban mainland, however, can you see as much wildlife as in the coral reefs that surround it. Those submarine gardens are amazing to behold, with their yellow staghorn coral, purple sea fans, and brilliant orange sponges. But even more impressive are the hundreds of fish and invertebrate species: dark-green moray eels, delicate sea stars, massive brown groupers, multicolored parrot fish, spotted eagle rays, spiny lobsters, bright red squirrel fish, and, of course, the occasional octopus. Whether you slip into tepid Caribbean waters, hike into a cool mountain valley, or navigate a coastal estuary, you can't help but be impressed by Cuba's varied wild things.

accepted in all government restaurants and hotels. For price categories, *see* the chart *under* Lodging *in* Smart Travel Tips A to Z.

Scuba Diving and Snorkeling

Diving possibilities range from coral formations just off shore to the isolated, hard-to-access, coral-ringed islands of the Jardines de la Reina, protected within a vast marine park off Cuba's southern shore. Reefs to the west are accessible from the Península de Ancón, Cienfuegos, and nearby Guajimico, which have dozens of dive spots between them. Playa Santa Lucía, the region's second-best scuba destination, has 35 dive spots nearby, including dozens of shipwrecks. Cayos Coco and Guillermo, in the heart of the northern Jardines del Rey, offer access to miles of coral reef teeming with marine life. The island is ideal for experienced scuba divers, but catamaran trips from Playa Ancón, Cayo Coco, and Santa Lucía make amazing snorkeling available to neophytes, and you can swim to the coral from the lodge on Cayo Las Brujas and Cienfuegos's Faro Luna.

Exploring Central Cuba

The region is easy to reach and explore, thanks to the central, mostly flat highway that traverses the island from Havana to eastern Cuba. The road becomes only slightly hilly east of Santa Clara, where it passes near the northern extreme of the Sierra de Escambray, the verdant mountain range that dominates the southern corner of Villa Clara and about half of Cienfuegos and Sancti Spíritus provinces. Various roads wind into the mountains from Trinidad and Cienfuegos. One connects the two cities via Topes de Collantes; another, more direct route runs along the coast. The more easterly provincial capitals of Ciego de Ávila and Camagüey are surrounded by flat ranch land, with roads running north and northeast to the coast.

Numbers in the text correspond to numbers in the margin and on the Central Cuba, Trinidad, and Camagüey maps.

Great Itineraries

IF YOU HAVE 3 DAYS

Drive or take a bus to the colonial city of ⚌ **Trinidad** ⑥–⑫ for a day of exploring. On day two, hit the beaches of the ⚌ **Península de Ancón** ⑭ or head into the mountains at ⚌ **Topes de Collantes** ⑮. Spend the third morning in the **Valle de los Ingenios** ⑬ before returning to Havana. Alternatively, you could drive to ⚌ **Santa Clara** ①, exploring that city by day and continuing to ⚌ **Remedios** ② for the night. The next day, after touring Remedios, head to the reefs and beaches of **Cayo Las Brujas** ③ for the second night and third morning.

IF YOU HAVE 5 DAYS

Drive or take a bus from Havana to the 19th-century city of ⚌ **Cienfuegos** ④ and explore its historic center. On day two, visit the Castillo de Jagua or nearby beaches. On day three, depart early for colonial ⚌ **Trinidad** ⑥–⑫. Spend day four in the city or visiting nearby attractions. Head to either ⚌ **Sancti Spíritus** ⑯ or ⚌ **Santa Clara** ① for the last night.

IF YOU HAVE 7 DAYS

Fly from Havana to ⚌ **Camagüey** ㉑–㉖ and explore its historic center. On the afternoon of the second day, rent a car and drive to the coastal resort of ⚌ **Playa Santa Lucía** ㉗, dedicating day three to sea, sand, and sun. On the fourth day, drive or take a bus to ⚌ **Sancti Spíritus** ⑤ or ⚌ **Trinidad** ⑥–⑫. If you spent the night in Sancti Spíritus, drive or take a bus to Trinidad on day five, stopping at the **Valle de los Ingenios** ⑬. Spend the sixth morning exploring Trinidad or the ⚌ **Península de Ancón** ⑭, and then travel by car or bus to the lively, 19th-century city of

⛶ **Cienfuegos** ④. On day seven, cross the bay to the Castillo de Jagua, enjoy a good lunch, then head for Havana.

When to Tour

The rainy season runs roughly from May to October, the dry season from November to April. The fact that most visitors head here in January and February has more to do with Canadian cold fronts than Santa Lucía sunshine. The rainy season is actually a great time to visit because all is green and crowds are thinner. The busiest months are July–August and January–March, with the last week of December and Easter week being peak. Rates during these times rise and yet rooms book up, making reservations essential.

VILLA CLARA, CIENFUEGOS, AND SANCTI SPÍRITUS PROVINCES

These three provinces contain several historic cities, half a dozen beaches, and natural attractions that range from highland forests to coral reefs. The wonderfully preserved, 18th-century city of Trinidad may be the most spectacular of the colonial towns, but Cienfuegos, Sancti Spíritus, and Remedios all have enough ancient architecture to transport you back in time—and they have fewer visitors. Beaches line the shores just to the south of Trinidad and Cienfuegos, where the ocean holds dozens of dive spots and good angling. In the exuberant valleys of the Sierra de Escambray, the crashing of crystalline waterfalls mixes with the songs of brightly colored birds.

Santa Clara

❶ *258 km (160 mi) southeast of Havana; 61 km (38 mi) northeast of Cienfuegos; 88 km (26 mi) north of Trinidad.*

The capital of Villa Clara Province is a pleasant city of 200,000, with a busy center where cobbled streets are lined with historic buildings and a periphery of factories and modern apartment buildings. Santa Clara was the site of a decisive battle during the last days of 1958, and the remains of the quintessential revolutionary, Che Guevara, rest in a monument at the edge of town. But you need merely visit the central plaza of this provincial capital to discover that its history stretches back centuries and that it has a good bit going on today.

Settled in 1689 by a group of landowners from nearby Remedios, Santa Clara's rich agricultural land and fortuitous location between Havana and eastern Cuba have made it a relatively affluent provincial center. It has Cuba's third-largest university, whose students are probably responsible for the city's reputation for being liberal (it's one of the few Cuban towns with a very visible gay presence). But Santa Clara also appears to be a historically secular city, judging from the absence of a church on its central plaza.

Most of the museums and monuments surround **Parque Vidal,** Santa Clara's central plaza. The streets that border it are closed to traffic, and locals gather here at night and on weekends, when concerts are often held in the kiosk or on the street in front of the Casa de la Cultura. On the park's northeast end stands the stately **Palacio Provincial,** built in 1912 to house the provincial government, but now the city's library. Across the park from the library is the **Palacio Municipal,** or town hall, a structure dating from 1922. The neoclassical building next to the Palacio Municipal was originally an elite social club but is now a government cultural center, the **Casa de la Cultura;** climb its marble staircase to the old ballroom, which is still lovely despite decades of neglect.

Near the southern end of Parque Vidal stands a statue of Marta Abreu, a 19th-century philanthropist who financed, among other things, the construction of the city's main theater, the **Teatro la Caridad** (☎ 422/5548). Set on the park's northwest corner, it was completed in 1885. The oldest building on Parque Vidal is the **Museo de Artes Decorativos,** a former home built in the 1820s that's now open to the public. The house itself is half the attraction, with its marble floors, fluted columns, and hand-painted tiles. Its rooms hold an array of antiques—including crystal, china, statues, and furniture—that date from several centuries. ✉ *Northwest corner of Parque Vidal,* ☎ *42/20–5368.* 🖾 *$2.* ⊙ *Mon. and Wed.–Thurs. 9–noon and 1–6, Fri.–Sat. 1 PM–10 PM, Sun. 6 PM–10 PM.*

★ Santa Clara's most popular attraction is the **Monumento Che Guevara,** a massive bronze sculpture of revolutionary Ernesto "Che" Guevara. The museum here chronicles Che's eventful life, from his happy childhood in Argentina to his 1967 assassination in Bolivia, concentrating on his involvement in the Cuban Revolution. The mausoleum next door holds the remains of Che and 16 others who fought and died with him in the mountains of Bolivia—they weren't discovered and identified by forensic anthropologists until 1997, and didn't arrive in Cuba until 1998. ✉ *Plaza de la Revolución, southwest end of Calle Rafael Trista,* ☎ *no phone.* 🖾 *Free.* ⊙ *Tues.–Sat. 8 AM–9 PM, Sun. 8–5.*

On the north side of Santa Clara, just across the Río Cubanicay, is the **Tren Blindado,** a military train that was carrying soldiers and weapons when it was derailed by Che and a group of rebels on the morning of December 28, 1958—a decisive moment in the Cuban Revolution. Guevara's troops went on to take the city, cutting Havana off from the eastern half of the country, which prompted Batista's flight from Cuba and Castro's victory—all in a matter of days. Several train cars, some containing displays, lie in the grass next to the tracks in memory of that battle; the bulldozer used to destroy the tracks stands on a nearby cement slab. ✉ *Northern end of Calle Independencia,* ☎ *no phone.* 🖾 *Free.* ⊙ *Mon.–Sat. 8–6, Sun. 9–noon.*

Dining and Lodging

The best hotels are well outside Santa Clara, near the peripheral highway called the Circunvalción, but budget travelers can choose from several casas particulares near Parque Vidal. **Omelio Moreno** (✉ Calle San Cristóbal 4, ☎ 42/21–6941) and his wife rent two spotless, air-conditioned rooms on the second floor of their house one block south of Parque Vidal. They also serve meals. **Orlando Cordero** (✉ Calle R. Pardo/Buenviaje 16, ☎ 42/20–6456) rents two well-equipped, spacious rooms half a block east of Parque Vidal; be sure to check out his rooftop terrace. The rooms that **Orlando Garcia** (✉ Calle R. Pardo/Buenviaje 7, ☎ 42/20–6761) rents are a bit dark, but he's an excellent host and offers meals at his rooftop paladar.

¢–$ ✕ **La Concha.** Its only decoration may be a pastoral mural covering one wall, but locals are drawn to this popular restaurant on the western edge of town by the food, the prices, and (perhaps) the air-conditioning—not the decor. The menu is a mix of Cuban and Italian dishes, with such local standards as *escalope de puerco* (breaded pork) as well as a selection of pastas and pizzas. ✉ *Carretera Central, esquina de Calle Danielito,* ☎ *42/21–8120. No credit cards.*

¢ 🏨 **La Granjita.** On a 5-hectare (12-acre) farm—the name means "little farm"—near Santa Clara's airport, this tranquil resort has plenty of fresh air and birdsong. Rooms are in two-story octagonal duplexes, with bright tile floors, hardwood furniture, and lots of windows overlooking shady lawns. You can follow trails through patches of forest, orchards, and pastures on foot or on horseback. A kidney-shape pool lies next to the reception area, and a large restaurant nearby offers buffets as well as a menu of Cuban dishes. ⊠ *Carretera la Maleza, 3 km (2 mi) northwest of Santa Clara,* ☎ *42/21–8190,* FAX *42/21–8192,* WEB *www.cubanacan.cu. 75 rooms. Restaurant, bars, pool, massage, horseback riding. MC, V.*

¢　🏨 **Santa Clara Libre.** This large, ugly hotel on Parque Vidal has two room sizes: tiny and not quite so tiny. They may not have been redecorated since the Revolution, but they're clean and have the basic amenities—in fact, those in front have nice views of the plaza and city beyond. For the best vistas, however, head for the rooftop bar; the basement disco is a popular nightspot. ⊠ *Parque Vidal 6,* ☎ *42/20–7548,* FAX *42/20–5171. 75 rooms. Bar, dance club. MC, V.*

Nightlife and the Arts

El Boulevard, the pedestrian mall on Calle Independencia, just north of Parque Vidal, has several bars and sidewalk cafés that are popular weekend spots. **Bar Club Boulevard** (⊠ Calle Independencia 225, ☎ 42/21–6236), at the eastern end of El Boulevard, is *the* place for live music; shows start at 10 PM.

The **Casa de la Cultura** (⊠ Parque Vidal 5, ☎ 42/21–7181) hosts several concerts a week at 9 PM and a street concert every Sunday at 4 PM. Occasional music and dance performances, as well as the historic La Marquesa bar, provide the perfect excuses to visit the lovely **Teatro la Caridad** (⊠ Parque Vidal 3, ☎ 42/20–5548).

Shopping

Stop by **ARTEX** (⊠ Parque Vidal 6, ☎ 42/20–6278) for Cuban music, T-shirts, and other souvenirs. The **Fondo de Bienes Culturales** (⊠ Calle Estebez 9, just north of Parque Vidal, ☎ 42/20–4195) sells such local handicrafts as straw hats, leather bags, and knickknacks.

Remedios

❷ *45 km (27 mi) northeast of Santa Clara.*

San Juan de Remedios is one of Cuba's oldest towns. Founded in 1515 on the northern coast, it was moved inland to its current location in 1524, following harassment by pirates. Toward the end of the 17th century, a group of wealthy citizens tried to move Remedios still farther inland, but most of the townspeople resisted; those who wanted to move went on to found Santa Clara, which became the province's principal city. Remedios slipped into its shadow and has retained a sleepy, unspoiled atmosphere.

Though small (20,000 inhabitants), Remedios is culturally rich and remarkably well preserved. It's actually amazing that the city has survived at all, considering that its most famous tradition is Las Parrandas: an incendiary festival celebrated on Christmas Eve that practically reduces the entire town to ashes year after year. Legend has it that the festival began in the 1820s when a parish priest, who worried that not enough people where attending Christmas mass, sent a group of boys through the streets banging drums and making noise to wake people up and get them into the pews. The tradition has developed into an all-night festival lit by homemade lanterns and fireworks and animated by brass bands; its participants are cheered still more by copious food and drink.

Remedios's geographic heart is **Plaza Marti,** a tidy park shaded by royal palms and other tropical trees and surrounded by 18th- and 19th-century architecture. **La Iglesia de San Juan Bautista** (Church of St. John

CHE GUEVARA: REVOLUTIONARY ICON

When the United States blockaded Cuba in 1961, Everywhere in Cuba, you encounter the legendary visage of Che Guevara in beard and beret—an image captured by the Cuban photographer Korda in the early days of the Revolution—on billboards, walls, posters, T-shirts, key chains, watches, and buttons. That same face also often adorns walls in universities, bars, and coffeehouses throughout Latin America and Europe. For students and leftists, Che represents idealism, rebellion, and dedication to a higher cause. He was a renaissance revolutionary—doctor, writer, soldier, photographer, statesman—who continues to be studied and mythicized. Jean-Paul Sartre called him "the most complete human being of our age," but for those who have suffered the wrath of Communism, he's just a pretty face on a heartless system, and for millions he has become a mere fashion statement. In Cuba, however, Che is the communist equivalent of a saint.

Ernesto Guevara was born into a middle-class family in El Rosario, Argentina, on June 14, 1928; che, the Argentine term for "buddy," became his nickname in Cuba years later. A precocious child who suffered from asthma at an early age, he learned to read when he was five and was devouring the works of Karl Marx and Cuban intellectual José Martí at the age of 15; by age 20 he was studying medicine at the University of Buenos Aires. In 1952, Guevara took a break from med school to travel around South America on a motorbike, and upon graduating he hit the road again, heading north to Central America. He was in Guatemala when the left-leaning government of Jacobo Arbenz was overthrown by a CIA-orchestrated coup, and he fled to Mexico a sworn enemy of U.S. imperialism.

In Mexico he joined Fidel Castro's small revolutionary army as a doctor, and sailed to Cuba aboard the Granma in 1956. Che displayed an innate talent for guerrilla warfare (he later wrote two books on the subject) and was soon promoted to field commander. He led troops in the Sierra de Escambray, and in a battle that ensured dictator Fulgencio Batista's defeat, he and his rebels derailed a military train in Santa Clara. Following his victorious entrance into Havana, the eloquent and charismatic Argentine captured the hearts of the Cuban masses and became Castro's confidant (Castro even declared him a Cuban citizen). Not only did Che serve as the country's minister of finance and minister of industry, he represented Cuba abroad. He became one of the socialist government's main architects, expounding a theory of the New Man, who would create a society based on equality and solidarity.

Perhaps driven by a desire to spread revolution, Guevara renounced his government positions in 1965 and left to fight with rebel forces in the Congo. From Africa he traveled to Bolivia, where he joined yet another rebel army. He and his band of guerrillas were captured—with help from the CIA—and executed by the Bolivian army on October 9, 1967. The location of their mass grave was a secret for three decades, and Che's remains weren't found and identified till 1997, when they were flown to Cuba and placed with pageantry in the mausoleum of the monument to him in Santa Clara.

the Baptist) is a squat colonial structure with a massive bell tower on the plaza's eastern end. Its splendidly restored 18th-century interior (head for the back door, as the main doors are usually shut) includes high arches, an elaborate beamed cedar ceiling, and gilt-wood altars. Although its stone floor dates from 1550, most of the chapel was rebuilt in 1752; it underwent extensive renovation in the 1940s, including the construction of a new main altar using parts of the original baroque altar. The smaller altar to the right is dedicated to the Virgin de la Caridad, Cuba's patron saint. The gilt shrines along the walls are dedicated to various saints; note the pregnant Virgin, brought from Seville in the 1700s, to the left of the main door. ☎ *No phone.* ✉ *Donation suggested.* ⊙ *Mon.–Sat. 8–noon and 3–6, Sun. 4–6.*

To the northwest of the plaza is the stout **Iglesia del Buen Viaje** (Church of the Good Voyage), which was built by mariners to protect an image of the Virgin Mary found floating in the ocean. The original structure, constructed in 1770, burned down in the 19th century and was replaced by today's version. It's a lovely edifice but is no longer used for mass, and is thus never opened to the public. In front of it stands a monument that bears some likeness to the Statue of Liberty; it's dedicated to local martyrs of Cuba's wars of independence.

On the northern side of Plaza Martí you'll find one of the city's best-preserved colonial buildings. The former home of composer Alejandro García Caturla is now the **Museo de la Música**, a museum dedicated to his life. Built in 1875, the house has a small central patio planted with palms and surrounded by rooms that contain antique furnishings or exhibits on the composer's works. ✉ *Calle Camilo Cienfuegos 5,* ☎ *no phone.* ✉ *$1.* ⊙ *Tues.–Sat. 9–noon and 1–5, Sun. 9–noon.*

If you can't be in Remedios on December 24 for Las Parrandas celebrations, you'll have to settle for a visit to the **Museo de las Parrandas.** The city is divided into two neighborhoods—El Carmen and El Salvador—each of which creates its own floats, costumes, lanterns, and fireworks as part of an informal competition during the festival. Though no winner is ever declared, most townspeople will tell you that not only does their neighborhood win every year, but the rest of Remedios isn't even good competition. The museum has faded photos and paraphernalia from past Parrandas. ✉ *Calle Máximo Gómez 71, 1½ blocks west of Plaza Martí,* ☎ *42/39–5400.* ✉ *$1.* ⊙ *Tues.–Sat. 9–noon and 1–5, Sun. 9–1.*

Dining and Lodging

Remedios is a one-hotel town, but it has several casas particulares, most of which are west of Plaza Martí. The airy rooms in the second-floor apartment belonging to **Gladys Aponte** (✉ Calle Brigadier Gonzales 32A, ☎ 42/39–5398) have great city views. The decoration reflects Gladys's devotion to Santería (a blend of Catholicism and African religious beliefs). Though the 1950s house that **Jorge Ribero** lives in (✉ Calle Brigadier Gonzales 32A, ☎ 42/39–5331) seems out of place in this colonial town, its spacious rooms are among Remedios's most comfortable accommodations.

¢ ✕ **El Louvre.** This small café with a hardwood bar, brass lamps, and wooden ceiling has been in business since 1866. The view, overlooking Plaza Martí, probably isn't much different than when it opened, and it still serves *ponche de la parroquia,* a rum-and-milk cocktail that wily young men once gave to chaperones. (Once drunk, the chaperones would be less likely to interfere should the young men try to steal kisses from their girlfriends.) Though the menu has a wide array of beverages, dishes are limited to sandwiches, pollo *frito* (fried), and *bistéc* *de puerco* (grilled pork). ✉ *Calle Máximo Gómez 122*, ☎ *no phone. No credit cards.*

¢ ✕🍴 **Hotel Mascotte.** Although such alterations as gleaming white-tile
★ floors detract from its historic atmosphere, this late-19th-century inn
is still charming. The thick square columns, high arches, and abundant
potted plants in the public areas will enchant you. Guest rooms have
tile floors and modern wooden furniture. The five in front have high
ceilings and small balconies overlooking Plaza Martí; those in the
back have no windows and are cramped. The restaurant (¢–$$) serves
quality Cuban cuisine; try the bistec *en cazuela* (in a red sauce) or a
seafood dish. ✉ *Calle Máximo Gómez 112*, ☎ *42/39–5144. 10 rooms.
Restaurant, bar. MC, V.*

Shopping

A small selection of wood sculptures and other local handicrafts is avail-
able at the **Fondo de Bienes Culturales** (☎ 42/39–5617), across Calle
Máximo Gómez from the Hotel Mascotte.

Cayo Las Brujas

❸ *50 km (30 mi) northeast of Remedios.*

A *piedraplen* (causeway) traverses the shallow waters of Bahía Buena
Vista (Buena Vista Bay) from the mainland to Cayo Las Brujas and be-
yond to the larger Cayo Santa María—both in the western half of the
Jardines del Rey archipelago. Cayo Santa María is being developed on
a grand scale, with giant, all-inclusive beach resorts. Perhaps Cayo Las
Brujas's salvation from mass tourism is the result of some kind of spell.

Brujas (pronounced "brew-haas") means "witches," and local legend
tells of the clandestine love affair between a fisherman's daughter and
a young man. One day he arrived late to their meeting place only to
discover a hoary witch in place of his tender love. A statue of the maiden
now stares at sea from atop a coral bluff next to the island's one, small
hotel—the Villa Las Brujas.

Cayo Las Brujas remains enchanted, but the current spell is cast by the
sun as it shines on this key's beige beach, which is backed by dense fo-
liage and fronted by crystalline waters, coral reefs, and uninhabited
islets. There's good snorkeling around the point, and a larger reef lies
across just the channel, in front of Cayo Francés. The hotel rents
snorkeling equipment, kayaks, and catamarans, and offers trips to dive
spots and a pristine beach on Cayo Borracho. You can visit Cayo Las
Brujas on a day trip, but you'll have to pay $5 to cross the piedraplen.
If you spend the night, bring insect repellent.

Lodging

$$ 🍴 **Villa Las Brujas.** Wooden buildings scattered along a coral bluff house
★ this intimate resort's spacious rooms. Tiles, drapes, and cushions
throughout are done in earthtones that evoke the surrounding land-
scape; abundant windows and balconies allow sun and sea breezes inside. All guest rooms have original art, wicker furniture, and satellite
TV; most have ocean views. The thatch-roof restaurant ($–$$) has a
panorama of beach and sea; the menu is short and dominated by
seafood. ✉ *Cayo Las Brujas*, ☎ *42/20–7599 or 7/66–6777 in Havana*,
FAX *42/20–4199*, WEB *www.cubaweb.gaviota.cu. 24 rooms. Restaurant,
beach, snorkeling, windsurfing, boating, motorbikes. MC, V.*

Cienfuegos

❹ *232 km (144 mi) southeast of Havana; 106 km (66 mi) southwest of
Remedios; 80 km (48 mi) northwest of Trinidad.*

Cienfuegos is an attractive, laid-back port city of 110,000 people that overlooks a deep bay of the same name. Its small historic core is surrounded by a gray ring of cement-block housing and industrial buildings, beyond which lie fields of sugarcane and the dark green mass of the Sierra de Escambray.

A relatively young provincial capital, Cienfuegos was founded in 1819 by immigrants from Bordeaux as part of a Spanish scheme to establish a city in a region that had long been the haunt of pirates. Originally dubbed Fernandina de Jagua ("Fernandina" honors Spain's King Ferdinand and "Jagua" was the indigenous name for the region), the city was later named after General José Cienfuegos (a colonial governor of the province). It quickly became an important port; sugar plantations came to cover its hinterlands, and slaves were imported to work on them. Families who made fortunes from cane and human bondage built mansions (known locally as *palacios* or palaces), many of which still stand.

Cienfuegos's French roots are reflected in some of its architecture, and are celebrated every April with a Francophile festival. Nevertheless, it's a very Cuban city where the breeze often carries the melodies of local hero Benny Moré, one of the giants of the Cuban music *son*.

Cienfuegos's main artery, Calle 37, is called El Prado in the old part of town, where it's flanked by late-19th-century colonnades and divided by a wide, landscaped median. To the south, Calle 37 runs roughly parallel to the waterfront **Malecón,** where locals stroll at night. Note the illuminated billboard near the Malecón; it has an image of Moré and a line from one of his songs: *"Cienfuegos es la ciudad que más me gusta a mi"* ("Cienfuegos is the city I like most.") The palm-lined promenade stretches south to Punta Gorda, a point dominated by the mansions once owned by sugar barons and ending in a small park surrounded by water where people gather on weekends to swim and relax.

Most of the important buildings of Cienfuegos surround the central **Parque José Martí,** which contains an impressive marble statue, carved in 1902, of the Cuban revolutionary and intellectual for whom it was named. Near the park's western end is a tiny replica of the Arc de Triomphe, a nod to the city's French heritage, and just south of the Martí statue stands a domed kiosk, where the municipal band sometimes gives weekend concerts. East of the park, Avenida 54 is a pedestrian mall—lined with shops and restaurants—called El Boulevard.

The stately building southeast of the bandstand used to be the Casino Español, an elite club built in the late 19th century. It now houses the **Museo Provincial,** a museum dedicated to local history and furnished with antiques that once belonged to some of the casino's most respected members. ⊠ *Av. 54 y Calle 27,* ☎ *432/9722.* 🖼 *$1.* ☉ *Tues.–Sun. 8–4:30.*

At the park's southwest corner stands the Palacio Ferrer, an elaborate mansion built in 1917 by Spanish businessman José Ferrer and now the **Casa de Cultura.** The corner room on the second floor was once used by Enrico Caruso, and a spiral staircase leads from here up to a tower that offers a nice view of the plaza. Local musicians and dancers often rehearse here. ⊠ *Av. 54 y Calle 25,* ☎ *432/6584.* 🖼 *$1.* ☉ *Mon.–Sat. 9–7.*

NEED A
BREAK?
El Palatino (⊠ Av. 54, esquina de Calle 27, ☎ 432/45–1244), the low building with the fat pillars south of Parque Martí's bandstand, dates from the 1840s. Today it's a popular tavern, the perfect place for a

When you pack your MCI Calling Card, it's like packing your loved ones along too.

Your MCI Calling Card is the easy way to stay in touch when you travel. Use it to call to and from over 125 countries. Plus, every time you call, you can earn frequent flier miles. So wherever your travels take you, call home with your MCI Calling Card. It's even easy to get one. Just visit **www.mci.com/worldphone.**

EASY TO CALL WORLDWIDE

1. Just enter the WorldPhone® access number of the country you're calling from.

2. Enter or give the operator your MCI Calling Card number.

3. Enter or give the number you're calling.

Aruba ⊹	800-888-8
Bahamas ⊹	1-800-888-8000

Barbados ⊹	1-800-888-8000
Bermuda ⊹	1-800-888-8000
British Virgin Islands ⊹	1-800-888-8000
Canada	1-800-888-8000
Mexico	01-800-021-8000
Puerto Rico	1-800-888-8000
United States	1-800-888-8000
U.S. Virgin Islands	1-800-888-8000

⊹ Limited availability.

EARN FREQUENT FLIER MILES

MCI®

SEE THE WORLD
IN FULL COLOR

Fodor's Exploring Guides bring all the great sights vividly to life with hundreds of photographs, fascinating historical background, and colorful anecdotes. Detailed maps and practical information keep you headed in the right direction.

Pair a **Fodor's** Exploring Guide with your trusted Gold Guide for a complete planning package.

quick Cuban coffee, a *mojito* (rum, lime juice, and mint), or light lunch. Live music shows are common in the afternoon and early evening.

The **Catedral de la Purísima Concepción,** the city's bright yellow cathedral, with its high central bell tower reminiscent of a minaret, was consecrated in 1869. Its interior is less impressive than the renovated exterior, but it does feature a statue of the Virgin of the Immaculate Conception—the city's patron saint—and stained-glass windows from France that depict the 12 apostles. ⊠ *Av. 56 y Calle 29, east of Parque Martí,* ☎ *no phone.* ⊠ *Free.* ⊙ *Daily 7–3.*

The **Teatro Tomás Terry,** the city's principal theater, was built in 1889 and named for the millionaire whose fortune funded its construction. If you can't come for a concert or dance performance, you can admire the painted ceilings, statues, and carved hardwoods for a small fee. ⊠ *Av. 56, No. 2703, north of Parque Martí,* ☎ *432/3361.* ⊠ *$1.* ⊙ *Daily 9–6.*

★ Of Punta Gorda's various palacios, the most impressive is the **Palacio de Valle,** built in 1917 by the sugar baron Asisclo del Valle. It's a sumptuous structure full of ornate relief work, crystal chandeliers, hand-painted tiles, Italian-marble columns, French windows, and carved Cuban hardwoods. Though the mansion's design is eclectic, its foremost inspiration was the Alhambra—the Moorish palace in southern Spain. It now houses the city's best restaurant on the ground floor and a rooftop bar that's the perfect spot from which to watch the sun set. ⊠ *Av. 0 y Calle 37,* ☎ *432/45–1226.* ⊠ *$1.* ⊙ *Daily 11–10.*

★ ☾ Above a fishing village overlooking the narrow entrance to the Bahía de Cienfuegos (35 km/21 mi south of the historical center) is the **Castillo de Jagua,** a Spanish fortress built in 1745 to keep out pirates who had grown accustomed to trading with locals. It's completely refurbished (even the drawbridge works), and has a historical museum with weapons and other antiques. The dungeon houses a bar and restaurant. On your way down, note the small chamber beneath the steps; prisoners were chained and tortured here. Considering the existence of this chamber, and a working drawbridge, it's not advisable to try sneaking out without paying your bill. ⊠ *Jagua,* ☎ *439/6420.* ⊠ *$1.* ⊙ *Tues.–Sat. 9–5, Sun. 9–1.*

Cienfuegos's **Jardín Botánico** (Botanical Garden) covers 94 hectares (232 acres) and contains more than 2,000 plant species, most of which are from other countries. Created at the turn of the last century by U.S. sugar farmer Edwin Atkins, the garden was administered by Harvard University until 1962, when it was taken over by the Cuban Academy of Science. It includes palms, bamboos, and other tropical trees as well as medicinal plants and a forest reserve that's home to many native animals. Guides are available (only one speaks English), and tips are greatly appreciated. ⊠ *16 km/10 mi east of Cienfuegos,* ☎ *432/45115.* ⊠ *$2.50.* ⊙ *Daily 8–5.*

☾ The **Delfinario** offers daily performances by trained dolphins and sea lions and the opportunity to swim with captive dolphins in an estuary near Playa Rancho Luna, the beach closest to Cienfuegos. Call for show times. ⊠ *18 km/11 mi southeast of Cienfuegos,* ☎ *432/04–8120.* ⊠ *$5; $40 to swim with dolphins.* ⊙ *Daily 9–4.*

OFF THE BEATEN PATH
EL NICHO – This cool, luxuriant valley full of idyllic swimming holes makes an excellent day trip from Cienfuegos. The entrance to the region is marked by a rustic restaurant. From here, footpaths lead to a series of pools filled with emerald waters and two crystalline waterfalls sur-

rounded by greenery. Be on the lookout for the great lizard cuckoo, the emerald hummingbird, and the Cuban trogon—the national bird. The tour company Rumbos offers cheap excursions here, which are the best option since the road is often too rough for most vehicles. ⊠ *55 km/34 mi east of Cienfuegos,* ☎ *no phone.* ☎ *$2.* ⊙ *Daily 8–6.*

Beaches

The coast southeast of Cienfuegos has several nice beaches, the nearest of which is the public **Playa Rancho Luna,** a pale crescent flanked by rocky points 18 km (11 mi) southeast of town. It has hotels to the west and east of it and an extensive coral reef wrapped around the point directly to the west—you can rent snorkeling equipment at the Faro Luna Diving Center there. A smaller beach, also called Rancho Luna, lies just around the point to the east.

Dining and Lodging

Cienfuegos's accommodations range from a historic inn downtown to beach hotels with ocean views. There are also a number of rooms for rent in private homes, the nicest of which are on the point beyond the Hotel Jagua. **Angel e Isabel** (⊠ Calle 34, No. 24, ☎ no phone) are a young couple who live in an old house near La Punta; they have three rooms in a newer, separate building in back. Rooms have private baths and air-conditioning, and they open onto a small, manicured yard overlooking the sea. The bright green **Casa Lolita** (⊠ Av. 52, No. 5312, ☎ 432/7568), run by Maritza and Leandro, is an 80-year-old house with simple rooms three blocks south of the bus station. **Juan Napolis** (⊠ Calle 35, No. 22, ☎ 432/3196) rents two basic rooms that share a bath; he also has a small garden on the water. **Villa Lagarto** (⊠ Calle 35, No. 4B, ☎ 432/9966) is the best casa particular in town. Its three modern rooms have air-conditioning and private baths; they overlook the sea and a park called La Punta. Friendly hosts Tony and Maylin serve unforgettable meals; if their rooms are booked, they can arrange rentals elsewhere in the neighborhood.

$$–$$$$ ✕ **Palacio de Valle.** Elegance abounds on the ground floor of Cienfuegos's
★   most gracious mansion, with its ornate arches, marble columns, and crystal chandeliers. And there's usually someone playing the restaurant's grand piano. The food may play second fiddle to ambience, but it's still some of the best in town. The specialty is langosta, which is prepared five different ways; other choices include *sopa de mariscos* (seafood soup), *camarones al pincho* (shrimp shish kebab), and even filet mignon. Try to arrive early enough to enjoy a sunset cocktail on the roof deck. ⊠ *Av. 0 y Calle 37, Cienfuegos,* ☎ *432/3021 or 432/ 3025. MC, V.*

$–$$$$ ✕ **La Cueva del Camarón.** In any other neighborhood, this mansion would be impressive, but since it practically sits in the shadow of the Palacio de Valle, it looks like a failed attempt at keeping up with the Joneses. Nevertheless, its bright interior—full of shiny marble, colorful tiles, and carved hardwoods—makes it an elegant place to dine, and the waterfront terrace in back is a great spot for lunch. The menu is strong on seafood, with dishes ranging from *pescado al camaron* (fish fillet in a white shrimp sauce) to a *grillada mixta* (mixed grill) that contains lobster, fish, and prawns. ⊠ *Av. 2 y Calle 37, Cienfuegos,* ☎ *432/ 45–1128. MC, V.*

$ ✕ **Paladar Aché.** The plastic chairs and tables and pink walls of this tiny private eatery don't hold a candle to the brilliance of the city's mansion restaurants, but your meal here will be prepared by the owner instead of by underpaid government employees. The state only lets the owners serve chicken and pork, which are, consequently, prepared several ways and come with lots of arroz congrí and other Cuban side dishes. The paladar is in a yellow house 2½ blocks east of the Malecón and a block south of the Bahía Service Station. If you let a Cuban lead you here or you arrive in a taxi, the prices will be inflated to cover their commission. ⊠ *Av. 38, No. 4106, Cienfuegos,* ☎ *no phone. No credit cards. Closed Sun.*

$ ✕🏠 **Hotel Jagua.** This six-story cement structure dating from the 1950s towers over the palacios of Punta Gorda (it stands in what was once the Palacio de Valle's garden). Rooms view the bay and the city—a more pleasant sight at night by day thanks to an oil refinery and other industry. The decor is bright and modern, with white-tile floors and colorful bedspreads. The restaurant ($–$$) has buffets—serving Italian food one time, Cuban another—when there are groups and offers a Continental menu when it's quiet. There's also a tiny museum dedicated to the city's Austurian heritage. ⊠ *Punta Gorda, Cienfuegos,* ☎ *432/45–1003,* FAX *432/45–1245,* WEB *www.grancaribe.cu. 145 rooms. Restaurant, bar, pool. MC, V.*

$ 🏠 **La Union.** Inaugurated in 1869, this stately hotel in the heart of Cienfuegos is Cuba's oldest. Photos in the foyer show it as a center of activity in the early 1900s, but it was neglected after the Revolution and was in ruins before the government rebuilt it in 1999. The result is a new hotel done in 19th-century style, with wide arches, painted columns, and quiet courtyards populated with potted plants. Rooms have high ceilings, white-tile floors, faux antiques, and modern amenities. The bright-blue restaurant serves an inventive selection of Cuban cuisine and fresh seafood. Each night, live music enhances the city views in the rooftop bar. ⊠ *Calle 31, esquina de Av. 54, Cienfuegos,* ☎ *432/45–1020,* FAX *432/45–1685,* WEB *www.cubanacan.cu. 49 rooms. Restaurant, 2 bars, minibars, pool, massage, sauna, gym, shop, car rental. MC, V. CP.*

¢   🏠 **Faro Luna.** Most of the rooms at this hotel just west of Playa Rancho Luna have ocean views, especially those in the two-story bungalows. Guest quarters are bright and spacious, with wicker furniture, colorful bedspreads, and large balconies. The main building has a small restaurant-bar that serves typical Cuban dishes and seafood. Next to it is a tiled pool surrounded by coconut palms. Though it's a bit of a walk to the beach, the hotel has its own dive center, which arranges trips to dozens of offshore reefs and wrecks. ⊠ *Playa Rancho Luna, 16 km/10 mi southeast of Cienfuegos,* ☎ *432/45–1030,* FAX *432/45–1162,* WEB *www.cubanacan.cu. 40 rooms. Restaurant, bar, pool, dive shop. MC, V.*

Nightlife and the Arts

After the sun has set, several spots along El Boulevard (Avenida 54) get busy. Local musicians perform nightly at the **Café Cantante Benny Moré** (Av. 54 y El Prado, ☎ no phone). The **Disco Club Benny Moré** (Av. 54, e/Calle 29 y Calle 31, ☎ 432/45–1105) rocks till the wee hours every night but Monday. The bar on the roof of the **Hotel Union** (⊠ Calle 31, esquina de Av. 54, ☎ 432/45–1020) has live jazz on Tuesday and Thursday and traditional Cuban music Wednesday, Friday, and Saturday; shows start at 9:30 PM.

Jardines de la UNEAC (Calle 25 e/Av. 54 y Av. 56, ☎ no phone), a garden venue near the Casa de la Cultura, occasionally has performances by local bands, either in the afternoon or evening. The rooftop bar at the **Palacio de Valle** (⊠ Av. 0 y Calle 37, ☎ 432/45–1226) is a great spot for a sunset drink and often has live music. **El Palatino** (Av. 54 e/Calle 25 y Calle 27, ☎ 432/45–1244), the historic bar overlooking Parque Martí, usually has live music in the afternoon and evening. The stately **Teatro Tomás Terry** (Av. 56, No. 2703, ☎ 432/3361) hosts frequent concerts and dance performances.

Outdoor Activities and Sports

FISHING

The fishing in the waters off Cienfuegos is good, with abundant mahimahi, wahoo, jacks, and other fighters. The **Marina Puertosol Cienfuegos** (⊠ Punta Gorda, ☎ 432/45–1241) has small charter boats equipped with basic gear for amazingly low rates.

HORSEBACK RIDING

Hacienda La Vega (⊠ 50 km/30 mi southeast of Cienfuegos on road to Trinidad, ☎ no phone), a working cattle ranch, runs a three-hour, horseback tour through pastures and forest; it includes a swim on a secluded beach and a dairy tour. You can hire horses and a guide at the ranch, or you can go on a half-day tour offered by Rumbos. Costs average around $20 per person.

SCUBA DIVING

The ocean around Cienfuegos has dozens of dive sites, from shallow reefs to deep shipwrecks. Because the edge of the platform is relatively close to shore, the waters are frequented by big fish. The coral is healthy and well developed—one column stands 7 m (23 ft) high—and visibility varies from 15 to 40 m (45 to 120 ft). The **Centro de Buceo Faro Luna** (Faro Luna Diving Center; ☎ 432/45–1340) is next to the hotel of the same name on Playa Rancho Luna, 16 km (10 mi) southeast of Cienfuegos. It costs about $5 a day to rent snorkeling gear and $10 a day for scuba equipment. The center runs one-tank boat dives ($25 per person) to roughly 30 sites; it also offers certification courses for $200.

Shopping

Casa Arco (⊠ Av. 54, No. 3301, ☎ no phone) offers a decent selection of music, as well as a few T-shirts and other souvenirs. The historic **Casa del Fundador** (⊠ Calle 28, esquina de Av. 54, ☎ 432/45–2134), a colonial house overlooking Parque Martí, has an excellent selection of cigars, but also sells rum, coffee, T-shirts, CDs, and other souvenirs. **El Embajador** (⊠ Av. 54 y Calle 33, ☎ 432/45–1343) specializes in rum, coffee, and cigars. The **Galería Moroya** (⊠ Av. 54, No. 2506, ☎ 432/45–1208), a colonial house south of Parque Martí, is packed with paintings, sculptures, clothes, and handicrafts.

Guajimico

⑤ *42 km (25 mi) southeast of Cienfuegos; 43 km (26 mi) northwest of Trinidad.*

The tiny agricultural community of Guajimico has little to offer in and of itself, but it sits in a wild area halfway between Cienfuegos and Trinidad where the natural attractions range from patches of tropical forest to offshore coral reefs. The cattle ranch of **Hacienda La Vega**, 50 km (30 mi) southeast of Cienfuegos and 8 km (5 mi) east of Villa Guajimico, runs horseback tours that pass through forests and pastures, and stop at an isolated beach for a swim. Tranquil **Playa Inglés** is a pale, steep beach lined with sea-grape trees. It's 10 km (6 mi) east of Villa Guajimico and is visited almost exclusively by Cubans, who stay in rustic bungalows or camp; most of the time it's deserted.

Lodging

¢ ▦ **Villa Guajimico.** Overlooking the emerald waters of the Río Jutia ★ estuary, this dive resort and nature lodge consists of comfortable bungalows scattered through the forest or behind a tiny, man-made beach. Each has a barrel-tile roof, a small porch, tile floors, and hardwood furniture. The pool, open-air bar, and air-conditioned restaurant all have ocean views. Birds sing in the surrounding forest, and there are coral formations submerged a shell's toss from shore. ⊠ *42 km/25 mi southeast of Cienfuegos, Guajimico,* ☎ *432/45–1251 or 7/66–2523 in Havana,* FAX *432/45–1226. 61 bungalows. Restaurant, bar, pool, beach, dive shop, snorkeling, boating. MC, V.*

Trinidad

❻–⓬ *85 km (51 mi) southeast of Cienfuegos; 407 km (244 mi) southeast of Havana; 70 km (42 mi) southwest of Sancti Spíritus.*

Trinidad seems to have weathered three centuries with hardly a wrinkle. Its enchanting cobblestone streets are lined with houses that have brightly painted adobe walls and wooden shutters. Its historic center, which covers more than 50 blocks, is like a vast, meticulously maintained museum full of restored mansions and manicured plazas. Yet it's also a lively town of 60,000, where the locals frequently pull their chairs out onto the street to gossip, and where the air rings with the songs of birds perched in wicker cages and of bands performing in bars or restaurants.

The city was founded in 1514 by the conquistador Diego Velázquez and named for the Holy Trinity. It grew little until the 17th century, when its inhabitants began trading with pirates. Between 1750 and 1825, the population rose from 6,000 to 12,000, as thousands of slaves were brought in to work on sugar plantations in the nearby Valle de los Ingenios. Wealthy families built mansions, filled them with imported treasures, and sent their children to European schools. By the second half of the 19th century, however, Trinidad's star began to fade as sugar prices fell, the struggles for independence began, and slavery ended. By the early 1900s, Trinidad was impoverished and isolated. But the neglect that prevailed during the first half of the 20th century has helped the city retain its colonial ambience. In 1988, the United Nations declared the historic center a World Heritage Site, and during the past decade the government has worked hard to restore the colonial architecture.

Most people who visit Trinidad stay on the nearby Península de Ancón, but the advantages of staying in the city include many cultural sights and vibrant nightlife. Day-trip options—through such tour operators as Cubánacan and Rumbos—include treks to the beaches of Ancón, hikes in the Sierra de Escambray, train rides through sugar plantations, and sailing or diving excursions to Cayo Blanco. (Note that like many Cuban cities, Trinidad's streets go by pre- and postrevolutionary names; both are cited in addresses below.)

Exploring Trinidad

A GOOD WALK

An appropriate place to begin your tour is the **Museo Histórico** ⑥. One block northeast along Calle Simón Bolívar (Desengaño) is the **Museo de Arqueología** ⑦, on the northwest corner of **Plaza Mayor** ⑧, the city's central square. From the Museo de Arqueología, walk north a block to the thick columns of the **Museo Romántico** ⑨ on the plaza's northeastern edge. From here follow Simón Bolívar north a block to Calle Fernando Hernández (Cristo) and the Antiguo Convento de San Francisco, Trinidad's most famous landmark, which now houses the **Museo de la Lucha Contra Bandidos** ⑩. Return to the Plaza Mayor along Fernando Hernández. Just beyond the Museo Romántico is the city's cathedral, **La Santísima Trinidad** ⑪. On the plaza's southwestern side and across from the Museo de Arqueología is the **Museo de Arquitectura** ⑫.

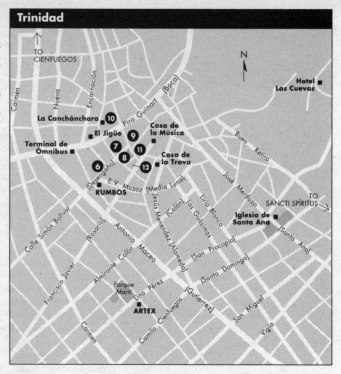

TIMING

You can follow this tour in 20 minutes without stopping. If you visit all the museums and monuments, plan on spending the better part of a day.

SIGHTS TO SEE

❼ Museo de Arqueología. The Archaeology Museum is in a mansion built by local merchant Andrés Padrón in 1734. Within its restored rooms you'll find unremarkable exhibits on the region's original inhabitants and the flora and fauna on which they depended for survival. There's also a small display on slavery. ✉ *Calle Simón Bolívar (Desengaño) y Calle Ruben Martínez Villena (Real del Jigüe)*, ☎ *419/3420.* ◼ *$2.* ⊙ *Mon.–Sat. 9–5.*

⓬ Museo de Arquitectura. Exhibits on the city's development and its most important 18th- and 19th-century buildings fill the rooms of a sky-blue 18th-century house, once the home of the Sánchez Iznaga family. Don't miss the lovely garden patio. ✉ *Calle Fernando Hernández (Cristo)*, ☎ *419/3208.* ◼ *$1.* ⊙ *Sat.–Thurs. 9–5.*

★ ❻ Museo Histórico. Set in the impressive Palacio Cantero, which was built by a sugar baron in 1830, the History Museum's displays trace the development of Trinidad from its founding by Diego Velázquez to the early years of the Revolutionary government. Two rooms are furnished with antiques, and elaborate murals cover some of the walls. A lookout platform atop the building's large tower affords a wonderful view. ✉ *Calle Simón Bolívar (Desengaño) y Calle Peña*, ☎ *419/ 4460.* ◼ *$2; $1 fee for photos.* ⊙ *Sun.–Fri. 9–5.*

❿ Museo de la Lucha Contra Bandidos. The tall, yellow bell tower—all that remains of the original 18th-century church and Franciscan monastery—is Trinidad's most famous landmark, adorning postcards, brochures, and T-shirts. You can climb the tower for a sweeping view of the city. The museum's displays explain the suppression of "bandits," who waged guerrilla warfare—with a little help from their friends at the CIA—from the Sierra de Escambray for the first six years of Castro's Revolutionary government. ✉ *Calle Fernando Hernádez (Cristo) y Calle Piro Guinart (Boca),* ☎ *419/4121.* ☜ *$1.* ⊙ *Tues.– Sun. 9–5.*

<table>
<tr><td>NEED A
BREAK?</td><td>Want to quench your thirst? Pop into **La Canchánchara**, a lively bar in an 18th-century building behind the Museo de la Lucha Contra los Bandidos. There's usually a live band playing in the shady patio, and there are always plenty of soft drinks, cold beer, and such Cuban cocktails as the mojito and the local specialty *canchánchara* (rum, lime juice, and honey).</td></tr>
</table>

★ ⑨ **Museo Romántico.** Rather than the stuff of Cupid's arrows, the romance in this museum's name refers to the one that Trinidad's prominent families had with their precious things. A great variety of antiques—most imported from Europe—fill the 14 rooms of this imposing mansion. Built in 1808, the house belonged to Count Burnet, though nearly all the antiques in it came from the homes of other families. Don't miss the view from the second-floor balcony. ✉ *Calle Fernando Hernádez (Cristo) y Calle Simón Bolívar (Desengaño),* ☎ *419/4363.* ☜ *$2.* ⊙ *Tues.–Sun. 9–5.*

★ ⑧ **Plaza Mayor.** The heart of the historic center, this charming little park is dominated by royal palms and has cast-iron benches, ceramic urns, the marble statue of a pale lady, and two brass greyhounds that were probably once cannons. It's surrounded by houses that once belonged to sugar barons and merchants, many of which now contain museums. ✉ *Calle Simón Bolívar (Desengaño), e/Calle Fernando Hernández (Cristo) y Calle Ruben Martínez Villena (Real de Jigüe).*

⑪ **La Santisima Trinidad.** Although the city's cathedral was consecrated in 1892, the building took the better part of the 19th century to complete (it was built to replace the 17th-century church that was destroyed by a hurricane). Don't let the rather bleak exterior (or limited hours) deter you from stepping inside; its interesting interior is replete with hardwood altars that date from the early 20th century and various colonial icons. ✉ *Calle Fernando Hernández (Cristo),* ☎ *no phone.* ⊙ *Mon.– Sat. 11:30–1.*

Dining and Lodging

There's a restaurant on practically every block of the historic center, but the food tends to lag behind the ambience. There are only three legal paladares in town, two of which are included here. Casas particulares are the only historic center lodging options; although they're abundant, quality varies greatly. Those listed below are good bets, but try to find them on your own; local hustlers earn commissions by leading you to a casa particulare or paladar. Turn down their offers to help, or risk being led astray.

Carlos Zerquera (✉ Calle Fernando Hernández/Cristo 54, ☎ 419/3634), Trinidad's official historian, lives next to the Museo Romántico in a house befitting his profession. He rents two rooms with private baths and offers you meals as well as the use of a washing machine. **Concepción Télles** (✉ Calle Piro Guinart/Boca 159, ☎ 419/2562) rents two large rooms in a colonial house with a garden. **María Antioneta Becquer** (✉ Calle Simón Bolivar/Desengaño 459, ☎ 419/3490), a.k.a. Tica, has two attractive rooms with two beds each in her blue house on the Plaza Mayor. You can use her kitchen, but she's a great cook. Her sister, María Elena, next door, has two comfortable, air-conditioned rooms. **María Pomares** (✉ Calle Zerquera/Rosario 361, ☎ 419/2164) rents two rooms in her 19th-century home down the hill from the Casa de la Trova; the one upstairs has three beds and a sun deck. **Osvaldo Saroza** (✉ Calle Izquierdo/Gloria 124, ☎ 419/3025) rents one room in his lovely home near the bus station.

$ ✕ **Paladar Estela.** This popular paladar, 1½ blocks up the hill from the Museo Románico, serves generous portions of *cerdo asado a la criolla* (seasoned, roast pork) and other Cuban fare. Your choice of entrée comes with several salads, arroz congrí, potatoes, fruit, and coffee—all for a very palatable price. Tables sit on or around a nicely planted interior patio. ✉ *Calle Simón Bolívar (Desengaño) 557,* ☎ *419/4329. No credit cards. Closed Sun. No lunch.*

$ ✕ **Sol y Son.** Trinidad's best paladar is a few blocks south of the Plaza
★ Mayor in an elegant 19th-century home. Upon entering, you may feel as if you've stepped into an antiques shop, but at the back is a garden courtyard complete with candlelight and taped music. The menu is surprisingly varied, with several vegetarian dishes and such rare ingredients as olives. The service and ambience are first rate, but it's the food that keeps this tiny restaurant packed. ✉ *Calle Simón Bolívar (Desengaño) 283,* ☎ *419/4504. No credit cards.*

¢–$$ ✕ **Restaurante El Jigüe.** Set in the Plazuela de Jigüe, a tiny plaza shaded by one tree, this colorful and historic restaurant (dating from 1720) seems to say "come on in." Its bright interior has high ceilings, chandeliers, and landscapes hung on white walls. The menu ranges from bistec de cerdo grillé to *enchilado de* langosta (in a red sauce). The specialty, *pollo al jigüe,* is a Cuban version of chicken cacciatore. ✉ *Calle Ruben Martínez Villena (Real de Jigüe) 69,* ☎ *419/4315. No credit cards.*

¢–$$ ✕ **Restaurante El Mesón del Regidor.** Down the hill from the Plaza Mayor, across from the Museo Histórico, this building is as historic as any in Trinidad: wooden ceilings, brass lamps, terra-cotta floors. The menu is traditional to match the address—bistec de cerdo grillé, *bistec de res en cazuela* (stewed beef), *filet de pescado grille* (sauteed fish fillet). Sometimes there's live music at lunchtime. ✉ *Calle Simon Bolívar (Desengaño) 424,* ☎ *419/6456. No credit cards.*

¢ ▥ **Hotel Las Cuevas.** On a grassy hill at the northern edge of town,
★ this collection of cement duplexes enjoys a sweeping panorama of Trinidad's red-tile roofs, the Península de Ancón, and the blue Caribbean beyond. The name means "the caves," and caverns riddle the ground beneath the hotel; one of them is a museum, another holds the discotheque. Rooms are above and below the modern reception area, next to which is the main restaurant, which usually serves buffets; a smaller café overlooks the pool, atop the hill. Most rooms are small, but they have porches. Those behind the pool are more spacious, but those in the lower H and F groups have the best views. ✉ *Calle Lino Pérez (San Procopio),* ☎ *419/4013 through 419/4019,* FAX *419/6161. 112 rooms. 2 restaurants, bar, pool, dance club. MC, V.*

¢ ▥ **Hotel la Ronda.** Though it caters mostly to Cubans, some of the rooms in this older hotel several blocks east of the historic center have been fixed up for visitors from abroad, which means such amenities as satellite TV and minirefrigerators. Guest rooms are stuffy, but public areas are pleasant, especially the rooftop and the central patio bars. ✉ *Calle José Martí (Jesús María) 238,* ☎ *419/4011. 17 rooms. Restaurant, 2 bars. No credit cards.*

Nightlife and the Arts

The open-air theater in the **ARTEX** (✉ Calle Lino Pérez/San Procopio 306, ☎ 419/6479), just north of Parque Martí, has live music and varied shows nightly at 10. The **Casa de la Música** (☏ 419/3414), behind the cathedral, has nightly concerts at 9 PM with complete bar service The **Casa de la Trova** (☏ 419/4135), two blocks east of the Plaza Mayor, has live music in the afternoon and after 10 PM for $1.

Trinidad's most popular dance spot is the subterranean **Cueva Ayala** (✉ Calle Lino Pérez/San Procopio, ☏ 419/4013), beneath the Hotel las Cuevas. The **Galería de Arte Universal** (✉ Calle Ruben Martínez Villena/Real de Jigüe y Calle Simon Bolívar/Desengaño, ☏ 419/4432) is an extensive art gallery on the south side of the Plaza Mayor. The open-air theater in the **Ruinas del Teatro Brunel** (✉ Calle Antonio Maceo/Gutiérrez, e/ Calle Simón Bolívar/Desengaño y Calle Francisco Javier/Rosario, ☏ 419/3994) has a nightly folk dancing and music show at 10.

Outdoor Activities and Sports

To explore a few of the area's 30 dive spots; contact the **Centro de Buceo Purtosol** (Puertosol Dive Center; ☏ 419/6205), on the Península de Ancón. Equipment rentals run about $60 a day; boat dives and certification courses are also available.

Shopping

Local artisans sell their wares from stalls on side streets near the Canchánchora, the Museo Histórica, and the Casa de la Trova. They not only offer the best deals, but all the money goes to the artist, rather than a fraction, as is the case with the government stores. The shop inside the **Casa de la Música** (☏ 419/3414), behind the cathedral, has an extensive selection of Cuban music. The **Casa del Tabaco** (✉ Calle Antonio Maceo/Gutiérrez y Calle Francisco Javier/Rosario, ☏ 419/6256) is the place for cigars, rum, and coffee. The **Fondo de Bienes Culturales** (✉ Calle Simón Bolívar/Desengaño 418, ☏ 419/3590), in a colonial house across from the Museo Histórico, sells paintings and handicrafts by local artists.

El Valle de los Ingenios

⑬ *3 km (2 mi) to 12 km (7 mi) east of Trinidad.*

Just east of Trinidad, the road winds its way through the verdant Valley of the Sugar Mills, where Trinidad's colonial fortunes were made. Just 3 km (2 mi) outside of Trinidad on the left is a *mirador* (scenic overlook) with an open-air restaurant and observation tower that affords an view of pale-green cane fields and the darker Sierra de Escambray beyond—a panorama best photographed in the morning. Twelve kilometers (seven miles) beyond the lookout just outside of Trinidad is **Manaca Iznaga,** where an 18th-century farmhouse that once belonged to one of the region's wealthiest families stands next to the Torre de Iznaga, a 43-m (141-ft) tower built in the early 1800s. Legend has it that the two Iznaga sons were in love with a beautiful slave girl, and their father told one to build a tower and the other to dig a well, with the promise that whoever built higher or dug deeper could have her. But when they were done, both the tower and well were 43 m, so the old man got the girl. The tower actually had a much more practical purpose: it was a place from which to keep an eye on the thousands of slaves who worked the surrounding plantations. The large bell that was rung when slaves tried to escape lies on the ground near the farmhouse.

Dining

$ ✕ **Restaurante Manaca.** The Manaca Iznaga family's former manor house is now occupied by a restaurant. The building's ochre walls, square columns, wood-beam ceiling, and terra-cotta floors lend considerable colonial ambience. There's an old sugar mill out back, and scattered on the lawn in front are the cauldrons used to boil down molasses. Lunches are usually accompanied by the music of an excellent little band. The specialty is *puntas de cerdo a la Iznaga* (strips of pork loin in a tomato-vegetable sauce), but the menu includes everything from fresh seafood to grilled chicken. ✉ *Manaca Iznaga*, ☎ *419/7241. No credit cards. No dinner.*

Península de Ancón

⑭ *12 km (7 mi) south of Trinidad.*

The beaches that line the southern edge of this narrow peninsula, which curves eastward into the Caribbean, are two of the best in the province. Most people who visit Trinidad actually stay here; it lies conveniently close to the historic city, and the area's largest hotels overlook its pale sands. The first beach on the peninsula is **Playa María Aguilar,** a short strand shaded by a few palm trees and cropped by rocky points. The ocean is littered with coral boulders, part of a colorful reef that wraps around the point to the east, making this the peninsula's best snorkeling beach. **Playa Ancón,** to the east of Playa María Aguilar, is the peninsula's most appealing beach, with more than a mile of beige sand sloping into aquamarine water. A 45-minute boat ride to the southeast of the peninsula is the island of **Cayo Blanco,** which has a white-sand beach and a vast coral reef off shore. Several boats visit the island on day trips offered by local hotels and tour operators.

Lodging

$$$ 🏨 **Brisas Trinidad del Mar.** Its many arches, columns, Spanish tiles, and pastel colors give this all-inclusive resort a Disneyesque look. Rooms have tile floors, small balconies, and paintings of Trinidad street scenes on the walls. About half face the ocean, most of the rest have views of a pool that's surrounded by palm trees and lounge chairs. The main restaurant serves mediocre buffets, but there's also a beach grill that serves seafood at night (reservations are required). ✉ *Playa Ancón,* ☎ *419/6500 through 419/6507,* ℻ *419/6565,* 🌐 *www.cubanacan.cu. 241 rooms. 2 restaurants, bar, snack bar, bar, pool, 2 tennis courts, gym, beach, boating. MC, V. All-inclusive.*

$ 🏨 **Hotel Ancón.** This massive beachfront complex is practically two hotels. Rooms in the main building are unattractive little boxes, the best of which have tiny balconies overlooking the sea. Those in the Modulo Nuevo—the newer, two-story buildings next door—are spacious, tastefully furnished, and have large balconies. The crazy thing is that all rooms cost the same, so request one (with an ocean view) in the Modulo Nuevo. The beach is a long, narrow strip of white sand shaded by thatched parasols. The restaurants are on the ground floor of the main building, next to which are a large pool, tennis courts, and other facilities. ✉ *Playa Ancón,* ☎ *419/6120,* ℻ *419/6151. 279 rooms. 3 restaurants, 2 bars, pool, 2 tennis courts, beach, boating. MC, V. All-inclusive.*

¢ 🏨 **Hotel Costasur.** The peninsula's oldest hotel was undergoing a piecemeal renovation at this writing, but it was still the best deal on the beach. The most expensive lodgings are the two-room bungalows scattered along a lawn overlooking the ocean, with lots of windows and small porches. Less expensive superior rooms are in a cement building; they're smaller than the bungalows, but are colorful and have sea-view balconies. Standard rooms—smaller still and farther from the beach—cost slightly less. ✉ *Playa María Aguilar,* ☎ *419/6172,* ℻ *419/6173. 131 rooms. 2 restaurants, bar, pool, volleyball, beach, boating, bicycles. MC, V. BP.*

Outdoor Activities and Sports

The ocean around the Península de Ancón holds plenty of coral, the most accessible of which lies a mere 300 m (985 ft) offshore from the Hotel Costasur. The **Centro de Buceo Puertosol** (☎ 419/6205), in the marina across from the Hotel Ancón, takes people to more than 20 dive spots ($60 for equipment rental), including a shipwreck and several large coral reefs; it also offers certification courses ($200). The marina also offers deep-sea fishing.

Topes de Collantes

⑮ *21 km (12 mi) north of Trinidad.*

High in the Sierra de Escambray, at the end of a road that winds its way north from Trinidad, this sylvan enclave has long been a health resort. It's also the perfect base for a hike. At an altitude of 800 m (2,600 ft) above sea level, the climate is refreshing (the average temperature is 21°C/70°F), and regular precipitation keeps everything green. Because the area receives mostly Cuban tourism, the accommodations and restaurants aren't as good as those in Trinidad and Ancón, but the rates are reasonable. If you don't want to spend the night, the tour operator Rumbos offers day trips from Trinidad.

The mountains around Topes de Collantes are covered with a mosaic of coffee farms and patches of forest that are protected within the **Parque Natural Escambray.** This nature preserve has several deep, lush valleys that are home to such birds as the Cuban parrot, the emerald hummingbird, and the trogon. Several trails lead to waterfalls; the most accessible is the **Salto de Caburní,** just a 2 km (1 mi) hike along a trail that starts at the Villa Caburní hotel, 2 km (1 mi) north of Topes de Collantes. The spectacular **Salto de Rocío** cascades down a rock face about 17 km (10 mi) north of Topes. Tours (the only way to visit) truck you to a point just 2 km (1 mi) from the falls. The grotto of **La Batata,** several kilometers west of Topes, has a river running out of it with a swimming hole; you can visit on a 7-km (4-mi) guided hike that passes a lookout point.

Lodging

¢ ⊞ **Los Helechos.** The name means "the ferns," a nod to the tree ferns that abound in the surrounding forest. Although you'd think that rooms here would offer views of all the greenery, few do. This place was originally a boarding school, and the best and brightest quarters are in the main building, a three-story, cement structure with a frightful paint job. Rooms here have balconies, tile floors, wicker furniture, and tacky Chinese curtains. A simple restaurant serves cheap Cuban food, and just down the hill is a large, indoor pool. ⊠ *Topes de Collantes,* ☎ *42/40330,* FAX *42/40117,* WEB *www.gaviota.cubaweb.cu. 58 rooms. Restaurant, bar, pool, sauna, bowling, gym, dance club. No credit cards.*

Outdoor Activities and Sports

Enjoying the great outdoors is about the only thing to do in Topes de Collantes, and hiking is the way to do it. **Gaviota Tours** (☎ 42/40117) offers inexpensive excursions to the waterfalls; La Batata; and Hacienda Codina, a nearby farm.

Sancti Spíritus

⑯ *70 km (42 mi) northeast of Trinidad; 360 km (224 mi) southeast of Havana; 92 km (55 mi) southeast of Santa Clara.*

The provincial capital of Sancti Spíritus is a lesser Trinidad—its historic center is much smaller, but it also receives a mere fraction of the visitors that flock to its more famous neighbor. It's a tranquil, traditional city, where bicycles and horse-drawn taxis make up much of the traffic and the locals hang out in the central plaza at night. It also has some splendid colonial architecture, much of which the government has restored and painted, including two small museums in colonial homes.

The oldest part of Sancti Spíritus extends northward from the muddy Río Yayabo to the **Plaza Serafín Sánchez,** a shady central park surrounded by 18th- and 19th-century architecture, including the town library and a museum with displays on the province's history.

The neoclassical **Biblioteca,** on Plaza Serafín Sánchez's southwest corner, is the most conspicuous edifice. Built in 1929 by the city's wealthiest citizens as an exclusive club, it became a public library following the Revolution, and was meticulously restored in 1998. On the second floor in the former ballroom, students now read beneath painted columns and crystal chandeliers. Be sure to check out the view from the balcony. ⊠ *Calle Máximo Gómez 1 Norte,* ☎ *41/2–3313.* 🖃 *Free.* ⊙ *Weekdays 8 AM–9 PM, Sat. 8–4.*

To the north of the Biblioteca, a house built by one of the city's first mayors in 1740 is now the **Museo Provincial** (Provincial Museum). The building itself, with its decorated walls and high wooden ceilings, is as much an attraction as the exhibits it holds, which are devoted primarily to the wars of independence and the Revolution. There are also some gruesome reminders of the days of slavery. ⊠ *Calle Máximo Gómez 3 Norte,* ☎ *41/27435.* 🖃 *$1.* ⊙ *Tues.–Sat. 9–5, Sun. 9–noon.*

For several blocks south of the Plaza Serafín Sánchez, **Calle Independencia** is a pedestrian mall lined with an array of shops, a couple of banks, and the main post office. The mall ends in front of the 19th-century Colonia Español building, to the west of which is Sancti Spíritus's ancient church, the Iglesia Parroquial Mayor.

Built in 1680, the **Iglesia Parroquial Mayor del Espíritu Santo** (⊠ Calle Jesús Méndez y Calle Rodríguez, ☎ 41/24855), is one of Cuba's oldest churches. Its massive bell tower is visible from much of Sancti Spíritus, and though its interior is sparsely decorated—a carved wooden ceiling and a blue-and-gold wooden arch framing a simple altar—it's extremely well preserved. Down the hill behind the church is **Calle el Llano,** a steep, cobbled street lined with some of the city's oldest houses, most of which are private homes. At the bottom of the hill stands the Quinta Santa Elena, a former farmhouse that dates from 1719. It's now a restaurant, and its shaded front terrace has the best view of the 19th-century stone bridge that spans the Río Yayabo.

★   The meticulously restored mansion that now houses the **Museo de Arte Colonial** (Museum of Colonial Art) was long the property of the Valle Iznaga family, who owned sugar plantations, processing plants, a railroad, and a port, among other things. Dating from 1744, it's furnished with antiques from several centuries, most of which belonged to the Valle Iznagas, so the house appears much as it might have for a party a century ago—the music rooms is full of instruments, the dining room is set for a banquet, and the kitchen is ready for the cooking to begin. ⊠ *Calle Plácido 74,* ☎ *41/25455.* 🖃 *$2; $1 fee for photos.* ⊙ *Tues., Wed., Fri. 9–5, Thurs. and Sat. 2–10.*

Dining and Lodging

Sancti Spíritus has a small selection of quality casas particulares, all of which are on or near Plaza Serafín Sánchez. **Omaida Echemendia** (⊠ Calle Maceo 4 Sur, ☎ 41/24336), rents three small rooms with private baths and air-conditioning on a quiet street three blocks east of the Hotel Plaza. **La Pantera** (✉ Calle Independencia 50 Norte, ☎ 41/ 25435) is Cristobalina Barreto's attractive second-floor home a block north of Plaza Serafín Sánchez; she rents two spacious rooms with balconies and a quiet rooftop apartment. All quarters have private baths, air-conditioning, TVs, and mini-refrigerators. **Ricardo Rodríguez** (✉ Calle Independencia 17 Sur, ☎ no phone) rents rooms in two second-floor apartments—one overlooking the plaza and one on the pedestrian mall. Both have high ceilings, private baths, and good views.

¢–$ ✕ **Restaurante Meson de la Plaza.** This refurbished 19th-century building overlooks Plaza Serafín Sánchez and the porticos of the colonial buildings that surround it. It's an impressive edifice, with large arched doorways. Seating is at sturdy wooden tables, a couple of which have views of the Iglesia Parroquial Mayor. The menu is traditional Cuban with a few twists, such as *garbanzo mesonero* (garbanzo and pork soup) and *ternero a la villa* (veal stewed in a clay pot). ✉ *Calle Máximo Gómez 34,* ☎ *41/28546. MC, V.*

¢–$ ✕ **Restaurante Quinta Santa Elena.** Set between the muddy Río Yayabo and the Calle el Llano, this ancient yellow manor house with a large, tree-shaded terrace is an inspiring spot. Seating is available on the terrace, for a river view, or inside, where the terra-cotta floors, thick columns, and wide arches attest to the building's more than 280 years. Specialties are *pollo a la quinta* (chicken in a vegetable tomato sauce) and *vaca frita* (strips of beef sautéed with onions), and an array of *criolla* dishes. ✉ *End of Calle el Llano,* ☎ *41/29167. No credit cards.*

¢ ✕🏠 **Villa Rancho Hatuey.** Here dozens of two-story, cement bungalows spread around verdant grounds have spacious rooms with white-tile floors, queen-size beds, and lots of windows. The main building houses the reception, a tiny bar, and the restaurant (¢–$), which serves such Cuban classics as *pierna asada* (roast pork) and *ternero guisado* (stewed veal), as well as a few Continental dishes. On weekends, light sleepers should request a room at the back of the property, since the discotheque next to the reception area stays open late. ✉ *Carretera Central, 5 km/3 mi north of Sancti Spíritus,* ☎ *41/28315,* 𝖥𝖠𝖷 *41/ 28830,* WEB *www.cubanacan.cu. 76 rooms. Restaurant, bar, pool, dance club. MC, V.*

¢ 🏠 **Hotel Plaza.** The historic Hotel Plaza, which overlooks the Plaza Serafín Sánchez, has undergone an extensive renovation with mixed results. The airy public spaces—with their arches, wicker furniture, and potted plants—are charming, but guest rooms are somewhat tacky. Those in the old wing have high ceilings, but newer rooms in back are small and dark; opt for one in front (Room 201, 202, 210, or 211), as they have small balconies and park views. There's a verdant patio bar next to the lobby and a restaurant in back, but you're better off dining elsewhere. ✉ *Calle Independencia 1 Norte,* ☎ *41/27102. 28 rooms. Restaurant, bar. MC, V.*

Nightlife and the Arts

Admission is $1 to the concerts and folk-dance performance that are sometimes held at the **Casa de la Cultura** (Calle Cervantes 72, ☎ 41/ 23772). The **Casa de la Trova** (✉ Calle Máximo Gómez 26 Sur, ☎ 41/26802) has live music shows starting at 10 PM Wednesday through Saturday, and on Sunday afternoons. Admission is $1. **Galería Oscar Fernandez Morera** (✉ Calle Céspedes 26 Sur, ☎ 41/23117), the main art gallery with painting and sculpture by local artists, closes for lunch and on Monday. If you want to dance, head for the discotheque at the **Villa Rancho Hatuey** (✉ Carretera Central, 5 km/3 mi north of Sancti Spíritus, ☎ 41/28315).

Outdoor Activities and Sports

The Zaza Reservoir, 10 km (6 mi) southeast of Sancti Spíritus, is re-
puted to have world-class bass fishing. The **Hotel Horizontes Zaza** (☎
41/25490), on the reservoir, can arrange excursions. The best place for
bird-watching is the **Reserva Ecológica El Naranjal,** a protected, mountainous area 20 km (12 mi) south of Sancti Spíritus and near the town
of Banao.

Shopping

Galería Arcada (✉ Calle Independencia 55 Sur, ☎ 41/27106), a colonial house on the pedestrian mall, sells a wide array of local handicrafts,
from paintings to wood sculptures and leather goods. The **Tienda el Manje**
(✉ Calle Cervantes 11 ☎ 41/23772), in the Casa de la Cultura, sells
locally made jewelry, papier-mâché items, and paintings.

CIEGO DE ÁVILA AND CAMAGÜEY PROVINCES

These two provinces are known for their white-sand beaches, which
are lapped by clear waters rich in marine life. But there's more to the
region than sun, sand, and deep-blue sea. On the mainland of Ciego
de Ávila Province you'll find bass-laden lakes; off its northern shore,
the mangrove shallows of Cayo Coco and Cayo Guillermo are often
filled with flamingos. In Camagüey Province, between the northern keys
and the coastal resort of Santa Lucía, there are enough coral reefs and
wrecks to keep a scuba diver submerged for weeks. The sportfishing
here is legendary (it was Hemingway's favorite angling area), and the
eponymous provincial capital is steeped in history and rich in culture.

Ciego de Ávila

🛈 *430 km (258 mi) southeast of Havana; 74 km (44 mi) east of Sancti
Spíritus; 90 km (54 mi) south of Cayo Coco; 100 km (60 mi) northwest of Camagüey.*

Most people simply pass through this provincial capital—an ordinary,
torrid city of 100,000—en route to Cayo Coco and Cayo Guillermo
to the north, Camagüey to the east, or the port of Júcaro to the south.
Founded in the 16th century, Ciego de Ávila didn't grow much till the
early part of 20th century, which is when most of its historic structures
were built. Ciego de Ávila's principal buildings are near the central **Parque Martí.** One block west of Parque Martí on Calle Independencia is
the **Casa de la Cultura,** a cultural center housed in what was once the
Colonia Español, an elite social club. One block south of Parque Martí
is the **Teatro Principal,** a renovated theater built in 1923.

The simple **Museo Provincial,** four blocks west of Parque Martí, has
exhibits on local history, including a model of La Trocha, the barrier
across the country built by the Spanish during the Ten Years' War (the
nation's first attempt at independence from Spain). ✉ *Calle José Antonio Echeverría 25,* ☎ *33/28431.* ▣ *$1.* ◷ *Tues.–Sat. 8–noon and
1–5.*

Ⓒ Two blocks northwest of the Museo Provincial is **El Fortín** (✉ Calle 1
y Calle Máximo Gómez), one of the small forts that dotted La Trocha's
length.

Dining and Lodging

¢ ✕▥ **Hotel Sevilla.** The stately Sevilla, a half block from Parque Martí,
was completed in 1920, which makes it one of the town's oldest buildings. Renovated just a few years ago, its shiny lobby has high arches,

stained glass, and potted plants. The restaurant, which occupies most of the lobby, serves a small selection of decent Cuban cuisine at bargain prices. Rooms are small but authentic, with high ceilings and colorful tile floors. Although those on the street have small balconies, they don't have hot water; second-floor rooms are your best bet. ⊠ *Calle Independencia 57,* ☎ *33/25603. 24 rooms. Restaurant, dance club. No credit cards.*

The Arts
Weekend nights often see concerts or dance performances in the **Casa de la Cultura** (⊠ Calle Independencia 76, ☎ 33/23974). The **Casa de la Trova** (⊠ Calle Libertad y Calle Simón Reyes, ☎ no phone) has live music every night but Tuesday.

Outdoor Activities and Sports
The vast, uninhabited keys of the Jardines de la Reina archipelago to the south of Ciego de Ávila and Camagüey provinces were once the haunt of pirates (five colonial shipwrecks are submerged here) and are now a protected area dedicated to scuba diving. The Jardines de la Reina's only accommodations are on the **Floating Hotel Tortuga** (☎ FAX 33/98104 or 33/56–6569, WEB www.puertosol.net), run by Puertosol's Avalón dive center. Anchored near Cayo Anclitas, the hotel is accessible by boat from Júcaro, a small port 30 km (18 mi) south of Ciego de Ávila. It's a stationary boat that sleeps 22 people in simple quarters and provides family-style meals and access to 32 pristine dive spots.

Shopping
The **Fondo de Bienes Culturales** (⊠ Calle Simón Reyes 17, ☎ 33/25616), two blocks west of Parque Martí, sells handicrafts and paintings by local artists.

Morón

⑱ *35 km (21 mi) north of Ciego de Ávila; 55 km (33 mi) south of Cayo Coco.*

Morón is a more pleasant town than Ciego de Ávila, as it has half the population and twice the historic architecture. It's also the nearest city to Cayo Coco and Cayo Guillermo and their resorts. Many people also use the city as a base for bass fishing. Oddly though, bass are called *trucha* in Cuba, though it's the Spanish term for "trout." Because it lies on an important tourist route, the colonnades of neoclassic buildings that line its main street, Calle Martí, got a fresh paint job several years ago.

Morón was the operations center for a private railroad, and its handsome **train station,** built in 1923, is a structure worth admiring; nearby stand the stately homes of the railway's administrators. Morón is known as the "City of the Rooster" (after a cocky public official in the Spanish town for which it was named), and thus has a large steel sculpture of a cockerel, **El Gallo de Morón,** that crows (thanks to a recorded broadcast) twice daily, at 6 AM and 6 PM. It's on Calle Martí near the south end of town. The **Museo Caonabo** (⊠ Calle Martí 374, ☎ 335/54510) has an extensive collection of pre-Columbian artifacts housed in a neoclassical pink building dating from 1919. It's open Tuesday through Saturday 10 to 6 and Sunday 8 to noon; admission is $1.

Laguna la Redonda, a shallow lake 14 km (8 mi) north of Morón, is a renowned fishing spot, and its narrow canals that wind between the silt roots of giant mangroves make an interesting boat ride. A small marina offers 45-minute boat trips (for one to four people) and half-day fishing excursions complete with tackle. The **Laguna de la Leche,**

5 km (3 mi) north of Morón, is much larger than Laguna la Redonda. Named for its milky water (*leche* means "milk"), it has better bird-watching than fishing.

Dining and Lodging

¢–$ ✕ **Restaurant Las Fuentes.** This charming restaurant is in an old residence near the north end of Morón's main drag. Cowhide chairs and wooden tables surround a small courtyard full of potted plants and *fuentes* (fountains), for which the restaurant is named. Paintings literally cover the walls, and set in the back corner is a small bar. The menu ranges from *bistec de res* (steak) to *camarón al pincho* (shrimp kebab). ⊠ *Calle Martí, e/Calle Libertad y Calle Agramonte*, ☎ *335/5758. No credit cards.*

¢ 🏠 **Club de Caza y Pesca.** In an elegant, restored mansion near the train station, this small hotel specializes in fishing packages and provides guests with guides, licenses, and gear. The building was originally the home of the railroad administrator, which seems to have been a lucrative job given the structure's marble floors and gracious staircase and columns. Upstairs guest rooms have large windows, high ceilings, blue-tile baths, minibars, and satellite TVs. There's a small pool out back, and a restaurant on the ground floor. ⊠ *Calle Cristóbal Colón 41,* ☎ *335/2236,* 𝖥𝖠𝖷 *335/2228,* 𝖶𝖤𝖡 *www.horizontes.cu. 7 rooms. Restaurant, bar, pool, fishing. MC, V.*

Nightlife

The **Casa de la Trova** (⊠ Calle Libertad 74, ☎ 335/4158) has live music every night but Monday. Shows start around 9.

Cayo Coco and Cayo Guillermo

★ ⑲–⑳ *55 km (33 mi) and 88 km (53 mi) north of Morón.*

These two green islands, set in the turquoise sea some 27 km (16 mi) north of the mainland, have more than a dozen white-sand beaches, twice that many coral reefs, and mangrove shallows that attract great flocks of flamingos. Ernest Hemingway made frequent fishing trips to these keys and described them in *Islands in the Stream.* Long uninhabited, and visited only by local fishermen and the occasional millionaire, the islands now have half a dozen modern beach resorts, with more under construction.

A causeway traverses the shallow Bahía de Perros (Bay of Dogs) south of Cayo Coco; from this key, shorter causeways stretch west to Cayo Guillermo and east to the undeveloped Cayo Romano. All three islands are covered with a thick scrub vegetation; mangrove swamps line their southern shores, and bleached-sand beaches scallop their northern edges. The fishing is good; in addition to the marlin that so fascinated Papa, there are wahoo, tuna, mahimahi, and sailfish. Sportfishing charters are available out of the marinas on both keys; you can arrange them at any hotel. The diving (particularly off Cayo Guillermo) is even better than the angling, with dozens of healthy coral reefs inhabited by hundreds of fish species—from the delicate butterfly fish to the menacing barracuda—as well as a dizzying array of invertebrates. Visibility averages 20–35 m (66–115 ft).

Cayo Coco was named for the white ibis, a pale wader called the *coco* in Cuba, but its mangroves and sandy shallows attract dozens of species, including flamingos (which gather by the hundreds in the shallow bay to the south), roseate spoonbills, tricolored herons, and reddish egrets. The island's roughly 90 indigenous bird species are joined by another 120 migrants between November and April, and its forests are also home to everything from wild pigs to anole lizards.

Despite its varied wildlife, most people visit Cayo Coco for its swaths of sugary sand shaded by coconut palms and washed by cerulean sea—the stuff of travel posters in Toronto storefronts or the daydreams of snowbound accountants. Nine beaches run for a total of 21 km (12 mi) along the northern coast, and only two of them have hotels. The most spectacular beaches are Playa Flamingo, with its extensive sandbars, and nearby Playa Prohibida (Forbidden Beach)—a protected area backed by dunes covered with scrubby native palms.

NEED A BREAK? About 10 km (6 mi) south of Cayo Coco, on a tiny islet along which the causeway passes, is **Paradero La Silla**—a rustic snack bar that's as good a place to bird-watch as it is to wet your whistle. The wooden tower next to it overlooks shallows where flamingos, herons, and other leggy waders regularly hunt for their dinner. Cold drinks and light meals are served under a thatched roof.

Cayo Guillermo's beaches are narrow, but still captivating. The ocean in front of them is so shallow that you can wade out more than 90 m (290 ft). Its nicest beach is Playa Pilar, which was named after Hemingway's old fishing boat. Stretching along the key's northwest end, this beach is backed by 20-m (66-ft) dunes and overlooks Cayo Media Luna, an islet where Fulgencio Batista once had a vacation home. Cayo Guillermo has excellent skin diving, with 37 dive spots nearby.

Lodging

The hotels on Cayo Coco and Cayo Guillermo are megaresorts of the type found throughout the Caribbean. A stay here will put you in full vacation mode, with meals, snacks, drinks, and everything from beach chairs to sea kayaks included in the rates. In addition, all have amphitheaters—where the nightly entertainment ranges from Cuban folk dancing to fashion shows—and dance clubs. They're also very kid-friendly, since all of them have children's programs.

$$$$ ⚑ **Hotel Tryp.** Cayo Coco's original hotel, the Tryp is a miniature city, with several pools, more than 20 bars and restaurants, and nearly a thousand rooms spread along a mile of pale beach. The hotel consists of two compounds, each with its own reception: the original complex, to the west, has more charm, with large rooms in Spanish-style structures surrounded by gardens; the newer wing has a modern, open-air lobby that overlooks a vast pool area with sculptures, fountains, and a sunken bar. Rooms throughout are done in earth tones and have tile floors, balconies, and large baths with tubs. ⊠ *Cayo Coco, due north of causeway,* ☎ *33/30–1300,* ℻ *33/30–1386,* WEB *www.solmeliacuba.com. 972 rooms. 8 restaurants, 11 bars, 2 cafés, 4 pools, beauty salon, massage, sauna, 6 tennis courts, aerobics, gym, horseback riding, Ping-Pong, volleyball, beach, dive shop, snorkeling, windsurfing, boating, fishing, motorbikes, shops, billiards, cabaret, nightclub, children's programs (ages 4–12), travel services, car rental. MC, V. All-inclusive, BP, MAP.*

$$$$ ⚑ **Iberostar Daiquiri.** Second only to its white beach, which extends into blue-green shallows, is this hotel's airy lobby set beneath a soaring wooden roof and adorned with shiny marble floors, painted columns, tinted glass, and a small bar surrounded by tropical greenery. Restaurants and three-story buildings with guest quarters surround the circular pool, which has a sunken bar beneath a thatched roof. Rooms have beige-tile floors, wood furniture, original art, and small balconies; about half have ocean views. ⊠ *Cayo Guillermo,* ☎ *33/30–1650,* ℻ *33/30–1645. 312 rooms. 3 restaurants, 3 bars, pool, massage, sauna, 2 tennis courts, aerobics, gym, horseback riding, volleyball, beach, snorkeling, windsurfing, boating, fishing, bicycles, mo-*

torbikes, shops, cabaret, children's programs (ages 4–12), travel services, car rental. MC, V. All-inclusive.

$$$$ ⊡ **Sol Club Cayo Guillermo.** The colonial era meets the new millen-
★   nium here. The spacious lobby has a high, beamed ceiling, thick square
columns, and a traditional Spanish fountain at its center. But beyond
glass doors lies a pool surrounded by coconut palms and tropical gardens. The spacious rooms—in one- and two-story buildings scattered
around the grounds—have fanciful pastel interiors, Caribbean-style furniture, and sliding doors that open onto covered porches or balconies.
Restaurants range from an eatery serving very European buffets to a
thatched beach grill, and the food is excellent—the only things not included in the rates are lobster and certain wines. This is the best destination for divers, since it has a modern dive center and plenty of reefs
nearby. ⊠ *Cayo Guillermo,* ☎ *33/30–1760,* 𝖥𝖠𝖷 *33/30–1748,* 𝖶𝖤𝖡
*www.solmeliacuba.com. 264 rooms. 3 restaurants, 2 bars, snack bar,
pool, sauna, 2 tennis courts, aerobics, gym, horseback riding, volleyball, beach, dive shop, snorkeling, boating, fishing, bicycles, motorbikes, shops, cabaret, nightclub, children's programs (ages 5–13),
travel services, car rental. MC, V. All-inclusive.*

Camagüey

㉑–㉖ *535 km (321 mi) southeast of Havana; 174 km (104 mi) southeast of
Ciego de Ávila; and 255 km (153 mi) northwest of Holguín.*

Cuba's third-largest city (population 315,000) and the capital of the
country's biggest province, Camagüey is a sprawling but tranquil town
of narrow, cobbled streets—lined with an eclectic mix of architecture—converging on plazas dominated by colonial churches. The *camagüeyanos,* as its citizens are known, are proud of their city and its
nearly five centuries of history. They're accommodating to the few foreigners who pass this way, which makes it that much more pleasant
to visit.

Camagüey was one of the seven villas founded by Diego Velázquez at
the beginning of the 16th century. Originally called Puerto del Príncipe
(Prince's Port), it started out on the northern coast and was moved twice,
reaching its current location in 1528. It wasn't until the early 1900s
that it took the name Camagüey, after a tree common to the region.
As the vast plain surrounding it was converted to ranchland, the city
became a prosperous commercial center. During the 17th and 18th centuries, buccaneers and pirates, led by the likes of Henry Morgan,
marched inland and sacked the city several times. As protection against
such invasions, Camagüey was transformed into a maze of narrow streets
that facilitated ambushing attackers in the old days but today only make
it easier for visitors to get lost.

As sugar exports came to complement ranching profits, Camagüey developed a criollo upper class that was supportive of the independence
movements that swept the country in the 19th century. Some of its most
fortunate sons took up arms against the Spanish, and many paid dearly
for their treason. The most famous of these rebels was Ignacio Agramonte; after he was killed by the Spanish, his body was burned in public. Agramonte consequently became the town hero.

As the city is set in a fairly dry, flat region, for centuries the camagüeyanos
drank rainwater collected in giant ceramic vessels called *tinajones.* In
the early 20th century, when a water system was finally built, it's estimated that there were 1,900 such containers, more than enough to
give Camagüey its nickname "City of the Tinajones." Those giant jugs
are now displayed all over town, and the need for them gave birth to

a ceramic-making tradition. One popular legend has it that if a local maiden gives a visitor water from a tinajón, he'll fall in love with her and never leave. Whether or not the same applies to women who accept drinks from local lads is unclear, but caution is advised.

Exploring Camagüey

A GOOD WALK

Start out at the central **Plaza de los Trabajadores** ㉑, dominated to the east by the **Catedral Nuestra Señora de la Merced** ㉒, and to the south by the **Casa Natal de Ignacio Agramonte** ㉓. From here, walk three blocks northeast to the **Iglesia de la Nuestra Señora de la Soledad** ㉔. From this church, head south down the quiet Calle Maceo, crossing the tiny Plaza Maceo to Independencia, and continuing one block south to **Parque Ignacio Agramonte** ㉕. After visiting the sights around the park, walk south from the Casa de la Trova along Calle Cisneros, veering right just after crossing Calle Raúl Lamar, and taking the next left onto Calle Hurtado to the **Plaza de San Juan de Dios** ㉖.

TIMING

This route should take 40 minutes to walk, without stops; with stops you can just about visit everything in half a day. If you dally, perhaps stopping for a meal and listening to a few songs in the Casa de la Trova, you can stretch the tour into a full day.

SIGHTS TO SEE

㉓ **Casa Natal de Ignacio Agramonte.** This yellow colonial building with a high, wooden balcony was probably one of the tallest structures in town when Ignacio Agramonte was born to a wealthy ranching family here in 1841. Agramonte grew to become a general in the Ten Years' War. When he was killed in battle in 1873, he ascended to the rank of hero. Though only half of the original house remains, it has been restored and converted to a museum. Its courtyard has a tinajón in every corner, and upstairs rooms are furnished with period pieces or filled with displays about the wars for independence. ⊠ *Av. Ignacio Agramonte 59,* ☎ *32/29–7116.* 🖃 *$2.* ☉ *Tues.–Sat. 10–6, Sun. 8–noon.*

★ ㉒ **Catedral Nuestra Señora de la Merced.** Originally erected in 1748, this church was reconstructed in 1848, repaired after a fire in 1906, and renovated yet again in 1998. The clock on its facade was the city's first public timepiece, made in Barcelona in 1773; its current machinery was imported from the United States in 1901. The church's interior has massive square columns and a vaulted ceiling decorated with faded art nouveau frescoes dating from 1915. The painted wooden altar was made in 1909, to replace one destroyed by the fire, but the paintings on the walls around it date from the 18th and 19th centuries. To the right of the altar is the Santo Sepulcro: a Christ figure in a glass casket that was made in 1762 using the silver from 22,000 Mexican coins. It's carried out of the cathedral and back every Good Friday in a religious procession that was prohibited for nearly four decades. The crypts beneath the altar have been partially excavated and converted into a tiny museum of tombs, icons, and other antiquities; it's not for the claustrophobic. If the church is closed, enter through the convent next door. ⊠ *Calle Independencia y Av. Ignacio Agramonte,* ☎ *no phone.* 🖃 *Free.* ☉ *Mon.–Sat. 9:30–11:30 and 2:30–6, Sun. 9–noon.*

㉔ **Iglesia de la Nuestra Señora de la Soledad.** The weathered exterior of this 18th-century church dedicated to Our Lady of Solitude belies its well-preserved interior. Thick, square columns rise into high arches decorated with lovely floral frescoes, above which is a *mudejar* wooden ceiling with ornate carved beams. According to legend, a statue of the Virgin fell from a wagon at this spot in the late 1600s; seeing it as a

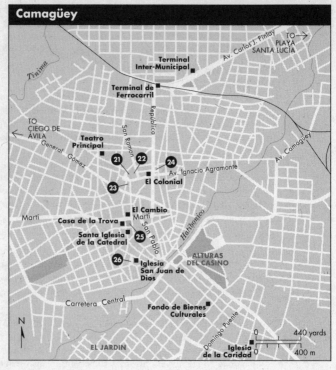

sign from heaven, the locals built a hermitage for it, which was later replaced by this church, completed in 1776. ✉ *Calle República y Av. Ignacio Agramonte,* ☎ *32/29–2392.* ⊙ *Mon.–Sat. 6–11 and 4–6, Sun. 6–noon.*

㉕ Parque Ignacio Agramonte. Originally the city's central square, or Plaza de las Armas, this didn't become a proper park until 1912. Note the bronze statue of Agramonte on his steed at its center. In the park's southwestern corner is a 19th-century house that's now the Casa de la Trova, whose courtyard hosts performances by local musicians every day but Monday. The neoclassical building to the north is the Biblioteca (Library); a few doors farther north is the Palacio Municipal (Town Hall), which was originally erected in 1730 but almost completely rebuilt in 1906; local artists often exhibit in its foyer. ✉ *Calle Martí, e/Calle Cisneros y Calle Independencia.*

Built in 1864, the **Santa Iglesia de la Catedral**—on the southeastern edge of the park—replaced one built in 1617, and has seen several renovations. The most recent one took 15 years, and included replacing the wood-beam ceiling. Its refurbished exterior is an attractive beige and yellow. The most impressive aspect of the spacious interior is the large wood-and-marble altar, behind which shine stained glass and a statue of the Virgin Mary. ✉ *No phone.* ✉ *Free.* ⊙ *Weekdays 8–11 and 4–6, Sun. 10–noon.*

NEED A
BREAK?

The historic bar **El Cambio** (✉ Calle Martí y Calle Independencia, ☎ no phone), across from the Parque Agramonte's northeast corner, is a convenient stop for a little liquid refreshment. Dating from 1909, this proletarian watering hole has a wild interior paint job, ceramic work by local artists, stone floors, and a simple wooden bar.

★ ❷ **Plaza de San Juan de Dios.** This splendid cobbled square, surrounded by meticulously restored 18th- and 19th-century buildings (most still private homes), has been declared a national monument. On its eastern edge, the old **Hospital de San Juan de Dios** now holds the offices of several cultural organizations. In the portico of its large garden you'll find a simple museum with exhibits on the building's history, some old photos, and surgical instruments from days of yore—thank goodness for modern medicine. More interesting is the view from the roof. ☎ *32/29–1388.* ☒ *$1.* ☉ *Weekdays 9–5.*

Also on the plaza is Camagüey's oldest church, the **Iglesia de San Juan de Dios,** which was built in 1728 to replace the original (1686) St. John's. It underwent some structural changes in 1847 and an extensive restoration in 1986. Its simple, traditional interior has a terra-cotta floor, white-stucco walls, and a sloped wooden ceiling. Four ancient hardwood altars stand along the walls, each of them dedicated to a different saint—St. John's is the second on the left. The main altar is dedicated to the Holy Trinity, and is unique in that the Holy Spirit is represented as a man instead of as the usual dove. ☎ *no phone.* ☒ *Free.* ☉ *Mon.–Sat. 7–11 and 3–6.*

❷ **Plaza de los Trabajadores.** Before the Revolution, the Workers Plaza was known as the Plaza de La Merced, after the church and convent that define its eastern edge. It's a distinctly Cuban spot, with a large mural of Che Guevara, whose eternally youthful visage stares past the ancient facade of La Merced. A kapok tree towers over the plaza's center, and in the southwest corner stands the stately La Popular, built in 1928, and the seat of a local cultural society. ☒ *Calle Fernando Hernández y Calle Simón Bolívar.*

Dining and Lodging

Most of Camagüey's casas particulares are near the bus terminal, on the Carretera Central. There are, however, several nice ones in the historic center. **Alfredo and Milagros** (☒ Calle Cisneros 124, esquina de Calle San Clemente, ☎ 32/29–7436) rent three modern rooms a block northeast of the Plaza de San Juan. Though slightly tacky, the place is spotless and has a courtyard. **Manolo Venegas** (☒ Calle Independencia 251, ☎ 32/29–4606) and his neighbor Dalgis Fernández have two spacious, second-floor apartments above tiny Plaza Maceo, one block north of Parque Ignacio Agramonte. Manolo's three rooms have the best views, but Dalgis's two have high ceilings, private baths, and access to a sundeck.

¢–$ ✕ **La Campana de Toledo.** Set in a restored 18th-century house over-
★ looking the timeless Plaza de San Juan de Dios, this restaurant was named for the *campana* (bell) that hangs in its courtyard, which was apparently brought to Camagüey from Toledo, Spain, by a merchant who lived here. Seating is either in the courtyard, which is shaded by trees and decorated with tinajones, or in the front of the house, with a view of the plaza. The Cuban dishes include *boliche mechado* (roast tenderloin stuffed with bacon and served in a light sauce), a specialty here; all come with arroz congrí. ☒ *Plaza San Juan de Dios 18,* ☎ *32/29–5888. No credit cards.*

¢–$ ✕ **Restaurante Don Ronquilo.** A few steps from the Iglesia de la Soledad, this open-air restaurant has several tables overlooking a courtyard and a dozen more in back, surrounded by potted plants and colored glass. The menu is Cuban, but includes variations on common themes. Try the *bistec mayoral* (steak in a wine sauce on toast) and *pollo grillé al huerto* (half a grilled chicken with vegetables). ☒ *Av. Ignacio Agramonte 406,* ☎ *32/28–5239. No credit cards.*

¢ 🖫 **Gran Hotel.** This stately, five-story building in Camagüey's historic
★ heart has been a hotel since 1938. Its bright lobby has chandeliers hung
from high ceilings and various other antiques, the elevator being one
of them. Rooms also have high ceilings and old tile floors; those facing the street are the biggest, but they can be noisy at night. Although
the fifth-floor restaurant is lovely (it's furnished with antiques and surrounded by windows and glass doors that open onto a wraparound
balcony), the food often disappoints. Even if you stay elsewhere, stop
in for a sunset drink at the rooftop bar. ⊠ *Calle Maceo 67,* ☎ *32/29–
2094. 72 rooms. Restaurant, 3 bars, pool. MC, V.*

¢ 🖫 **Hotel Camagüey.** Though devoid of ambience, this 1970s structure
southeast of town is quieter than the city's downtown lodgings during the week, though its open-air disco rocks on weekends. Rooms are
basic boxes with wicker furniture, colorful bedspreads, and picture windows. Those in back have balconies overlooking a few trees, and are
quieter. ⊠ *Carretera Central Este, Km 4,* ☎ *32/28–7267,* 🖷 *32/28–
7180.* 𝚆𝙴𝙱 *www.horizontes.cu. 142 rooms. Restaurant, 2 bars, pool,
dance club. MC, V. BP.*

¢ 🖫 **Hotel Colón.** The Colón was inaugurated in 1927 and completely
refurbished in 2001. The lobby is a jewel, with ornate columns, a marble staircase, and a dark wooden bar and front desk. The patio in back—
surrounded by painted columns and lit by antique street lamps—is
flanked by the main bar, restaurant, and some rooms. Most rooms are
on the second floor, and though they're small, they have new furniture
and tile baths. The two that face the street, with tiny balconies, are the
biggest, though noisiest. ⊠ *Calle República 472,* ☎ *32/28–3368 or
32/28–3346. 48 rooms. Restaurant, 2 bars. MC, V.*

Nightlife and the Arts

At the **Casa de la Trova** (⊠ Calle Cisneros 171, ☎ 32/29–1357), on
Parque Ignacio Agramonte, local musicians perform Cuban son in an
18th-century courtyard every day but Monday from 2 to 5 and 9 to
midnight. The bar in the **Galería Colonial** (⊠ Av. Ignacio Agramonte
406, ☎ 32/28–5239) has live music Friday through Sunday starting
at 10 PM. The city's most popular dance club is the open-air discotheque at the **Hotel Camagüey** (⊠ Carretera Central, Km 4, ☎ 32/
28–7267); it's closed on Monday and Tuesday. The impressive **Teatro
Principal** (⊠ Calle Padre Valencia 64, ☎ 32/29–3048), two blocks northwest of the Plaza de los Trabajadores, hosts monthly performances by
the city's renowned ballet, regular concerts by the symphony orchestra, and occasional shows by the *ballet folclórico* (folkloric ballet).

Outdoor Activities and Sports

You can hike the forests and explore the caves (including the Cueva
del Indio, with its pre-Columbian drawings) of the **Sierra de Cubitas,**
a protected area 45 km (27 mi) northwest of Camagüey. Make arrangements through the tour operator Rumbos.

Shopping

The large store run by the artists' association **ACAA** (⊠ Calle Padre
Valencia 2, ☎ no phone), on the northern end of the Plaza de los Trabajadores, has an extensive selection of ceramics and other handicrafts. The **Fondo de Bienes Culturales** (⊠ Av. de la Libertad y Calle
Vega, ☎ no phone) sells ceramics, straw work, and other handicrafts.
The **Galéria Colonial** (⊠ Av. Ignacio Agramonte 406, ☎ 32/28–5454),
in front of the Iglesia de la Soledad, has two stores in it: one sells T-
shirts and other souvenirs, and the other sells cigars, rum, and coffee.

En Route Halfway between Camagüey and Santa Lucía, next to the Saramajuacan
River, stand the ruins of **Santa Isabel,** a 19th-century sugar mill that
was destroyed by the Spanish when its owner—a cousin of Ignacio Agra-

monte—joined the rebel army. An open-air restaurant next to the ruins serves light food, varied refreshments, and *guarapo* (fresh sugarcane juice).

Playa Santa Lucía

★ ㉗ *128 km (77 mi) northeast of Camagüey.*

Originally a simple fishing and salt-collecting village east of the Bahía de Nuevitas, Santa Lucía has been attracting tourists for decades, and all you need is a glimpse of the beach to understand why. Its 20 km (12 mi) swath of white sand, shaded by coconut palms and lapped by blue-green waters, is as impressive as any beach on the island. About a mile offshore is a barrier reef that beckons both divers and snorkelers, and in the Bahía de Nuevitas are the ruins of a Spanish fort and other reminders of the days when pirates threatened the region. The tourist area consists of five hotels and other facilities scattered along a 2-km (1-mi) stretch of beach just west of town.

If you desire a wider—and perhaps even whiter—beach than Playa Santa Lucía, you can drive or take a taxi 4 km (2 mi) west to **Playa los Cocos,** next to the fishing village of La Boca. This idyllic swath of sun-bleached silica slopes into aquamarine waters at the mouth of the Bahía de Nuevitas, and is shaded by abundant *cocos* (coconut palms), hence its name. The lagoon behind La Boca is a feeding area for flamingos, which you may be able to spot on your way there. **Cayo Sabinal,** just west of the Bahía de Nuevitas, has deserted beaches, a working lighthouse, and the ruins of a Spanish fortress.

Dining and Lodging

$$–$$$$ ✕ **Restaurante la Alfonsina.** At the end of a long dock, this simple restaurant under a thatched roof has the best views in town, not to mention the best ventilation. Though it belongs to the Club Santa Lucía hotel, it's open to guests from other hotels, and is one of the few places in Cuba that has live lobster. The menu includes an array of seafood dishes, but the langosta, which is prepared a number of ways, is your best bet. ⊠ *Club Santa Lucía, Playa Santa Lucía,* ☎ *32/36–5146. Reservations essential. No credit cards.*

$$–$$$ 🏨 **Club Santa Lucía.** Although this resort lines a wide swath of sugary sand shaded by palms and thatched parasols, few of its rooms have ocean views. The Coral Suites—spacious, beach-front bungalows with large balconies—are the best rooms by far. Junior suites are big but are set back from the beach in two-story buildings; standard rooms are so far from the sea that most view the road. The bar, two restaurants, and amphitheater surround a large, blue-tile pool with a rocky waterfall at one end. Though billed as all-inclusive, you have to pay for meals in two of the five restaurants (the one that serves seafood and the pizzeria) and to enter the dance club. ⊠ *Playa Santa Lucía,* ☎ *32/36–5284,* 🅵🅰🆇 *32/36–5147. 222 rooms, 20 suites. 5 restaurants, 1 bar, pool, massage, sauna, tennis court, aerobics, gym, horseback riding, volleyball, snorkeling, boating, jet skiing, motorbikes, shops, cabaret, dance club, children's programs (ages 3–12), travel services, car rental. MC, V. All-inclusive.*

$$ 🏨 **Hotel Cuatro Vientos.** The architecture is a mix of Cuban and Spanish, with arches, marble floors, barrel-tile and thatched roofs, and murals by Camagüey artists. Rooms are in two-story buildings scattered around vast, luxuriant grounds. They have white-tile floors, hardwood furniture, large baths with tubs, and sliding glass doors that open either onto balconies or porches with views of the gardens, pool, or sea. Buffet meals are included in rates, as are drinks at the main bar; but you must pay your own way at the beach grill and discotheque.

✉ *Playa Santa Lucía,* ☎ *32/33–6317 or 32/36–5120,* FAX *32/36–5142,* WEB *www.vnet/hotelesc. 412 rooms. 2 restaurants, 2 bars, pool, massage, sauna, 2 tennis courts, gym, volleyball, snorkeling, boating, fishing, motorbikes, shops, billiards, cabaret, children's programs (ages 3–12), travel services, car rental. MC, V. All-inclusive.*

¢ 🏨 **Villa Tararaco.** Built in 1956, this small hotel is Santa Lucía's oldest, but it's well maintained. The lobby, restaurant, and bar are in a spacious cement building with an ocean view, and the food and drink are incredibly cheap. Rooms are in a low, cross-shape building nearby, but only half—those with numbers beginning with 2 or 3—have ocean views. They're small but comfortable, with wicker furniture, tiny porches, and such amenities as air-conditioning and satellite TV. A thatched bar and grill sit on the beach nearby. The entire place belongs to a hotel school, so the staff is young and friendly. ✉ *Marina, Playa Santa Lucía,* ☎ *32/33–6410 or 32/33–6310,* FAX *32/36–5166. 31 rooms. Restaurants, bar, grill, air-conditioning. MC, V.*

Nightlife and the Arts

The **Centro Cultural Mar Verde** (✉ By entrance to Villa Caracol, on main road west of Club Santa Lucía, ☎ 32/33–6205) has high-season courtyard concerts by musicians from Camagüey. It functions as a dance club other nights. **La Jungla** (☎ 32/36–5284), the discotheque at the Club Santa Lucía, is the town's most popular dance club.

Outdoor Activities and Sports

FISHING

The ocean off Playa Santa Lucía has good fishing, with everything from sailfish to snapper. The **Marlin Marina** (☎ 32/36–5294) offers both trolling and bottom-fishing charters. Basic gear is provided; charters cost $100–$200 a day, depending on the type of boat.

SCUBA DIVING

With a barrier reef 2 km (1 mi) offshore, many shipwrecks nearby, and average visibility of about 25 m (66 ft), Playa Santa Lucía is a world-class dive destination. The **Sharks' Friends Diving Center** (☎ 32/36–5182), just west of the hotels, runs trips to 35 different spots, including 24 shipwrecks, the oldest of which dates from the 1800s. The center's most famous dive is a shark-feeding show, but it costs twice what the others do. It also offers a day trip to Cayo Caguamas, in the Jardines de la Reina. One-tank boat dives cost $35, equipment rental included; shark-feeding trips costs $50. Basic certification courses run about $200.

Shopping

The **Centro Comercial** (☎ 32/33–6204), a small shopping center on the beach next to the Club Santa Lucía, has a number of tiny shops that sell souvenirs, tobacco, rum, coffee, and film. The **Centro Cultural Mar Verde** (☎ 32/33–6205), on the main road, has two excellent shops: one sells a good selection of Cuban music, books, and musical instruments; the other, paintings, sculptures, and ceramics by Camagüey artists.

CENTRAL CUBA A TO Z

To research prices and get advice from other travelers, visit www. fodors.com.

AIR TRAVEL

Havana may be the main international hub, but in winter, Canadian charter flights arrive almost daily in Ceinfuegos, Ciego de Ávila, and Camagüey. Those charters can be much cheaper than scheduled flights to Havana, especially if you wait for a last minute deal. At this writing, there were also flights from Havana to Cienfuegos, Ciego de Ávila, Camagüey, and Cayo Coco.

AIRPORTS

Cienfuegos's international airport, Aeropuerto Jaime Gonzalez, is 8 km (5 mi) northeast of town, just past Caonoa. Trinidad's tiny airport, 2 km (1 mi) south of town on the road to Casilda, is served only by domestic charters. Ciego de Ávila's international airport, Aeropuerto Máximo Gómez, is 24 km (13 mi) north of town, near Ceballos. Cayo Coco has a small domestic airport 12 km (7 mi) west of the hotels. Camagüey's international airport, Aeropuerto Ignacio Agramonte, is 9 km (5 mi) northeast of town on the road to Nuevitas. Taxis and car-rental representatives meet every flight.

➤ AIRPORT INFORMATION: **Aeropuerto Cayo Coco** (✉ ☎ 33/30–1165). **Aeropuerto Ignacio Agramonte** (☎ 32/26–1010). **Aeropuerto Jaime Gonzalez** (☎ 322/61889). **Aeropuerto Máximo Gómez** (☎ 332/5717). **Aeropuerto de Trinidad** (☎ 419/6393).

CARRIERS

International flights to the region are charters, most of which run only during the winter months. Canada 3000 and Skyservice Airlines both fly from Toronto to Ciego de Ávila. Air Transat flies to Ciego de Ávila from Toronto, Montréal, Calgary, Edmonton, and Halifax, and to Camagüey and Cienfuegos from Toronto and Montréal. Monarch Airlines flies from London to Ciego de Ávila during the winter months. Because most of their flights are in the high season, charter companies work with local tour operators instead of maintaining offices in the central provinces.

Cubana has several flights a week from Havana to Cienfuegos and Ciego de Ávila and daily flights to Camagüey. Aero Caribbean has daily flights from Havana to Cayo Coco.

➤ AIRLINES AND CONTACTS: **Aero Caribbean** (☎ 33/30–1165 in Cayo Coco). **Cubana** (☎ 419/2296 in Trinidad, 33/25316 in Ciego de Ávila, 32/29–1338 or 32/29–2156 in Camagüey).

BOAT AND FERRY TRAVEL

Thousands of people visit Cuba on private boats every year, and there are a number of marinas in the central provinces with mooring space, electricity, water, diesel, and other services. The largest operation is Puertosol, with marinas in Cienfuegos, Trinidad, and Cayo Guillermo. Marlin is number two, with marinas in Cayo Coco and Playa Santa Lucía. A rusty ferry crosses the bay from Cienfuegos to the Castillo de Jagua daily at 8, 11, 3, and 5:20. The trip takes about 40 minutes and costs 50¢.

➤ BOAT AND FERRY INFORMATION: **Cienfuegos Ferry** (✉ Av. 46 y Calle 25, ☎ no phone). **Marina Marlin** (☎ 33/30–1323 on Cayo Coco, 32/36–5294 in Playa Santa Lucía). **Marina Puerto Sol** (☎ 432/45–1241 in Cienfuegos, 419/6205 in Playa Ancón, 33/30–1738 on Cayo Guillermo).

BUS TRAVEL

Air-conditioned Viazul buses depart from Havana for Trinidad daily at 8:15 and 1, stopping in Cienfuegos four hours later. Buses depart from Havana for Santiago at 5 and 8 PM, stopping in Santa Clara (about 2½ hours later), Sancti Spíritus (4½ hours), Ciego de Ávila (5½) hours, and Camagüey (7 hours). There's also a bus from Varadero to Trinidad departing at 7:30 (6 hours). Buses depart from Trinidad for Havana at 7:45 and 3, Varadero at 2:30, and Santiago at 8:15. Tickets must be purchased ahead of time.

Less comfortable (no air-conditioning) Astro buses, which have offices in most major terminals, serve the same routes for less money, but because of vehicle and gas shortages, they're sometimes cancelled and often run late. Always call ahead. Astro does, however, cover routes that Viazul doesn't, and may offer seats when Viazul is full—several seats on every bus are reserved for tourists. At this writing, there were departures from Havana for Cienfuegos at noon (returning at 10 AM); for Santa Clara at 8 PM (returning at 12:30 PM); and for Sancti Spíritus, Ciego de Ávila, and Camagüey at 9:20 AM and 7:45 PM (returning at 12:30 and 11:30 PM, 10:30 AM and 9:30 PM, 8 AM, and 7 PM, respectively). From Havana, buses take 4½ hours to reach Cienfuegos, 3½ hours to Santa Clara, 4½ hours to Sancti Spíritus, 5½ hours to Trinidad, 7½ hours to Ciego de Ávila, and 9½ hours to Camagüey.

From Santa Clara there are daily departures for Varadero at 9 AM, for Cienfuegos at 7:20 and 11:20 AM, Sancti Spíritus at 8 AM and 5 PM, Trinidad at 1:20, and Ciego de Ávila and Camagüey at 7 PM. Daily buses to Remedios depart at 6:40 and 9 AM and 2:30 from Santa Clara's Terminal Provincial. From Cienfuegos, buses depart daily for Santa Clara at 5:30 and 9 AM, Trinidad at 6:30 and 11:30 AM, and Cumanayagua at 6:30 AM. From Sancti Spíritus, departures for Santa Clara are at 6 AM and 2 PM, for Trinidad every other day at noon, and for Ciego de Ávila and Camagüey every other day at 7 AM. Buses leave Trinidad for Sancti Spíritus daily at 7 AM and Cienfuegos daily at 9 and 2:15, and Santa Clara every other day at 5 PM. Ciego de Ávila has daily departures for Camagüey at 5 AM and 4:40 PM, Sancti Spíritus and Cienfuegos at 7 AM, and Morón at 4 PM. From Camagüey, departures for Cienfuegos are at 4:30 PM on odd days and 8 AM on even days, for Sancti Spíritus every other day at noon, and for Santa Clara every other day at 7 AM. Buses leave Camagüey's Terminal Inter-Municipal for Playa Santa Lucía at 5:30 AM, returning at 8 AM.

► BUS INFORMATION: **Camagüey Terminal Inter-Provincial** (⊠ Carretera Central y Calle Peru, ☎ 32/27–2302). **Camagüey Terminal Inter-Municipal** (⊠ Av. Finlay, ☎ 32/28–1525). **Ciego de Ávila Terminal Inter-Provincial** (⊠ Carretera Central, ☎ 33/25109). **Cienfuegos** (⊠ Calle 49 y Av. 56, ☎ 432/5720). **Sancti Spíritus Terminal** (⊠ Calle Masso, 3 km/2 mi south of town, ☎ 41/24142). **Santa Clara Terminal Inter-Provincial** (⊠ Carretera Central, ☎ 42/29–2114). **Santa Clara Terminal Inter-Municipal** (⊠ Carretera Central at Amparo, ☎ 42/20–3470). **Terminal de Omnibuses de la Habana** (⊠ Av. Rancho Boyeros, ☎ 7/70–3397). **Trinidad Terminal** (⊠ Calle Piro Guinart, e/Calle Izquierdo y Calle Maceo/Gúttierez, ☎ 419/4448). **Viazul** (⊠ Av. 26 y Calle Zoológico, Havana, ☎ 7/81–1413, 🕸 www.viazul.cu).

CAR RENTAL
Rental-car rates are as high. Several companies are well represented in the region, so shopping around is an option.

► LOCAL AGENCIES: **Cubacar/Veracuba** (⊠ Aeropuerto Máximo Gómez, Ciego de Ávila, ☎ 33/30–8143; ⊠ Punta Gorda, Cienfuegos, ☎ 432/45–1645; ⊠ Av. Turística, Playa Santa Lucía, ☎ 32/36–5216; ⊠ Calle Trista y Calle Amparo, Santa Clara, ☎ 42/20–2020; ⊠ Calle José Martí/Jesús María 256, Trinidad, ☎ 419/6317). **Havanautos** (⊠ Carretera Central, Camagüey, ☎ 32/22–8270; ⊠ Hotel Tryp, Cayo Coco, ☎ 33/30–1386; ⊠ Aeropuerto Máximo Gómez, Ciego de Ávila, ☎ 33/52114; ⊠ Punta Gorda, Cienfuegos, ☎ 432/45–1211; ⊠ Carretera Casilda, Trinidad, ☎ 419/6301). **Micar** (⊠ Calle A, No. 20, Camagüey, ☎ 32/27–2439; ⊠ Calle Libertad, Ciego de Ávila, ☎ 33/26–6157; ⊠ Punta Gorda, Cienfuegos, ☎ 432/45–1605; ⊠ Calle Virtudes, esquina de Calle Independencia, Santa Clara, ☎ 42/20–4570). **Transtur** (⊠ Av. Monaco Sur, Camagüey, ☎ 32/27–1208; ⊠ Cayo Coco, ☎ 33/

30–1175; ✉ Calle 125, Cienfuegos, ☎ 432/45–1172; ✉ Parque Serafín Sánchez, Sancti Spíritus, ☎ 41/28544; ✉ Carretera Camajuani, Santa Clara, ☎ 42/20–4100).

CAR TRAVEL

Central Cuba's roads are generally in good repair. The four-lane highway that connects Havana to Santa Clara and Jatibonico and the two-lane road that continues east to Ciego de Ávila and Camagüey form an east–west aorta through which little traffic flows. Peripheral arteries head south to Cienfuegos and north from Ciego de Ávila to Cayos Coco and Guillermo, and from Camagüey to Santa Lucía. The old road loops south from the highway to Sancti Spíritus at Cabaiguan, continuing east toward Ciego de Ávila; another good road heads southwest from Sancti Spíritus to Trinidad. Cienfuegos and Trinidad are connected via Topes de Collantes by a rough mountain road and a smoother, more direct coastal route.

Driving within central Cuba's towns can be confusing. There are many one-way streets, and intersections aren't always well marked. If you have any doubts about where you're going, just ask someone; people are happy to help strangers. Traffic is invariably light—mostly bicycles and horse-drawn taxis—and parking spaces are abundant and free.

EMERGENCY SERVICES

If your rental car breaks down, contact the rental agency immediately. There are plenty of police along the main roads, but many don't have vehicles, so you're most likely to be helped by a concerned citizen. Cubans are very good about stopping for accidents and breakdowns, and helping out in general.

GASOLINE

All major towns and cities have gas stations—Cupet-Cimex or Oro Negro—most of which are open 24 hours a day.

EMERGENCIES

Servimed, which provides medical services for tourists, has access to medicines you won't find in the pharmacies. The nurses and doctors assigned to every hotel are local Servimed representatives. Asistur offers travel insurance to tourists and can help during medical and other emergencies. The region has several decompression chambers, in case of a diving accident.

➤ CONTACTS: **Ambulance** (☎ 32/29–2860 in Camagüey, 185 in Ciego de Ávila, 432/5019 in Cienfuegos, 41/24462 in Sancti Spíritus, 42/20–3965 in Santa Clara, 419/2362 in Trinidad). **Asistur** (☎ 33/30–8173 in Cayo Coco, 33/30–8150 in Ciego Ávila, 432/6402 in Cienfuegos, 42/20–6529 in Santa Clara). **Fire** (☎ 115). **Police** (☎ 116). **Servimed** (☎ 432/45–1623 in Cienfuegos, 335/33–5680 in Morón, 419/6240 in Trinidad).

HEALTH

It's best to drink bottled water in central Cuba. Note that the big resorts have filter systems, so that the water at their bars is safe to drink. The problem is finding bottles for them to fill up so that you have drinking water in your room. The region's most common health risks are heat stroke and sunburn; drink plenty of fluids and use sunscreen.

MAIL AND SHIPPING

You can mail letters and make international calls from local *correo* (post office) branches, which are open weekdays 8 AM–6 PM.

➤ POST OFFICES: **Camagüey** (✉ Calle Cisneros, e/Av. Agramonte y Calle Gómez, ☎ 32/29–5312). **Ciego de Ávila** (✉ Calle República y Calle

4, ☎ 33/27510). **Cienfuegos** (✉ Av. 54, No. 3514, ☎ 432/45–1259). **Sancti Spíritus** (✉ Calle Independencia Sur 8, ☎ 41/23134). **Santa Clara** (✉ Calle Colón 10, ☎ 42/20–3119). **Trinidad** (✉ Calle Maceo/Gutiérrez 418, ☎ 419/2149).

MONEY MATTERS

The Banco Financiero Internacional, Cuba's biggest commercial bank, has branches in all the region's cities. It will exchange most European currencies and Canadian dollars into U.S. dollars and give cash advances on credit cards not issued by U.S. banks. All big beach resorts change money, and many have bank branches in them.

➤ EXCHANGE SERVICES: **Banco Financiero Internacional** (✉ Calle Independencia 221, Camagüey, ☎ 32/29–4846; ✉ Calle H. Castillo 14, Ciego de Ávila, ☎ 33/26–6310; ✉ Av. 54 y Calle 29, Cienfuegos, ☎ 432/45–1657; ✉ Calle Independencia 2, Sancti Spíritus, ☎ 41/28477; ✉ Calle Cuba 6, Santa Clara, ☎ 42/20–7450; ✉ Hotel Ancón, Trinidad, ☎ 419/6107).

SAFETY

Although central Cuba is quite safe on the whole, you should always keep an eye on your things.

LOCAL SCAMS

The influx of tourists in Trinidad has resulted in an abundance of *jineteros,* "hello-friend" hustlers who make their living "helping" tourists. They can be aggressive and have been known to tell tourists that the casa particular or paladar they're looking for is closed, or simply take them somewhere else and tell them it's the place they were looking for (Trinidad has an overabundance of illegal paladares). You may encounter similar tactics in Cienfuegos.

TAXIS

Cubataxi and Transtur taxis are usually parked outside every major hotel. They have dollar meters and are relatively expensive. Cheaper Cuban taxis that ply the main routes aren't supposed to pick up tourists but usually will if away from the hotels and traffic police. Unfortunately, Cienfuegos's charming horse-drawn taxis risk a hefty fine if they pick up tourists, so they don't.

➤ LOCAL COMPANIES: **Cubataxi** (☎ 32/28–1247 in Camagüey, 32/33–6196 in Playa Santa Lucía). **Transtur** (☎ 32/27–1015 in Camagüey, 33/30–1175 in Cayo Coco, 33/26–6229 in Ciego de Ávila, 432/45–1600 in Cienfuegos, 41/28533 in Sancti Spíritus, 42/20–4100 in Santa Clara, 419/6454 in Trinidad).

TELEPHONES

Although you can make local and international calls from most hotels, it's considerably cheaper to call from a public phone using the ETECSA (Cuban phone company) cards that are sold at most hotels, post offices, and phone centers. There should be a rate chart posted next to phones that accept these cards. Area codes for central Cuba are: Villa Clara 42, Cienfuegos 432, Trinidad 419, Sancti Spíritus 41, Ciego de Ávila and Cayos 33, Morón 335, Camagüey 32.

➤ PHONE CENTERS: **Camagüey** (✉ Calle Avellaneda 271). **Ciego de Ávila** (✉ Edificio H. Castillo, Calle 12, Plantas). **Cienfuegos** (✉ Calle 37, e/Av. 0 y Av. 1; ✉ Calle 31, e/Av. 54 y Av. 56). **Morón** (✉ Calle Céspedes 5). **Playa Santa Lucía** (✉ Av. Turística). **Sancti Spíritus** (✉ Parque Serafín Sánchez). **Santa Clara** (✉ Av. Barrero 6). **Trinidad** (✉ Parque Martí, ☎ 419/2149).

TOURS

The tour operators Cubanácan and Rumbos (and, to some extent, Cubatur) provide a variety of local tours. They have representatives in all the large hotels as well as in regional offices.

➤ TOUR COMPANIES: **Cubánacan** (✉ Hotel Tryp, Cayo Coco, ☎ 33/30–1217; ✉ Av. 54, No. 1208, Cienfuegos, ☎ 432/45–1680; ✉ Casa 38 Residencial, Playa Santa Lucía, ☎ 32/33–6412; ✉ Calle Maceo 453, Santa Clara, ☎ 42/20–5189; ✉ Calle José Martí/Jesús María y Calle Colón, Trinidad, ☎ 419/6302). **Cubatur** (✉ Av. 37 y Av. 0, Cienfuegos, ☎ 432/45–1242; ✉ Calle Tararaco, Playa Santa Lucía, ☎ 32/33–6291; ✉ Calle Máximo Gómez 7, Sancti Spíritus, ☎ 41/28518). **Rumbos** (✉ Calle Lopez Recio 108, Camagüey, ☎ 32/29–7229; ✉ Complejo Rocarena, Cayo Coco, ☎ 33/30–1414; ✉ Carretera Central, Ciego de Ávila, ☎ 33/26–6643; ✉ Av. 20, No. 3905, Cienfuegos ☎ 432/45–1121; ✉ Playa Santa Lucía, ☎ 32/33–6106; ✉ Calle Roloff, Sancti Spíritus, ☎ 41/28388; ✉ Calle Independencia 167, Santa Clara, ☎ 42/21–7292; ✉ Calle Maceo/Gutiérrez y Calle Simón Bolívar/Desengaño, Trinidad, ☎ 419/6444).

TRAIN TRAVEL

Though it is often late and occasionally cancelled, train service in central Cuba is quite extensive. Foreigners must pay for their tickets in dollars at the Ladis office in the station. The train to Cienfuegos departs from Havana's Coubre station at 1:25 PM and arrives 10 hours later, returning at 1 PM. Trains to Santiago de Cuba, which stop in Santa Clara, Ciego de Ávila, and Camagüey, depart from Havana's Terminal Central at 4:40 PM, with a faster, air-conditioned *especial* at 7:30 PM; there's also an especial to Santiago that departs from Coubre at 10:40 AM. The train to Sancti Spíritus departs and returns at 10 AM. Trains depart from Camagüey for Havana at 10:30 AM, 1:30, 7:50 and 10:40 PM, stopping in Ciego de Ávila (2–3 hours) and Santa Clara (4–6 hours).

➤ TRAIN INFORMATION: **Camagüey Terminal** (✉ Calle Quiones y Calle Padre Olalla, ☎ 32/28–3214). **Ciego de Ávila Terminal** (✉ Calle Van Horne y Calle Simón Reyes, ☎ 33/23313). **Cienfuegos Terminal** (✉ Calle 49 y Av. 58, ☎ 432/5495). **Santa Clara Terminal** (✉ Calle Pedro Estévez, north of town, ☎ 42/20–2895).

VISITOR INFORMATION

Trinidad is the only town that has an Infotur office, but tour agency desks in the lobbies of most hotels can provide basic information, and you may be able to pick up a map and other printed materials at the provincial offices of the Ministry of Tourism, MINTUR.

➤ TOURIST INFORMATION: **Infotur** (✉ Calle Simón Bolívar/Desengaño y Calle Maceo/Gutiérrez, Trinidad, ☎ 419/2149). **MINTUR** (✉ Carretera Central y Calle Céspedes, Camagüey, ☎ 32/27–1712; ✉ Calle Máximo Gómez 82, Ciego de Ávila, ☎ 33/23335; ✉ El Prado y Av. 20, Cienfuegos, ☎ 423/45–1627).

5   EASTERN CUBA

The region known as Oriente has a variety
of sublimely beautiful settings—from palm-
lined beaches to the city of Santiago—the
metaphorical seat of the Cuban soul—to the
majestic Sierra Maestra. The sagas that
unfolded here lent great drama to the
island's history, and Cubans speak of the
area with awe.

EASTERN CUBA IS FULL OF TALES about rebellion and revolution. The stories go back all the way to the 16th century, when Hatuey, a Taíno Indian chief, rose up against the Spaniards and was captured and burned at the stake near Baracoa in 1523. On October 10, 1868, Carlos Manuel de Céspedes freed the slaves on his plantation near Bayamo and proclaimed Cuba's independence from Spain, launching the Ten Years' War. In 1895, patriot and poet José Martí landed on the south coast of the Bahía de Guantánamo; he was killed shortly thereafter in a battle against the Spanish at Dos Ríos in Granma Province. The region is the birthplace of Fidel Castro (who was born in Holguín Province) and his Revolution. Granma Province itself takes its name from the boat that carried Castro and 81 revolutionaries back to Cuba from exile in Mexico in 1956. Although their landing—at Playa las Coloradas in the province's southwestern corner—was disastrous, the survivors fled to the Sierra Maestra, the eastern mountain range, and continued their fight.

By John Marino

Updated by Michael de Zayas

In this region you'll find Cuba's "second city," Santiago de Cuba, which has always been as open to French, African, and Caribbean creole influences as it has to those of Havana. It explodes during the July carnival, a weeklong festival of music, dancing, and merrymaking. One of the country's great pleasures may be enjoying a *mojíto* (light rum, sugar, mint, and soda) on the balcony of Santiago's Hotel Casa Granda. From here, you can watch the goings-on in the Parque Céspedes, the city's historic heart and the hub for *santiagueros* (as locals are called). The city also sizzles at night, when musicians share a microphone at the Casa de la Trova.

Resorts rise in many a cove on Holguín's northern coast, especially around Guardalavaca. The white-sand beaches here, and their dark-sand counterparts on Granma's southern coast, draw Canadians and Europeans seeking isolated vacations. Along both shores, water-sports outfitters stand ready to help sailors, fishermen, scuba divers, and snorkelers.

From the Caribbean Sea 32 km (20 mi) north to the Atlantic, a legendary highway known as La Farola cuts a sinuous path through jungle. At its northern end, El Yunque, an anvil-shape mountain, rises into the clouds. Beyond, in the far reaches of Guantánamo Province, are more coastal enclaves, including quirky Baracoa, site of the first Spanish settlement. Throughout the region, hiking trails seem to lead through history to colorful hamlets and old rebel outposts that appear lost in verdant jungle or rugged mountains.

Pleasures and Pastimes

Arts and Culture

Santiago, arguably Cuba's cultural capital, is the birthplace of *son*, a forerunner of salsa. You can catch live-music performances at hotels, theaters, clubs, and the Casa de la Trova. The city's musical energy is highlighted in the late July carnival celebration. Santiago is also home to all types of *teatro*—from children's theater to modern dramas—as well as to poets and painters. It's Old City has a good number of art galleries and crafts shops. Works by artisans in Baracoa, which still seems influenced by its Taíno predecessors, are also noteworthy.

Dining

Because of shortages, the best meals are served at expensive resorts that cater to tourists. Outside of such complexes, good bets are the privately operated *paladares*, which serve *comida criolla* (the island's own mix-

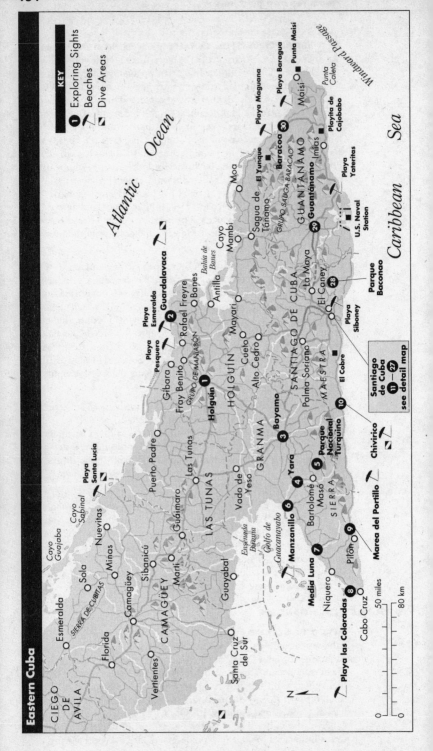

Eastern Cuba

KEY

● Exploring Sights

⌐ Beaches

⚑ Dive Areas

ture of Spanish and New World cuisines). Roasted pork or chicken and stewed or spiced beef are common main courses. They're usually served with *arroz* (rice) and red-kidney or black beans or fried sweet bananas or plantains.

Santiago is known for its roast pig and its marinated *yuca* (cassava or manioc). Other eastern Cuba specialties include *fufú*, a mashed plantain side dish laced with crumbs of crispy pork, and *prú*, a soft drink made from pine needles, sugar, roots, and herbs. Baracoa's cuisine is closer to that found elsewhere in the Caribbean in that it relies heavily on the coconut. Fish and shellfish, for example, are served in a flavorful orange coconut sauce. *Bacán* is mashed plantain and coconut stuffed with pork, wrapped in plantain leaves, and then cooked. All along the roadsides, children sell *cucurucho*, a desert of shredded coconut, fruits, nuts, and sugar ingeniously wrapped in a palm leaf.

Hotel restaurants tend to serve such standard Continental fare as roast beef and potatoes, creamy casseroles, and paella. Chinese cuisine and Italian food (mostly pizza and pastas) are also available. The closest thing to a Western-style chain restaurant you're likely to see is Pizza Nova, a Canadian pizzeria chain (there are branches in Santiago and Guardalavaca). Most hotels serve breakfast from 7 AM to 10 AM and, coincidentally, also keep those hours (7 PM–10 PM) in the evening for dinner. Cuban meals are relaxed; reservations are rarely required. The most conservative regulation involves not wearing swimsuits to certain restaurants.

The U.S. dollar is the most reliable form of payment. Credit cards *not* affiliated with U.S. banks or companies are accepted in all government restaurants, though never in paladares. For price categories, *see* the chart *under* Dining *in* Smart Travel Tips A to Z.

Scuba Diving and Snorkeling
The diving and snorkeling opportunities are best on the northern coast, near Guardalavaca, where there are a number of outfitters affiliated with hotels. The waters here are perfect for snorkeling, and you'll find an abundance of coral formations and colorful fish just off the shore.

Lodging
Santiago de Cuba has extraordinary lodgings, from the historic, well-situated Hotel Casa Granda to the postmodern Hotel Meliá Santiago de Cuba. Hidden in the decaying elegance of Vista Alegre are some fine *casas particulares* (private homes that rent out rooms to guests), as well as more conventional lodgings.

In sleepy Baracoa your options range from a hotel in a fort to a small, oceanside guest house whose former owner ironically fled to Cuba from Russia after the Russian Revolution. She once hosted such guests as Errol Flynn and Che Guevara.

Top-notch resorts line the southern coast from Santiago de Cuba to Marea del Portillo. Most of them charge flat, all-inclusive rates. The prices are economical, and the quality of the service and the food is better than average. To the north, Guardalavaca is becoming a haven for Europeans and Canadians. It has a handful of mostly all-inclusive resorts and a few free-standing restaurants and discos. This area offers the perfect beach vacation, *and* it's a convenient place from which to explore Santiago and Baracoa.

Credit cards *not* affiliated with U.S. banks or companies are accepted in most major hotels. For price categories, *see* the chart *under* Lodging *in* Smart Travel Tips A to Z.

Exploring Eastern Cuba

The spirit of eastern Cuba, the birthplace of rum and revolution, is intoxicating. The region includes the provinces of Granma, Holguín, Santiago, and Guantánamo. Together with Las Tunas, they once composed the single province of Oriente, a moniker still used for the whole area today.

The provincial capital of Holguín is a good regional hub—one that's quite close to the beautiful beaches of Guardalavaca. South of it lies Bayamo, the capital of Granma Province and the gateway to the Sierra Maestra. Directly west is the colorful port town of Manzanillo, with a wide *malecón* (bay-side boulevard) and a beautiful historic center. An hour's drive south brings you to Playa las Coloradas, where Castro landed in 1956. About 40 minutes east of here is Marea del Portillo, with two lovely resorts on Mediterranean-like beaches. From here the road hugs the southern coast while snaking along in the shadow of the Sierra Maestra to Santiago de Cuba. The Baconao Nature Reserve—which has several beaches, restaurants, hotels, and other attractions—is just 45 minutes east of here.

Santiago is the gateway to Guantánamo Province. Although famous for its U.S. military base, the province's most outstanding attraction is the colonial town of Baracoa, near Cuba's easternmost point. The town is a 260-km (161-mi) drive from Santiago along the awesome La Farola Highway, which brought Baracoa in contact with the rest of Cuba when it was constructed during the 1970s. Pine-covered highlands, jungle-covered foothills, miles of beaches, and surging rivers fill the area around Baracoa. El Yunque looms over the city. The mountain was a sacred place for the indigenous Taínos, and their imprint is still strongly felt in Baracoa. Locals still boast of their Taíno blood, evident in their features.

Great Itineraries

IF YOU HAVE 3 DAYS

Spend two days touring ☷ **Santiago de Cuba** ⑪–㉗, taking in its many historical sights, shopping in its many stores and galleries, and seeing live-music shows in its many venues. On the third day visit **Parque Baconao** ㉘, a nature preserve just east of the city.

IF YOU HAVE 5 DAYS

Spend two days exploring ☷ **Santiago de Cuba** ⑪–㉗. On the third day, head east for a day trip to **Parque Baconao** ㉘. Rise early on the fourth day and take the gorgeous south coast road west for an overnight trip to the beach town of **Marea del Portillo** ⑨, where the Sierra Maestra crashes into the Caribbean Sea.

IF YOU HAVE 7 DAYS

Spend three days exploring ☷ **Santiago de Cuba** ⑪–㉗. On the fourth day, head east, visiting **Parque Baconao** ㉘ and stopping in ☷ **Guantánamo** ㉙ for the night. The next day continue your journey east along La Farola Highway to **Baracoa** ㉚. Spend the fifth and sixth days exploring the town and El Yunque or the Playa Maguana before returning to Santiago on the seventh day.

When to Tour

Although peak season is technically December through April, July is a hectic month owing to Santiago's carnival and the Festival del Caribe. Make reservations well in advance during these peak times. The spring and fall off-seasons see prices drop by as much as 25% in places, though hotels may offer fewer amenities (some may even close entirely). Discounts during these times may not be as great in Guardalavaca—one of the driest spots in the off-season—and Santiago, which tends to draw visitors year-round.

HOLGUÍN AND GRANMA PROVINCES

These two provinces northeast of Santiago have acres of sugar and banana plantations, rice paddies, and cattle fields. The eponymous provincial capital of Holguín Province affords a look at a typical Cuban city. But the province is best known for Guardalavaca, a north coast town on a white-sand beach. Although small, it has top-notch resorts, watersports outfitters, and tour operators; nearby, you'll find several other beaches and attractions.

Granma Province has the most varied landscapes—from the forbidding peaks of the Sierra Maestra to the dry south coast—and was also the sight of events that were important not only to the Revolution, but also to Cuba's earlier struggles for independence. Both its capital, Bayamo, and the port town of Manzanillo are interesting stops filled with historic structures. The coastal road south leads to beaches and natural reserves at Playa las Coloradas, where Castro's rebels landed in the yacht *Granma*. The province is also a gateway to the Sierra Maestra via the Bayamo–Manzanillo roadway. These mountains crash down along the south coast and rise from a jungle interior. The road winds along an awesome turquoise shore in the shadow of steep, muscular rock.

Holguín

❶ *734 km (456 mi) southeast of Havana; 134 km (83 mi) northwest of Santiago de Cuba.*

"Holguín was for me . . . absolute boredom," wrote Reinaldo Arenas in *Before Night Falls,* an autobiography that became Julian Schnabel's Academy Award–nominated film in 2000. "The town was flat, commercial, square, with absolutely no mystery or personality. . . . I saw Holguín as a gigantic tomb, its low houses looked like pantheons punished by the sun."

Holguín, Cuba's fourth-largest city, has gotten worse in the four decades since Arenas lived here. The "low houses" of which he speaks have all been added onto illegally using whatever materials their owners could acquire. The result has been an aesthetic collapse, where piles of bricks and cinder blocks lie in the street and structures are bare of paint. Still, if you seek insight into a Cuban city that has been bypassed by tourism, Holguín is an interesting study. It's also a good gateway to the beach resorts at Guardalavaca 50 km (31 mi) north.

Holguín's small historic district hugs the **Plaza Calixto García,** a square graced by large trees and a marble bust of Calixto García, a local general in the Ten Years' War (1868–78) for independence from Spain. It's lined with colonial buildings containing residences, small shops, the Casa de la Trova (where music is often performed), the Teatro Comandante Eddy Sunoi, and the Centro de Arte Salón Moncada, with its occasional painting and photography exhibits. The **Museo Historia Provincial,** in the former Casino Español at the plaza's north end, contains an exhibit of pre-Columbian artifacts as well as displays on the Revolution and the province's role in it. Locally, the redbrick building is known as La Periquera (The Parrot Cage), because brightly dressed Spanish officers peered through its barred windows while the city was under siege by General García's troops in 1868. ✉ *198 Calle Frexes,* ☎ *no phone.* ⌚ *$1.* ☺ *Mon.–Sat. noon–7.*

You can learn more about the Ten Years' War and its local patriot, General Calixto García, at his birthplace. The **Casa Natal Calixto García** contains some of his belongings. ⊠ *147 Calle Miro, just off Plaza Calixto García,* ☏ *no phone.* ☑ *$1.* ☉ *Tues.–Sun. 9–4.*

The **Museo de la Historia Natural Carlos de la Torre,** a Moorish-style structure with beautiful ceramic tile work, contains preserved specimens of Cuban wildlife. Be sure to check out the snail-shell collection. ⊠ *Calle Maceo, ½ block south of Plaza Calixto García,* ☏ *no phone.* ☑ *$1.* ☉ *Tues.–Sat. 8–6, Sun. 8–noon.*

The **Plaza Julio Grave de Peralta,** locally called Parque de las Flores (Flower Park), is bounded by Luz Caballero, Aricios, Maceo, and Libertad streets. On its northern end are murals of Cuban patriots of the Revolution and previous wars of independence. Look for the portrait of a youthful Fidel; it may be the only one you'll see in Cuba. The Catedral de San Isidorio, on Calle Libertad, dates from 1720.

Exactly 456 steps lead up to the **Loma de la Cruz,** a hill named for the large white cross that has graced it since 1790. From here you have a lovely view of Holguín and the surrounding limestone hills. There are also artisan shops and a snack bar. ⊠ *Staircase is on Calle Maceo, 10 blocks north of Plaza San José.*

The **Plaza de la Revolución,** 3 km (2 mi) northeast of central Holguín, has a marble bust of local hero General Calixto García and his marble mausoleum. This wide, open park is used for political rallies and other events. Look for the white colonial building containing the Communist Party headquarters.

OFF THE
BEATEN PATH

FINCA MAYABE – Just southeast of Holguín a rural road takes you to the hilly Mayabe sector. Here you'll find Finca Mayabe, a re-creation of a farm with fruit trees, animals (horseback riding is a possibility), and a hotel, Mirador de Mayabe, with a bar-restaurant.

FINCA MANACAS – Fidel Castro was born at Finca Manacas in the town of Biran, 60 km (37 mi) southeast of Holguín. Although the two-story house isn't open to visitors, you can get a special pass (free) to enter the premises from the Communist Party headquarters in Holguín. Castro's father leased land here from the United Fruit Company and raised sugarcane. The property eventually encompassed 26,000 acres and included a cattle farm, a repair shop, a store, and other facilities.

Dining and Lodging

¢   ✕🏠 **Hotel Pernik.** Partially paid for by the Bulgarian government (it's named for a town in Bulgaria), this Soviet-inspired hotel has more than 200 rooms and plenty of amenities. For a lively atmosphere, head to the pool. For better-than-average Cuban specialties and frequent live-music performances, head to the main restaurant ($), Sofia—named after the Bulgarian capital, of course. ⊠ *Av. Dimitrov y Av. XX Aniversario,* ☏ *24/48–1011,* 𝖥𝖠𝖷 *24/48–1667. 202 rooms. 2 restaurants, 2 bars, pool, beauty salon, massage, shop, nightclub, airport shuttle, car rental, travel services. MC, V.*

¢   ✕🏠 **Mirador de Mayabe.** You can stay in one of the hillside cabins or
★   in the gracious Casa del Pancho, whose beautifully appointed rooms have balconies. Either way, chances are you'll have a good view of Holguín Valley. The on-site bar-restaurant, Taberna Pancho ($), serves decent fare, although its biggest draw may be its mascot: a beer-drinking donkey named Poncho. (In the rainy season, mosquitoes are a problem here; bring plenty of bug spray.) ⊠ *Loma del Mayabe, La Cuaba,*

☎ 24/42–2160, FAX 24/42–5347, *4 rooms, 20 cabins. Restaurant, bar, pool, beauty salon, shop, travel services. MC, V.*

En Route The road to Guardalavaca passes through the Plaza de la Revolución and rolling farmland as it runs out of town. Near Gibara, a dusty port town 28 km (17 mi) north of Holguín, the **Silla de Gibara** (Saddle of Gibara) rises from the flatlands. Locals believe that this is the land mass first sighted by Columbus when he discovered Cuba; Baracoans, however, hotly dispute this, claiming that he saw El Yunque, near Cuba's eastern tip.

As you continue north to Guardalavaca, you'll pass through sugar country. If you go through the town of Rafael Freyre, take the road that runs by the large sugar mill to **Bahía Bariay,** which is where Columbus supposedly landed. Two monuments commemorate the event: one at Playa Blanca, a white-sand stretch, and another at Fray Benito.

Guardalavaca

❷ *70 km (43 mi) northeast of Holguín.*

The north coast of Holguín Province has some of eastern Cuba's finest beaches. Guardalavaca, a funny name that translates as "guard the cow," is the most famous of these. (One theory behind its name is that it was a place where cows were herded and guarded during pirate attacks.) Its biggest draws are its opportunities for sunning, swimming, sailing, and scuba diving. You'll find a handful of hotels, restaurants, and discos along a single road, behind which is a beautiful white-sand beach. You can make arrangements to participate in water sports, go horseback riding, or visit the Bahía de Naranjo aquarium through your hotel.

Five kilometers (3 miles) west of Playa Guardalavaca, heading back toward Holguín along the main road, is **Playa Esmerelda,** a beach that the Spanish chain Sol has claimed as its own with three all-inclusive hotels. Just 1 km (½ mi) west of Playa Esmerelda is **Bahía de Naranjo** (Orange Tree Bay), an inlet with mangrove islands. At a snack bar here you can buy tickets for the boat to an aquarium in the middle of the bay. The $12 fee includes the boat ride, entrance to the facility, and a dolphin show daily at noon; for an additional $40 you can take a 15-minute swim with the dolphins.

Twelve kilometers (7 miles) west of Bahía de Naranjo along the Carretera Holguín–Guardalavaca (Holguín–Guardalavaca Highway) is **Playa Pesquero,** a cove whose shallow, clear waters and white sands are surrounded by greenery; indeed, the area is often referred to as the Costa Verde (Green Coast). If you stay in one of the resorts here, consider renting a car for a day trip into the interior.

Guardalavaca is part of the county of **Banes,** whose urban center is 20 km (12 mi) southeast of Playa Guardalavaca. Castro married his first wife at the Iglesia de Nuestra Senora de la Caridad on the town's Plaza Martí. Fulgencio Batista, the dictator Castro eventually toppled, lived here in 1901. But Banes is best known for its archaeological treasures. The **Museo Indocuban** has one of Cuba's largest collections of such indigenous artifacts as pottery, jewelry, and tools. There are also murals depicting Indian life. ⊠ *Calle General Marrero 305, esquina de Av. José Martí, Banes,* ☎ *no phone.* 🎫 *$1.* ◯ *Tues.–Sat. 9–5, Sun. 8–noon.*

Dining and Lodging

$-$$ ✕ **El Cayuelo.** At the end of a dirt road that runs off the main road to Banes, you'll find this beachfront restaurant. You can't go wrong by ordering one of the local seafood specialties. Afterward, walk in the shade of sea-grape trees and discover your own Guardalavaca. ⊠ *Playa Guardalavaca,* ☎ 24/30422. *No credit cards.*

¢–$ ✕ **El Ancla.** The specialty here is seafood, prepared according to local recipes. The restaurant is set above a charming stretch of sand on the western end of town. ⊠ *Playa Guardalavaca,* ☎ 24/30237. *MC, V.*

¢–$ ✕ **Pizza Nova.** This Canadian chain restaurant serves quality pasta dishes, salads, and pizza in a low-key, outdoor setting. Look for the yellow sign near a park that hosts an artisans fair by day. ⊠ *Playa Guardalavaca,* ☎ 24/30137. *MC, V.*

$$$$ 🏨 **Breezes Costa Verde.** If you seek a fun-loving, contemporary beach
★ vacation, don't pass up this Canadian-run resort. By day you can take a dip in one of several lovely swimming pools or follow the boardwalk past protected marshlands to the beach, with its gleaming white sand and clear, shallow waters that are good for snorkeling. At night you can sample daiquirís of any flavor at one of six bars or spend some time dancing at the disco before retiring to your spacious, modern guest quarters. Other amenities include ample buffets and a colorful day-care center. ⊠ *Off Carretera Holguín–Guardalavaca, Playa Pesquero,* ☎ *24/30520, 800/701–5923 in Canada, or 800/GO–SUPER in the U.S.,* FAX *24/20525,* WEB *www.superclubscuba.net. 464 rooms, 16 suites. 4 restaurants, 6 bars, in-room safes, minibars, 3 pools, wading pool, hair salon, outdoor hot tub, massage, sauna, 8 tennis courts, gym, beach, snorkeling, windsurfing, boating, waterskiing, bicycles, shop, dance club, recreation room, video games, baby-sitting, children's programs, nursery, laundry service, weddings, travel services, car rental, airport shuttle. MC, V. All-inclusive.*

$$$$ 🏨 **Las Brisas Club Resort.** Easy access to a white-sand beach, wide-open public spaces, and elegant swimming pools make this resort a solid choice for a relaxing vacation. Rooms—in the original five-story building or in the newer, breezier villas—have tile work and fairly new furnishings, though the decor is on the tacky side. Nonguests can pay a day charge to use the facilities. ⊠ *Playa Guardalavaca,* ☎ *24/30218,* FAX *24/30018. 450 rooms. 8 restaurants, 6 bars, in-room safes, 2 pools, 4 tennis courts, gym, bicycles, outdoor hot tub, children's activities, beach, horseback riding, snorkeling, windsurfing, boating, jet skiing, waterskiing, fishing, shops, nightclub, children's programs, travel services, car rental. MC, V. All-inclusive.*

$$$$ 🏨 **Meliá Río de Oro.** This Spanish-operated resort has raised the bar
★ for luxury along Holguín's coast. Playa Esmerelda is a short walk away, and you have access to two small private beaches on protected coves. The beaches are lined with native trees, and there's an excellent coral reef just offshore. Golf carts, on call 24 hours, whisk you from your door to the beach or the pool complex. Two oceanside Garden Villas ($600) have their own beach, pool, lookout tower, and butler, making them the most luxurious accommodations in Cuba. ⊠ *Carretera Holguín–Guardalavaca, Playa Esmerelda,* ☎ *24/30102,* FAX *24/30035,* WEB *www.solmelia.com. 250 rooms, 8 suites, 2 villas. 3 restaurants, 4 bars, minibars, pool, beauty salon, health club, 3 tennis courts, driving range, dive shop, dock, snorkeling, windsurfing, fishing, shop, nightclub, baby-sitting, children's programs, car rental, travel services, airport shuttle. MC, V. All-inclusive.*

$$$$ 🏨 **Sol Club Río de Luna and Sol Club Río de Mares.** These sister resorts on the Bahía de Naranjo inlet 3 km (2 mi) west of Guardalavaca have the luxurious sands of Playa Esmeralda all to themselves. The setting and the many amenities are the real draws: rooms at Río de Luna are slightly outmoded and drab, though large and well kept. At this writing, however, change was afoot. Río de Mares was slated to undergo extensive renovations, so its rooms may soon top those of other area resorts. ⊠ *Carretera Holguín–Guardalavaca, Playa Esmeralda,* ☎ *24/*

30030, FAX *24/30035,* WEB *www.solmelia.com. Río de Luna: 218 rooms, 8 suites. Río de Mares: 232 rooms, 10 suites. 6 restaurants, 8 bars, in-room safes, pool, beauty salon, 2 tennis courts, health club, beach, dive shop, dock, snorkeling, windsurfing, boating, jet skiing, waterskiing, fishing, shop, nightclub, travel services, car rental. MC, V. All-inclusive.*

¢ ⊡ **Villa Cabañas.** The cheapest option—by far—on the coast is this collection of no-frills bungalows on the same traffic loop as Pizza Nova and La Roca Disco, just feet from the beach. Many of the rooms have been recently occupied by a clinic and other ventures, but those that remain provide a simple haven. A shady central thatched hut, beside a modest but pleasant garden, serves burgers. ⊠ *Playa Guardalavaca,* ☎ *24/30144. 35 rooms. Restaurant, bar, café, air-conditioning. No credit cards.*

Nightlife and the Arts

La Roca Disco (☎ 24/30167), at the west end of Playa Guardalavaca, has a dance floor that's open to the breezes and an outdoor terrace with ocean views; after the disco's flashing lights, the twinkling stars are soothing.

Outdoor Activities and Sports

Base Nautica Marlin Guardalavaca (⊠ Carretera Guardalavaca–Holguín, Rafael Freyre, Playa Guardalavaca, ☎ 24/30185) offers boat rides, waterskiing, snorkeling, scuba diving, and deep-sea fishing. They also rent catamarans and windsurfers. **Beach Club Atlántico** (⊠ Playa Guardalavaca, ☎ no phone) offers waterskiing ($1 per minute), deep-sea fishing trips ($250 for 5 hours), sunset cruises, glass-bottom rides, and scuba diving. **Marina Bahía de Naranjo** (⊠ Carretera Guardalavaca–Holguín, ☎ 24/30132) has boat rentals and services for boaters, such as mooring space, electricity, water, and diesel.

Shopping

Artisans hawk their wares in a park near the Pizza Nova restaurant at the center of town (it's after the turnoff for Cubanacán Atlántico and near the Havanautos car-rental booth). The fair is held daily from dawn to dusk. The **Centro Commercial** (☎ no phone), fronting the beach near Guardalavaca's western end, may be in an ugly building, but it sells plenty of consumer goods (to anyone with dollars) and has a crafts shop that's worth a look.

Bayamo

❸ *71 km (44 mi) south of Holguín; 127 km (79 mi) northwest of Santiago.*

Bayamo, the capital of Granma Province, is descended from one of Spain's first seven villas: the 1513 settlement of Villa de San Salvador de Bayamo, which was near present-day Yara before being moved to its current location. There's little evidence left of its colonial beginnings. In 1869, the townspeople burned Bayamo to the ground rather than let it fall into Spanish hands during the Ten Years' War.

Parque Céspedes is a charming square with large trees and long marble benches. It's still a center of local life, and a good place to drink in the rhythms of a quiet Cuban town. Horse-drawn carriage rides are available from here.

At the square's center is the granite-and-bronze **statue of Carlos Manuel de Céspedes,** the hero of the Ten Years' War. He wrote the famous Grito de Yara (Shout of Yara)—a declaration of independence from Spain—which he read aloud on October 10, 1868, after freeing his slaves. Look also for the **statue of Perucho Figueredo,** who wrote Cuba's national anthem; its words describe the valor of the local townspeople: *Run to the battle, Bayamenses / Let the motherland proudly watch you / Don't fear death / To die for the motherland is to live.* On the east side of the square is the **Poder Popular,** the old town hall where Céspedes abolished slavery after founding an independent republic briefly in 1868.

The **Casa de Carlos Manuel de Céspedes,** a two-story house on the plaza's north side, is the birthplace of Céspedes. It has been a museum since 1968, the centennial anniversary of the signing of the Cuban Declaration of Independence, and is filled with period furniture and the belongings of this Cuban patriot. Also on display is the printing press on which Céspedes published Cuba's first independent newspaper. ☒ *Calle Maceo 57,* ☏ *no phone.* ☎ *$1.* ☉ *Tues.–Sat. 9–5, Sun. 9–1.*

On the plaza's north side is the **Museo Provincial,** which is housed in the birthplace of composer Manuel Muñoz Cedeño. He wrote "La Bayamesa," a tribute to the beauty of the town's women, who are, tradition holds, among Cuba's loveliest. There are exhibits on the region's colonial history and its geography. ☒ *Calle Maceo 55,* ☏ *no phone.* ☎ *$1* ☉ *Tues.–Sat. 9–5, Sun. 9–1.*

One of Bayamo's most peaceful spots is the **Plaza de Himno** (Anthem Square), northwest of Parque Céspedes. The plaza is dominated by the **Iglesia de San Salvador.** First built in 1613 and rebuilt several times starting in 1740, the church is famous as the first place "La Bayamesa" was sung in 1868. Its stone-and-wood interior has been restored, and it's open to visitors late in the afternoon, before the 5 PM mass. The plaza is also the home of **Casa de la Nacionalidad Cubana,** the town's archives. It's not officially open to the public, but you can ask questions of the staff and maybe have a peek at the antique furniture and interior courtyard. A list of cultural events happening around town is usually posted here. Southeast of the plaza is the **Iglesia de San Juan Evangelista,** a church that was partially destroyed in the 1869 fire but whose tower remains intact. The **Retablo de los Heroes** is a monument to Cuban independence fighters, from Céspedes to Celia Sánchez (who, in addition to being a revolutionary, was also Castro's lover and confidante).

NEED A BREAK?	After seeing Bayamo's historic sights, duck into the **Islazul Café** (☒ North side of Parque Céspedes, ☏ no phone) for a drink and snack. **La Bodega** (☒ Plaza de Himno, ☏ no phone) is a good stop for some wine.

Dining and Lodging

¢ ✕🛏 **Villa Bayamo.** This attractive complex is 6 km (4 mi) outside the city on the road to Manzanillo. The restaurant, El Tamarindo (¢–$), is famous for its roast pork. ☒ *Carretera via Manzanillo, Calle Mabay,* ☏ *24/42–3102. 12 rooms, 12 cabins. Restaurant, bar, pool, nightclub. MC, V.*

¢ 🛏 **Hotel Sierra Maestra.** Although it looks unkempt and institutional from the outside, inside this hotel is well maintained. The lobby is a little noisy (music blasts from speakers), but the rooms are comfortable and have satellite TVs. The restaurant serves meals that are filling, if uninspired. ☒ *Carretera Central, Km 7.5,* ☏ *24/48–2230 or 24/48–1643. 204 rooms. Restaurant, bar, pool, shop, nightclub, travel services. MC, V.*

Nightlife and the Arts

Adjacent to the Hotel Sierra Maestra is the **Cabaret Bayamo** (☒ Carretera Central, ☏ 23/42–5111), where high-stepping, costumed dancers perform at nightly dinner shows. Another cabaret is inside the hotel, but it isn't as highly charged as the Bayamo.

Shopping

Stop by the **Casa Le Fondo de Bienes Culturales** (✉ Plaza de Himno, ☎ no phone) for beautiful ceramics, paintings, and leatherwork.

Yara

❹ *46 km (29 mi) west of Bayamo, 23 km (14 mi) east of Manzanillo.*

West of Bayamo, the road to Manzanillo passes through banana farms and cane fields. The biggest settlement between the two cities is Yara, a striking sugar town in the shadow of the Sierra Maestra. The road into it is lined with palm and mango trees; it takes you past worn wooden plantation houses—made brittle by the tropical heat and sun—a sugar mill, and a train station. The town was first settled by Diego Velázquez in 1513, but it is most famous for being *the* Yara in Céspedes' Grito de Yara and as the place where Céspedes fought his first battle against the Spanish in 1868.

The **Museo Municipal,** just off the main square, has displays on the town's history. ✉ *Calle Grito de Yara 107,* ☎ *no phone.* 🎫 *50¢.* ☼ *Tues.– Sat. 9–5, Sun. 9–1.*

En Route The few people who live in the isolated Sierra Maestra region seem as rugged as the terrain. Along the road out of Yara you'll see thatch-roof huts, farmers guiding ox-drawn plows through fields, men pulling small, crop-filled carts up steep hills, and boys struggling on bicycles with an armful of farm tools. There's a frontier feeling here, accentuated, perhaps, by the popularity of cowboy hats in the area. From Yara, it's 15 km (9 mi) to Bartolomé Masó, where the road then climbs to Providencia. At an intersection here, turn left and continue on to Santo Domingo, the base for exploring the Sierra Maestra, especially the Parque Nacional Turquino.

Parque Nacional Turquino

★ ❺ *Entrance at Santo Domingo, roughly 30 km (19 mi) south of Yara.*

The Sierra Maestra was the base of Castro's rebel army, and a tour through its dramatic terrain makes it clear why the revolutionaries chose it as a place to hide from—and launch clandestine strikes against—Batista's forces. Its massive spine, averaging 1,372 m (4,500 ft) in height, cuts 130 km (81 mi) across Oriente, throwing a shadow over the southern coast from southwest Granma Province to Santiago de Cuba. The range is covered by moist, tropical forests with huge ferns and towering bamboos. It's cut by steep ravines, rocky valleys, and rushing rivers, and its peaks are often covered with clouds. Its history and majesty are preserved in the Parque Nacional Turquino.

Santo Domingo, on the banks of the Río Yara and in a valley between two steep mountainsides, is a hub for visits to the park. The village has restaurants, accommodations, and shops with provisions. You can hire a guide (they're obligatory, but charge only about $5 a day) and buy a $10 permit to enter the park at the Villa Santo Domingo hotel. Note: there have been reports that you need the $10 permit to enter the park, but the manager at the Villa Santo Domingo says that, with a guide, such a permit isn't necessary. It's best to call ahead to find out what you need and to make sure that the park is open; if the Cuban National Institute of Science or another agency is conducting research, the park may be closed to visitors.

It's a steep 5 km (3 mi) ascent from Santo Domingo village to the **Alto del Naranjo**—a parking lot with beautiful views—which marks the park entrance. If you haven't hired a guide in Santo Domingo, you can do so at the visitors center here.

★   The **Comandancia de la Plata,** the revolutionary headquarters, is just 3 km (2 mi) west of the park's entrance. A relaxing, one-hour walk on a clearly marked trail along a ridge brings you to a remote forest clearing. Here you'll find Castro's command post, hospital, and residence—built with an escape route into an adjacent creek. This is the perfect trek if you have limited time: you can get a taste of the region in the morning and return to the lowlands by early afternoon.

The summit of **Pico Turquino,** Cuba's highest peak at 1,974 m (6,476 ft), is 13 km (8 mi) from the Comandancia de la Plata. A journey here involves a night of camping, typically at a tent camp at the mountain's base. Cooks are sometimes available, but you have to bring your own food. Showers and fog alternate with sun and daytime heat, and humidity alternates with chilly windy nights, so in addition to good hiking boots you need clothing that you can layer and a lightweight rain jacket.

Dining and Lodging

¢   ✕🏨 **Villa Balcón de la Sierra.** This complex in the town of Providencia rents rooms in 10 cabins with wonderful views. The restaurant serves basic fare. ⊠ *Municipio Bartolomé Masó, Providencia,* ☎ *23/59–5180. 20 rooms. Restaurant, bar, pool, hiking. No credit cards.*

¢   ✕🏨 **Villa Santo Domingo.** Its rooms may be on the musty side with
★   furnishings that have seen better days, but this is *the* starting point for trips into the Sierra Maestra. The modest cabins are along the bank of the Río Yara, and the friendly ambience and cool, fresh mountain air make for a pleasant stay. The basic bar-restaurant serves hearty meals: breakfast is likely to be fried eggs served with rice and beans, dinner may well be barbecued chicken—again, with rice and beans. You can hire guides here for trips to the Parque Nacional Turquino or go for a horseback ride along the river and on mountain trails. ⊠ *Municipio Bartolomé Masó, Santo Domingo,* ☎ *23/42–5321. 20 cabins. Restaurant, bar, hiking, horseback riding, game room. No credit cards.*

Manzanillo

❻   *70 km (43 mi) west of Bayamo.*

The charming, cheerful port of Manzanillo stretches 3 km (2 mi) along the Bahía de Guacanayabo. It has a beautiful historic district whose pastel-painted structures have elements of Moorish architecture. And while you're here you'll undoubtedly hear some street-organ music; the instruments were first imported to Cuba through this city, which is still full of them.

The main plaza, **Parque Céspedes,** is the best place to experience Manzanillo's unique sense of style. It's dominated by a central bandstand, with colorful, intricately painted tiles and a domed top. Many of the fine buildings surrounding the plaza are Moorish-inspired. You'll also find a café, an art gallery, shops, and the Casa de la Cultura, which has art exhibits, live-music shows, and other cultural events. The **Museo Histórico Municipal** has displays on local history and popular culture. One exhibit is dedicated to Taty Labernia, who was so famous for her renditions of *boleros* (traditional Cuban songs descended from troubadour ballads) that they called her La Reina del Bolero (The Queen of the Bolero). ⊠ *Calle Bartolomé Masó,* ☎ *no phone.* 🎟 *$1.* ☉ *Tues.–Sat. 9–5.*

To reach the **Monumento Celia,** a monument to revolutionary hero Celia Sánchez, a longtime confidante of Fidel Castro, you climb a beautiful staircase lined with Moorish-style residences. ⊠ *Calle Caridad y Calle Martí.*

🐾 Wandering the bay-side malecón and exploring its adjacent **Parque de Recreación Bartolomé Masó** is a great way to spend an afternoon. This small park features rides and snack vendors in a shady clearing on the shore. It's lit up at night and is particularly lively on weekends.

In the sugar country just 13 km (8 mi) south of Manzanillo is **La Demajagua,** the farm where poet, patriot, and cane farmer Carlos Manuel de Céspedes freed his slaves and called for rebellion against Spain. There's a large monument at the entrance to the estate, and you can see the bell used by Céspedes to summon his slaves to freedom. The **Museo Histórico La Demajagua,** in Céspedes's former home, displays documents, photos, and other artifacts. ☎ *no phone.* 🎟 *$1.* ☉ *Daily 9–5.*

Lodging
¢ 🏨 **Hotel Guacanaybo.** On a bluff overlooking the bay, this modest, Soviet-inspired hotel offers the best accommodations, amenities (including satellite TV), and food you're likely to find in the area. All rooms have bay views and small balconies. ⊠ *Av. Camilio Cienfuegos,* ☎ *23/ 54012, 104 rooms, 4 suites. Restaurant, bar, pool, health club, shop, nightclub, travel services. MC, V.*

Media Luna

❼ *40 km (25 mi) southwest of Manzanillo.*

The road south from Manzanillo passes through cane fields and smoking sugar mills to the town where Celia Sánchez was born. Eight kilometers (5 miles) south of this town lies the turnoff to Pilón, the beach resort Marea del Portillo, and the beautiful south-coast road to Santiago de Cuba.

On the road to Pilón you'll find the **Casa Natal de Celia Sánchez,** the simple white-and-green house where Sánchez was born in 1920. The patio at the back is beautiful; you can rest here after seeing the exhibits of her eclectic clothing as well as photos, documents, and other mementos chronicling her life as a rebel. ⊠ *Carretera de Pilón,* ☎ *no phone.* 🎟 *$1.* ☉ *Tues.–Sat. 9–5, Sun. 9–1.*

Playa las Coloradas

❽ *30 km (19 mi) southwest of Media Luna.*

Throughout Granma Province, signs marking municipal limits bear the town name and an image of the *Granma,* the boat that carried Castro and his rebels to Cuba in their 1956 "invasion" of the island. Playa las Coloradas is the beach where it all began.

Even in its decline, **Niquero,** the area hub, is beautiful. The local Communist Party headquarters is in a stone mansion, seemingly immune to the decay affecting the French-style plantation houses, playful Victorian homes, and Spanish colonial buildings that surround it. The road to Playa las Coloradas heads straight through town, passing some of these structures. (Although there are a restaurant and small bungalows for rent here, operating hours are sporadic, especially in the off-season. Your best bet is to spend the night in Manzanillo or at one of the fine resorts in Marea del Portillo.)

★ Playa las Coloradas is at the start of the **Parque Nacional Desembarco del Granma,** the national park honoring the *Granma* landing. It sprawls across Cuba's southwestern end and is covered by woodlands, by a dry region of cacti and steep terraces, and by lagoons filled with marine life. The **Monumento de Desembarcadero,** near the park's entrance, is a huge replica of the *Granma* built on the exact spot where Castro and his rebels ran aground. You'll find a map showing the rebels' escape route, some revolutionary slogans, and a stage used for political events. The main road through the park runs from the monument to Oriente's southwestern tip. There are well-marked hikes off it, including the Morlotte-Fustete Trail, which leads to caves and sinkholes, and the Sendero Arqueologico Natural El Guage, which takes about two hours to hike and which passes mangroves, coastline, and areas purported to have Taíno remains.

Down a road exploding with bougainvillea you eventually get to Oriente's southwest corner, which is marked by the 33-m-high (108-ft-high) **Faro de Santa Cruz** (Santa Cruz Lighthouse), built in 1877. Cabo Cruz is the pretty, but poor, fishing town that surrounds it. The rocky coast is flanked by exceptionally blue water. Fishermen work over nets in wooden boats along the shore. It's a beautiful picture, and the last stop on this coastal road.

Marea del Portillo

9 *110 km (68 mi) east of Manzanillo; 19 km (12 mi) east of Pilón.*

The road to Pilón moves into the southern shadow of the Sierra Maestra near Marea del Portillo; here sugar country gives way to a dry, craggy coastline, punctuated by green pastures, palm trees, and surging rivers. Marea del Portillo is a great place from which to explore this beautiful region. You'll be well attended at the two resorts, whose all-inclusive rates are a bargain by Caribbean standards. (Note that only one of them is open in the off-season.) Water-sports activities abound, nightlife entertainment is supplied on site, and there are plenty of stunning beaches.

Dining and Lodging

¢ ✕🏨 ★ **Hotel Farallón del Caribe.** The nicest of Marea del Portillo's two resorts is filled with airy terraces, and each room has satellite TV, as well as a balcony overlooking the beach or the lagoon and mountains. You'll find many on-site amenities, including a pool on a terrace above the beach. The food served at the breakfast and dinner buffets (¢–$) is a cut above that offered by other hotels in the region. ⊠ *Carretera de Pilón, Km 14,* ☎ *23/59–4003,* ℻ *23/59–7080. 140 rooms. Restaurant, bar, pool, health club, beach, dive shop, snorkeling, windsurfing, boating, jet skiing, waterskiing, fishing, shop, nightclub, travel services, car rental. MC, V. All-inclusive.*

¢ 🏨 **Villa Marea del Portillo.** This hotel is close to the beach and is jam-packed with amenities. Open public spaces look out to the sea or mountain greenery. You'll find rooms and suites in a main building, as well as villas scattered throughout the grounds. All accommodations are spacious and have contemporary furnishings and satellite TV. ⊠ *Carretera de Pilón, Km 14,* ☎ *23/59–7001. 70 rooms, 4 suites, 56 villas. Restaurant, bar, pool, 2 tennis courts, exercise room, hiking, beach, dive shop, dock, snorkeling, windsurfing, boating, jet skiing, waterskiing, fishing, shop, nightclub, travel services, car rental. MC, V. All-inclusive.*

En Route   Beyond Marea del Portillo the road swings along the coast, with the green cliffs and ravines of the Sierra Maestra on one side and the sparkling blue Caribbean and dark-sand coast on the other. The route passes small coves, coastal villages, and budding resorts. Hawks circle overhead, and your biggest traffic concern is the occasional stray

FROM THE *GRANMA* TO HAVANA

On November 25, 1956, Castro and 81 other heavily armed men set sail from Mexico in a boat designed for 25 unarmed passengers. The idea was to "invade" Cuba and drive Batista from power, but it was a rough trip—filled with food shortages and seasickness. Mechanical problems delayed the landing two days beyond schedule. The rebels missed an important rendezvous with sympathizers who were organized by Celia Sánchez and were to take them deep into the interior of the Sierra Maestra.

Batista's troops got word of the plan and attacked as soon as the rebels landed, killing or capturing most of them. (Only Castro, his brother Raúl, Che Guevara, and 15 others escaped.) After the attack, Batista's flacks announced Castro's death, which made international news. But Batista, who knew the truth, dispatched troops to the area to hunt Castro down.

From his base camp in the Sierra Maestra, Castro sent patrols of as few as eight men to attack rural outposts, targets that were relatively easy but greatly symbolic (such rural guards had harassed locals since the the days of Spanish rule). Throughout 1957, Castro and his forces were increasingly successful; he garnered more local support (and knowledge of the rugged terrains) and mounted attacks on larger installations. As the rebellion in the countryside gained momentum, resistance and acts of terrorism in urban areas increased as well. When the regime shut down universities in response to student activism, students channeled their anger into riots. Batista retaliated with a vengeance, but this only isolated him

further. In addition, there were several conspiracies to overthrow the dictator on the part of his own military leaders. The U.S. government, which had long been a Batista ally, began withdrawing its support. The regime was crumbling—a fact that seemed clear to everyone but Batista.

In July 1958, leaders of several insurgent groups met in Caracas, Venezuela, to discuss uniting their efforts. Under the Pact of Caracas Castro emerged as the leader of the Revolution. Later that summer Batista sent more than 10,000 troops to the Sierra Maestra; despite heavy attacks by air, land, and sea, his large offensive failed. By fall, military desertions had greatly increased (in several cases, soldiers surrendered without one shot being fired), and forces loyal to Batista were frantically trying to return to western Cuba. With the desertions, arms and equipment fell into the hands of an increasingly bold citizenry. Uprisings throughout the island became more common.

In December 1958, Che Guevara and a band of rebels (locals among them) successfully derailed a military train carrying soldiers and weapons in Santa Clara, capital of Villa Clara Province. The rebels marched through central Cuba just as a military coup seized control of the government. Batista fled to the Dominican Republic on January 1, 1959. Upon hearing of his flight, the army simply stopped fighting. Rebel forces advanced unchallenged, the 26th of July Movement leaders denounced the leadership instituted by the coup, and Fidel Castro arrived victoriously in Havana one week after Batista's flight.

herd of sheep or cattle. About 30 km (18 mi) beyond Marea del Portillo is the Río de la Plata, the site of the rebels' first attack on Batista's troops. The small **Museo de la Plata** (☎ no phone), just off the road, tells the story. It's open Tuesday–Saturday 9–4; admission is $1.

Chivirico

⑩ *70 km (43 mi) east of Marea del Portillo; 60 km (37 mi) west of Santiago de Cuba.*

A little more than halfway to Santiago lies Chivirico, a beach town with two fine all-inclusive resorts. The beaches here offer all kinds of watersports activities; the diving is particularly noteworthy owing to several area wrecks and the deep Cayman Trench.

Lodging

$$–$$$$ 🏨 **Los Galeones.** At this intimate resort on a coastal hilltop, the large
★   rooms count king-size beds, satellite TVs, and fine views among their features. A lovely pool and sundeck and a charming restaurant also make this one of the nicer properties around. Note that a stay here enables you to use the facilities at the Sierra Mar, and there are discounts of up to 50% in the off-season. ⊠ *Playa Sevilla, Guamá,* ☎ *226/62–9110,* ℻ *226/62–6160. 200 rooms. Restaurant, bar, pool, barbershop, beauty salon, hot tub, massage, sauna, spa, aerobics, exercise room, Ping-Pong, volleyball, beach, dive shop, dock, snorkeling, windsurfing, boating, jet skiing, waterskiing, fishing, bicycles, shop, nightclub, travel services. MC, V. All-inclusive.*

$$ 🏨 **Sierra Mar.** High-quality food and service are among this resort's
★   hallmarks. It's on a bluff overlooking a beach 10 km (6 mi) east of town. Rooms have top-flight amenities, including air-conditioning and satellite TV. Open terraces and the pool deck overlook the beach and the mountains. In the off-season, discounts are as much as 50%. ⊠ *Playa Sevilla, Guamá,* ☎ *226/62–9110,* ℻ *226/62–9007. 200 rooms. Restaurant, bar, in-room safes, pool, barbershop, beauty salon, hot tub, massage, sauna, spa, aerobics, archery, exercise room, hiking, horseback riding, Ping-Pong, volleyball, beach, dive shop, dock, snorkeling, windsurfing, boating, jet skiing, waterskiing, fishing, bicycles, shop, nightclub, travel services, car rental. MC, V. All-inclusive.*

SANTIAGO DE CUBA AND GUANTÁNAMO PROVINCES

Santiago Province is home to the Sierra Maestra to the west, the Cordillera de la Gran Piedra to the east, and the Sierra de Cristal to the north. Although rugged and sparsely populated, the province is Oriente's geographic and cultural center. The region's most important city, Santiago de Cuba, sits on a wide, south-coast bay, smack in the middle of the province. Founded in 1514, it was Cuba's first capital and still rivals Havana in terms of art, culture, music, and historical sights. Nearby beaches line the coast of the Baconao Nature Reserve.

Most famous for being the site of the U.S. Naval Base—one of the few remaining outposts of the Cold War—Guantánamo Province embodies Oriente's untamed spirit. Much of the region is within the protected biosphere reserve known as the Cuchilla del Toa, and its topography varies from a flat arid coastal zone to rain forest to pine-covered mountains. The main destination, Baracoa, was only reachable by water until the 1970s, when Castro had the Farola Highway built over a formidable mountain range. Much of the east coast is still remote, served only by a string of country roads.

Santiago de Cuba

★ **⑪**–**㉗**   *860 km (534 mi) southeast of Havana; 86 km (53 mi) southwest of Guantánamo.*

To earn the title Hero City, Santiago has played an important role in island history, from the beginnings of the wars for independence to Castro. Yet it also has an independent spirit, bred through its isolation from Havana and its tradition of trading with and welcoming settlers from neighboring Caribbean islands.

The city's unique architecture blends Caribbean, Spanish and other European influences. The African roots of its people are among the most pronounced in Cuba, and this adds considerable flavor to the food as well as a lyrical lilt to the Spanish that's spoken here. There's often music in the air, from hypnotizing Cuban salsa to the folksy *nueva trova* to the latest Latin ballads.

Exploring the Centro Histórico

At the center of the city's historic district you'll find Parque Céspedes. The plaza and the streets just off it form the city's cultural heart. They're filled with museums, art galleries, bookstores, and spots where the music never seems to stop. Note that, as in many Cuban cities, Santiago's streets often go by pre- and postrevolutionary names; both are provided in addresses below.

A GOOD TOUR (OR TWO)

Start your tour at **Parque Céspedes** ⑪, a large, busy plaza. Shop- and vendor-lined Calle Heredia runs along the plaza's southern edge, which is dominated by the Santa Ifigenia Basilica Metropolitana. On the park's north side is the colonial Poder Popular. From here, follow Calle Aguilera (Marino) east, crossing Calle Félix Peña (Santo Tomás) to the **Casa de Don Diego Velázquez** ⑫. Take Félix Peña south to the intersection of Calle Bartolomé Masó (San Basilio). Turn right and walk 2½ blocks to the **Balcón de Velázquez** ⑬. After taking in the stunning city and bay views, you can visit two sights slightly off the path or continue on the walking tour. If you head west on Bartolomé Masó to Avenida Jesús Menéndez, you'll come to the **Fábrica de Tabaco César Escalante.** This is a good jumping-off point for a cab trip 14 km (9 mi) southeast to the **Castillo del Morro.**

Alternatively, you could continue walking south from the Balcón de Velázquez along **Calle Padre Pico** ⑭. Follow Padre Pico still farther south to Calle Diego Palacios and the revolutionary **Museo Lucha Clandestina** ⑮. After touring the museum, retrace your steps to Parque Céspedes and Calle Heredia. Walk east roughly 2½ blocks beyond the park to reach the **Casa Natal de José María Heredia** ⑯. From here, art and history lovers can head one block north to the **Museo Bacardí** ⑰, between Calle Hartman (San Félix) and Calle Pío Rosado (Comisaria); rum lovers can go one block south to the **Museo del Ron** ⑱, and culture mavens can walk 1½ blocks west to the **Museo de Carnaval** ⑲. From the Museo de Carnaval, walk one block east along Calle Heredia; at Calle Maya Rodriguez (Reloj) turn left and continue to the intersection of Calle Aguilera and the charming **Plaza Dolores** ⑳—the perfect place to rest your feet. Four blocks east on Calle Aguilera is **Plaza de Marte** ㉑, which marks the east end of the Old City.

TIMING

If you wear your most comfortable shoes, get an early start, and are selective about which museums you explore (or visit each only briefly), you can just about squeeze the walking portions of this tour into a seven-hour day. If you have the time, break this tour up into two days—see-

170

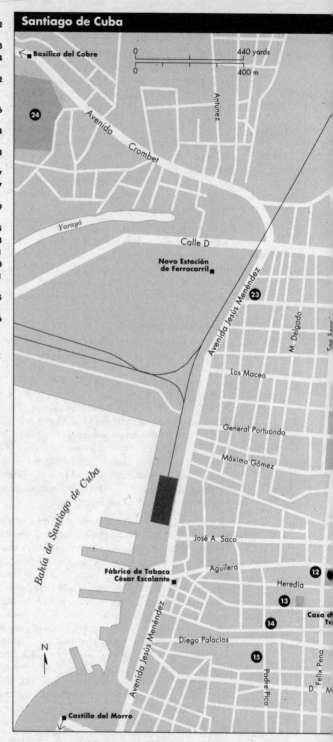

Santiago de Cuba

Basílica del Cobre

0   440 yards
0   400 m

Avenida Crombet

Antúnez

(24)

Yarayó

Calle D

Novo Estación
de Ferrocarril

Avenida Jesús Menéndez

M. Delgado

(23)

Los Maceo

General Portuondo

Máximo Gómez

Bahía de Santiago de Cuba

José A. Saco

Aguilera

(12)

Fábrica de Tabaca
César Escalante

Heredia

(13)

Casa d
Tr

(14)

Avenida Jesús Menéndez

Diego Palacios

Padre Pico

Felix Pena

(15)

N

Castillo del Morro

D

ing the sights just west of Parque Céspedes and visiting the Castillo San Juan on one day and then following the walk to the many museums east of Parque Céspedes on another. Be sure to paint the historic center red at least one night during your visit—perhaps taking in a show at the Casa de la Trova or the Casa del Estudiante.

SIGHTS TO SEE

⑬ Balcón de Velázquez. Once used by authorities to monitor boat traffic, today this ceramic-tiled terrace is simply a great place to linger while taking in views of both the city and the bay. Music shows and other events are often held here, particularly on weekend evenings. ⊠ *Calle Bartolomé Masó (San Basilio) y Calle Corona.*

⑭ Calle Padre Pico. The climb up the stone steps to this street will reward you with more than just dramatic views. It's part of the Tivoli neighborhood, where 18th-century French colonial mansions sit side by side with 16th-century structures. Locals gather on its shady edges to gossip, play dominoes, or watch visitors like you make their ascent.

★ ⑫ Casa de Don Diego Velázquez. Constructed in 1516, this may well be Cuba's oldest house. Diego Velázquez, the Spanish conquistador who founded Santiago de Cuba and was the island's first governor, lived upstairs. Inside you'll find period beds, desks, chests, and other furniture. On the first floor is a gold foundry. Memorable are the star-shaped Moorish carvings on the wooden windows and balconies, and the original interior patio with its well and rain-collecting *tinajón* vessel. An adjacent house is filled with antiques intended to convey the French and English decorative and architectural influences—such as the radial stained glass above the courtyard doors—in the late 19th-century. ⊠ *Calle Félix Peña (Santo Tomás) 612,* ☏ *no phone.* ☞ *$2.* ☉ *Daily 9–4:45.*

⑯ Casa Natal de José María Heredia. This Spanish colonial mansion was the birthplace of poet José María Heredia, who, because of his pro-independence writings, is considered Cuba's first national poet. Heredia died in 1839 at age 36, while exiled in Mexico. The house, now just a fraction of its original size, displays period furniture and some of the poet's works and belongings. The home's traditional interior patio is planted with trees and plants—including orange, myrtle, palm, and jasmine—associated with Heredia's verse. A marble plaque on the house's Calle Heredia facade excerpts one of the poet's most famous works, "Niágara" ("Ode to Niagara Falls"). ⊠ *Calle Heredia 260,* ☏ *no phone.* ☞ *$1.* ☉ *Tues.–Sun. 9–5.*

OFF THE BEATEN PATH

CASTILLO DEL MORRO – Sixteen kilometers (10 miles) south of Santiago is the Spanish fortress known as El Morro. It dates from 1640 and was designed by Giovanni Antonelli, the Italian architect and engineer responsible for fortresses bearing the same name in both Havana and San Juan, Puerto Rico. Dominating a bluff at the entrance to the Bahía de Santiago de Cuba, El Morro was built to ward off pirates (and rebuilt after a 1662 attack by the English pirate Henry Morgan). Inside you'll find a museum with exhibits on, appropriately enough, pirates. There are wonderful views from interior rooms, which have wooden floors and stone walls, as well as from various terraces. From the lowest terrace, the view of the fortress itself, formed from the sheer face of the bluff, is powerful. The way into the structure takes you down and then back up a 207-step staircase; a drawbridge over a moat leads to the entrance. In the middle of glittering Santiago Bay you're sure to notice Cayo Granda, a small island with colorful homes and long docks. You can reach it by taking Carretera Ciudamar, which runs along the bay from El Morro (it can also take you back to Santiago). Not far down the road, at a hut resembling a bus stop, you can pick up a ferry (5¢) that runs from 7 AM to 9 PM. ⊠ *Ruta Turística (Carretera del Morro), El Morro,* ☎ *no phone.* 🎫 *$1.* ⊙ *Daily 9–4.*

FÁBRICA DE TABACO CÉSAR ESCALANTE – If Cubanos are your passion, a trip to this small cigar factory, where locals roll stogies in the traditional way, is a must. To visit, you must hire a guide ($3) through the Rumbos travel agency in Parque Céspedes. A plaza, Parque Alameda, is nearby and across the street is the stately Aduana (Customs House). ⊠ *Av. Jesús Menéndez 703, esquina de Calle Bartolomé Masó (San Basilio),* ☎ *no phone.* 🎫 *Free (but only with guide).* ⊙ *Mon.–Sat. 7–4.*

★ ⑰ **Museo Bacardí.** Cuba's oldest museum was founded in 1899 by Emilio Bacardí Moreau, the former Santiago mayor whose rum-making family fled to Puerto Rico after the Revolution. Although the neoclassical structure's interior was horrendously remodeled in 1968—destroying many elegant details and cutting off air circulation—the collection it contains is fantastic. The basement, which you enter from the side of the building, has artifacts—including mummies and a shrunken head—from indigenous cultures throughout the Americas. In the first-floor displays of colonial objects, the antique weapons and brutal relics of the slave trade are especially thought-provoking. Step outside a door to a cobblestone alley, along which are houses from the 16th to the 19th centuries. Around the corner is a traditional colonial patio. The second-floor art gallery has works from the 19th and early 20th centuries. ⊠ *Calle Pío Rosado (Comisaria) y Calle Aguilera,* ☎ *226/62–8402.* 🎫 *$2.* ⊙ *Mon. 2–8, Tues.–Sat. 10–8, Sun. 10–5.*

★ ☛ ⑲ **Museo de Carnaval.** The spirit of one of the Caribbean's most vibrant street parties, Santiago's annual July carnival, is recalled in photos and newspaper clippings, floats, costumes, and musical instruments. For a true sense of what carnival is like, stop by at 4 PM Tuesday through Saturday or 11 AM on Sunday for a performance by music and dance troupes. The 45-minute spectacle of colorful costume, Afro-Cuban rhythms, and stirring song will have you planning your next trip to coincide with the main event. ⊠ *Calle Heredia 303,* ☎ *no phone,* 🎫 *$1.* ⊙ *Tues.–Sat. 9–8, Sun. 9–7.*

⑮ **Museo Lucha Clandestina.** This museum is in a 19th-century building that was once the city's police headquarters. It was attacked by Frank País and a band of rebels on November 30, 1958. Displays give you a complete overview of Castro's Revolution, and the architecture and bay views are as compelling as the exhibits. ⊠ *Calle General Jesús Rabí 1,* ☎ *226/62–4689.* 🎫 *$1.* ⊙ *Tues.–Sat. 9–5, Sun. 9–noon.*

⑱ **Museo del Ron.** Exhibits here take you through the rum-making process. You'll also find displays of antique rum paraphernalia and bottles. In the same building (but accessible only through an entrance around the corner) is the **Taberna del Ron,** which sells rum products and gifts. ⊠ *Calle Bartolomé Masó (San Basilio) 358,* ☎ *no phone.* 🎫 *$1.* ⊙ *Tues.–Sun. 9–6.*

★ ⑪ **Parque Céspedes.** At times it seems that Santiago's main activity is the curious stare down that takes place in Parque Céspedes between mojíto-sipping tourists at the Hotel Casa Granda's café and white-hatted locals, who sit across the way. Long the central meeting place for santiagueros, this large plaza is always abuzz with sound and movement. Musicians wander past and around its shady benches, which are occupied from early in the morning to late in the evening. At the park's center is a large bronze statue of Carlos Manuel de Céspedes, whose Grito de Yara declared Cuba's independence from Spain in 1868 and began the Ten Years' War.

The twin towers and central dome of the neoclassical **Santa Ifigenia Basilica Metropolitana** loom over the southern edge of Parque Céspedes. Since this area is atop a hill, the cathedral's profile is visible from afar and creates a recognizable silhouette. Although it was first built on this site in 1523, the current building dates primarily from 1922. Inside, the painted ceiling has been beautifully restored and there are several noteworthy works of religious art, including a sculpture of Cuba's patron saint, La Virgen de la Caridad. A two-room museum near the east entrance (open Monday–Saturday 9:30–5:30, $1) displays objects relating to the history of the Catholic church in Cuba. ⊠ *Calle Heredia,* ☎ *no phone.* ✍ *Donation suggested.* ☉ *Daily 8–10 and 5–7:30. Mass Mon. and Wed. 6:30 PM, Sat. 5 PM, Sun. 9 AM, and 6:30 PM.*

Poder Popular. On the north side of Parque Céspedes, this colonial structure (not open to the public) was where Castro gave his victory speech on January 2, 1959. Occasionally it hosts exhibits and special performances. Draped across the front of the building is a huge red and black banner reading M 26-7, referring to Castro's July 26 storming of the Moncada barracks. ⊠ *Calle Aguilera.*

⁂⓪ Plaza Dolores. Four blocks from Parque Céspedes, this long, shady plaza—the city's former marketplace—is ringed with cafés, open-air restaurants, and 18th-century homes with noteworthy wooden balconies. It takes its name from the church overlooking its eastern end, the Iglesia de Nuestra Señora de los Dolores, which was renovated and turned into a concert hall.

㉑ Plaza de Marte. For a memorable photo, visit this park at the edge of the Old City. Children ride in colorful carts pulled by goats—a pleasure formerly enjoyed in Parque Céspedes. This relaxed square, filled with families and sweets vendors, captures the rhythm of Santiago life.

Exploring Metropolitan Santiago de Cuba

If you have an extra day, take in some of metropolitan Santiago's sights. There are several places of interest on and near the bay just to the north of the Centro Histórico. Avenida de las Américas edges modern Santiago's northern perimeter before arcing sharply southeast. Along and just off this boulevard are several noteworthy contemporary and historical sights.

A GOOD DRIVE

Start at the **Antiguo Cuartel Moncada** ㉒ for a taste of revolution. Next head northwest for a taste of rum: take Paseo de Martí to Avenida Jesús Menéndez and follow it south two blocks to the **Fábrica de Ron Caney** ㉓, opposite the modernist Santiago train station. From here take Menéndez north to Avenida Crombet; veer left and follow Crombet to the **Cementerio Santa Ifigenia** ㉔ and the wondrous José Martí memorial. The cemetery is a good jumping-off point for the 20 km (12 mi) trip northwest of Santiago to the **Basilica del Cobre.** Alternatively, you could cut north from the cemetery through the Centro Urbano José Martí, a housing project that captures the spirit of socialist life, to Avenida Las Américas. This wide boulevard arcs past the large Universidad de Oriente (Eastern Cuba University) just before passing through the **Plaza de la Revolución** ㉕. Follow Las Américas to the traffic circle formed by it, Avenida Victoriano Garzón, Avenida Raúl Pujol, and Avenida Manduley. Travel around to Avenida Manduley and the elegant neighborhood of **Reparto Vista Alegre** ㉖. Just south of here is the famous **Loma de San Juan** ㉗.

TIMING

Excluding the trip to El Cobre, you can follow this tour in a day. You'll save money and your sanity by hiring a car and driver rather than renting a car and driving yourself. A taxi will charge roughly $30 for this tour. In addition, many hotels offer half-day Havanatur excursions that hit many of these sights.

SIGHTS TO SEE

㉒ Antiguo Cuartel Moncada. On July 26, 1953, Castro and 100 men attempted to storm this former army barracks. It was carnival time in Santiago; the streets were full of revelers, and Castro had hoped that security would be lax. Unfortunately, his hopes were dashed, and the rebels were either killed or captured. Castro, who fled to the mountains, was eventually caught, tried, and imprisoned on the Isla de la Juventud off western Cuba's south coast. Although unsuccessful, the attack ignited the sparks of Castro's Revolution. He wrote his famous speech "La Historia me Absolverá" ("History Will Absolve Me"), which was smuggled out of prison, printed, and distributed throughout the island. Although luck had not been on his side in 1953, it certainly was in 1955, when Batista granted many political prisoners their freedom. Castro left for the United States, where he began soliciting support for his 26th of July Movement (named in honor of the ill-fated barracks attack) to rid Cuba of Batista's regime. From there, he took his cause to Mexico. In 1956, just a year after being released from prison, Castro made his historic journey from Mexico to Cuba aboard the *Granma*.

Today the former stronghold of Batista's troops contains a grammar school and the **Museo de 26 de Julio.** The bullet holes surrounding the doorway to the museum are re-creations of those left after the original attack, which were quickly patched over by Batista's men. The exhibits here tell, in Spanish, the entire story of the attack and the events that followed. They're among the nation's most comprehensive ones on revolutionary history. Take the guided tour (it's customary to tip docents $1). ☒ *Av. General Portuondo y Av. Moncada, Reparto Sueño,* ☏ *226/62–0157.* ☒ *$2.* ☉ *Daily 9–9.*

OFF THE
BEATEN PATH

BASILICA DEL COBRE – After a 20 km (12 mi) drive through the countryside northwest of Santiago you'll see the red-tile tower of La Basilica de Nuestra Senora de la Caridad del Cobre—dedicated to Cuba's patron saint in 1916—before the turn-off to the copper mining town in which it is set. The story of the Virgin dates from the early 1600s, when three men in a boat first saw her floating on water; several other area sightings were followed by tales of the Virgin's miraculous powers. (Her image has also been blended with that of Óchún, the *orisha*, or goddess, of love in the Santería religion.) Each September, pilgrims journey here—sometimes crawling uphill for miles on their knees—on the Virgin's feast day (September 12). Her shrine is filled with gifts from the faithful, including Ernest Hemingway's Nobel Prize, which he left here in 1952. A staircase at the back of the cathedral leads to the chapel containing the Virgin's wooden image. In front of the cathedral you'll find a plaque commemorating Pope John Paul's visit here during his 1998 trip to Cuba. ☒ *Carretera Central,* ☏ *no phone.* ☒ *$1 suggested donation.* ☉ *Daily 6:30–6.*

㉔ Cementerio Santa Ifigenia. This cemetery is home to the majestic mausoleum of the great poet-patriot in the wars of independence, José Martí. The structure is true to Martí's wishes (expressed in one of his poems) that he be buried below the flag of Cuba and surrounded by roses. Marble steps lead to the tomb, above which is a domed tower. Other highlights include a memorial to Cuban soldiers who have fallen in battle and the tombs of Carlos Manuel de Céspedes and those who died in the Moncada Barracks attack. You need a guide ($1) to enter. ☒ *Av.*

Crombet, Reparto Santa Ifigenia, ☎ no phone. 🎫 Free (but only with guide). ⊙ Daily dawn–dusk.

㉓ **Fábrica de Ron Caney.** Cuba's oldest rum distillery, a former Bacardí family enterprise, now makes Havana Club. The on-site shop—which has a bar, live music, and free samples—is the central attraction. ⊠ *Av. Jesús Menéndez y Calle Gonzalo de Quesada, Centro Histórico,* ☎ *no phone.* 🎫 *Free.* ⊙ *Mon.–Sat. 9–6.*

㉗ **Loma de San Juan.** Made famous by Teddy Roosevelt and his Rough Riders, San Juan Hill lies just south of Reparto Vista Alegre. Today it's a park, in the Reparto San Juan neighborhood, covered by monuments left by U.S. and Cuban militaries, dedicated to the to the battle fought here during the Spanish-American War. It's a lovely passive spot, with amusements for small children in the **Parque de Diversiones**—identifiable by its large Ferris wheel—at the base of the hill. It also marks the official start of the Baconao Nature Reserve, which covers the mountain and coastal regions east of Santiago. Nearby you'll find the **Parque Zoológico** (⊠ Av. Raúl Pujol, near San Juan Hill, ☎ no phone), which has animals from around the world. It's open Tuesday–Sunday 1–5, and admission is $1.

㉕ **Plaza de la Revolución.** Just about every city on the island has a Revolution Square, perhaps the most prominent markers of Cuban socialism. This one in the Reparto Sueño neighborhood was the site of Pope John Paul's address to Santiago during his visit. Towering above the plaza is the dramatic **monument to Major General Antonio Maceo,** one of the heroes of the wars of independence. It shows the general on his horse, going down in a battlefield portrayed by 23 steel machetes that rise from the ground around him. The small **Exhibición de la Plaza de la Revolución** (Av. de las Americas and Av. de los Libertadores, ☎ no phone) has artifacts as well as holograms that represent important dates in Maceo's life. You can view the displays Tuesday through Saturday from 9 to 5 and Sunday from 9 to 1; admission is $1.

★ ㉖ **Reparto Vista Alegre.** This elegant neighborhood of mansions is a place of historical splendor. French-inspired plantation homes, stately Spanish colonial mansions, even art deco gems are beautifully decaying amid riotous vegetation under the clear Caribbean sun. Chevy Bel Airs and Cadillacs from the late 1950s roll down the wide, quiet streets where time seems to have frozen four decades ago, just before the Revolution. The district, framed in bougainvillea and hibiscus, resembles Havana's Vedado and older residential neighborhoods in Miami. Look for the four-story, peach **Palacio de Pioneros** (⊠ Av. Manduley y Calle 11), a mansion that once belonged to rum baron Pepe Bosch but now is a school for Young Pioneers. The building is easy to find thanks to the Soviet MIG fighter jet in the front yard.

Dining

$–$$$$ ✕ **Restaurant Zun Zún.** The well-prepared seafood dishes and extensive wine list befit Zun Zún's elegant Vista Alegre setting. You can dine outdoors on a wraparound porch adorned with potted ferns or inside amid the unique decor of the house's former owner, an Arab merchant. ⊠ *Av. Manduley 159, Reparto Vista Alegre,* ☎ *226/64–1528. MC, V.*

$–$$$ ✕ **La Maison.** This white, neoclassical mansion contains clothing stores,
★ a restaurant, and cafés. The west wing's Cafeteria Las Arecas, open 10 AM to 1 AM, serves mediocre pizza and pasta dishes but is a great place to relax with a drink either before or after browsing in the boutique. The restaurant at the back of the house, open from noon to 10 PM, offers seafood (paella is a specialty) as well as steaks. Though it's the last thing you'd expect to encounter in Cuba, a dozen male and fe-

male models walk the runway in nightly (10:30–11:20) fashion shows in the east wing café; admission is $5. ⊠ *Av. Manduley 52, esquina de Calle 1, Reparto Vista Alegre,* ☎ *226/64–1117. MC, V. Closed Sun.*

$–$$$ ✕ **Restaurant Don Antonio.** Although this state-run spot serves much of the same flavorless food as its many state-run neighbors, its setting in a restored colonial mansion on Plaza Dolores is terrific. Ceiling fans spin slowly overhead from a lofty wooden ceiling, and large windows open to the plaza's northwest corner. ⊠ *Calle Aguilera y Calle Porfirio Valiente, Plaza Dolores, Centro Histórico,* ☎ *226/65–2205. MC, V.*

$–$$$ ✕ **La Teresina.** The Italian fare—pizza, pastas, and seafood dishes—is good by local standards. The white-tile, European café–style setting overlooking the plaza is pleasant, and the staff is friendly. ⊠ *Calle Aguilera, Plaza Dolores, Centro Histórico,* ☎ *226/65–2205. MC, V.*

¢ ✕ **1900 Santiago.** In the former mansion of the rum-making Bacardí family, this restaurant is a Santiago standard. Although the dishes lack a sense of adventure, you can't beat the ambience. The formal dining room, with its antique furnishings, is particularly striking; the informal back patio, whose offerings vary only slightly from those inside, is a good spot for a drink. The restaurant accepts only pesos, but the staff will change dollars on the spot. ⊠ *Calle Bartolomé Masó (San Basilio) 354, e/Calle Pío Rosado/Comisaria y Calle Hartman/San Félix, Centro Histórico,* ☎ *226/62–3507. No credit cards.*

¢ ✕ **Taberna de Dolores.** Conversation and music linger in the air at this
★ authentically Cuban restaurant. Long white flowers known as *campanitas blancas* hang from the trellis of a broad interior courtyard. A marble staircase leads up to a narrow second floor and its long bar. Diners at tables on the balcony survey Plaza Dolores. The *cerdo frito* (fried pork) isn't $15, it's 15 pesos (75¢). ⊠ *Calle Aguilera y Calle Maya Rodriguez/Reloj, Plaza Dolores, Centro Histórico,* ☎ *226/62–3913. No credit cards.*

Lodging

Santiago has some fine casas particulares, particularly in the Vista Alegre neighborhood. On a leisurely stroll through this barrio you can pick out a favorite house; if you're lucky, it will have a sticker with a blue triangle on its door, which means it's a licensed, private lodging establishment. Most such homes charge $15 for one person, and $20 for two. **Guadalupe and José** (⊠ Calle 6, No. 307, Reparto Vista Alegre, ☎ 226/64–3118) have two air-conditioned rooms with bath. Rates are $20 per room (no credit cards) per night. **Mireya Guerra López** (⊠ Calle 6, No. 252, Reparto Vista Alegre, ☎ 226/64–1904) offers two nice rooms with air-conditioning and private bath; the nightly rate is $20 (no credit cards).

$$$$ ⊞ **Hotel Casa Granda.** From here, the only hotel in the Centro Histórico,
★ you can see Parque Céspedes, with its wandering musicians and guayabera-clad men in conversation. The hotel's second-floor porch—adorned with plants, crimson and gray awnings, a black-and-white tile floor, and a large wooden bar—is a great people-watching spot. Even if you don't stay here, be sure to stop by for a mojíto or a light meal (they make good *cubanos,* roast pork and ham sandwiches served with pickles and a salad). The formal dining room offers delectable seafood and steak dishes. The fifth-floor rooftop terrace, which has buffets for breakfast, lunch, and dinner, has views of the bay as well as the Old City beyond. Although guest rooms don't have the same elegant aura as the rest of the structure—the furniture isn't new and quarters are on the small side—they're still among the best in the city. ⊠ *Calle Heredia 201, Parque Céspedes,* ☎ *226/68–6600,* ℻ *226/68–6035. 55 rooms, 3 suites. 2 restaurants, bar, room service, shop, travel services. BP. MC, V.*

$$ 🏨 **Meliá Santiago de Cuba.** With the look of a tropical erector set, this red, white, and blue high-rise is either playfully appealing or pompously postmodern, depending on your point of view. However controversial the exterior might be, no one argues about whether this Spanish-run hotel's service and amenities are top-notch—they simply are. Rooms are large and modern, with great city views from the upper floors. The vast lobby, cast in green marble, includes two restaurants and a business center with Internet access—almost unheard of—for a mere $5 an hour. The lobby leads outdoors to a palm-lined pool complex surrounded by bars and restaurants. The buffet breakfasts and dinners at the main restaurant are good, and the house band, Aldo y Su Grupo, is hot; be sure to catch their happy-hour set at the rooftop nightclub. ⊠ *Av. de las Américas, e/Av. Manduley y Av. Cuarto, Reparto Sueño,* ☏ *226/68–7070,* FAX *226/68–7170,* WEB *www.solmelia.com. 270 rooms, 30 junior suites. 4 restaurants, 3 bars, pool, barbershop, beauty salon, sauna, 4 tennis courts, basketball, gym, massage, shops, nightclub, travel services, business services, meeting rooms, parking (fee). BP. MC, V.*

¢–$ 🏨 **Hotel Versalles.** The Versalles is on a hill 2 km (1 mi) from the airport just south of Santiago on the road to El Morro. There are nice views of the city from here, and it's quiet at night. All accommodations have satellite TVs; rooms are slightly cheaper than cabins. ⊠ *Ruta Turistica (Carretera del Morro), Km 1, Alturas del Versalles,* ☏ *226/ 69–1016,* FAX *226/68–6039. 46 rooms, 14 cabins. Restaurant, bar, pool, health club, shop, nightclub, travel services, car rental. MC, V.*

¢ 🏨 **Hotel Balcón del Caribe.** On a coastal cliff a few minutes' walk from El Morro, this hotel has spectacular views. The staff is friendly, and the San Pedro del Mar Cabaret next door has nightly spectaculars. All guest quarters have satellite TV; some have minibars. You'll need a car to reach Santiago, 6 km (4 mi) away, but the drive is splendid. ⊠ *Ruta Turistica (Carretera del Morro), Km 7, El Morro,* ☏ *226/69–1011. 72 rooms, 22 cabins. Restaurant, bar, pool, shop, travel services. BP. MC, V.*

¢ 🏨 **Hotel San Juan.** The setting is bucolic: at the foot of San Juan Hill and surrounded by trees and fields. Rooms in the villa-style accommodations are appealing and all have satellite TV. You can spend time by the rectangular pool; on the pleasant terrace; or in the bar, which is open 24 hours and has live music in the evening. ⊠ *Carretera a Siboney, Km 1.5, Reparto San Juan,* ☏ *226/68–7200,* FAX *226/68–7017. 112 rooms. Restaurant, bar, pool, barbershop, beauty salon, sauna, health club, travel services. BP. MC, V.*

¢ 🏨 **Villa Santiago.** At the edge of the Vista Alegre neighborhood are these 12 houses, all former residences built in the 1950s. A stay here is similar to a stay in a casa particular, except the houses are run by the state-owned Gaviota tour operator. Three to six rooms are available in each house; all are comfortable and well maintained. The service is reliable. ⊠ *Av. Manduley 502, esquina de Calle 19, Reparto Vista Alegre,* ☏ *226/64–1368,* FAX *226/68–6166. 47 rooms. Restaurant, 3 bars, minibars, pool, shop, travel services, free parking. BP. MC, V.*

Nightlife and the Arts

CARNIVAL

Carnival began as a celebration by slaves who were given respite from their labors at Easter time. Despite its initial link with a Christian holiday, the rhythms and rituals of this festival (now celebrated in July here) have their roots in pagan Africa. Neighborhood associations called *carabalís* compete to build the most colorful floats, create the most inspired costumes, and stage the most spectacular processions. Men dress in colorful outfits and wear papier-mâché masks; women don bikinis and wraps of see-through silk and feathers. The primal rumba beat—accentuated by maracas, Chinese coronets, and wooden flutes—

drives the processions, which take place throughout the city. The biggest day is St. James's Day (July 25), and celebrations usually begin the Saturday before.

The **Balle Folklórico Cutumba** (✉ Av. José A. Sacó 170, Centro Histórico, ☎ 226/62–5860) practices in the morning and late afternoon Tuesday–Saturday. There's also a show every Sunday at 10:30 AM; admission is $3. **Carabalí Izuama** (✉ Calle Pío Rosado/Comisaria, e/Calle los Maceo y Calle San Antonio, Centro Histórico, ☎ no phone) welcomes visitors to its practice sessions. You can also watch members of **La Tumba Francesca** (✉ Calle los Maceo 501, at San Bartolomé, Centro Histórico, ☎ no phone) rehearse.

FILM

When's the last time you paid $1 to see a movie? That's what Santiago's main movie theater charges, the **Cine Rialto** (✉ Calle Félix Peña/Santo Tomás, just off Parque Céspedes, Centro Histórico, ☎ no phone). It plays dated foreign films and U.S. action flicks.

MUSIC

Street musicians often perform (just follow your ears) for tips along Calle Heredia and in Parque Céspedes. This central plaza is also the best place to see the excellent Santiago Municipal Band (their rendition of "La Virgen Guerrera" is haunting); try to catch a performance early Sunday evening.

Next to El Morro, **Cabaret San Pedro del Mar** (✉ Ruta Turistica (Carretera del Morro), El Morro, ☎ 226/69–1287) has shows every night but Monday and Tuesday for $10. Although they aren't as extravagant as others in the city, they're well orchestrated and take place on a terrace overlooking the ocean. **Casa del Estudiante** (✉ Calle Heredia 204, Centro Histórico, ☎ no phone) has live music on Saturday and Sunday evenings; admission is 1$. The folksy *trova* combines African rhythms with Spanish guitar, and the lyrics explore themes of romance or social protest. The **Casa de la Trova** (✉ Calle Heredia 208, Centro Histórico, ☎ 226/65–2689) has daily shows where groups play in one of four shifts: 10 AM–2 PM, 3–7, 8:30–10, and 10 PM–2 AM. Admission is $1–$2, and drinks and sandwiches are sold.

The **Claqueta Bar** (✉ Calle Félix Peña/Santo Tomás 654, Centro Histórico, ☎ no phone), just off Parque Céspedes, serves cheap drinks on its outdoor terrace; sometimes there's live music here weekend evenings. Early in the evening, a band plays at the bar-café on the porch of the **Hotel Casa Granda** (✉ Calle Heredia 201, Parque Céspedes, Centro Histórico, ☎ 226/68–6600). Its rooftop bar often has live-music shows and is also a nice spot for a drink. Aldo y Su Grupo, the outstanding (and friendly) house band at the **Hotel Meliá Santiago de Cuba** (✉ Av. de las Américas, e/Av. Manduley y Av. Cuarto, Reparto Sueño, ☎ 226/68–7070) specializes in salsa. They perform their happy-hour set from 6–9 at the terrace bar outside the main restaurant. At 10 they head up to the rooftop nightclub, where things really sizzle.

The **Teatro Heredia** (✉ Av. de las Américas y Av. de los Desfiles, Reparto Sueño, ☎ 226/64–3134) hosts performances of classical and Cuban music and opera as well as poetry readings. There are also children's shows here on weekend mornings. The **Tropicana Santiago** (✉ Circunvalación, 4 km/2 mi north of Hotel Meliá Santiago de Cuba, Reparto Sueño, ☎ 226/64–3036) puts on a full cabaret, with dozens of dancers—men in Spandex, women in feathers and jeweled bikinis—floating through the colored lights and tropical decor. Most hotels offer cabaret packages for $30 (including transport, entrance, and one drink).

Outdoor Activities and Sports

You can arrange day trips to the area immediately east of Santiago, which encompasses the sprawling Baconao Natural Reserve. There are beaches and plenty of hiking opportunities here. The beach zone west of Santiago, along the coastal road into Granma Province, is also just a day trip away.

Nonguests can use the sports facilities at the **Hotel Meliá Santiago de Cuba** (⊠ Av. de las Américas, e/Av. Manduley y Av. Cuarto, Reparto Sueño, ☎ 226/68–7070)—including pools and tennis and basketball courts—for a $10 fee; equipment rentals are also available. **Marina Marlin** (⊠ Punta Gorda, ☎ 226/69–1446) can arrange water-sports equipment rentals and boat trips. It offers bay tours, day-long excursions (including lunch) to area beaches, and full-day fishing charters.

Despite the continued chill in official United States–Cuba relations, all of Cuba is crazy about the American pastime of baseball. You can catch the madness at **Estadio Guillermón Moncada** (⊠ Av. de las Américas, Reparto Sueño, ☎ 226/64–1090 or 226/64–1078), the stadium of the hometown team, the Santiago Orientales. The season runs November through March, and games are played Tuesday and Thursday at 7:30 PM, Saturday at 1:30 and 7:30 PM, and Sunday at 1:30.

Shopping

Santiago and its environs have some of the best arts and crafts in the region—from surrealist oil paintings to stuffed dolls to wood carvings. The city's painters are particularly good; if you buy an artwork, just remember to purchase a $10 export permit from the artist.

Parque Céspedes, the heart of the historic district, is ringed by stores and art galleries, including one that's housed in an elegant former casino, the erstwhile Club San Carlos. **Calle Heredia,** which runs along the south side of Parque Céspedes, is lined with bookstores, galleries, and shops (including those in the Casa de la Trova and the Casa del Estudiante) that purvey crafts and music. Artists also sell their creations from stands set up along this street. The road to and the area around **El Morro** has its share of artisans hawking their wares.

Arte Universal (⊠ Calle 1, e/Calle M y Calle Terraza, Reparto Vista Alegre, ☎ no phone), has art exhibits (and works for sale) Monday–Saturday 9–7 and Sunday 9–5. Admission is $1. **Boutique La Casona** (⊠ Av. Manduley y Calle 1, Reparto Vista Alegre, ☎ 226/64–1117), in La Maison, a mansion turned restaurant and emporium, has clothing, tobacco, and electronics shops within. It's open Monday through Saturday 10–6. At **Casa del Caribe** (⊠ Calle 13, No. 154, esquina de Calle 5, Reparto Vista Alegre, ☎ 226/64–2285) you can buy books or take a course on Cuban or Caribbean culture.

Cubartesania (⊠ Calle Bartolomé Masó/San Basilio y Calle Félix Peña/Santo Tomás, Centro Histórico, ☎ no phone), just off Parque Céspedes, is a state-run store that sells high-quality paintings, prints, and a wide selection of crafts. **Foto Service** (⊠ Calle General Lacret y Calle Heredia, Centro Histórico, ☎ no phone, ☺ open daily 9–9) sells cheap bottled water and American cigarettes, chocolate, and toothpaste. It also sells and develops film.

Parque Baconao

28 *10 km (5 mi) east of Parque Céspedes to San Juan Hill and beginning of Parque Baconao.*

The Baconao Biosphere Reserve starts at San Juan Hill in Santiago and covers some 800 square km (309 square mi) east of the city. In addition to beaches and mountains, it contains several museums, a flower farm, and an artist colony—among other things. From Santiago, take the Carretera de Siboney, and follow the signs to Playa Siboney, a Caribbean beach 19 km (12 mi) southeast of town.

La Gran Piedra, a gigantic rock offshoot of the Sierra Maestra, rises 1,200 m (3,900 ft) and offers views of Haiti and Jamaica on clear days. Visibility is best first thing in the morning. The cutoff to it from the Carretera de Siboney is right beyond the Prado de las Esculturas, a contemporary sculpture garden that's one of several points of interest near La Gran Piedra. The road to the peak climbs about 15 km (9 mi), passing from lush jungle vegetation—with towering bamboo and palms that block out the sun—to scrub forest open to the rays and affording great views. The road ends at a hotel and restaurant; a large stairway leads to the rock peak from here. To one side of the peak is the Jardín la Idalia, a colorful farm with gardens full of tropical flowers. It's sometimes called the "Jardín Ave de Paraíso" for the bird of paradise flowers that grow here.

Two kilometers (1 mile) east of La Gran Piedra is the **Museo la Isabelica,** housed in a former plantation. Its exhibits depict the life of a French coffee farmer—one of many who settled in this region during the Haitian revolution in 1792. The museum is open daily 9–4, and admission is $1.

The **Museo Granjita Siboney,** a few kilometers east of the cutoff to La Gran Piedra, is housed in the farmhouse where Castro and his cohorts met (having hid their weapons in a well here) before attacking the Moncada Barracks. The farmhouse is on a large, shady piece of land. The museum inside commemorates the event with photos, news articles, documents, blood-stained clothing, and weapons. Twenty-six memorials to the attack line the road from here to Santiago. ⊠ *Carretera de Siboney, Km 13.5,* ☎ *226/69–8360.* ⊡ *$1.* ☉ *Tues.–Sun. 9–5.*

☾ The **Valle de la Prehistoria** (Prehistoric Valley) is a park of rolling green fields, filled with life-size replicas of dinosaurs, Cro-Magnon man, and other prehistoric creatures. The park, whose towering sculptures are made of cement poured over wood and metal frames, is divided into different eras: from Paleozoic to Mesozoic to Cenozoic. There's also a natural science museum. Some people have dismissed the place as tacky, but it's hard not to have fun here. (Just watch the kids.) ⊠ *Carretera de Baconao, Km 22,* ☎ *no phone.* ⊡ *$1 entrance fee; $1 fee for taking pictures.* ☉ *Daily 8–7.*

☾ The **Museo Nacional de Transporte,** an antique car museum, has classic American vehicles from Model T Fords to 1958 Thunderbirds. The car in which Fidel Castro rode to attack the Moncada Barracks and a Cadillac belonging to Cuban singer Beny Moré are here. Across the street is a toy museum. ⊠ *Carretera de Baconao, Km 24,* ☎ *no phone.* ⊡ *$1 (joint admission with toy museum).* ☉ *Daily 8–5.*

☾ At the **Aquario Baconao** you can see sharks, seals, eels, turtles, and other marine life. The highlight is the dolphin pool and show; for an extra $20, you can also swim with the dolphins. ⊠ *Carretera de Baconao, Km 26, Playa Larga,* ☎ *no phone.* ⊡ *$3.* ☉ *Tues.–Sun. 9–4.*

The **Laguna Baconao,** a 4-square-km (2-square-mi) circular lagoon surrounded by mountains, is literally the last stop along the Carretera de Baconao. There's a crocodile farm here ($1 to enter), and you can arrange boat trips on the lagoon.

Dining and Lodging

¢–$ ✕ **La Rueda.** This eatery at the entrance to the town of Playa Siboney is rustic. But you can't beat the barbecued meats and seafood prepared the Cuban way. There's also a bar here. ⊠ *Playa Siboney,* ☎ *226/63– 9352. MC, V.*

¢–$$ ▥ **Hotel Bucanero.** The area's nicest resort is less than an hour's drive from Santiago. It's built around a pristine beach surrounded by cliffs. Rooms, which have cable TV and other amenities, are in secluded, single-story structures spread out along the shore. Interior and exterior color schemes match the terra-cotta bluffs that rise from the sea. ⊠ *Carretera de Baconao, Km 4.5, Arroyo La Costa,* ☎ *226/62–8130 or 226/68–6363,* FAX *226/68–6070. 200 rooms. Restaurant, bar, pool, barbershop, beauty salon, hot tub, sauna, 4 tennis courts, health club, volleyball, beach, dive shop, snorkeling, windsurfing, boating, jet skiing, waterskiing, fishing, shops, nightclub, travel services. MC, V. All-inclusive.*

$ ▥ **Hotel Carisol Resort.** Rooms here (equipped with satellite TV) either face the sea or the mountains. The resort has a nice beach and all the facilities you need. In addition, the food and the service are both good. ⊠ *Carretera Baconao, Km 10, Playa Cazonal,* ☎ *226/62–8519,* FAX *226/62–7191. 120 rooms. Restaurant, bar, pool, 2 tennis courts, health club, hiking, beach, dive shop, snorkeling, windsurfing, boating, jet skiing, waterskiing, fishing, shops, nightclub, travel services. MC, V. All-inclusive.*

¢ ▥ **Balneario del Sol.** Guest quarters are either in rooms or in four-room cabins that dot the grounds; all have amenities like satellite TV. Be sure to check out the saltwater pool, which extends out to the coastal cliffs that front the property. ⊠ *Carretera Baconao, Km 38.5, Playa Larga,* ☎ *226/69–8113 or 226/69–8124. 115 rooms, 24 cabins. Restaurant, bar, 2 pools, 2 tennis courts, health club, beach, dive shop, snorkeling, windsurfing, boating, jet skiing, waterskiing, fishing, shops, nightclub, recreation room, travel services. MC, V.*

¢ ▥ **Villa La Gran Piedra.** Here 22 self-contained villas (with satellite TV) are spread out along a cliff-side ridge of La Gran Piedra. The restaurant-bar is in a country lodge. ⊠ *Carretera de la Gran Piedra, Km 14,* ☎ *226/65913. 22 cabins. Restaurant, bar, kitchenettes, pool. MC, V.*

Outdoor Activities and Sports

BEACHES

You can visit **Playa Bacajagua** for a nominal fee. Gray cliffs surround the white sands of **Playa Bucanero,** which is for the exclusive use of guests at the Hotel Bucanero. **Playa Daiquirí,** which gave its name to the famous drink first made here in 1898, was the landing site of Teddy Roosevelt and his Rough Riders. The beach itself is unattractive and is reserved for military use during parts of the year. **Playa Siboney** is a clean, dark-sand beach as well as a town with charming wooden vacation homes. There are a couple of nice casas particulares and paladares here as well as traditional lodging and dining options. It's a good spot for a lunch stop. **Playa Sigua** is known for its two good restaurants: Casa del Pedro del Cojo, specializing in creole dishes, and Los Coraldes, whose forte is seafood. There's also a marina where you can gear up to fish, snorkel, sail, and windsurf.

RODEO

For a cowboy rodeo Cuban style, stop by the **Finca Guajira Rodeo** (⊠ 3 km/2 mi beyond the Playa Siboney turn-off onto Carretera de Baconao, opposite El Oasis, ☎ no phone). Competitions are held Tuesday through Thursday, Saturday, and Sunday at 9 AM and 2 PM, and entrance costs $5. Horseback rides are also available here.

Shopping

There are *artesanía* vendors nearly everywhere you look in Baconao. Good-quality art is often sold (at good prices) beside roads. The artist colony **El Oasis** (⊠ 3 km/2 mi beyond the Playa Siboney turn-off onto Carretera de Baconao, ☏ no phone) is a logical shopping stop. Several artists keep their workshop/home/gallery open every day until around dusk. The artists are much more interesting than the professional gallery staffs in the city; prices are better than in the cities, too.

Guantánamo

㉙ *86 km (53 mi) northeast of Santiago.*

Despite its scenic parks and aging manses on wide palm-lined streets, many feel that the eponymous provincial capital is ugly and boring. The people, however, are beautiful and vibrant. Much of the populace is descended from immigrants from Haiti, Jamaica, and other Caribbean nations, who came to cut cane in the late 18th and early 19th centuries. Some residents still speak English.

The town is also the home base of the Orquestra Revé, and local musicians, who mix modern tropical music and traditional Afro-Cuban drumming known as *son-changuí,* play around town. The traditional lyrics to Cuba's most famous song, "Guantanamera," are about a beautiful woman from here.

The **Guantánamo Naval Base** rims the two entrances to Guantánamo Bay 25 km (16 mi) south of the capital. It's behind a virtual no-man's land of minefields and barbed wire planted by Castro to keep determined Cubans on the island. Your best chance of seeing it is from Alturas de Malone, high above the city. The United States has controlled the base since 1903, when it was granted an indefinite lease under the Platt Amendment. The terms were changed in 1939, but America remains in the role of an unwanted tenant, standing on extremely beneficial terms. It pays a bit more than $4,000 a year in rent, but the checks to the Cuban government remain uncashed (they're supposedly kept in one of Castro's desk drawers).

Although closed to Cuba since Castro took power in 1959, the base has, in recent years, been used as a way station for Haitian and Cuban refugees. (A plan to house refugees from the Kosovo war here was scrapped as insensitive due to cultural and climatic differences between this tropical island and the refugees' Eastern European homeland.) Inside the base, the 7,000 military personnel and their families live with all the comforts of home, including a golf course, several pools, sports facilities, shopping malls, a McDonald's, an airport, and marina facilities.

Dining and Lodging

¢ ✕🏨 **Hotel Guantánamo.** Although nondescript, this hotel is really the only game in town. The food and accommodations are adequate; rooms have satellite TV and other standard amenities. To witness a surreal scene of local life, check out the frigid (the air-conditioning may well be turned up higher than any other establishment in Cuba) second-floor bar. ⊠ *Calle 13 y Calle Ahogado, Plaza Mariana Grajales,* ☏ *21/38–1015 or 21/38–1025,* 🆀🆇 *21/38–2406. 124 rooms. Restaurant, 2 bars, pool, shop, game room, beauty salon, nightclub, travel services. MC, V.*

En Route Beyond Guantánamo, the road to Baracoa skitters along a dry region whose rocky shore is cut with coves and small beaches. The highway meets the Caribbean Sea at **Playa Yateritas,** one of the area's most pop-

THE CUBAN AMERICANS

After Castro's Revolution, thousands of Cubans fled the island. The first exiles were close associates of dictator Fulgencio Batista. But by late 1962, 250,000 Cubans—disenfranchised by Castro's austere reforms—had left their homeland. Most were white upper- and middle-class professionals. As Castro embraced communism, many of his fellow guerillas became disillusioned and also left; later, they were joined by gay Cubans, writers, and artists.

During the 1980 Mariel Boat Lift, the U.S. accepted thousands more Cubans; it was later discovered that many were convicts and other "undesirables" whom Castro had released from prisons and psychiatric wards. Since then, still more rank-and-file Cubans—including New York Yankees pitcher Orlando "El Duque" Hernández—have braved strong currents, bad weather, and sharks making the 145-km (90-mi) journey to Florida on makeshift wooden rafts. Today there are about 750,000 Cuban-born U.S. citizens, most of whom live in Miami, elsewhere in south Florida, New Jersey, and Puerto Rico.

Cuban-Americans have excelled at achieving the American dream while retaining their culture. Many frown on Castro and his regime, and such organizations as the Cuban American National Foundation have lobbied to keep the U.S. trade embargo in effect. Still, a growing number of Cuban-Americans believe that current U.S. policies are hurting Cuba more than those of Castro. Groups such as Cambio Cubano have called for an open dialogue with Castro to encourage democracy. To learn more about the current debates, contact the Center for Cuban Studies (124 W. 23rd St., New York, NY 10011, 212/242–0559), which publishes *Cuba Update*.

ular stretches, with light sand and a protected coastline. Thirty km (19 mi) beyond Playa Yateritas is the roadside town of **Imías,** which has a small beach. Ten km (6 mi) from Imías is **Cajobabo,** a hamlet that was, on April 11, 1895, the landing site of José Martí and five other patriots who came to conquer Cuba after years of exile. A huge billboard points toward Playita Cajobabo, the beach where they landed. You'll find a museum with exhibits on the event as well as a restaurant here.

Just after the billboard pointing the way from Cajobabo to Martí's landing site, the road turns north toward Baracoa, and the famous highway known as La Farola climbs the **Sierra del Purial** to Baracoa. It twists through deep valleys, slithers past cascading rivers, and winds over bare peaks. The few *miradores* (lookouts) along the way are good places for a picnic lunch or a snack bought from roadside vendors who sell fresh fruit, crafts, and cucurucho. Near the summit, the road passes through stands of tall pines before dropping into tropical vegetation. As the road nears Baracoa, majestic El Yunque—a massive green mountain shelf—comes into view.

Baracoa

 ★ *164 km (102 mi) northeast of Guantánamo; 250 km (155 mi) northeast of Santiago.*

Cuba's first Spanish settlement was founded in 1512 by Diego Velázquez, who went on to settle six other cities. Today Baracoa is one of the island's most charming towns. Its historic center is bounded by three fortresses and El Malecón, a wide ocean-side roadway (La Farola runs into it) bordered by sea-grape trees and coral coastline on one side and buildings—some historic, some modern and sterile—on the other.

One of Baracoa's three fortresses, **Fuerte Matachín,** was completed in 1802. Today it houses the **Museo Histórico Matachin,** whose displays discuss the city's history, including its Taíno roots. There are examples of Taíno pottery, sculpture, and other artifacts; exhibits on famous citizens; and displays explaining the community's role in the wars of independence and the Revolution. ⊠ *Calle Martí y El Malecón,* ☎ *no phone.* ⌸ *$1.* ☉ *Daily 8–noon and 2–6.*

The **Plaza de Antonio Maceo Grajales** is a nice shady spot with a central monument to its namesake, a local general who fought in the Ten Years' War. A block over, at another shady plaza on El Malecón, is a striking monument to Columbus's landing. Cuba was Columbus's second stop on his first trip to the Americas, and Baracoans claim it was El Yunque that he described before landing. From here you can walk along El Malecón, or hitch a ride on one of the horse-drawn carts—more utilitarian than charming—that ply the route.

NEED A BREAK?	While you're on El Malecón, be sure to stop by the **Hotel La Rusa** (⊠ Av. Máximo Gómez 161, ☎ 21/43011), a charming guest house with a colorful history. In the lobby you can see some of the personal effects of the house's former owner, a Russian woman who fled the Bolshevik Revolution and wound up living in Baracoa, only to become a supporter of Castro's movement. There's a small bar-restaurant here with tables overlooking the water.

In Baracoa's historic heart, the **Plaza Independencia,** note the large bust of the Indian chief Hatuey—Cuba's first rebel—who fought against the Spanish and was burned at the stake for his audacity in 1512. The plaza is home to the **Catedral de Nuestra Señora de la Asunción** (⊠ Calle Antonio Maceo 152, ☎ no phone). Built in 1833, the church is best known for preserving the Cruz de la Parra that Columbus supposedly used to name and claim Cuba for Spain. (Scientific tests have confirmed that it is, indeed, old enough to have been brought by the discoverer.) The cross is also said to have magical powers.

El Castillo de Seboruco, a fortress that now houses the Hotel El Castillo, dominates a hill overlooking Baracoa. Although construction on it started in 1739, the fort wasn't finished until nearly 200 years later. Even if you don't stay here, stop by for the views of El Yunque and the city. Baracoa's third fortress, **Fuerte de la Punta,** was built in 1803 on a spit of land over the entrance to the bay. The fortress now contains the Restaurant La Punta.

Five km (3 mi) west of town, where the Río Duaba empties into the sea, the **Duaba obelisk** marks the spot where Antonio Maceo landed with a group of rebels in 1885, during the Second War of Independence. The **Finca Duaba,** is a replica of a typical Cuban plantation, where you can get a taste of country life. A tour takes you past mango and coconut trees as well as coffee and cocoa crops. You'll also visit a typical *bohío,* or peasant's hut, where staff members actually live. A rustic restaurant serves a good comida criolla lunch for about $10 per person. To get here, 7 km (4 mi) west of town take a left at the Campismo El Yunque and follow the dirt road to the right. ⊠ *Ruta Duaba,* ☎ *no phone.* ⌸ *$1.* ☉ *Tues.–Sun. 9–4.*

About 40 km (25 mi) east of the city, the province narrows to its east-ernmost point, **Punta Maisí,** marked by a lighthouse and small village.

Dining and Lodging

¢–$ ✕ **Restaurant La Punta.** At this restaurant in the Fuerte de la Punta you can dine on traditional food 24 hours a day. Tables are set within the old fort walls. Just outside are wonderful bay views. Live music and dance shows take place nightly. ⊠ *Av. Los Mártires y El Malecón,* ☎ *no phone. MC, V.*

¢   ✕🏨 **Hotel Castillo.** El Castillo de Seboruco was renovated and trans-
★   formed into this charming hotel. Views are of Baracoa—from its quaint historic center to its malecón—El Yunque, and the sea. Even the pool and its terrace offer panoramic vistas, though a third-floor bar pro-vides some of the best perspectives. Rooms mix comfortable, classic antiques with modern conveniences, and the attentive staff provides top-notch service. The on-site Restaurant Duaba ($) has an airy din-ing room and an outdoor patio overlooking the pool. This is *the* place to try Baracoa's famous (and flavorful) cuisine, more Caribbean than Cuban. Recommended dishes include *dorado a la Santa Barbara* (dol-phinfish in a red coconut sauce) and *pollo en salsa caribeña* (chicken sautéed in a fruit and beer sauce). The full-course meal-of-the-day here costs a mere $8.95. ⊠ *Calle Calixto García, Loma El Paraíso,* ☎ *21/42147 or 21/42125,* ℻ *21/35–5518. 34 rooms. Restaurant, 2 bars, pool, shop, travel services, car rental. MC, V.*

¢   🏨 **Gaviota Villa Maguana.** If you like the idea of sitting in the shade
★   on a rocking chair steps from a secluded, palm-lined beach, this guest house is perfect. The sands here are white, and the waters are protected by a cove. The house is simple, offering such basic comforts as a com-mon TV lounge. As there are only four rooms, you must make reser-vations well in advance through the Hotel Castillo or any Gaviota office. ⊠ *Playa Maguana,* ☎ *21/42147 or 21/42125,* ℻ *21/35–5518. 4 rooms. Restaurant, refrigerator, beach. MC, V. BP.*

¢   🏨 **Hotel La Rusa.** The charming, rust-color La Rusa overlooks the ocean-side malecón. It takes its name from its former owner, Mima Rebenskaya, a Russian immigrant who made it her home. The woman is the inspi-ration of Alejo Carpentier's novel *The Rites of Spring.* In addition to the Cuban novelist, guests have included Errol Flynn, Fidel Castro, and poet Nicolas Guillén. A plaque in Room 203 commemorates Che Gue-vara's visit. You'll need to have a historic frame of mind, though, to feel truly at home in these old, spare rooms. ⊠ *Av. Máximo Gómez 161,* ☎ *21/43011. 13 rooms. Restaurant, bar, air-conditioning. MC, V.*

Nightlife and the Arts

The town band plays in Plaza Independencia every Sunday, and the adjacent Plaza Martí hosts weekend chess tournaments. If you get a late-night craving, try **Cafeteria El Parque** (⊠ Parque Independencia, ☎ no phone), which serves sandwiches 24 hours a day. It also has live music nightly. You can often catch live-music shows at the **Casa de la Cultura** (⊠ Calle Antonio Maceo 124, ☎ 21/42349).

The **Casa de la Trova** (⊠ Calle Antonio Maceo 149, ☎ no phone) is the best spot to hear live music. It's open nightly until about 2 AM, and admission is $1. Listen for *el nengen* or *el kiribá,* two styles of music that predate the Cuban son. **Discoteca 485** (⊠ Calle Antonio Maceo 141, ☎ no phone), at the north side of Parque Independencia, is Bara-coa's dancing hot spot.

Outdoor Activities and Sports

BEACHES

A series of dark-sand beaches stretches east of Baracoa, and there's 30 km (19 mi) of good cement road along the coast. About 20 km (12 mi) west of town, you'll find the lovely **Playa Maguana,** site of the Gaviota Villa Maguana hotel. Right outside the east end of town you'll cross the **Río Miel.** Legend has it that after swimming in these waters you'll fall in love in Baracoa and stay here forever. About 20 km (12 mi) east of town is **Playa Baragua,** one of the area's few light-sand beaches. Not far from here, the road passes beneath a natural arch called the Túnel de los Alemanes (Germans' Tunnel) before ending 25 km (16 mi) east of Baracoa, at the Río Yumurí and the adjacent village of the same name. The river tumbles out of a steep canyon. Boats ferry passengers across the river and up into the canyon for nominal fees.

RIVER RAFTING

Gaviota (Hotel Castillo, Calle Calixto García, Loma El Paraíso, ☎ 21/42147 or 21/42125) offers rafting trips along the Río Yumurí, 28 km (18 mi) east of town (7 hrs, $12); the Río Toa (5 hrs, $8); and the Río Duaba (4 hrs, $8).

HIKING

You can hike the mysterious El Yunque, an anvil-shape mountain covered in green jungle and mist. **Gaviota** (Hotel Castillo, Calle Calixto García, Loma El Paraíso, ☎ 21/42147 or 21/42125) offers an eight-hour trek (minimum of five people) for $8 per person.

Shopping

The works of Baracoa's many fine artisans and painters are often influenced by their Taíno ancestry. They sell their creations along the malecón and in the city's plazas. **Galería Yara** (✉ Calle Antonio Maceo 120, ☎ no phone) has an eclectic collection of paintings, jewelry, and crafts. Look for the round sign reading GALERÍA DE ARTE on the north side of Parque Independencia.

EASTERN CUBA A TO Z

To research prices and get advice from other travelers, visit www.fodors.com.

AIR TRAVEL

Holguín and Santiago have international airports, and there are smaller airports in Bayamo, Guantánamo, and Baracoa. Cubana has several daily flights between Havana and Santiago, a daily flight between Havana and Holguín and Santiago, and weekly flights from Santiago to Baracoa.

AIRPORTS AND TRANSFERS

Holguín's Aeropuerto Internacional Frank País is just south of the city. A taxi into town costs $10, and transfers are available to both Holguín and Guardalavaca. The airport also sees a good deal of international charter-flight service.

Santiago's Aeropuerto Internacional Antonio Maceo is 8 km (5 mi) south of the city center; a taxi ride into town will cost about $10. Havanatur operates an airport shuttle service, but you must make arrangements in advance; the costs are $15 round-trip, $10 one-way.

➤ AIRPORT INFORMATION: **Aeropuerto de Baracoa** (☎ 4/42580). **Aeropuerto de Bayamo** (☎ 23/42–4502). **Aeropuerto de Guantánamo** (☎ 21/35–5454). **Aeropuerto Internacional Antonio Maceo** (☎ 226/69–1014). **Aeropuerto Internacional Frank País** (☎ 24/46–2534).

CARRIERS

Cubana, the Cuban national airline, provides direct service between Santiago and Madrid, Spain; Paris, France; and Frankfurt, Germany. Sunholiday Tours flies from Montego Bay, Jamaica, to Santiago. Taíno

Air flies to Santiago from Santo Domingo, Dominican Republic, on Thursday and Sunday.

➤ AIRLINES AND CONTACTS: **Cubana** (✉ Edificio Pico de Cristal, Parque Calixto García, Holguín, ☎ 24/42–5707). **Sunholiday Tours** (☎ 809/952–5629 in Jamaica; 800/433–2920 in the United States). **Taíno Air** (☎ 809/687–7114 in Santo Domingo).

BUS TRAVEL

In general, city buses aren't recommended. They're crowded, poorly maintained, and slow—all this and tickets are still in great demand. Tourist buses, however, can take you on tours of all lengths. Most can be booked through your hotel or at local offices of Havanatur and other state travel agencies. Islazul has modern, air-conditioned buses that run from Santiago to Havana; trips cost $40 per person each way. You can make arrangements through Rumbos and other tour operators. Payment is accepted in cash and with major non-American credit cards.

➤ BUS INFORMATION: **Rumbos** (✉ Parque Céspedes, Santiago, ☎ 226/62–5969).

CAR RENTAL

Since public transportation is virtually nonexistent, it's soothing to know that renting a car is simple, and prices—about $50 a day with a $200 cash deposit—are on par with those elsewhere in the world. There are rental desks at most major hotels, at airports, and on main streets in tourist areas such as Guardalavaca. Although vehicles are readily available, employee organizational skills are dodgy, so it's best to reserve a day or two in advance.

Rental agencies include Cubacar, Micar, Transautos, and Viacar. All are run by the Cuban government, so the service they provide is similar. Peugeots and Fiats are the most common vehicles available; many outlets offer Jeep Suzukis, which are a few dollars cheaper. One-way rentals are common. If you'll be traveling far, insist on *kilometraje ilimitado* (unlimited mileage). Even if you have unlimited mileage, you'll be charged a return fee based on mileage (a one-way rental from Havana to Santiago will incur a return fee of roughly $100), which will be deducted from your deposit when you hand in your car. Before renting a car, ask whether you are expected to refill the gas tank, as policies on this vary.

➤ LOCAL AGENCIES: **Cubacar** (✉ Villa Marea del Portillo, Carretera de Pilón, Km 14, Marea del Portillo, ☎ 23/59–4201; ✉ Hotel Farallón del Caribe, Carretera de Pilón, Km 14, Marea del Portillo, ☎ 23/33–5301; ✉ Hotel Casa Granda, Calle Heredia 201, Parque Céspedes, Centro Histórico, Santiago, ☎ 226/64–2612; ✉ Meliá Santiago de Cuba, Av. de las Américas, e/Av. Manduley y Av. Cuarto, Reparto Sueño, Santiago, ☎ 226/64–2612). **Micar** (✉ Aeropuerto Internacional Frank País, Holguín, ☎ 24/48–1652; ✉ Hotel Pernik, Av. Dimitrov y Av. XX Aniversario, Holguín, ☎ 226/62–9194; ✉ Playa Guardalavaca, Guardalavaca, ☎ 24/46–8270; ✉ Parque Céspedes, Centro Histórico, Santiago, ☎ 24/30767). **Transautos** (✉ Hotel Casa Granda, Calle Heredia 201, Parque Céspedes, Centro Histórico, Santiago, ☎ 226/64–1121; ✉ Meliá Santiago de Cuba, Av. de las Américas and Av. Manduley, Reparto Sueño, Santiago, ☎ 226/69–2245; ✉ Aeropuerto Internacional Antonio Maceo, Santiago, ☎ 226/68–6107). **Viacar** (✉ Parque Céspedes Centro Histórico, Santiago, ☎ 226/62–4646).

CAR TRAVEL

The main routes into and out of eastern Cuba are well maintained, and once you're out of the cities traffic is light (your biggest concern will be the occasional stray sheep or cow). Renting a car is the best way to cover vast distances, but you're better off hiring a car and driver for short journeys. Note that signage is poor, and it's easy to get mixed up when passing through a city. Ask directions: Cubans will gladly help you out of a mess.

The Autopista Nacional runs from Havana to Santiago (860 km/534 mi) as well as between Santiago and Camagüey, 325 km (202 mi) to the west. You're much more likely to take the northern highway to Bayamo (127 km/79 mi) and then onward to Holguín (140 km/87 mi), the gateway to the north coast region. The stunning 200-km (124-mi) road that runs west from Santiago along the coast is squeezed between the Sierra Maestra and the Caribbean Sea. Equally impressive is the road east to Baracoa (250 km/155 mi), which runs along the arid coastline before turning north and becoming La Farola highway, which winds through mountains.

EMERGENCY SERVICES

In the event of a breakdown or highway emergency, call your rental agency.

GASOLINE

There are state-run Servi-Cupet gas stations along major routes. Many are open 24 hours and sell food and beverages; only dollars are accepted. Stations are also abundant in cities. Gas costs about 90¢ per liter, but there is a big black market. At stations, you may be accosted by teenagers offering to sell you gasoline from private tanks at substantial discounts (usually 45¢ to 50¢ a liter). Although there's some risk of being scammed, many travelers have found the gas to be reliable, and you can save $15 filling a tank. A few precautions: check the size of the tank that's being filled, and make sure it's full; second, take a whiff of the gas to be sure it hasn't been diluted.

EMERGENCIES

Traveler's assistance for legal, financial, and medical problems is available through Asistur, which is open 24 hours a day. Santiago's Clínica Internacional is a medical clinic catering to foreigners, with an English-speaking staff on duty 24 hours a day. The clinic also has a fairly well-stocked pharmacy. In Guardalavaca, contact one of the big resorts, which have doctors on call during the day and other medical personnel on call 24 hours. In Holguín, the same is true at the Hotel Pernik, or you can try the state-run Hospital Lenin.

In Santiago, Farmacia Fereiro is open 24 hours a day. Bayamo's 24-hour pharmacy is Piloto. Elsewhere, pharmacy hours are more limited, though hotels stock basic first-aid and other medical supplies.

➤ GENERAL EMERGENCIES: **Ambulance** (☎ 113). **Asistur** (✉ Hotel Casa Granda, Parque Céspedes, Santiago, ☎ 226/68–6600). **Police** (☎ 116).
➤ MEDICAL EMERGENCIES: **Clínica Internacional** (✉ Calle 13 y Calle 14, Reparto Vista Alegre, Santiago, ☎ 226/64–2589). **Hospital Lenin** (✉ Av. Lenin s/n, Holguín, ☎ 24/42–5302).
➤ PHARMACIES: **Farmacia Fereiro** (✉ Av. Victoriano Garzón y Calle 10, Reparto Vista Alegre, Santiago, ☎ 226/62–2240). **Piloto** (✉ General García 53, Bayamo).

MAIL AND SHIPPING

Cuban mail, although affordable, is very slow; time-sensitive material should be sent by international mail services. Many major hotels have desks for international express mail.
➤ POST OFFICES: **Baracoa** (✉ Calle Maceo 286). **Bayamo** (✉ Parque Céspedes). **Holguín** (✉ Calle Libertad 183 y Calle Frexes). **Santiago** (✉ Calle Aguilera y Calle Calrín, Centro Histórico).

SAFETY

There's very little crime in eastern Cuba (tourists are particularly safe). In Santiago you may be bothered by panhandlers, particularly around Parque Céspedes, or by young men wanting to serve as your guide or refer you to a casa particular or to a paladar. Ignore their advice, and try to remain polite. The same can occur in isolated Baracoa: as you approach the town by car, for example, teens on bicycles ride alongside, trying to make a commission on a private home stay. Stay calm; they're harmless.

TAXIS

Modern, well-maintained tourist taxis, which charge dollars, congregate in front of hotels, transportation hubs, and major sights. Private cabs with yellow plates are much cheaper, and you can hire them for a day of driving around town for about $25. The famous *bicitaxis,* or bicycle taxis, are a relaxing way to see the sights. Regardless of which type of taxi you choose, settle on a price before you board.

In Holguín, Turistaxi is a reliable cab company. In Santiago, contact Taxis Cubalse, Transgaviota, or Turistaxi.
➤ LOCAL COMPANIES: **Taxis Cubalse** (☎ 226/64–1165). **Transgaviota** (☎ 226/64–1465). **Turistaxi** (☎ 24/42–4187 in Holguín or 226/63–1389 in Santiago).

TELEPHONES

All major hotels have international phone service. You can also make international calls at phone offices. Holguín's two phone centers are open daily 8 AM–10 PM. Bayamo's Centro Telefónico is open daily 8 AM–11 PM. In Santiago, the Centro de Llamadas Internacionales is open 24 hours a day. To make international calls in Guantánamo, your best bet is the Hotel Guantánamo. Baracoa's post office/communications center is open daily 8 AM–10 PM.

Your best bet for calling the United States is to purchase an ETESCA phone card, with rates fixed at $2 per minute. To call Cuba from abroad, dial the international access number, then 53 (Cuba's country code), and the local code: 4 for Baracoa, 21 for Guantánamo, 23 for all of Granma province, 24 for all of Holguín province, 226 for Santiago de Cuba.
➤ PHONE CENTERS: **Centro de Llamadas Internacionales** (✉ Parque Céspedes, Centro Histórico, Santiago). **Centro Telefónico** (✉ Av. Miguel Enrico Capote y Calle Saco, Bayamo). **Holguín Phone Center** (✉ Parque Calixto García, ☎ no phone; ✉ Calle Martí y Calle Máximo Gómez). **Hotel Guantánamo** (✉ Calle 13 y Calle Ahogado, Plaza Mariana Grajales, Guantánamo, ☎ 21/38–1015). **Communications Center** (✉ Calle Antonio Maceo 136, Plaza Independencia, Baracoa).

TOURS

Major hotels throughout the region have tour desks where you can book everything from flights to rental cars to tours. Santiago operators serve all the town's sights as well as such surrounding areas as Baconao and El Cobre. You can also arrange tours to Baracoa, Marea del Portillo, and Guardalavaca. Companies include Havanatur, Rumbos, Tour and Travel, and Gaviota.
➤ TOUR COMPANIES: **Gaviota** (✉ Hotel Castillo, Calle Calixto García, Loma El Paraíso, Baracoa, ☎ 21/42147 or 21/42125). **Havanatur** (✉ Calle 8, No. 54, Reparto Vista Alegre, Santiago, ☎ 226/64–3603 or 226/68–7281; ✉ Hotel Casa Granda, Parque Céspedes, Centro Histórico, Santiago, ☎ 226/64–3603). **Rumbos** (✉ Parque Céspedes, Centro Histórico, Santiago, ☎ 226/62–5969). **Tour and Travel** (✉ Parque Céspedes, Centro Histórico, Santiago, ☎ 226/62–2222).

TRAIN TRAVEL

An overnight *especial* train runs between Havana and Santiago (once daily in both directions), with stops at Las Tunas, Camagüey, Ciego de Ávila, Santa Clara, and Matanzas. Santiago is the only stop the train makes in eastern Cuba; nightly departures are at 9:35 PM. (Santiago's modern train station, the Estación de Ferrocarriles, is on the harbor, six blocks west of Parque Céspedes.) The trip takes about 15 hours and costs $42; payment is accepted only in cash. It's best to buy your ticket far as possible in advance. The older European-style coaches have air-conditioning and reclining seats. Although a food cart trundles by twice on the trip, you'll definitely need to bring food and bottled water.

Besides the especial train, a $31, non–air-conditioned train leaves from Santiago at 5 PM on odd-numbered days of the month and arrives in Havana at 7 AM. There's also rail service between Havana and Holguín, Bayamo, and Guantánamo. Most train stations are near a city's historic center. The one exception is Holguín, whose station is 15 km (9 mi) to the south in the town of Cacocum. Tickets can be bought at train stations.

➤ TRAIN INFORMATION: **Estación de Ferrocarriles** (✉ Av. Jesús Menéndez, Centro Histórico, Santiago, ☎ 226/62–2896).

VISITOR INFORMATION

The tour desks at major hotels throughout the region can provide you with travel information and assistance. Major state-run agencies include Rumbos and Cubanacán. Both of these arrange rental cars and other modes of transportation, tours, hotel stays, and, literally, any tourist service provided on the island.

➤ TOURIST INFORMATION: **Rumbos** (✉ Parque Céspedes, Centro Histórico, Santiago, ☎ 226/62–5969; ✉ Meliá Santiago de Cuba, Av. de las Americas y Calle M, Reparto Sueño, Santiago, ☎ 226/68–7040). **Cubanacán** (✉ Meliá Santiago de Cuba, Av. de las Americas y Calle M, Reparto Sueño, Santiago, ☎ 226/68–7040).

6 PORTRAITS OF CUBA

CUBA AT A GLANCE: A CHRONOLOGY

1000 BC   Guanahatabey Indians (possibly from the southeastern United States) begin to populate Cuba.

AD 900   Ciboney Indians (a South American Arawak group) begin arriving, gradually pushing the Guanahatabey to the western third of the island.

1400s   During the middle of the century, Taíno Indians (another, more advanced Arawak group) settle on the island; later in the century, Carib Indians (a warlike group believed to be from South America) challenge the Taíno, though they never actually settle on the island.

1492   Christopher Columbus, commissioned by King Ferdinand and Queen Isabella of Spain, "discovers" Cuba and claims it for the Spanish crown. Columbus believes he has discovered a shorter trade route to the Far East. At the time of his landing, the indigenous population is an estimated 112,000.

1508   Sebastian de Ocampo circumnavigates Cuba and determines that it is an island and not, as Columbus had suggested, part of the Asian mainland.

1511   Diego Velázquez arrives from Hispaniola with 300 soldiers and establishes the settlement of Baracoa. Velázquez becomes governor of Cuba and begins conquering the island's native people, including the great chieftain Hatuey.

1514   Havana is founded.

1520   Three hundred slaves arrive from Africa.

1538   The seat of government is moved to Havana.

1555   The French pirate Jacques de Sores burns Havana. This attack is one of many—by pirates seeking loot for themselves or buccaneers seeking booty for other European nations—that will occur in Cuba over the next 100 years. The Spanish monopoly on the island's imports and exports encourages some islanders to become involved in smuggling. Cuba's indigenous population now numbers 5,000; its African population is roughly 800.

1728   A university is established in Havana.

1740   Government authorities create the Real Compañía de Comercio to handle all Cuban imports and exports. The monopoly buys Cuban goods at a fixed price and resells them elsewhere at a tidy profit, sowing the seeds of discontent among creole (Cuban-born Spaniards) farmers and manufacturers.

1762   England captures Havana after a three-month attack at the end of the Seven Years' War (French and Indian War), during which Spain has been France's ally against England. The most important legacy left by the English during their brief occupation of the city is the removal of Spain's crippling trade restrictions. The English relinquish Havana to Spain in exchange for the territory of Florida.

1762–1870   Roughly 700,000 African slaves are brought to Cuba (most between 1811 and 1870) as sugar supplants cattle and tobacco as the island's major commodity.

1763   The first Cuban newspaper is published.

1764   Cuba's postal service is initiated.

1820–23 Various revolutions lead to the independence of the mainland Spanish colonies—from Mexico to Argentina.

1848 U.S. President James Polk offers $100 million for Cuba. Spain declines the offer.

1854 U.S. President Franklin Pierce makes an unsuccessful bid for the island. By this time, Cuba accounts for a third of the world's sugar production.

1868 The Ten Years' War, the first Cuban attempt at revolution against Spanish rule, begins when Carlos Manuel de Céspedes issues the Grito de Yara (a declaration of independence) on his plantation in eastern Cuba. It's largely a guerilla war—led on the political front by Céspedes and on the military front by the Dominican-born Máximo Gómez and the Cuban-born Antonio Maceo—and results in 200,000 deaths before the 1878 Treaty of El Zanjón, which guarantees a list of government reforms.

1886 Slavery is officially abolished.

1890–1895 American trade with and investment in Cuba increases significantly, particularly in relation to the sugar industry.

1892 The great poet, journalist, and lawyer José Martí founds the Partido Revolucionario Cubano (Cuban Revolutionary Party) and begins collaborating with Gómez and Maceo.

1893 Equal civil status of blacks and whites is proclaimed.

1895 Led by Martí, Gómez, and Maceo, Cuban rebels—angered by Spain's refusal to make reforms that had been promised at the end of the Ten Years' War—begin the Second War of Independence. Martí is killed in May, on his first day in battle.

1898 The USS *Maine* explodes in Havana Harbor, precipitating the Spanish-American War. This war lasts for less than four months, and Spain's loss marks the end of its holdings in the Caribbean.

1899 Cuba becomes an independent republic under U.S. protection.

1901 The U.S. Congress approves the Platt Amendment. Among its provisions are that the United States may institute military intervention in Cuba and that the United States will buy or lease land for a military installation on Cuban soil. Cuba accepts the terms of this amendment, though not without controversy.

1902–17 Although the U.S. occupation ends in 1902, U.S. involvement in Cuban affairs does not. As the fledgling nation hits political rough spots that threaten its stability, the Platt Amendment is invoked in 1912 and again in 1917.

1920 Sugar prices plummet. With the Cuban economy in turmoil, U.S. investors capitalize on cheap property.

1920–30 Cuban students and other intellectuals begin calling for political, economic, and education reforms. A period of *cubanismo* (Cuban nationalism) begins, as do calls for an end to the Platt Amendment and U.S. meddling. Student leader Julio Antonio Mella and others found the Cuban Communist Party in 1925.

1928 President Gerardo Machado, who had been in power for four years, has the constitution changed to allow a six- rather than four-year presidential term. His policies of persecuting critics—particularly students—make him seem more of a dictator to many islanders.

1929 While in exile in Mexico, Mella mysteriously dies (many point the finger at Machado) and becomes a martyr for the Cuban reform movement.

1933 President Machado is overthrown in a revolt led by Fulgencio Batista, then an army sergeant. The new government makes such populist reforms as the establishment of a department of labor, the institution of women's suffrage, and the opening of the university to all, regardless of income. It also nullifies the Platt Amendment (except for the lease of the naval base at Guantánamo).

1934 The Universidad de la Habana (University of Havana) is reopened after a three-year suspension of classes.

1940 After having ruled—since 1934—through a series of puppet presidents, Batista is elected president.

1945 Cuba becomes a member of the United Nations.

1950 Fidel Castro graduates from the University of Havana with a law degree after having participated in revolutionary activities throughout Latin America. He is nominated to run as the Orthodox Party's candidate to Cuba's House of Representatives.

1952 Fulgencio Batista cancels the upcoming elections, and institutes a police state. Castro's political career is put on hold, and his career as a Cuban revolutionary leader begins.

1953 Castro heads a disastrous attack on the Moncada Army Barracks in eastern Cuba on July 26. Most of the rebels are killed, and Castro is sentenced to 15 years in jail on the Isla de la Juventud.

1955 Batista grants amnesty to all political prisoners in Cuba. Upon his release, Castro sets out for Mexico.

1956 Castro and 81 would-be rebels sail from Mexico to Cuba aboard the yacht *Granma*. Their boat is met in Oriente Province by Batista's men. Only a handful of rebels, including Ernesto "Che" Guevara and Castro's brother Raúl, survive the landing. The rebels proceed to the jungle of the Sierra Maestra, where they establish their headquarters.

1957 The rebels win a series of small skirmishes. Public sentiment sways their way as the brutality of Batista's regime is made known to the world.

1958 Guevara leads the rebel capture of the central Cuban provincial capital of Santa Clara.

1959 Batista flees to the Dominican Republic on New Year's Day. Castro and his followers march to Havana, where they take control of the Cuban government.

1960 A game of political and economic cat-and-mouse ensues between Cuba, the United States, and the Soviet Union. After Castro signs a trade agreement with the U.S.S.R., U.S. oil companies based in Cuba refuse to refine the crude oil that's part of that trade agreement. In response, Castro nationalizes the American oil companies; America cancels the balance of Cuba's sugar quota; Castro appropriates all U.S. businesses and landholdings; the Soviets agree to purchase the balance of the U.S. sugar quota.

1961 In January, the U.S. government breaks relations with Cuba. Castro allies himself with the Soviet Union. In April, U.S.-trained Cuban exiles are deployed in the Bahía de Cochinos (Bay of Pigs) Invasion. It's expected that the invasion will spur a revolt against Castro. It does not.

1962 In late October the Soviet intent to install mid-range missiles in Cuba leads to a U.S. naval blockade of the island. The so-called Cuban Missile Crisis is resolved when the sites are ordered dismantled and shipped back to the Soviet Union by Soviet premier

Nikita Khruschev. In return, U.S. president John F. Kennedy promises not to attack Cuba. Trade embargoes are imposed.

1963   U.S. citizens are prohibited from traveling to Cuba, and conducting business with Cuba becomes illegal.

1965–67   Guevara leaves Cuba in 1965 to fight with rebel forces in the Congo. From Africa, he travels to Bolivia, where he joins another rebel army. He and his guerrillas are captured and executed by the Bolivian army on October 9, 1967.

1976   Castro is elected president, and a socialist constitution is approved. Castro turns his attention to the international stage, especially to Africa, where Cuban troops are sent.

1980   The Mariel Boat Lift results in an influx of 125,000 Cuban refugees to the United States. It's later discovered that many of those permitted to leave Cuba during this exodus were criminals, residents of psychiatric hospitals, and other "undesirables."

1988   Cuba withdraws its troops from Angola and strikes a peace accord with South Africa.

1991   Following the collapse of the U.S.S.R., Russia cuts economic support to Cuba, including generous oil subsidies. In the early 1990s Castro declares a "Special Period" and calls for Cubans to practice belt-tightening austerity.

1994   Another refugee exodus results in a revision of U.S. immigration policy regarding Cuban asylum-seekers.

1996   Castro receives an audience with Pope John Paul II at the Vatican. Cuban fighter planes attack an aircraft flying for the humanitarian organization Hermanos al Rescate (Brothers to the Rescue). In response, the United States passes the Helms-Burton Act, stating that the United States will not trade with countries doing business with Cuba. President Clinton declines to enforce the law's harshest sanctions.

1997   For the first time since the Revolution, Christmas is declared an official holiday in Cuba. Also in this year Che Guevara's remains are found, identified, and transported to Cuba for burial in a monument outside Santa Clara.

1998   Pope John Paul II visits Cuba.

1999–2000   Elián González, a 5-year-old Cuban boy, is rescued off the coast of Florida in November 1999. When it's discovered that his mother and stepfather died during their attempt to reach the United States, an international custody battle ensues. Despite efforts by the Cuban American community to keep him with relatives in Florida, he is forcibly removed from their home and reunited with his father, who takes Elián back to Cuba in May 2000. Also in 2000 the U.S. Congress passes legislation exempting food and medical supplies from the 37-year-long trade embargo.

2001   The U.S. House of Representatives votes to lift the ban on travel to Cuba for the second time, but observers predict the bill will be buried by conservative Republicans. The Bush administration increases the number of fines assessed for illegal travel to Cuba. In December, a ship containing $33 million worth of grain and meat arrives in Havana from the United States. Bought by the Cuban government, these goods replenish supplies depleted earlier in the year by Hurricane Michelle.

IRRESISTIBLE RHYTHMS

THE COURTYARD OF A 19th-century mansion-cum-restaurant rings with the music of an acoustic trio as they perform a spirited rendition of Compay Segundo's "Chan Chan" for a tour group. The percussionist's fluid hands work the taut skins of his drums, the guitarist strums to the polyphonous beat, and the *tres* player's fingers dance along its metal strings. As the tres solo ends, the musicians belt out the song's refrain: "De Alto Cedro voy para Marcané / Luego a Ceto voy para Mayarí" ("From Alto Cedro I head to Marcané / Then to Ceto and on to Mayarí").

Their performance of that popular ode to itinerancy would be enough to pack a mid-size nightclub in any northern metropolis, but the tourists hardly look up from their lunches. Perhaps they missed the album and film *Buena Vista Social Club,* both of which begin with that same song. Perhaps they missed breakfast. Whatever the reason for their indifference, they wouldn't be the first visitors to start taking the entertainment in Cuba for granted—good music is so common on the island that many travelers simply come to expect it.

Wherever you go in Cuba, you're likely to encounter some tantalizing tropical tune, be it the mellifluous harmonies of a guitar trio, the brassy refrains of an *orquesta,* or the irresistible rhythms of an Afro-Caribbean drum-and-dance troupe. Music is Cuba's pulse, and though the crumbling buildings and bus lines may give the impression of a nation suffering from some geriatric ailment, you need only step into a dance club or enjoy an impromptu concert at a *casa de la trova* to confirm the island's eternal youth. The number of musicians in Cuba seems surpassed only by the number of cigars, and there's hardly a citizen who doesn't dance.

Cuban music may have gained unprecedented popularity in North America and Europe following the release of the *Buena Vista Social Club,* but within Latin America the island has been synonymous with good music for nearly a century. Cuban styles, artists, and dance steps have dominated the airwaves and dance floors of the southern Americas for decades. As a music center, Havana stands shoulder to shoulder with Mexico City, Buenos Aires, and Rio de Janeiro—cities many times its size.

The group of veteran performers who collaborated on the Grammy-winning album *Buena Vista Social Club* drew on a vast and varied musical heritage. Subsequent solo albums by the likes of Compay Segundo (Francisco Repilado), Ibrahím Ferrer, Eliades Ochoa, Omara Portuondo, Barbarito Torres, and Rubén González dug deeper into the island's melodic gold mine, but in musical terms there's plenty more going on in Cuba. Such living legends as Ferrer and González may be the deans of Cuban music, but theirs is a university with campuses in every town and alumni on every street.

At the heart of Cuban music is a marriage of African and European traditions, the roots of which stretch back to the days when Havana was one of Spain's principal New World ports and one of the most important cargoes was human. African slaves brought with them the songs, dances, and rituals of their ancestors, which formed the basis for most of the island's musical styles. Cuba's two disparate musical traditions were originally kept separate—on Sunday, while the colonists danced the latest steps from France, the slave quarters pulsated with the drum beats of mother Africa—but it didn't take long for fusion to begin.

The Spanish gave the Africans European instruments, creating slave bands to entertain them. Slaves with talent saw in music a chance to escape the drudgery of manual labor and an opportunity for upward mobility; in fact, a colonial census of 1827 found that more than half of Havana's musicians were black. Spain provided the language and most of the instruments, but Africa gave Cuban music its soul. Even today, when a dance band performs at a popular Havana club—and the packed dance floor resembles a stormy sea of flesh—Africa reigns; Europe is a mere footman.

The fact that slaves from the same ethnicities were allowed to live together in groups called *cabildos* helped to preserve distinctive

African languages and cultures. These cabildos took their music to the streets of Havana and other cities on Christmas Eve and Epiphany (January 6). Such colorful celebrations were a popular subject of 19th-century engravings, which portray throngs of blacks in masks and elaborate costumes, drumming, dancing, and holding pagan idols on poles over the crowd. Although these spectacles offended conservatives (they were banned on several occasions in the late 19th and early 20th centuries) the tradition survived in the *carnavales* (carnivals) of Havana and Santiago, the *parrandas* (Christmas Eve parades) of Remedios, and in the private rituals of Santería and public *danzas afrocubanas* performed throughout the island.

The streets of Cuba's major cities have served as cradle and stage for many a musical form, such as the *guaracha,* a lively genre characterized by a shuffling rhythm and satirical, risqué lyrics. (The sexual innuendo common in guaracha lyrics is nothing new—back in 1801, an anonymous chronicler criticized the vulgarity of the guarachas he heard on the streets of Havana.) Two of the 20th century's great guaracha composers were Ñico Saquito (Antonio Fernández), whose humorous songs "María Cristina" and "Adiós Compay Gato" are Cuban standards, and Miguel Matamoros, whose Trío Matamoros popularized such tunes as "El Paralítico," and "La Mujer de Antonio."

Another genre born in the streets is the *pregón,* which is a descendent of the melodic announcements of *pregoneros,* ambulant vendors who sang about their wares as they wandered the city. Among the most popular pregones are "Frutas de Caney," and "El Manisero"—a 1940s classic composed by Moisés Simmons and made famous by Rita Montaner.

A musical style associated with rural Cuba is the *guajira,* a simple song with lyrics about country life (the words *guajiro/guajira* mean "man/woman from the country"). The most famous guajira is "Guantanamera," by Joseíto Fernández. Today its lyrics are usually several strophes from José Martí's *Versos Sencillos,* but when Fernández popularized this song on his weekly radio show he regularly invented new words. It consequently has countless verses, and is often used by Cuban musicians as a vehicle for poetic improvisation.

In the early part of the 20th century, the Cuban *bolero* (the local version of a Spanish form) was popular all over Latin America. Nearly every Cuban composer has penned at least a few boleros, which may be played by anything from a guitar duo to a dance band, but some of the genre's greatest stars have been Mexican and Puerto Rican. Boleros are slower, romantic songs with more complex lyrics than most Cuban music—the best provide melodramatic testimony to the ravages of unrequited love.

Lyrics may range from silly to suicidal, but a song's most important aspect is usually its rhythm, since more than listening to music, Cubans enjoy dancing to it. Most of the island's musical genres are danceable, and some, such as the *danzón,* were born in the dance hall. Created in the western city of Matanzas in the late 1800s, danzón was the craze of the early 20th century, with its sensual violin and flute melodies, syncopated bass, percussion, and piano. Danzón, in turn, begot the more pronounced rhythm of the *chachacha* (a genre created by band leader Enrique Jorrín in response to the way people moved to danzón), and the *mambo* (a style that made greater use of syncopation, percussion, and horns).

Cuba's most enduring and versatile genre, however, is the *son,* a form that originated in the eastern cities in the late 19th century and replaced danzón in Cuban dance halls during the first half of the 20th century. The son not only influenced the development of the mambo, and the danzón hybrid *danzonete,* but it also engendered the pan–Latin American *salsa.*

As the phonograph and radio connected Cuban artists to the world, the island experienced a boom in the export of music and musicians. Performers such as singer Rita Montaner and pianist Bola de Nieve toured Europe and the Americas during the 1930s and '40s, paving the way for an array of Cuban acts. Big band jazz had an impact on Cuban music during the '40s and '50s, when the horn sections of the island's *orquestas* expanded. But Cuban music also influenced that northern genre, especially thanks to percussionist and composer Chano Pozo, who moved to New York in 1946 and sowed the seeds of Latin jazz. One Cuban composer who was especially influenced by jazz was Dámasco Pérez Prado, dubbed the Mambo King, who composed wild, distinctive instrumental pieces with unimaginative titles such as "Mambo No. 8." A protégé of Pérez Prado named Benny Moré founded his own orchestra in 1950, and went on to become one of the country's most popular performers. A thin, dark man with a penchant for large hats, Moré was a musical giant whose memory is best preserved by the arrangements of Ibrahím Ferrer.

Although Cuban artists were affected by jazz, such genres as the mambo and son wielded their own influence, competing with swing on many of the world's dance floors. During the 1940s and '50s, Cuba had a plethora of dance bands, many of which spent years touring abroad. Among that era's great band leaders were flautist Arcaño Antonio, violinist Enrique Jorrín, trumpeter Felix Chapottín, and the blind guitarist Arsenio Rodríguez. The most enduring of those musical groups was probably the Sonora Matancera, which was founded in 1924. The Sonora worked with some of the island's best singers, among them Laíto Sureda, Orlando Vallejo, and the incomparable Celia Cruz. A living legend, Cruz continues to produce hits more than half a century after joining the Sonora, which she split with shortly after emigrating from Cuba.

Many musicians abandoned the island following the 1959 Revolution, after which the nation's musical focus shifted from dance hits to political ballads. But even the revolutionaries produced some memorable son: Carlos Puebla's 1960s paean to Che Guevara, "Hasta Siempre," remains one of the country's most popular songs. The '60s and '70s marked the rise of *nueva trova,* a less rhythmic genre known for the poetic quality and political intent of its lyrics. Cuba's two great *trovadores,* Silvio Rodríguez and Pablo Milanés, are immensely popular throughout Latin America, but they are as much poets as musicians, which makes it difficult for non-Spanish speakers to fully appreciate their genius.

Along with the historic cars that ply its roadways, Cuba has managed to preserve the sounds of the '40s and '50s. At the same time, the country has kept abreast of musical developments in the rest of Latin America. Popular dance bands such as Los Van Van, founded in the '70s, and the younger Charanga Habanera play salsa similar to that of Puerto Rico, Caracas, or Panama. The island has also stayed on the forefront of Latin jazz, producing such outstanding musicians as Chucho Valdéz, Arturo Sandoval, and Paquito Rivera, who played together in the group Irakere—Sandoval and Rivera emigrated to the United States years ago—and the younger pianist Gonzalo Rubalcaba, who lives in Spain.

Cuba continues to experiment with new genres. While the stars of Buena Vista fame draw their sounds from the golden years of the 1940s and '50s, younger musicians experiment with rock, reggae, and rap—often blending them with older styles to create new sounds. Bands that do a provocative job of spanning the centuries include Síntesis, which melds ancient African rhythms with rock, and the quartet Orishas, which has coined a son-based hip hop. But then, the secret of Cuban music has always been its variations on traditional themes, which is why the island's musical future is bound to be a reflection of its remarkable past.

— by David Dudenhoefer

IDEAS AND IMAGES

The Written Word

Havana's literary life, despite the restrictions on freedom of expression set forth in 1961 by El Comandante himself ("Within the Revolution, everything. Against the Revolution, nothing!"), seems vibrant and vigorous. Cuba and Havana in particular have always been inspirational to such writers as Graham Greene, Ernest Hemingway, Alejo Carpentier, and Guillermo Cabrera Infante. Drama, conflict, and eros steam from every crack and crevice in this Caribbean pressure cooker, a place where revolution and romance seem to make it hard *not* to write.

Nonfiction

The Reader's Companion to Cuba, edited by Alan Ryan, is a collection of colorful travel essays by such visitors to the island as John Muir, Frederic Remington, Anaïs Nin, Langston Hughes, Graham Greene, Martha Gellhorn, and Amiri Baraka. *Cuba: True Stories* is an anthology of more contemporary narratives edited by veteran travel writer Tom Miller. Miller's *Trading with the Enemy: A Yankee Travels through Castro's Cuba* is the product of an extended visit to the island in the early 1990s. *Mi Moto Fidel*, by Christopher Baker, is an opinionated travelogue that chronicles a three-month tour on a BMW motorcycle.

National Public Radio commentator Andrei Codrescu's *Ay, Cuba: A Socio-Erotic Journey* resulted from his two week visit in 1998 to cover the historic visit of Pope John Paul II. It's a very human, informative essay illustrated with photos by David Graham. Kenneth Triester's *Habaneros: Photographs of the People of Havana* was intended to be a photographic journal of the city's architecture, but evolved into a visual essay on its citizens. In *Havana Dreams*, Wendy Gimbel shows how the lives of four generations of women in one Cuban family were swept up in and transformed by the Revolution. Historian C. Peter Ripley made five trips to the island between 1991 and '97, interviewing dozens of people for his book *Conversations with Cuba*. Maria Lopez Vigil's *Cuba: Neither Heaven nor Hell*, published in 2000, provides a current, thorough assessment of the country's situation.

For a comprehensive (though dry) overview of the past, pick up *Cuba: A Short History*, edited by Leslie Bethell as part of *The Cambridge History of Latin America* series. Not as dry but just as comprehensive is *Cuba: From Columbus to Castro and Beyond* by Jaime Suchlicki. The Cuban Missile Crisis was a turning point in the uneasy history between Cuba and America. Robert F. Kennedy's *Thirteen Days: A Memoir of the Cuban Missile Crisis* provides an insider's view of the standoff. *The Kennedy Tapes: Inside the White House During the Cuban Missile Crisis* offers that view in the words of still other men who were there. And for that dictator's-eye-view you just can't get anywhere else, Fidel Castro himself is the author of more than 30 publications. Of the many books on Che, John Lee Anderson's *Che Guevara: A Revolutionary Life* is among the more recent, well-researched, and balanced. For those who prefer going to the source, there's the *Che Guevara Reader*, edited by David Deutschmann.

Bird-watchers should pick up *A Field Guide to the Birds of Cuba*, by Orlando H. Garrido and Arturo Kirkconnel. Alfonso Silva Lee's *Natural Cuba* is a general guide to the country's flora and fauna. Baseball fans will want to read *The Pride of Havana: A History of Cuban Baseball*, a lively mixture of politics and sport by Cuban-born author Roberto Gonzalez Echevarria. William P. Mara's *Cubans: The Ultimate Cigars* delves into the history and near-mythical appeal of Cuban stogies. For those of an epicurean mind, *A Taste of Old Cuba: More than 150 Recipes for Delicious, Authentic, and Traditional Dishes Highlighted with Reflections and Reminiscences*, by Maria Josefa Lluria de O'Higgins, and *The Flavor of Cuba: Traditional Recipes from the Cuban Kitchen*, by Laura Milera, may whet your appetite. *The Houses of Old Cuba*, by Lilian Llanes, is a lovely coffee-table book with more than 150 photos by Jean-Luc de Languarigue. A similar book with a wider scope is *Cuba: 400 Years of Architectural Heritage*, a collaboration by Rachel Carley and photographer Andrea Brizias. *Art Cuba: New Generations,* by Holly Black and Gerardo Mosque, is a colorful overview of the island's art scene, with photos of everything from paintings to performance pieces.

Fiction

As many an Ernest Hemingway fan will tell you, Papa wrote the bulk of his life-work in Cuba over a period of 20 years, including *For Whom the Bell Tolls, The Green Hills of Africa, Across the River and into the Trees,* and *A Moveable Feast.* His classic *The Old Man and the Sea* is set in Cuba, as are parts of *To Have and Have Not* and *Islands in the Stream.* Graham Greene's *Our Man in Havana* is an entertaining spy spoof that takes place in pre-revolutionary Cuba. A more contemporary novel set on the island is travel writer Pico Iyer's first attempt at fiction, *Cuba and the Night*—the setting is Cuba, the theme is love. Elmore Leonard (author of *Get Shorty* and *Out of Sight*) strays from his usual contemporary themes for *Cuba Libre,* which unfolds on the eve of the Spanish American War. In *Havana Bay,* by Martin Cruz Smith (author of *Gorky Park*), a Russian detective is sent to contemporary Havana to investigate the death of a colleague. John Blackthorn has written two suspenseful novels on Cuba: *Sins of the Fathers* and *I, Che Guevara.*

The most important Cuban writer of the 20th century was Alejo Carpentier, who continues to influence Latin American fiction. His most famous novel, *Explosion in the Cathedral,* is set in the Caribbean during the 18th century, but *The Chase* takes place in prerevolutionary Havana. The collection *Dream with No Name: Contemporary Fiction from Cuba,* edited by Esteban R. Rivera and Juan Ponce de Leon, has 19 short stories by authors ranging from the venerable Carpentier to contemporary writers. *Cubana: Contemporary Fiction by Cuban Women* is an anthology of 16 stories offering insight into the hearts of Cubanas and their world.

Havana resident Miguel Barnet (*Biography of a Runaway Slave* and *Rachel's Song*) may well be the island's most famous contemporary novelist. Abilio Estevez, who also lives in Havana, received praise for his first novel, *Thine Is The Kingdom,* a massive undertaking with a tremendous cast of characters. Reinaldo Arenas, whose memoir *Before Night Falls* was made into a film of the same name, wrote a number of novels before his 1990 death in New York, among them *Singing in the Well; The Palace of the White Skunks; Farewell to the Sea, a Novel of Cuba; Rosa: A Novel in Two Stories; Graveyard of the Angels;* and *The Doorman.* Two of the most important anti-Castro novelists are Zoe Valdés (*I Gave You All I Had, Cafe Nostalgia,* and *Yocandra in the Paradise of Nada: A Novel of Cuba*) and Guillermo Cabrera Infante (*Holy Smoke, Infante's Inferno, Mea Cuba,* and *Three Trapped Tigers*), exiled in, respectively, Paris and London.

There are several Cuban American writers whose fiction moves between the island and the U.S. expat community. Cristina García has written two novels: *Dreaming in Cuban*—about revolution, separation, and, of course, dreams—was nominated for the National Book Award; *The Agüero Sisters* centers around one sister who emigrated and one who stayed in Cuba. Journalist and novelist Achy Obejas explores themes Cuban and American in her short-story collection *We Came All the Way From Cuba So You Could Dress Like This?* and her two novels: *Days of Awe* and *Memory Mambo.* Ana Menendez's collection of short fiction titled *In Cuba I Was a German Shepherd* also digs into the fertile ground of the Cuban American dichotomy.

Captured on Camera

Cuban Cinema

Cuba's film industry—spearheaded by the Instituto Cubano del Arte y la Industria Cinematográfica (ICAIC; Cuban Institute of Art and Cinematography)—was originally established to create documentaries, newsreels, and feature films designed to spread revolutionary ideology throughout Cuba and other less-developed countries. But the ICAIC has accomplished much more than that. Two men, Colombian Nobel prize–winning novelist Gabriel García Márquez and Filmoteca director Alfredo Guevara have been key factors in that success story. Guevara (no relation to Che) is a dedicated Communist Party member and Castro crony who has managed to get films critical of the regime made and shown. García Marquez encouraged Castro to found the international film school in San Antonio de los Baños, just south of Havana, which has turned out a generation of fine filmmakers.

Must-See Movies

In *Fresa y Chocolate* (*Strawberry and Chocolate*), Cuban director Tomás Gutiérrez Alea (who died in 1996) tells the tale of Diego, a Cuban homosexual who falls in love with David, a younger heterosexual with all the prejudices associated with communist doctrine. (An interesting follow-up to this drama would be the documentary, *Gay Cuba,* an in-depth exploration of the lives of gays and lesbians on the island through the century.) In Gutiérrez Alea's last film, *Guantanamera,* a former university professor travels across the country with the body of her aunt and her funeral director husband, encountering, along the way, a former student who has become a truck driver. Two newer films feature *Fresa y Chocolate* star Jorge Perugorría: *Lista de Espera* (*Waiting List*), directed by Juan Carlos Tabío, is a comical, slightly Kafkaesque tale of a group of people stranded in a rural bus terminal; *Miel para Oshún* (*Honey for Oshún*), directed by Humberto Solás, tells the story of a man who was smuggled to America as a boy by his father and returns to the island to get to know his mother and Cuban culture. The U.S. production *Before Night Falls,* based on the memoir by Cuban writer Reinaldo Arenas and directed by painter Julian Schnabel, offers a dark but poignant view of Cuba's repression of homosexuals.

Soy Cuba (*I Am Cuba*) made its U.S. debut in 1995. Originally released in 1964, it was a Cuban-Soviet co-production. Awe at the sophisticated camera work of this anti-America propaganda film will be tempered by the clear view of hindsight (the propaganda seems naive and ineffective) and by the phonetically speaking "Americans." *Buena Vista Social Club* is Wim Wender's 1999 cinematic follow-up to Ry Cooder's 1996 collaboration with a group of brilliant semi-retired musicians in Havana. Cooder gave the compact disc he recorded in Cuba to Wenders while they were working together on the 1997 film *The End of Violence,* and Wenders became intrigued with this "very young music made by some very old people." He filmed, among others, Ibrahím Ferrer (81), Compay Segundo (91), Rubén González (80), and Pío Leyva (82) playing and discussing their music in Havana, Amsterdam, and New York.

If you need more of a musical fix, *A Night in Havana: Dizzy Gillespie in Cuba* captures the trumpeter's 1985 appearance in the fifth annual International Jazz Festival of Havana. The documentary includes Gillespie's explication of the Afro-Cuban musical connection meshed with performance footage.

Cuba has given many European and American commercial filmmakers an idea or two in the past 50 years. The movie based on Graham Greene's book *Our Man in Havana* is a Cold War classic. The kiss from one brother to another in Havana on the eve of the Revolution is one of the indelible images of *The Godfather, Part II.* In the 1979 action-adventure flick *Cuba,* Sean Connery plays a man hired to train Batista's soldiers to fight against Castro's guerillas. And Sydney Pollack's 1990 film *Havana* sees a professional gambler (Robert Redford) visit Cuba on the cusp of Batista's downfall.

SPANISH VOCABULARY

Words and Phrases

English	Spanish	Pronunciation

Basics

English	Spanish	Pronunciation
Yes/no	Sí/no	see/no
Please	Por favor	pore fah-**vore**
May I?	¿Me permite?	may pair-**mee**-tay
Thank you (very much)	(Muchas) gracias.	(**moo**-chas) **grah**-see-as
You're welcome	De nada	day **nah**-dah
Excuse me	Con permiso	con pair-**mee**-so
Pardon me	¿Perdón?	pair-**dohn**
Could you tell me?	¿Podría decirme?	po-dree-ah deh-**seer**-meh
I'm sorry	Lo siento	lo see-**en**-to
Good morning!	¡Buenos días!	**bway**-nohs **dee**-ahs
Good afternoon!	¡Buenas tardes!	**bway**-nahs **tar**-dess
Good evening!	¡Buenas noches!	**bway**-nahs **no**-chess
Goodbye!	¡Adiós!/¡Hasta luego!	ah-dee-**ohss**/**ah**-stah-**lwe**-go
Mr./Mrs.	Señor/Señora	sen-**yor**/sen-**yohr**-ah
Miss	Señorita	sen-yo-**ree**-tah
Pleased to meet you	Mucho gusto	**moo**-cho **goose**-to
How are you?	¿Cómo está usted?	**ko**-mo es-**tah** oo-**sted**
Very well, thank you.	Muy bien, gracias.	**moo**-ee bee-**en**, **grah**-see-as
And you?	¿Y usted?	ee oos-**ted**
Hello (on the telephone)	Diga	**dee**-gah

Numbers

1	un, uno	oon, **oo**-no
2	dos	dos
3	tres	tress
4	cuatro	**kwah**-tro
5	cinco	**sink**-oh
6	seis	saice
7	siete	see-**et**-eh
8	ocho	**o**-cho
9	nueve	new-**eh**-vey
10	diez	dee-**es**
11	once	**ohn**-seh
12	doce	**doh**-seh
13	trece	**treh**-seh
14	catorce	ka-**tohr**-seh

15	quince	**keen**-seh
16	dieciséis	dee-**es**-ee-**saice**
17	diecisiete	dee-**es**-ee-see-**et**-eh
18	dieciocho	dee-**es**-ee-**o**-cho
19	diecinueve	**dee-es**-ee-new-**ev**-ah
20	veinte	**vain**-teh
21	veinte y uno/veintiuno	**vain**-te-**oo**-noh
30	treinta	**train**-tah
32	treinta y dos	train-tay-**dohs**
40	cuarenta	kwah-**ren**-tah
43	cuarenta y tres	kwah-**ren**-tay-**tress**
50	cincuenta	seen-**kwen**-tah
54	cincuenta y cuatro	seen-**kwen**-tay **kwah**-tro
60	sesenta	sess-**en**-tah
65	sesenta y cinco	sess-**en**-tay **seen**-ko
70	setenta	set-**en**-tah
76	setenta y seis	set-**en**-tay **saice**
80	ochenta	oh-**chen**-tah
87	ochenta y siete	oh-**chen**-tay see-**yet**-eh
90	noventa	no-**ven**-tah
98	noventa y ocho	no-**ven**-tah-**o**-choh
100	cien	see-**en**
101	ciento uno	see-**en**-toh **oo**-noh
200	doscientos	doh-see-**en**-tohss
500	quinientos	keen-**yen**-tohss
700	setecientos	set-eh-see-**en**-tohss
900	novecientos	no-veh-see-**en**-tohss
1,000	mil	meel
2,000	dos mil	dohs meel
1,000,000	un millón	oon meel-**yohn**

Colors

black	negro	**neh**-groh
blue	azul	ah-**sool**
brown	café	kah-**feh**
green	verde	**ver**-deh
pink	rosa	**ro**-sah
purple	morado	mo-**rah**-doh
orange	naranja	na-**rahn**-hah
red	rojo	**roh**-hoh
white	blanco	**blahn**-koh
yellow	amarillo	ah-mah-**ree**-yoh

Days of the Week

Sunday	domingo	doe-**meen**-goh
Monday	lunes	**loo**-ness
Tuesday	martes	**mahr**-tess
Wednesday	miércoles	me-**air**-koh-less
Thursday	jueves	hoo-**ev**-ess

Friday	viernes	vee-**air**-ness
Saturday	sábado	**sah**-bah-doh

Months

January	enero	eh-**neh**-roh
February	febrero	feh-**breh**-roh
March	marzo	**mahr**-soh
April	abril	ah-**breel**
May	mayo	**my**-oh
June	junio	**hoo**-nee-oh
July	julio	**hoo**-lee-yoh
August	agosto	ah-**ghost**-toh
September	septiembre	sep-tee-**em**-breh
October	octubre	oak-**too**-breh
November	noviembre	no-vee-**em**-breh
December	diciembre	dee-see-**em**-breh

Useful phrases

Do you speak English?	¿Habla usted inglés?	**ah**-blah oos-**ted** in-**glehs**
I don't speak Spanish	No hablo español	no **ah**-bloh es-pahn-**yol**
I don't understand (you)	No entiendo	no en-tee-**en**-doh
I understand (you)	Entiendo	en-tee-**en**-doh
I don't know	No sé	no seh
I am American/ British	Soy americano (americana)/ inglés(a)	soy ah-meh-ree-**kah**-no (ah-meh-ree-**kah**-nah)/ in-**glehs** **(ah)**
What's your name?	¿Cómo se llama usted?	koh-mo seh **yah**-mah oos-**ted**?
My name is . . .	Me llamo . . .	may **yah**-moh
What time is it?	¿Qué hora es?	keh **o**-rah es?
It is one, two, three . . . o'clock.	Es la una. . . . Son las dos, tres	es la **oo**-nah/sohn lahs dohs, tress
Yes, please/No, thank you	Sí, por favor/No, gracias	**see** pohr fah-**vor**/no **grah**-see-us
How?	¿Cómo?	**koh**-mo?
When?	¿Cuándo?	**kwahn**-doh?
This/Next week	Esta semana/ la semana que entra	**es**-teh seh-**mah**-nah/lah seh-**mah**-nah keh **en**-trah
This/Next month	Este mes/el próximo mes	**es**-teh mehs/el **proke**-see-mo mehs
This/Next year	Este año/el año que viene	**es**-teh **ahn**-yo/el **ahn**-yo keh vee-**yen**-ay
Yesterday/today/ tomorrow	Ayer/hoy/mañana	ah-**yehr**/oy/mahn-**yah**-nah
This morning/ afternoon	Esta mañana/ tarde	**es**-tah mahn-**yah**-nah/**tar**-deh

Tonight	Esta noche	es-tah **no**-cheh
What?	¿Qué?	keh?
What is it?	¿Qué es esto?	keh es **es**-toh
Why?	¿Por qué?	pore **keh**
Who?	¿Quién?	kee-**yen**
Where is . . . ?	¿Dónde está . . . ?	**dohn**-deh es-**tah**
the train station?	la estación del tren?	la es-tah-see-**on** del **train**
the subway station?	la estación del Tren subterráneo?	la es-ta-see-**on** del trehn soob-tair-**ron**-a-o
the bus stop?	la parada del autobus?	la pah-**rah**-dah del oh-toh-**boos**
the post office?	la oficina de correos?	la oh-fee-**see**-nah deh koh-**reh**-os
the bank?	el banco?	el **bahn**-koh
the . . . hotel?	el hotel . . . ?	el oh-**tel**
the store?	la tienda . . . ?	la tee-**en**-dah
the cashier?	la caja?	la **kah**-hah
the . . . museum?	el museo . . . ?	el moo-**seh**-oh
the hospital?	el hospital?	el ohss-pee-**tal**
the elevator?	el ascensor?	el ah-**sen**-sohr
the bathroom?	el baño?	el **bahn**-yoh
Here/there	Aquí/allá	ah-**key**/ah-**yah**
Open/closed	Abierto/cerrado	ah-bee-**er**-toh/ ser-**ah**-doh
Left/right	Izquierda/derecha	iss-key-**er**-dah/ dare-**eh**-chah
Straight ahead	Derecho	dare-**eh**-choh
Is it near/far?	¿Está cerca/lejos?	es-**tah sehr**-kah/ **leh**-hoss
I'd like . . . a room	Quisiera . . . un cuarto/una habitación	kee-see-ehr-ah oon **kwahr**-toh/ **oo**-nah ah-bee-tah-see-**on**
the key	la llave	lah **yah**-veh
a newspaper	un periódico	oon pehr-ee-**oh**-dee-koh
a stamp	un sello de correo	oon **seh**-yo deh koh-**reh**-oh
I'd like to buy . . .	Quisiera comprar . . .	kee-see-**ehr**-ah kohm-**prahr**
cigarette	cigarrillo	ce-ga-**ree**-yoh
matches	cerillos	ser-**ee**-ohs
a dictionary	un diccionario	oon deek-see-oh-**nah**-ree-oh
soap	jabón	hah-**bohn**
sunglasses	gafas de sol	**ga**-fahs deh sohl
suntan lotion	loción bronceadora	loh-see-**ohn** brohn-seh-ah-**do**-rah
a map	un mapa	oon **mah**-pah
a magazine	una revista	**oon**-ah reh-**veess**-tah

paper	papel	pah-**pel**
envelopes	sobres	**so**-brehs
a postcard	una tarjeta postal	**oon**-ah tar-**het**-ah post-**ahl**
How much is it?	¿Cuánto cuesta?	**kwahn**-toh **kwes**-tah
It's expensive/ cheap	Está caro/barato	es-**tah kah**-roh/ bah-**rah**-toh
A little/a lot	Un poquito/ mucho	oon poh-**kee**-toh/ **moo**-choh
More/less	Más/menos	mahss/**men**-ohss
Enough/too much/too little	Suficiente/ demasiadó/ muy poco	soo-fee-see-**en**-teh/ deh-mah-see-**ah**-doh/**moo**-ee poh-koh
Telephone	Teléfono	tel-**ef**-oh-no
Telegram	Telegrama	teh-leh-**grah**-mah
I am ill	Estoy enfermo(a)	es-**toy** en-**fehr**-moh(mah)
Please call a doctor	Por favor llame a un medico	pohr fah-**vor ya**-meh ah oon **med**-ee-koh
Help!	¡Auxilio! ¡Ayuda! ¡Socorro!	owk-**see**-lee-oh/ ah-**yoo**-dah/ soh-**kohr**-roh
Fire!	¡Incendio!	en-**sen**-dee-oo
Caution!/Look out!	¡Cuidado!	kwee-**dah**-doh

On the Road

Avenue	Avenida	ah-ven-**ee**-dah
Broad, tree-lined boulevard	Bulevar	boo-leh-**var**
Fertile plain	Vega	**veh**-gah
Highway	Carretera	car-reh-**ter**-ah
Mountain pass, Street	Puerto Calle	poo-**ehr**-toh **cah**-yeh
Waterfront promenade	Rambla	**rahm**-blah
Wharf	Embarcadero	em-bar-cah-**deh**-ro

In Town

Cathedral	Catedral	cah-teh-**dral**
Church	Templo/Iglesia	**tem**-plo/ee-**glehs**-see-ah
City hall	Casa de gobierno	kah-sah deh go-bee-**ehr**-no
Door, gate	Puerta portón	poo-**ehr**-tah por-**ton**
Entrance/exit	Entrada/salida	en-**trah**-dah/sah-**lee**-dah
Inn, rustic bar, or restaurant	Taverna	tah-**vehr**-nah
Main square	Plaza principal	plah-thah prin-see-**pahl**

Market	Mercado	mer-**kah**-doh
Neighborhood	Barrio	**bahr**-ree-o
Traffic circle	Glorieta	glor-ee-**eh**-tah
Wine cellar, wine bar, or wine shop	Bodega	boh-**deh**-gah

Dining Out

A bottle of . . .	Una botella de . . .	**oo**-nah bo-**teh**-yah deh
A cup of . . .	Una taza de . . .	**oo**-nah **tah**-thah deh
A glass of . . .	Un vaso de . . .	oon **vah**-so deh
Ashtray	Un cenicero	oon sen-ee-**seh**-roh
Bill/check	La cuenta	lah **kwen**-tah
Bread	El pan	el pahn
Breakfast	El desayuno	el deh-sah-**yoon**-oh
Butter	La mantequilla	lah man-teh-**key**-yah
Cheers!	¡Salud!	sah-**lood**
Cocktail	Un aperitivo	oon ah-pehr-ee-**tee**-voh
Dinner	La cena	lah **seh**-nah
Dish	Un plato	oon **plah**-toh
Menu of the day	Menú del día	meh-**noo** del **dee**-ah
Enjoy!	¡Buen provecho!	bwehn pro-**veh**-cho
Fixed-price menu	Menú fijo o turistico	meh-**noo fee**-hoh oh too-**ree**-stee-coh
Fork	El tenedor	el ten-eh-**dor**
Is the tip included?	¿Está incluida la propina?	es-**tah** in-cloo-**ee**-dah lah pro-**pee**-nah
Knife	El cuchillo	el koo-**chee**-yo
Large portion of savory snacks	Raciónes	rah-see-**oh**-nehs
Lunch	La comida	lah koh-**mee**-dah
Menu	La carta, el menú	lah **cart**-ah, el meh-**noo**
Napkin	La servilleta	lah sehr-vee-**yet**-ah
Pepper	La pimienta	lah pee-me-**en**-tah
Please give me	Por favor déme	pore fah-**vor deh**-meh
Salt	La sal	lah sahl
Savory snacks	Tapas	**tah**-pahs
Spoon	Una cuchara	**oo**-nah koo-**chah**-rah
Sugar	El azúcar	el ah-**thu**-kar
Waiter!/Waitress!	¡Por favor Señor/Señorita!	pohr fah-**vor** sen-**yor**/sen-yor-**ee**-tah

INDEX

NOTES

NOTES

NOTES